MW00721075

You can sort records numerically, chronologically, and alphabetically. Turn to "Sorting Records," page 332, to find out how.

The creation of any database in Works begins with a field. Find out how to create a field in "Creating a Database," page 301.

Category number: 42

Inventory

No. 00001

Product ID	Supplier ID	Category ID	Product Name	English Name	Quantity Per Unit	Unit Price	Units In Stock
1	1	1	Chai	Dharamsala Tea	10 boxes x 20 bags	$18.00	39
2	1	1	Chang	Tibetan Barley Beer	24 - 12 oz bottles	$19.00	17
3	1	2	Aniseed Syrup	Licorice Syrup	12 - 550 ml bottles	$10.00	13
4	2	2	Anton's Cajun Seasoning	Anton's Cajun Seasoning	48 - 6 oz jars	$22.00	53
5	2	2	Chef Anton's Gumbo Mix	Chef Anton's Gumbo Mix	36 boxes	$21.35	0
6	3	2	Bob's Boysenberry Spread	Bob's Boysenberry Spread	12 - 8 oz jars	$25.00	120
7	3	7	Uncle Bob's Organic Dried	Uncle Bob's Organic Dried	12 - 1 lb pkgs.	$30.00	15
8	3	2	Northfork Cranberry Sauce	Northfork Cranberry Sauce	12 - 12 oz jars	$40.00	6
9	4	6	Mishi Kobe Niku	Mishi Kobe Beef	18 - 500 g pkgs.	$97.00	29
10	4	8	Ikura	Fish Roe	12 - 200 ml jars	$31.00	31
11	5	4	Queso Cabrales	Cabrales Cheese	1 kg pkg.	$21.00	22
12	5	4	Queso Manchego La Pastora	Manchego La Pastora Cheese	10 - 500 g pkgs.	$38.00	86
13	6	8	Konbu	Kelp Seaweed	2 kg box	$6.00	24
14	6	7	Tofu	Bean Curd	40 - 100 g pkgs.	$23.25	35
15	6	2	Genen Shouyu	Lite Sodium Soy Sauce	24 - 250 ml bottles	$15.50	39
16	7	3	Pavlova	Pavlova Meringue Dessert	32 - 500 g boxes	$17.45	29
17	7	6	Alice Mutton	Alice Springs Lamb	20 - 1 kg tins	$39.00	0
18	7	8	Carnarvon Tigers	Carnarvon Tiger Prawns	16 kg pkg.	$62.50	42
19	8	3	Teatime Chocolate Biscuits	Teatime Chocolate Biscuits	10 boxes x 12	$9.20	25
20	8	3	Sir Rodney's Marmalade	Sir Rodney's Marmalade	30 gift boxes	$81.00	40

You can design forms in Form Design view to increase the effectiveness of your presentation. See how in "Designing Database Forms in Form Design View," page 316.

You can use queries to zero in on information in a database. Learn how to construct a query in "Querying a Database to Find Information," page 339.

Neil J. Salkind started writing about computers when he related his experiences buying software through the mail in an article that appeared in *BYTE* magazine. From there, it was more articles, then books, and then books that are as much fun to write as the people who publish them are to work for, such as *Running Microsoft Works for Windows 95*. When he is not writing, he teaches at the University of Kansas; tries to answer his 11-year-old's questions about everything; e-mails his daughter, who is a sophomore at Smith College; and cooks for his wife of almost 30 years, Leni. When he's not doing one of the aforementioned things, he can be found reading, collecting first editions, or juggling in beautiful eastern Kansas.

Ad astra per asperum—To the stars with difficulty.

In-Depth Reference

and Inside Tips from

the Software Experts

RUNNING

Microsoft®

WORKS for Windows® 95

NEIL J. SALKIND

Microsoft Press

PUBLISHED BY
Microsoft Press
A Division of Microsoft Corporation
One Microsoft Way
Redmond, Washington 98052-6399

Copyright © 1995 by Neil J. Salkind and Microsoft Press

Library of Congress Cataloging-in-Publication Data
Salkind, Neil J.
   Running Microsoft Works for Windows 95 / Neil Salkind, JoAnne
Woodcock.
      p.   cm.
  Includes index.
  ISBN 1-55615-883-1
  1. Integrated software. 2. Microsoft Works for Windows.
3. Microsoft Windows 95. I. Woodcock, JoAnne. II. Title.
QA76.76.O63S3415 1995
005.369--dc20   95-38728
                                          CIP

Printed and bound in the United States of America.

1 2 3 4 5 6 7 8 9 QMQM 0 9 8 7 6 5

Distributed to the book trade in Canada by Macmillan of Canada, a division of Canada Publishing
Corporation.

A CIP catalogue record for this book is available from the British Library.

Microsoft Press books are available through booksellers and distributors worldwide. For further
information about international editions, contact your local Microsoft Corporation office. Or
contact Microsoft Press International directly at fax (206) 936-7329.

America Online is a registered trademark of America Online, Inc. Apple and Macintosh are registered
trademarks of Apple Computer, Inc. CompuServe is a registered trademark of CompuServe, Inc.
Microsoft, Microsoft Press, MS-DOS, and Windows are registered trademarks of Microsoft Corporation, and The Microsoft Network is operated by Microsoft Corporation on behalf of Microsoft Online
Services Partnership. All other trademarks and service marks are the property of their respective
owners.

Acquisitions Editor: Lucinda Rowley
Project Editor: Wallis Bolz
Manuscript and Technical Editors: Labrecque Publishing

Chapters at a Glance

Table of Contents

Part 2 Using the Word Processor   83

Table of Contents

Dedication

For Micah on his 11th birthday,
and Sara, on her 19th

May you live to see your world fulfilled,
May your desire be for worlds still to come,
And may you trust in generations past and yet to be.
May your heart be filled with intuition
And your words be filled with insight.
May songs of praise ever be upon your tongue
And your vision be a straight path before you.
May your eyes shine with the light of holy words
And your face reflect the brightness of the heavens . . .

—*Talmud, Berachot 17A*

Acknowledgments

Here's how the book world works. The author does his or her best to produce a good manuscript, and if they are fortunate enough to do so, then everything else (and I mean everything) depends on the long list of people in charge who copy-edit, produce, proofread, produce, and on and on. In the case of this book, I *hope* the manuscript that I initially produced was a good one, but I *know* that the long list of people who took it from there did a superb job.

At Microsoft, I want to thank Lucinda Rowley, Acquisitions Editor, for giving me the opportunity to revise *Running Works for Windows*. She's a cut above the best. So, too, is Wallis Bolz, Project Editor, who shepherded this project every step of the way and was responsive to my suggestions, both good and bad. At Labrecque Publishing Services, Terrence O'Donnell was the technical editor on the job, and if this book is a success, it will to a large extent be due to his excellent editing and keen eye for accuracy. If you think this book works, it's because of Terry's hard work and skill. If you think the book does not work, blame me. Thanks also go to Lisa Labrecque, who managed the production of the project, Mark Woodworth, who copy-edited the text, Curtis Philips, who produced the pages, and Andrea Fox, who proofread them. Finally, I thank the team of developers at Microsoft for putting together a wonderful set of integrated applications in Microsoft Works for Windows 95.

Introduction

You may already be aware that Microsoft Works has been around for years, operating on a variety of platforms such as MS-DOS, Apple DOS, and the Macintosh, among others. The most recent version is Works for Windows 95, and it's a special edition not only because of many new features, but also because it has been designed specifically for the Windows 95 operating system. This book covers Works 4. As you will see, the combination of Works and Windows provides you with a complete integrated software package, which runs on a graphical user operating system. Works gives you the power to do everything, from writing this week's shopping list using the word processor to figuring out how the national debt will be settled using the spreadsheet. And Windows allows you to do all of this in an easy-to-use multitasking environment.

While Works contains modules that offer the capabilities of several applications, you may not know how well they can all work together. The main modules—word processor, spreadsheet, and database—are integrated with one another so that information stored in or generated by one can easily be used by another. That means no retyping! Data can be easily copied from module to module. The other parts of Works, such as Draw, also provide you with tools that have many of the features offered by the best graphics and communications modules on the market. In all respects, Works is a complete package of computer applications. I hope you're reading this before you go out and spend $500 on a word processor and another $500 on a spreadsheet, and so on. Unless you're a high-powered turbo user, Works is really all you will need.

Whom This Book Is For

Almost anyone who is more concerned about getting a letter off to the IRS or a note to Aunt Gussie than recovering a lost file cluster will love Works and (I hope) this book. Throughout this book you will find the kind of information you need to understand the process of creating several different types of documents and then modifying them to fit your particular computing needs. Works has plenty of advanced features, and this latest version introduces enough new tools, especially TaskWizards, to make any one module competitive with dedicated word processors, spreadsheets, and databases. But its most important feature is its ease of use. You'll be up and running with Works in minutes. Really!

What's in This Book

Running Microsoft Works for Windows 95 is organized into seven parts, each of which takes you through the beginning and advanced features of a particular aspect of Works.

In Part 1, *Getting Started with Works*, you will learn how to start Works and explore some of the built-in features, such as TaskWizards and toolbars. You will learn how these features make Works such an easy and powerful tool to use.

Part 2, *Using the Word Processor*, introduces you to the word processor by showing you how to create a simple document. From there, the part goes on to describe more advanced features such as formatting text and incorporating graphics into your pages.

Part 3, *Using the Spreadsheet*, begins with the creation of a simple spreadsheet. It then shows you how to manage cell entries, design formulas, and work with functions. Finally, it ends with a startling display of charts. (How did you *do* that?)

Part 4, *Using the Database*, takes you through the steps of designing a database form, using the Form and List views to display your records, and creating reports to customize your printouts. If you've ever lost your first edition of *One Flew Over the Cuckoo's Nest*, your database of first editions will help you locate it and not lose it again.

Part 5, *Using Graphics*, shows you what Works can do with graphics, including special features such as WordArt that allow you to transform ordinary characters and words into interesting shapes and presentations. Here, you will also be introduced to the Microsoft Draw program.

Want to know the weather in Tokyo? How much one share of Marvel Comics is worth (about $30 today)? Or how to buy a perfume bottle from the Museum of Modern Art? In Part 6, *Using Works Communications*, you'll find out how to use Works and the communications tools it comes with.

Part 7, *Working Together*, shows you the true power of integrated applications. Create a chart using the spreadsheet, place it in a word-processed document, and then change the numbers the chart is based on two weeks later. Guess what? The chart you created in the spreadsheet changes as well. Applications and files can be connected in Works so that everything stays nicely in touch.

Finally, three appendixes summarize the spreadsheet and database functions available in Works, list available keystroke shortcuts to make your computing easier, and describe in detail how to install Works on your system.

Using This Book

In this book, when you see a key combination written with a hyphen, like this:

Ctrl-A

it means "hold down the first key and then press the second key." For example, Ctrl-A means "Hold down the Ctrl key and press A." When you see two keys names separated by a comma, like this:

Alt, F

it means "Press and release the first key, and then press the second."

TIP Throughout this book you'll find loads of tips on better use of Works. They are marked with this icon so you can't miss them.

See Also   Finally, wherever you encounter the "See Also" icon, you'll find references to other sections in the book that provide additional, related information.

Whatever you want with Works, you can have. I had fun writing this book, and I hope you have fun using it to learn how to use Works. I welcome e-mail from you, and I know that suggestions, ideas, criticisms, or any other feedback you offer will make the next edition of this book even better. So, enjoy the book and write me, snail mail me, or e-mail me with comments, questions, ideas for the next revision—just a great recipe for anything that includes chocolate. Best wishes. Good works to you!

Neil J. Salkind
Lawrence, KS
Internet: njs@falcon.cc.ukans.edu
CompuServe: 70404,365
September 13, 1995

Part 1

Getting Started with Works

In This Part

Whether you're new to computers, new to Windows 95, or just looking for new software to help you get your jobs done, you've come to the right place. Works for Windows 95 offers you everything you need in the leading integrated package. The combination of Works for Windows 95 and Windows 95 is a real winner. Works takes advantage of the computing power of Windows 95 as well as the neat new features that Windows 95 offers, such as longer file names and right-clicking. *Running Works for Windows 95* tells you all about them.

Want to write a letter or design a brochure? The word processing module will provide you all the tools you need. Or, if you need to create a budget or calculate your annual stock profits, turn to the spreadsheet. The last of the big three applications is the database, which lets you track information ranging from your book collection to a compendium of recipes. Works also gives you the tools to create graphics, as well as go "online" by connecting to the Microsoft Network or other online services, where you can access the Internet and send e-mail.

In Chapter 1, you'll see what Works is and what it can do for you. You'll also find out about the many ways you can access Help, to do your work as easily and efficiently as possible.

In Chapter 2, you'll learn all about using the Launcher, the Works for Windows 95 opening screen where you can choose from 39 TaskWizards (a fun kind of do-it-yourself document maker), select an already existing document (one you created in an earlier Works session), or use one of the Works modules presented in this part.

Chapter 1

Getting to Know Works

These are exciting times for Works users like you. Not only will this book show you how to use Microsoft Works for Windows 95, but, even better, you'll learn how Works operates with Windows 95, a newly designed operating system that lets you perform complex operations with a simple click or two of a mouse button. That's why the official name of Works is Works for Windows 95—the name says it all.

Since Windows 95 is so new, you may not yet be familiar with all its features. That shouldn't stop you from using Works for Windows 95 because Works for Windows 95 provides you with all the tools needed to create a variety of documents for business and personal use. Throughout *Running Works for Windows 95*, we'll also offer you tips to help make your Windows 95 activities easier, more enjoyable, and more efficient.

A Brief Tour of Works for Windows 95

You probably purchased Works because it's an integrated software package—a single program that contains a set of different parts you can use to create, work with, and organize letters, memos, lists, charts, budgets, and more.

Works offers the services of a word processor, a spreadsheet, a database, and a communications module—four parts that you would otherwise have to purchase separately. While you save money by buying and using such an integrated package, Works has one other major advantage. Because Works is an integrated package, the four different modules were designed to work together. You only need to learn one basic set of commands and one basic way of working with the program, and then apply what you know to any of the four modules. In addition, because Works is integrated, information from one module can be used by another.

See Also   For more information on Works' fourth module, *communications*, see Chapter 14, "Getting in Touch" page 435.

We assume that both Windows and Works for Windows 95 (which we'll call Works from here on) have already been installed on your hard drive. If they have not, turn to Appendix C, "Installing Microsoft Works for Windows 95," page 519, for instructions, or see your Windows 95 or Works for Windows 95 documentation.

If you are entirely new to Works and have little idea what it can do for you or how you can use it, you might want to take a general tour of what Works offers. The tour takes about 10 minutes and acquaints you with all the features that Works has to offer. Even if you've used Works before, there are enough new things about Works for Windows 95 that you may want to know about. The easiest way to find out about these is to take the tour. Besides, it's free and even has minivideos that show you how to do things. To start the tour, click Help and click Introduction To Works.

Welcome to Works

It's time to begin what you're really here for! In this chapter, you'll learn how to start Works, examine the options that are available even before you begin creating your first Works document, and learn how to use the Works online Help system. You'll also be introduced to three modules to help get you better acquainted with Works: the word processor, the spreadsheet, and the database.

Along the way, you'll see how the look of Windows extends to applications designed to work with it, and you will come to view Works as a set of valuable tools that help you work productively. That's what computers and good applications like Works are all about: providing the tools that let you concentrate on doing what you want to do, rather than on how you're supposed to do it.

Starting Works

When you install Works, Windows 95 places an entry on the Programs menu. Check your Programs menu for the Microsoft Works 4.0 entry, as shown in Figure 1-1. If it doesn't appear, Works has not been installed properly. During installation, you also have the option of placing a shortcut for Works on the desktop. A feature that is new to Windows 95, shortcuts are pointers to program and document icons. All you need to do is click on a shortcut icon; you won't even have to worry about the Program menu.

Start Works by following these steps.

1. Click on the Start menu.

2. Point to Programs.

3. Point to Microsoft Works 4.0.

4. Click Microsoft Works 4.0.

In a moment, you will see a licensing message, followed by the Works Task Launcher, as shown in Figure 1-2. The Task Launcher is a

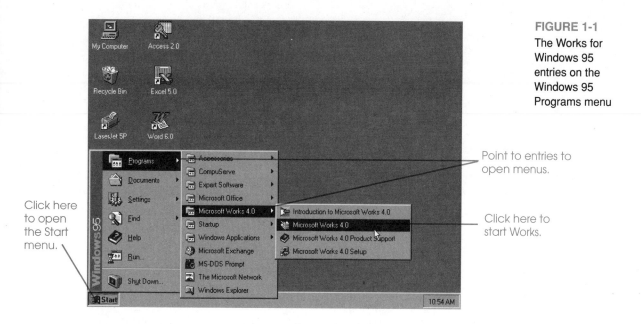

FIGURE 1-1
The Works for
Windows 95
entries on the
Windows 95
Programs menu

Point to entries to
open menus.

Click here
to open
the Start
menu.

Click here to
start Works.

dialog box that lets you select from any one of three options, depending
on how you want to work. We'll explore each of these options in detail in
Chapter 2.

Works
desktop

Click here to use
a TaskWizard.

Click here to open
an existing
document.

Click here to use
one of the Works
modules.

FIGURE 1-2
The Works for
Windows 95
opening screen and
Task Launcher

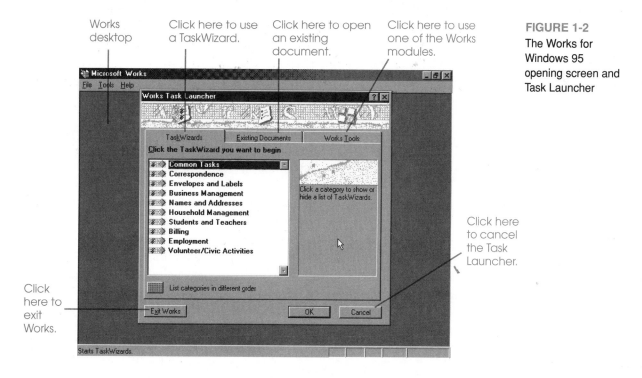

Click here
to cancel
the Task
Launcher.

Click
here to
exit
Works.

🪟 Locating Files and Creating Shortcuts

Shortcuts are easy to create. First, you must locate the file for which you want to create a shortcut. To begin locating a file, you can either double-click the My Computer icon on the Windows 95 desktop or you can select the Windows Explorer command on the Programs menu.

The My Computer icon opens a window that shows your computer's disk drive icons and some folders. You can double-click a disk drive icon, such as drive C, to open another window that shows its contents. Continue double-clicking folders, as necessary, to see their contents in windows until you see the icon and filename for the file you want.

The Windows Explorer alternative for locating a file allows you to peruse the contents of disk drives and folders in a single window. Simply click a device icon or folder listed in the Exploring window's left pane to see the contents of the drive or folder in the right pane.

Once you've located the file, you can create its shortcut by pointing to the file, clicking the right mouse button, and selecting the Shortcut command on the pop-up menu. Then you can place the shortcut anywhere you want on the desktop or within another folder. You can even place a shortcut on the Start menu by dragging the shortcut icon to the Start button.

The first option is to use one of the TaskWizards. These are Works tools that take you step by step through the creation of many different, useful, and interesting documents such as personalized letters, billing forms, and name and address collections. We'll walk you through a set of TaskWizards in Chapter 2.

As a second option, you can open and work with Existing Documents, such as a letter you previously created and want to use again. The more documents you create using Works, the larger your library of existing documents will be. A sizable library makes it easy for you to draw on previously created documents that you can use again as is, or slightly modify and use once more in a revised form.

Your third choice is to use Works Tools and begin the creation process from scratch. This option gives you total control from the start of what you will create, using the word processor, spreadsheet, database, or communications modules.

Figure 1-2 on page 7 also shows the Works desktop and the Works menus (File, Tools, and Help). These menus provide sets of commands that let you create new documents as well as retrieve previously created ones. These menus are available only when the Task Launcher is not present on the screen. Here's a quick survey of the commands offered on each of the menus.

See Also For more information on *TaskWizards*, see Chapter 2, "What Do You Want to Do?," page 43.

Opening, Closing, and Saving Documents

Although you might normally begin a Works module with the Works Tools option in the Task Launcher, the File menu offers an alternative. If you select New from the File menu, you'll see the Task Launcher (see Figure 1-2 on page 7), and you can select from one of the three options discussed above. If you select Open from the File menu, you can open a previously created document and even open those created using other applications that Works can read, such as Microsoft Word and Microsoft Excel.

The Close, Save, and Save As commands, respectively, let you close an open file, save a file under an existing name, and save a file under a new name in a different directory or on a different disk. These three commands are dimmed (grayed out) to indicate that you can't use them now—because you can't close or save a file when you haven't yet opened one.

The final command on the File menu, Exit Works, is the command you use to quit Works and return to Windows. If you want, you can double-click on the Control menu icon to accomplish the same thing.

While the final command on the File menu allows you to exit Works, other menu items listed there are not commands. Below the Exit command is a listing of up to the last four files that were opened in Works, from which you can select the one you want to open. In other words, if you finished working on a document yesterday and want to open that file once again, just click File, and then select the filename on the list at the bottom of the File menu.

Using the Address Book and Customizing Works

The Tools menu contains two commands: Address Book and Options.

The Address Book command opens the default Address Book, which is a database where you can store personal information like the names, addresses, and phone numbers of your friends and associates. Works uses the Address Book as a source of information for several of its TaskWizards, such as for the Wizard that prepares mailing labels. If an Address Book has not yet been created, Works will display an error message telling you so and give you the opportunity to prepare one. You can easily create an Address Book using a TaskWizard that guides you through preparing one, as you will do in Chapter 2.

The Options command presents you with a host of alternatives for customizing Works. When you select Options from the Tools menu, you will see a set of tabs in the Options dialog box like this.

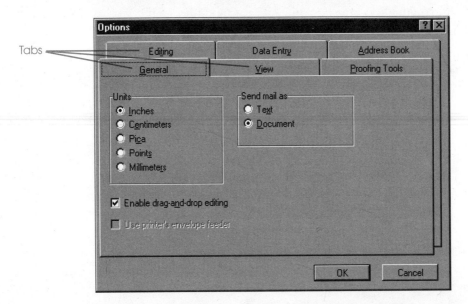

The General tab lets you select a unit of measure such as inches or centimeters or points, define whether you want e-mail (see Chapter 14) sent as text or as a document, and specify whether drag-and-drop editing is enabled.

▦ Using Drag-and-Drop

Drag-and-drop is an editing feature new to Windows 95. It allows you to select a portion of a document, drag the highlighted section, and drop it in a new location. No more cut and paste; just drag and drop to copy or move information from one location in a document to another location, or from one document to a different document.

The View tab enables you to set which aspects of Works you want to show on startup such as the status bar, Help, and if you want to save the current workspace.

The Proofing Tools tab lets you define the language in which the Spelling and Thesaurus tools will evaluate documents.

The Editing tab provides options for editing documents such as whether you want newly typed characters inserted into a document, or typed over existing characters. This tab also permits options such as the use of smart quotes "like this," rather than regular quotes "like this."

The Data Entry tab lets you adjust the number of decimal places in a value as it is entered, the way that values in cells (in the spreadsheet) are edited, and decide whether you want to hide zero values.

The Address Book tab allows you to select the Address Book that you want to use as the default since you can create and use more than one Address Book. If you haven't yet created an Address Book, you can run the Address Book TaskWizard from here.

As you use Works, you will see how modifying these options helps you personalize Works and make it work best for you. When you start using Works, leave these options set at the default and only change one or two at a time so that you can evaluate their effects. Don't change too many at once, or you won't know what's responsible for what changes.

TIP If you find that Works is performing a bit differently after someone else used your computer, perhaps some of the options have been changed. There's no way to switch back to all the default settings. Rather, you may have to go through and reset what you *think* might have been changed.

Getting Help in Works

You might find the Help menu to be your best friend if you don't know quite what the next step is in creating a letter to a client, a budget for the next quarter, or a database of suppliers. The Help menu consists of eight commands; each provides a unique method for viewing information about using Works. Let's take a brief look at these commands and, as an example, see how Help can assist you in learning how to enter a formula in a spreadsheet—a basic spreadsheet task.

Searching for Help by Topic

When you first select Contents on the Help menu, you'll see a Help Topics: Microsoft Works dialog box and an accompanying Help screen, which displays help information, as shown in Figure 1-3. The left-hand side of the screen lists topics on which you can get Works Help, organized by module. You click the module that contains the topic on which you want help. Once you find the topic you want help on, the steps necessary to complete the task are shown on the right-hand side of the screen under the title Help. You can then click on any topic and follow the detailed instructions.

For example, here's how to get help on creating a formula in the spreadsheet module using the Contents command.

1. Click Help, and then click Contents.

    When you do this, you'll see the Contents Help screen as shown in Figure 1-3. On the left-hand side is a listing of topics. On the right-hand side, under Help are step-by-step instructions for accomplishing the task.

2. Click Spreadsheet.

    When you do this, the topics under that module are revealed.

3. Click Calculating with formulas.

4. Click Formulas and functions.

Click here for a list of topics organized alphabetically.

Click here for a list of topics organized by module.

FIGURE 1-3
The Help Topics dialog box and Help screen

Click on any icon for help on a specific module.

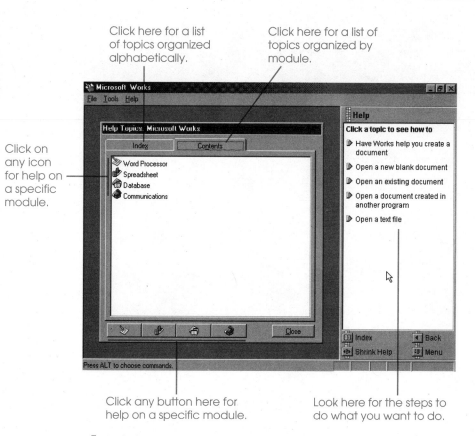

Click any button here for help on a specific module.

Look here for the steps to do what you want to do.

5. Click To type your own formula.

In the Help section, as you see in Figure 1-4 on the following page, are the three steps you will follow to enter your own formula in a spreadsheet cell. Just follow the listed steps, which will remain on screen until you shrink Help or hide Help (using the Hide Help command on the Help menu). You can continue to use Help while you work. The Help screen remains next to the module you are working in until you shrink or hide it.

TIP To quickly get to the Index or Help screens from within modules, press the F1 function key. The F1 key summons Help from virtually any operation in Works, and Windows too.

FIGURE 1-4
Step-by-step help
for typing your own
formula via
Contents

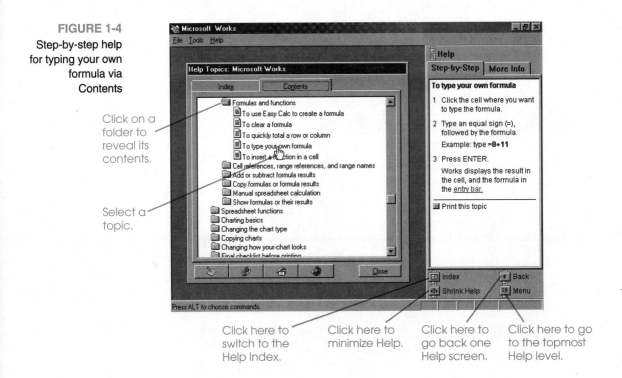

Click on a
folder to
reveal its
contents.

Select a
topic.

Click here to
switch to the
Help Index.

Click here to
minimize Help.

Click here to
go back one
Help screen.

Click here to go
to the topmost
Help level.

Searching for Help Using a Keyword

The Index offers a comprehensive, alphabetical listing of all the topics in Works Help across all four modules. The same information that is accessible through the Contents command that we just discussed is available through the Index commands as well, but there it is organized alphabetically. Contents is organized by module (word processor, spreadsheet, database, or communications) and, within each module, by general topic.

The best part of using the Index is that as you type a term for which you want help, Works Help continues to suggest related topics. For example, in Figure 1-5, we entered the term *formulas*, and Works located the first occurrence of that term. From there, we could select from the list in the bottom section of the Help Topics screen. Then, as we clicked through the different folders within the general category of formulas, we finally reached the specific topic we wanted, which was how to type a formula in a cell. Once the topic was clicked, a step-by-step description of how to type a formula appears in Help. Notice how the Step-by-Step Help screen in Figure 1-6 on page 16 is the same as the one you saw in Figure 1-4, yet there are two different ways to get there, depending on how much you know about what you want to find out. If you have a general idea of what

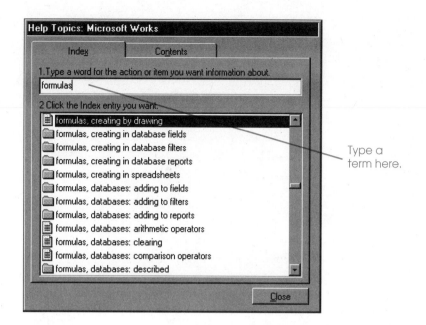

FIGURE 1-5

Typing a term to
move directly to
related topics

Type a
term here.

you want to do, use the Index command. It will generate lots of different
options as you type. If you are working in a particular module and want
to find out about a certain feature, use Contents.

TIP Want to find out what an Index entry does? Place
the mouse pointer on the entry and press the right
mouse button. You'll see an explanation of what the
topic in the Index covers.

Using the Help Screen to Navigate Through Help

At the bottom of the Help screen, in the lower right-hand corner, you will
see four buttons. Each of these assists you in navigating through
Works Help.

The Index button connects you to a comprehensive, A to Z index of
Works topics. Clicking this button is the same as clicking the Index tab.

The Back button lets you move back to the previous Help screen, a
valuable feature if you want to review what you have already seen help on.

The Shrink Help button minimizes the Help screen to an icon located in the lower right-hand corner of the desktop. You can click on this icon at any time to restore the Help screen to its original size.

Finally, the Menu button takes you back to the topmost and most general Help screen in the module you are working in. For example, if you are getting help in the spreadsheet module about creating formulas, clicking on the Menu icon will take you to the first screen in Help on spreadsheets. You can always get to the first Help screen in the module, whether it's word processing, spreadsheet, database, or communications, by clicking Menu.

Using Jump Words

In Figure 1-6, in the Step-by-Step area of the Help screen, you see the words *entry bar* underlined (and probably in color as well). This denotes a jump term. When a jump word is underlined in Help, you can find the definition of that word by placing the mouse pointer on the word and then clicking the left mouse button. You can see such a definition for *entry bar* in Figure 1-6. This is a quick and easy way to get basic definitions of important Works terms.

FIGURE 1-6

Clicking on a jump term to get a definition of it

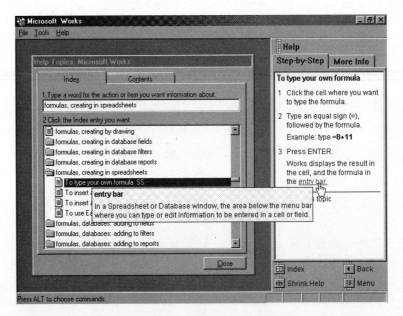

How to Use Help

Help on Help shows you how to use Help. When this command is selected, the Help screen lists a series of topics as shown in Figure 1-7, from which

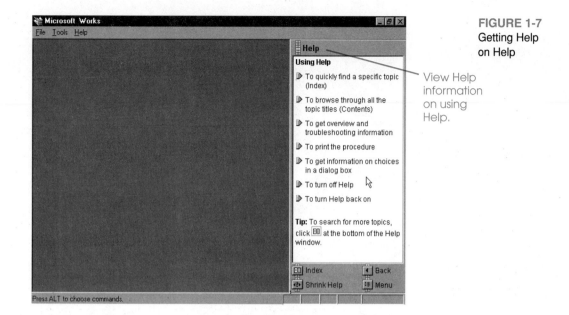

FIGURE 1-7
Getting Help
on Help

View Help
information
on using
Help.

you can begin to find the information you need. Click on any one of these topics and you'll be shown additional screens containing information on how to use the various Help features that we are describing in this section.

Hiding Help

If you no longer want Help visible on the screen while you are working, you can do one of two things. You can click the Shrink Help icon at the bottom of the Help screen. Or, you can select the Hide Help command from the Help menu. Both will get the Help screen out of the picture. The Shrink Help option keeps the icon in sight, should you want to see help quickly, without having to select it from the Help menu. The Hide Help command leaves nothing on the screen; in many of the illustrations that you will see later in this chapter, that command was used to hide Help.

Getting Context-Sensitive Help

There is another way to get help while using any of the many different dialog boxes that Works displays to get information from you. A dialog box is a Windows feature where you are asked to supply information so that Windows can continue. For example, in Figure 1-8 on the following page, you can see the dialog box used in the word processor module to create columns. To use context-sensitive help, follow these steps.

FIGURE 1-8
Using context-
sensitive help

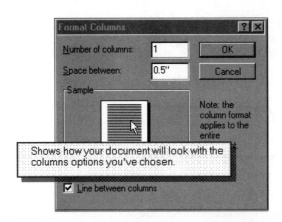

1. Open the dialog box for which you want help.

2. Click the question mark in the upper right-hand corner of the dialog box.

3. Click on whatever portion of the dialog box you want to see help about.

As shown in Figure 1-8, the Sample section was clicked and the purpose of that preview area of the dialog box is explained.

You can only use context-sensitive help within a dialog box.

Knowing Vital Information About Microsoft Works

Finally, the people who designed this terrific package get a chance to plug their good work. When you select About Microsoft Works from the Help menu, you get a screen telling you the version in which you are working, your serial number, and general information about using Works. Why is such information important? First, if you ever need to call Microsoft's technical support, you will have to give your serial number to verify that you have registered. Then in the course of getting help, you may very well need to tell the software engineer who is helping you what version of Works you are using.

Getting Help from the Online Works Forum

On your Windows 95 desktop is a small icon labeled The Microsoft Network. This is your gateway to e-mail, the Internet, and much more. One of the places it can take you is the Microsoft Works Forum, a place where Works users share ideas, tips and tricks, information about new releases,

---

Multiple Product Compatible

You probably know that Microsoft manufactures many other software products such as Microsoft Word and Microsoft Excel. Several of these are combined into Microsoft's successful Office package. Works for Windows 95 is completely compatible with all these programs. For example, you can use the spreadsheet module in Works to read a spreadsheet created with Microsoft Excel. And, you can use Works to read a document created with Microsoft Word.

This high degree of compatibility enables you to easily exchange files from one application to another without losing any information or without necessitating any change in format.

---

unique documents created using Works, and more. You can get there by simply clicking on the Launch Works Forum command on the Help menu. But to connect successfully, you must first be a member of The Microsoft Network. And to do that, you need to double-click on the Microsoft Network icon and then click Connect. Windows 95 will take it from there and sign you up.

Once you are signed up, select the Launch Works Forum command on the Help menu and see how useful the information contributed by Works users just like you can be.

Good Words to You:
The Works Word Processor

Although computers originated as elaborate calculating machines, they are most commonly used today for processing words, not numbers. Of all applications, the word processor is the most popular—so it's a good module to try out first. The Works word processor is remarkably adaptable in many ways, particularly in its ability to insert drawings, spreadsheet charts, and database records into a document. That's the useful, integrated nature of Works. You can even create links to charts and other items so that changes in them are automatically reflected in the word-processed document to which they are linked. And keep in mind that many of the skills you'll learn in this section, such as working with document windows, apply to every module.

To keep the screen simple, we'll start the word processor by telling Works you want to open a new file. Here's how to do it.

1. Start Works if necessary.

2. Click the Works Tools tab in the Task Launcher.

   In a moment, you'll see the word processor's opening screen shown in Figure 1-9. Works Help is automatically available and will remain on the screen unless you turn it off by selecting Hide Help from the Help menu or clicking the Shrink Help icon.

   You'll notice in Figure 1-9 that the opening screen has many familiar Windows characteristics including minimize, maximize, and close buttons, a menu bar, a toolbar, and a work area. Specific to the word processor, you can see a place to enter a header (text that will appear at the top of every page), and both a Page control (for moving between pages) and a Zoom control at the bottom of the screen.

   In the document window, Works displays Unsaved Document 1, the default name for your first new word processing document, be it a letter, memo, or report. Until you name and save a new file, Works always gives it a generic name and number. The default name for an unsaved document created using the word processor is Unsaved Document 1—so named to remind you to save it, if you choose to. When you save a document, you can use up to 255 characters to name the file.

FIGURE 1-9
The Works word
processor
opening screen

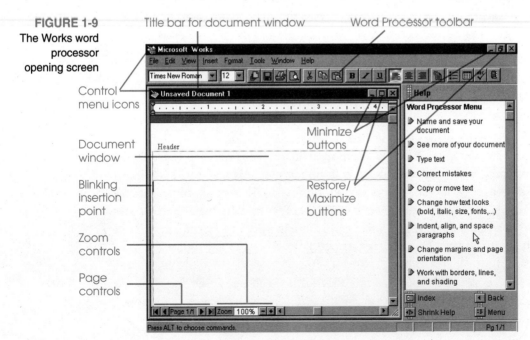

Title bar for document window

Word Processor toolbar

Control menu icons

Document window

Blinking insertion point

Zoom controls

Page controls

Minimize buttons

Restore/ Maximize buttons

TIP Applications such as Works for Windows 95 assign extensions to files, but you won't see them unless you point to the filename in the Explorer or My Computer window, click the right mouse button, and select the Properties command on the pop-up menu.

Notice the two Control menu icons available on your screen. The Control menu box in the top left corner controls the application, or Works, window. Clicking once on that icon reveals a menu of commands that control the application window. Double-clicking on it closes Works. The Control menu icon for the document window, if it has been maximized, appears to the left of the File menu. Otherwise, the Control menu icon appears on the left end of the document window's title bar. Clicking once on that icon reveals a menu of commands that control the document window or determine where you create your document. Double-clicking on this icon closes the document window and returns you to the Task Launcher.

The Application Window

Across the top of the Works application window you'll see a more extensive set of menu names than the three you first saw when starting Works. Just below the menu bar is one of Works' most useful on-screen features, the toolbar.

With the toolbar you can quickly and easily carry out common actions using the mouse. Instead of choosing commands from a menu, you simply click a button on the toolbar to achieve the same result. Once you become accustomed to its speed and responsiveness, the toolbar quickly proves indispensable.

Any Windows 95 application offers many different ways to execute a command, and Works is no exception. You might be able to complete a task by accessing a menu command, by using a keyboard shortcut, or by clicking on a button on the toolbar. You should use whichever method you like the best.

TIP   If you can't recognize what command is associated with a button on the toolbar, move your mouse on top of the button. After a moment, a short description is displayed to tell you what the button will do.

If these messages do not appear for you, open the Tools menu, choose the Customize Toolbar command, and then select the Enable ToolTips command.

Each Works module has its own toolbar. As we progress through those modules later, you'll see how each differs and how each can greatly increase your Works effectiveness.

See Also   For more information on *toolbars*, see "About the Toolbars" on page 37 of this chapter.

The Document Window

You create your word-processed document, including text and graphics, in the document window. At the top is a space to insert a header, and in the left corner of the document window's workspace you'll see a blinking vertical line called the *insertion point*. This line marks the place where text will appear when you begin typing. Try typing some text. If you make a mistake, use the Backspace or arrow keys to move to the error and retype. For the example in this chapter, we typed the following words:

```
This is the first document I've created with the Works
word processor.
```

As you type, the insertion point moves to the right, staying one space ahead of each new character.

The Changing Pointer

Somewhere else in the document window you should also see the mouse pointer. (If you don't see it, move the mouse around a little bit.) The mouse pointer changes shape in different parts of the screen depending on its location. In the word processor, the mouse pointer can take four important shapes:

A vertical line with short crossbars at the top and bottom. This is called an I-beam cursor and is the shape of the mouse pointer when you are entering text.

The arrow, which you have already seen, is the shape of the mouse pointer when you are making a selection from the toolbar or Help.

A double-headed arrow. This is the shape of the cursor when you are changing the size of the document window by placing the mouse pointer on the right or bottom edge and dragging the edge to the left or up.

A "cross" of sorts, with parallel lines as the horizontal bar and a double-headed arrow as the vertical bar. This is called a split cursor and on the screen is labeled ADJUST. It is used to split the document window into separate panes for viewing different parts of a document at the same time.

Each of these shapes indicates the task the pointer can perform. Within the document workspace, the mouse pointer appears as an I-beam cursor. You can easily move the insertion point to the location where you want to insert text or select text for editing by moving the mouse cursor to the desired location, and clicking. Practice moving the insertion point and highlighting as follows.

1. Place the pointer just in front of a letter in your document.

2. Click the left mouse button and watch as the insertion point jumps to that position.

3. Double-click the mouse. (The pointer should still be in the same position.)

    A dark highlight covers the entire word to which you are pointing, indicating that it is selected. We did this to highlight the word *document*, as you see in Figure 1-10 on the next page. We've hidden Help so that more of the document window shows.

You can also highlight text by holding down the left mouse button and dragging the mouse cursor across the text to be selected. Let's look at how the pointer changes its appearance within a Works document.

1. Move the pointer to the menu bar.
    Notice that the pointer changes to an arrow.

2. Point to a menu and click to open it. The menu opens.

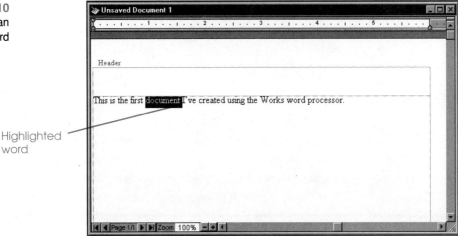

Highlighted
word

3. Now move the pointer into the document workspace. Make sure you're not anywhere within the menu.

4. Click to close the menu.

This is how to use the mouse pointer for its usual point-and-click function. Because a menu was open and Works expected you to choose a command, the mouse pointer remained an arrow even though you moved it back into the document workspace. When you closed the menu, indicating that you were finished with it, the mouse pointer returned to its I-beam shape.

For a preview of the last shape (a cross), do the following.

1. Move the mouse pointer to the small rectangle (the split box) just above the up scroll arrow in the vertical scroll bar.

2. When you see the split cursor, hold down the left mouse button and drag down toward the middle of the screen. Then release the mouse button.

As you can see in Figure 1-11 the mouse pointer (labeled ADJUST on the screen) splits a window into two panes. When you split a window, you can scroll each pane independently to view different parts of a long document. This is a great feature to use when you need to work in one part of a long document, yet see what's in another part of the same document.

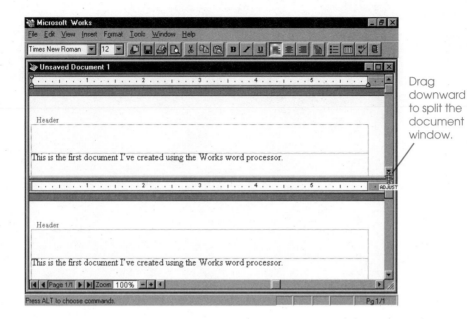

FIGURE 1-11
Splitting a window

Drag
downward
to split the
document
window.

As you'll see later, the mouse pointer assumes other shapes in the spreadsheet and database. When you explore these applications in detail, you'll see how the shape of the mouse pointer gives you visual clues as to what it can do.

TIP To remove the split and return to a single window, place the mouse pointer on the horizontal split bar separating the two panes. Double-click, or drag the split bar off the screen.

Managing Document Windows

Every time you open a document, whether it's a new or an existing file, Works opens a document window. As in Windows, you can choose to cascade document windows (overlapping them on the screen), or you can choose to tile them (placing them side by side in the available space). You can maximize a document window to fill the application workspace, or you can minimize it and reduce it to an out-of-the-way icon.

To see how easily you can work with multiple documents, open a second window by following these steps. The Unsaved Document 1 document window should still be the active window.

FIGURE 1-12
Tiling more than
one window

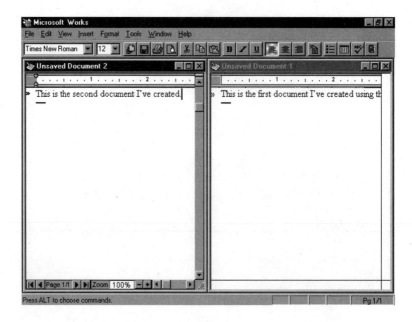

1. Click File, and then click New.

2. Click the Word Processor button to create another word processing document named Unsaved Document 2.

3. When the second window opens, distinguish it from the first by typing some different text. In our example, we typed the following text:

   `This is the second document I've created.`

4. Open the Window menu, and then choose Tile to see both windows. The windows appear side by side as shown in Figure 1-12.

TIP   Whenever more than one window is open, only one can be active. The active window is always the one with the title bar appearing in color. The inactive window (or windows) is the one that has a dimmed title bar.

Tiling windows makes it easier to work with two or more documents. Each window is equipped with its own title bar, scroll bars, and control buttons, so you can manipulate each as you choose. To switch from one document to another, just click in the window you want.

To clear the screen a bit, close the second document window without saving your sample text by following these steps.

1. Make the Unsaved Document 2 window active.

2. Double-click on its Control menu icon, or click the File menu and then click Close.

   Works displays this Microsoft Works dialog box.

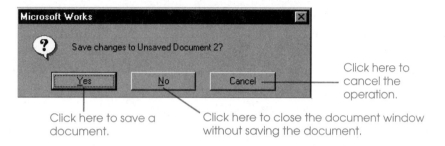

Click here to cancel the operation.

Click here to save a document.

Click here to close the document window without saving the document.

3. Choose No to discard this practice document.

These steps are the way to "toss out" an unnamed document you no longer want. You can eliminate the empty space left by the closed document by maximizing the remaining active one or by clicking Tile on the Window menu.

TIP The Microsoft Works dialog box is extremely important since you are only one step away from throwing out or discarding all of your work in the current document. Make sure this is what you really want to do. Works is asking you if you want to save your work, before you close the document. If you answer No, be sure this is what you want to do.

That's enough of the word processor for now. Let's move on and get acquainted with the Works spreadsheet module.

Your Electronic Ledger: The Works Spreadsheet

The Works spreadsheet lets you work with and manipulate numeric data, such as financial statements, budget projections, and salary information. Because much of the work you do with numbers involves calculations, the spreadsheet enables you to build formulas to add, subtract, multiply, work out percentages, and perform many other simple and complex calculations. The spreadsheet is also the ideal tool for creating tables and charts.

For certain calculations, such as averages, loan payments, and return on investments, the spreadsheet even includes predesigned formulas called functions that you can use by simply plugging your numbers into the formulas and letting Works take care of the rest.

You can experiment with different possibilities (the so-called "what-if" scenarios) to see which of several alternatives works best for you. For example, you can calculate the difference in payments on a loan extending 5, 10, and 15 years. How do those payments fit into your current budget? Which payment comes closest to your projected future income? For that matter, what *is* your projected future income?

The spreadsheet can't decide any of these things for you, but it can help you see the figures more clearly, especially if you use it to transform those numbers into a graph or chart that illustrates what you see numerically.

You can start the spreadsheet while the word processor is running by following these steps.

1. Click File, and then choose New.

2. Click the Spreadsheet button.

A new document window appears, as shown in Figure 1-13, containing a blank document named Unsaved Spreadsheet 1 and a rectangular grid of small boxes called cells.

A spreadsheet consists of rows and columns. Each place where a row and column intersect is called a *cell*. Each of the cells on your screen can contain a numeric value, an item of text, or a formula that performs a calculation.

Notice the letters across the top of the window. Each letter refers to one vertical column of cells on the spreadsheet. Similarly, you can see numbers running down the left side of the window. Each of these numbers

Column   Cell   Spreadsheet toolbar

FIGURE 1-13
A new spreadsheet
document window

Highlight

Row

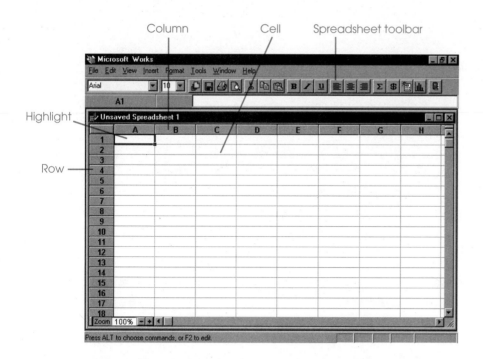

refers to one horizontal row of cells. Because each cell occupies a unique position in the spreadsheet, it has its own address that indicates the column and row intersection where the cell is located. For example, the cell in the top left corner of the spreadsheet (currently outlined by a double-lined box called the *highlight*) is cell A1 because it is in column A and in row 1. You and Works use cell addresses whenever you want to refer to a specific cell or group of cells. Notice also that the spreadsheet opening screen contains the regular complement of Windows elements such as a toolbar (though it's different from the one you've seen so far), scroll bars, menus, a work area, and maximize, minimize, and close buttons.

Recall that the mouse pointer looks like a slender I in a word processor document. In the spreadsheet, it looks like a chubby cross. But as with the word processor, the mouse pointer changes as it does its job. Move it around on the screen and you'll notice it changing shape, depending on the screen region it touches.

Entering and Calculating Numbers

You've probably noticed that the toolbar in the spreadsheet looks different from the toolbar in the word processor. Specifically, several buttons toward the right side of the toolbar have changed.

In the word processor, buttons control features such as the use of bullets (•) in a list, the insertion of tables, and the use of the spelling checker. These buttons aren't needed in the spreadsheet, so they are replaced by other buttons that let you automatically sum a column or row of numbers, format numbers as currency, and create charts with just a few clicks.

Let's try out some of these buttons now. Follow these steps.

1. Verify that the highlight is in the top left corner of the grid (cell A1). If not, just move the mouse pointer there and click.

2. Type some numbers in cell A1. We entered *123* in our example.

3. Press the Down arrow key to enter the number and, at the same time, move the highlight down one cell.

4. Type some other numbers in cell A2, and press the Down arrow key again. We typed *456*.

5. Type some other numbers in cell A3, and press the Down arrow key once more. We typed *789*.

   The spreadsheet should appear as shown in Figure 1-14.

FIGURE 1-14

Entering numbers
in a spreadsheet

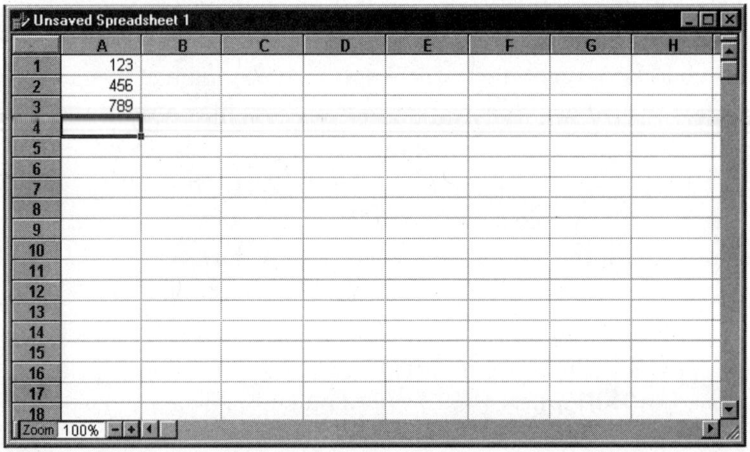

The numbers in our example are rather plain at the moment. Let's have Works display the numbers as dollar values by using the toolbar.

1. Select cells in which you've entered data by placing the mouse pointer in the first cell, pressing the left mouse button, and dragging the mouse pointer to the last cell. In our example we highlighted cells A1, A2, and A3.

2. Click the right mouse button and click the Format command on the pop-up menu.

    When you do this, you will see the Format Cells dialog box shown in Figure 1-15. Here you make selections to format selected cells in a variety of ways.

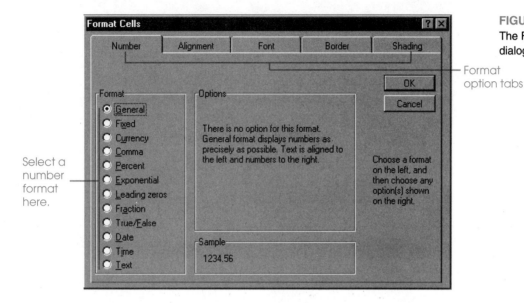

Select a
number
format
here.

FIGURE 1-15
The Format Cells
dialog box

Format
option tabs

3. Click the Currency button, and then click OK.

    Works automatically formats all three cells as currency.

4. Click the New Chart button (second from the right that looks like a bar chart) on the toolbar.

    You'll see the New Chart dialog box.

5. Click OK. Then click OK.

▨ Clicking the Right Mouse Button

One of the neatest features that Windows 95 offers is the set of options on a pop-up menu that become available when you click or press the right mouse button. In Works, clicking the right mouse button in a spreadsheet cell lets you cut, copy, or paste text; insert or delete rows or columns; format and select cells; and more. Always click the right mouse button in any Works document just to see what you might be able to do.

A new document window opens, displaying the chart shown in Figure 1-16.

FIGURE 1-16
The easiest way to
create a chart

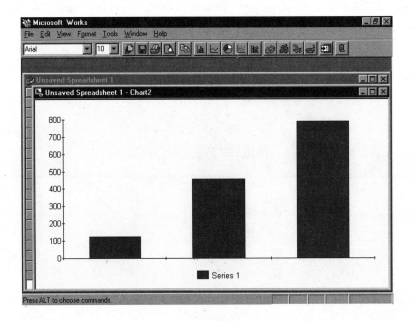

This is how to turn the numbers into a graphic display. If anything can demonstrate the ease with which Works can help you master data, creating a chart can. Return to the spreadsheet document by opening the Window menu, and then choosing Unsaved Spreadsheet 1.

That's enough for now with the spreadsheet, so let's close it up and move on to the database. Follow these steps to close the spreadsheet.

1. Click File, click Close, and then click No.

    Since the chart is linked to the spreadsheet, both will close and not be saved.

Your Electronic Filing Cabinet: The Works Database

With the word processor you can write anything from a letter of congratulations to a complicated, multilevel bid proposal. With the spreadsheet you can track numbers ranging from pennies to your Fortune 500 stocks.

What's left? A place to organize information into lists and manipulate it as well. You can keep lists of any kind, for any purpose, but you will most likely keep lists of entries you want to sort in some way, from names and addresses to warehouse inventories, catalog items, or a lifetime list of bird species spotted in your backyard.

All these lists can be turned over to the Works database, a far more organized and efficient list maker than most humans. A database is a set of records related to a particular topic. Each record forms a unit of information made up of from one to several fields. Each field contains one piece of data about the record. To see how the database works, we can create a sample database with three fields—Last Name, First Name, and Dept—which form records for several employees. Here's the information that we will place in our sample database.

Last Name	First Name	Dept.
Dillon	Mariane	Accounting
Tanaka	George	Accounting
Mayer	Oscar	Sales
Donatello	Raphael	Graphic Arts
Smith	Georgia	Sales

The spreadsheet helps you by manipulating numbers, calculating formulas, and creating charts. Similarly, the Works database sorts records for you, finds specific entries, and even examines records to find those that match qualifications you specify. If you want, the database can calculate averages, find the highest and lowest values in a given field, or generate a report.

To start the database, follow these steps.

1. Click File, and then choose New.

2. Click the Database button.

You'll see a new screen, a new document name (Unsaved Database 1), and a new and different toolbar. Works presents you with a blank slate but, unlike the word processor, the database opens with the Create Database dialog box over the document window, as shown in Figure 1-17 on the next page.

You then proceed to define each of the fields that you are going to add to the database, and select the format (General, Number, Date, and so on) for the data that will be entered in that field. You create the fields that will hold the data for each of the records in your database on this form. You can arrange the fields in any way, much as you would when creating a paper-based form for employee information, test scores, insurance coverage, or any other set of records.

FIGURE 1-17

The opening
database window
and Create
Database
dialog box

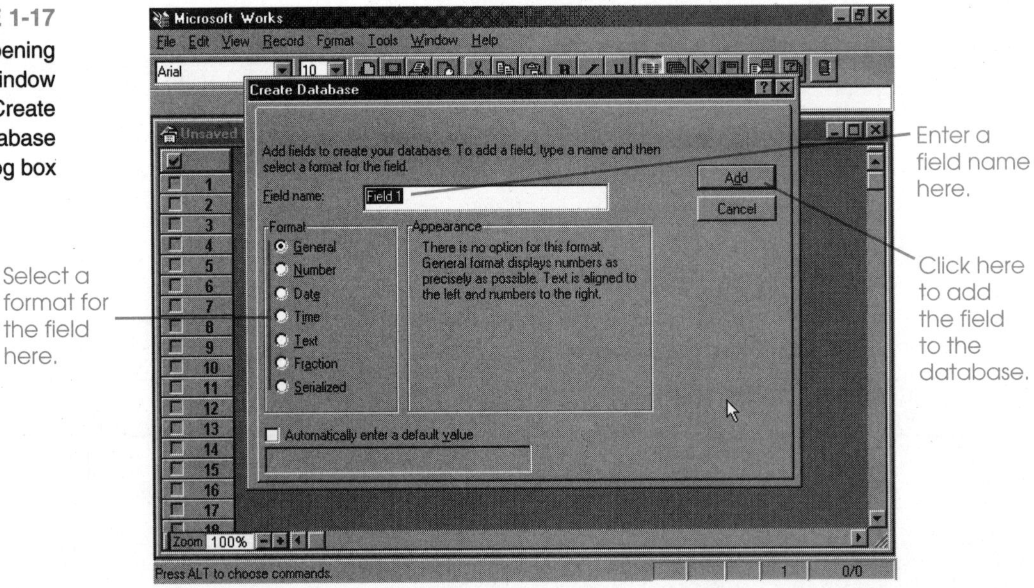

Select a
format for
the field
here.

Enter a
field name
here.

Click here
to add
the field
to the
database.

Unlike the other Works applications, the database has four views. In Figure 1-18, you see the database in the List view, which displays groups of records in a spreadsheet-like format. In Form view you can use a form to enter information one record at a time. In Form Design view, you can customize the form's layout and use borders, colors, and even objects. Finally, in Report view you can add and delete fields, group records in any fashion you want, and also perform calculations; Report view also generates a printable report listing selected records and calculations you choose to include. Several buttons on the toolbar let you quickly change views, or you can select a view from the View menu.

Entering Records and Viewing a Database

Let's create a form for the data shown earlier. The first thing you need to do is type the field names.

1. Type a name for the first field and click Add. This is the definition of field #1. We entered *Last Name* in our example.

2. Type a name for the second field and click Add. We entered *First Name* in our example.

3. Type a name for the next field and click Add. We entered *Dept.* in our example.

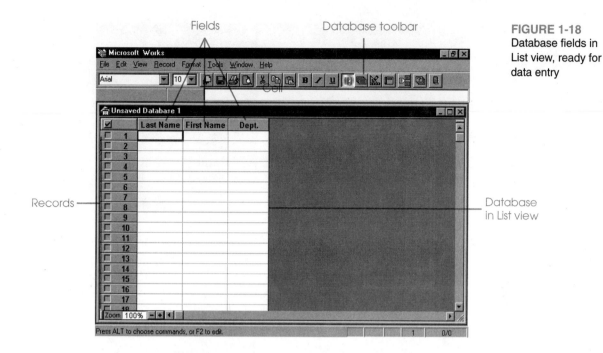

Fields   Database toolbar

FIGURE 1-18
Database fields in
List view, ready for
data entry

Records

Database
in List view

4. Click Done when you have added all the fields you want.

     An example of a database in List view, ready for data entry, appears as shown in Figure 1-18.

Now you're ready to enter some data. To do so, follow these steps.

1. Click the first field (or column) in the row that is numbered 1.

2. Type a last name for the first employee and press Tab. In our example we entered the name *Dillon*.

     The highlight moves to the next field, First Name.

3. Type a first name and press Tab. We entered the name *Mariane* in our example.

4. Type a department title and press Tab to start a new record. We entered the title *Accounting* in our example.

5. Create at least three additional records. Press Enter when you complete the last record. We entered the four additional records you see in Figure 1-19 on the next page.

FIGURE 1-19
The database
containing
data entries

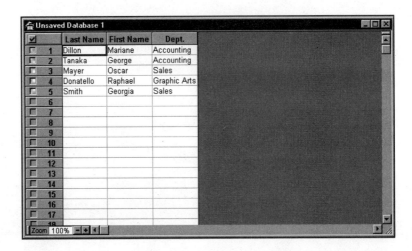

The default view is List view, which is what you see in Figure 1-18 on the preceding page with the completed database shown in Figure 1-19.

Finding information in a database is the result of posing a *query*, which is a question you specify for the database to search for records. Performing a query in Works involves using a filter where you filter out those records you don't want, based on certain criteria. Here's how to perform a simple query using a filter.

1. Click Tools, and then click Filters, or click the Filters button on the toolbar.

2. Type a name for the filter and click OK.

    In this example, we typed *Accounting* since we will be searching the database for all those people who work in the Accounting Department. Here, we are simply telling Works the name of the filter. We are not yet defining what we will be searching for.

3. Click on the top Field Name drop-down menu, and select the appropriate field name. In our example we selected the Dept. field.

    The field name appears in the Filter dialog box's Field Name box, as you see on the following page.

4. Click in the Compare To text box and type a department title. We entered the title *Accounting* in our example.

5. Click Apply Filter.

    Works will go through the database and select only those records that meet the selected criterion. In our example Works selects

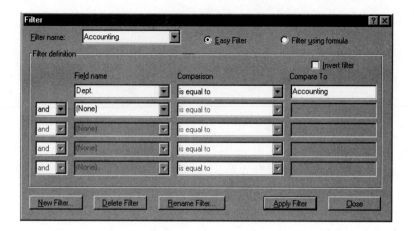

those records with the word Accounting in the Dept. field. In this case Works selects records for Mariane Dillion and George Tanaka, the only employees in the database who work in Accounting.

See Also For more information on *using filters to query a database*, see "Fashioning a Query and Using Filters" in Chapter 10, page 340.

About the Toolbars

Each of the Works modules—word processor, spreadsheet, database, and communications—has its own toolbar. Other parts of Works have more specialized toolbars. The toolbars contain sets of buttons that perform tasks—generally, those tasks that are used more often than others. These buttons provide shortcuts to corresponding commands that you can select from menus. For example, all the toolbars contain this Save button:

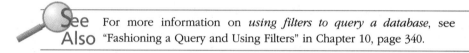

So instead of clicking File, and then clicking Save to save changes to a document, you can simply click the Save button to do the same thing.

Although each module's toolbar varies somewhat from the others, all of them contain several of the same buttons. For example, in addition to the Save button we just mentioned, all four modules also contain the Task Launcher button you see here:

In addition to the buttons common to all or some of the modules, each toolbar comes with several buttons that perform tasks that are specific to the module. For example, only on the word processor module's toolbar will you see this Spelling Checker button:

Similarly, only on the spreadsheet module's toolbar will you see this New Chart button:

And, the database and communications modules also contain unique buttons for tasks specific to those modules.

Customizing the Toolbars

A specific toolbar might not have all the buttons you want. Moreover, buttons that you never use might be there. For example, you might never need to use the Bullets button on the word processor's toolbar, but you might like a button that double-spaces text. In other words, you want to customize the toolbar to fit the way you work. To make room on the toolbar for a new button, you might have to first remove one or more buttons you don't want; then you can add one or more new ones. In this example, we'll remove the Bullets button from the word processor module's toolbar and add a new one that double-spaces text. Here's how you do it.

1. Click Tools, and then click Customize Toolbar, or double-click on any blank space on the toolbar.

When you do this, you'll see this Customize Works Toolbar dialog box:

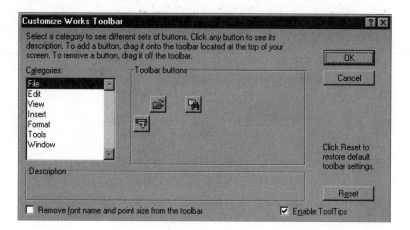

Unless this dialog box is active, you can't remove or add buttons.

2. Position the mouse pointer on the Customize Works Toolbar title bar and drag the dialog box downward so that you can see the toolbar you want to change.

3. To remove any button, simply drag it off the toolbar. For example, you can drag the Bullets button (fourth from the right) off the toolbar.

4. Select the category of the button you want to add from the list in the Categories box. In our example, we would select Format.

When you select a category, you see the buttons that are available in that category to add to the toolbar.

TIP To find out what a button does, place the mouse pointer on the button, and then press and hold down the mouse button (or just click it). A description of the button's function appears in the Description box.

5. Drag the button you want to add—in this example, the button that sets spacing for a selection to two lines—to its new location on the toolbar. You can add as many buttons as you make space for.

6. Click OK in the Customize Works Toolbar dialog box, and you've added a button!

A Works toolbar can't be moved to a new location in a window, nor can you create a totally new toolbar. If you find that you want to return to the button arrangement on the original toolbar, just click Reset in the Customize Works Toolbar dialog box.

Combining Data from Applications

As a final exercise, try moving a few records from your database into the word-processed "document" you created earlier.

In the past, transferring data between documents created by different applications was one of the most difficult and frustrating activities in personal computing. With Works, it's a breeze—thanks to Windows and a special Windows feature called the Clipboard.

About the Clipboard

Earlier in this chapter, we explained that Windows and Works form a partnership to help you get things done. Although you can't see the Clipboard, it forms an important part of Windows.

The Clipboard is a portion of your computer's memory that Windows sets aside specifically for holding data that you want to move from one part of the document to another part of that same document, or from one document to another. After you place information on the Clipboard, whether it's text or a graphic, one paragraph or several pages, that information remains in your computer's memory and is available to programs that can accept it until you place new data on the Clipboard.

To move data from document to document, you use a process called cut and paste. Cut and paste is the electronic equivalent of scissors and tape. You've no doubt snipped text from a letter, report, or proposal and reorganized it or inserted parts of a different document by taping the pieces together in a new order. You use cut and paste in Windows applications such as Works in much the same way, but without the mess. Windows, in fact, is better than real-life cut and paste, because it lets you *copy* and paste as well.

You can rearrange or duplicate information across documents with only three basic commands in the Edit menu: Cut, Copy, and Paste; or you can use the corresponding buttons on the toolbar. Cut, as its name implies, removes information and places it on the Clipboard. Copy duplicates information, placing a copy on the Clipboard but leaving the original where it belongs. Paste inserts the contents of the Clipboard into an open document.

Using the Clipboard to Move Information Between Documents

To demonstrate how to move data between documents in two different Works modules, we'll provide an example that places information in two database records into a word-processed document, as follows:

1. Drag the mouse pointer to extend the highlight to cover the cells containing the information you want to copy.

2. Point to the selected records, click the right mouse button, and select Copy on the pop-up menu.

3. Click Window, and then click the window containing the document that will receive the information.

4. Place the insertion point where you want to insert the contents of the Clipboard.

5. Click the right mouse button, and then click Paste on the pop-up menu.

    The copied information appears in the receiving document as you see in Figure 1-20. That's all there is to it!

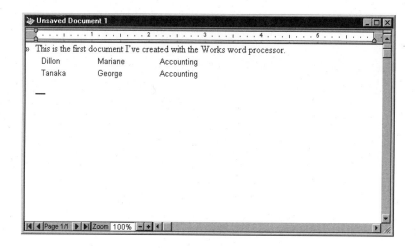

FIGURE 1-20

Pasting database information into the word processor

Now let's move on to Chapter 2, where we'll learn all about the Task Launcher and how TaskWizards can walk you through the creation of 40 different sophisticated and useful documents. If you need to clear your Works application window by closing open document windows, here's how to do it:

1. Close all open documents by clicking File, and then clicking Close for each.

2. When you are asked whether you want to save a document, choose the appropriate button: Yes, if you want to save your changes or No, if you don't.

    You'll be returned to the opening screen, the Works Task Launcher.

Coming Next

This chapter gave you a taste of what Works is all about, what the various modules can do for you, and how to use Works Help. Before we start a detailed discussion of how to use each of these modules, let's first turn to a set of powerful helpers, including Works TaskWizards. TaskWizards are tools that design personalized documents for you when you simply follow Works' step-by-step plans.

Chapter 2

What Do
You Want to Do?

You've had a good run through the modules, Works options, and Help features provided by Works for Windows 95. You already know that the Task Launcher is what you see on the Works opening screen. Through the Task Launcher, you can start a TaskWizard, open an existing document, or create a new document using one of the Works modules. In this chapter we will discuss each of these three options and give you examples of how they work.

Starting a TaskWizard

Perhaps the best feature of this new version of Works is how TaskWizards walk you through the creation of even the most complex documents. There are 39 TaskWizards, organized into different categories such as Common Tasks, Business Management, and Employment. In fact, TaskWizards can be such an important part of Works that many Works users will never create a document entirely from scratch; they will use the TaskWizards that are provided instead. Once a TaskWizard is created, it can be saved and further modified like any Works document, giving you even *more* flexibility.

A Directory of TaskWizards

The 39 TaskWizards are organized in 10 different categories. Some (such as the Letter and Statement TaskWizard) show up in more than one category. A list of what each one does is in Table 2-1, which describes each TaskWizard and the categories in which it is used.

TaskWizard Name	Description	Categories (Location)	Module It Uses
Accounts	Tracks accounts receivable, accounts payable, or checking accounts.	Business Management, Billing	
Address Book	Organize phone numbers, addresses, and other information about business clients, friends, family, or others.	Common Tasks, Names and Addresses, Household Management, Volunteer/Civic Activities	

TABLE 2-1

(continued)

TaskWizards, what they do, and where to find them

TABLE 2-1 *continued*

TaskWizard Name	Description	Categories (Location)	Module It Uses
Bibliography	Create a list of reference sources in specified bibliographic style.	Students and Teachers	
Bids	Create a form to estimate the costs of labor and/or materials.	Correspondence, Business Management, Billing	
Brochure	Create a side-fold or three-fold document for advertising purposes.	Correspondence, Business Management	
Business Inventory	Maintain an inventory of materials and equipment used in a business.	Business Management	
Certificate	Create a one-page certificate that acknowledges an individual.	Correspondence, Students and Teachers, Volunteer/Civic Activities	
Customers or Clients	Record information about clients.	Names and Addresses	
Employee Profile	Maintain a record of employee names, addresses, and other important information.	Business Management, Names and Addresses, Employment	
Employee Timesheet	Record weekly, bimonthly, or monthly time and wages for hourly employees.	Business Management, Employment	
Envelopes	Create envelopes and mailing labels from entries in the address book.	Envelopes and Labels	
Fax Cover Sheets	Create a one-page document that contains telephone numbers and routing information to accompany a fax.	Correspondence	

(continued)

TABLE 2-1 *continued*

TaskWizard Name	Description	Categories (Location)	Module It Uses
Flyer	Create a single-page advertisement.	Correspondence, Business Management	
Form Letter	Create a standardized letter to send to the people in the address book.	Correspondence	
Grade Book	Record student performance.	Students and Teachers	
Home Inventory	Create an inventory of possessions and their value.	Household Management	
Invoice	Create a form to calculate prices and to bill customers for goods and services.	Business Management, Billing	
Labels	Create mailing labels for address book entries.	Envelopes and Labels	
Letter	Create standard elements of a document that uses supplied text: current date, return address, recipient address, salutation, and signature block.	Common Tasks, Correspondence, Household Management, Employment, Volunteer/Civic Activities	
Letterhead	Personalize your stationery.	Common Tasks, Correspondence	
Memo	Create a memorandum for business or personal use.	Correspondence	
Mortgage/ Loan Analysis	Analyze the costs associated with a loan.	Business Management, Household Management	
Newsletter	Create a one-, two-, or three-column document.	Common Tasks, Correspondence, Business Management, Students and Teachers, Volunteer/Civic Activities	

(continued)

TABLE 2-1 *continued*

TaskWizard Name	Description	Categories (Location)	Module It Uses
Order Form	Create a form for customers to order goods.	Business Management, Billing	
Phone List	Create an organized list of phone numbers of friends, business associates, and others.	Names and Addresses, Household Management	
Price List	Create a document that informs customers of prices of products.	Business Management	
Proposal Forms	Create a single-page or multiple-page proposal.	Correspondence, Business Management, Billing	
Proposal Letter	Create a prewritten proposal, a cover letter, or a follow-up letter, plus guidelines for writing your own.	Correspondence, Business Management, Billing	
Quotations	Create a form to submit standard quotes, and customized quotes.	Correspondence, Business Management, Billing	
Resume (CV)	Create a summary of work and qualifications (curriculum vitae)	Common Tasks, Correspondence, Business Management, Students and Teachers, Employment	
Return Address Labels	Create mailing return address labels for your correspondence.	Envelopes and Labels	
Sales Contacts	Keep track of key information about customers.	Names and Addresses	
Schedule	Create a form to schedule classrooms, write lesson plans, and more.	Business Management, Students and Teachers	

(continued)

TABLE 2-1 *continued*

TaskWizard Name	Description	Categories (Location)	Module It Uses
School Reports/ Thesis	Create a report.	Students and Teachers	
Start from Scratch	Create a custom document with the word processor, spread-sheet, or database.	Common Tasks	
Statements	Create a monthly statement of overdue balances, showing purchases, payments, and credits.	Correspondence, Business Management, Billing	
Student & Membership Information	Record names, addresses, and other important student or member information.	Names and Addresses, Students and Teachers, Volunteer/Civic Activities	
Suppliers & Vendors	Track information about vendors and suppliers.	Business Management, Names and Addresses	
Tests	Create a true/false, multiple choice, or essay test from a preformatted layout.	Students and Teachers	

The general strategy for using a TaskWizard is to select the category you want to use, next select the specific TaskWizard, and then follow the steps as dictated by the TaskWizard when it runs. TaskWizards in effect are predesigned uses of the word processor, spreadsheet, and database modules within Works. For example, the Letter TaskWizard is based on the word processor, the Grade Book TaskWizard is based on the spreadsheet, and the Accounts TaskWizard on the database.

TABLE 2-2
TaskWizards used
for business,
school, and
personal activities
and the Works
module on which
they are based

	TaskWizard Based on the Word Processor	TaskWizard Based on the Spreadsheet	TaskWizard Based on the Database
Business	Statement	Price List	Accounts
Personal	Letterhead	Mortgage/ Loan Analysis	Address Book
School	Tests	Grade Book	Student Information

Let's look at three scenarios where TaskWizards can be used: one in which a small business uses Works to organize bookkeeping tasks, another in which personal documents are organized, and the third in a school setting in which grades and student information are tracked. In Table 2-2, you can see what the different TaskWizards are and note how they're organized within each scenario.

TIP You can always tell on which Works module a TaskWizard is based by examining the icon that accompanies it in the TaskWizards window. The little pad and pencil represents the word processor, the calculator represents the spreadsheet, and the cards represent the database.

Using TaskWizards in a Business Setting

Mike runs a juggling and kite business named Things-That-Fly, and as with any business, he has to send out statements, generate a price list for his customers, and keep his accounts current so that they can be billed. To accomplish these tasks, he will use three different TaskWizards. We'll begin with the Accounts TaskWizard.

Starting the Accounts TaskWizard

The Accounts TaskWizard provides an automated procedure for customizing documents that track receivable and payable activities.

1. Start Works.

2. If the Task Launcher is not already present on the screen, click File, and then click New.

3. Click the TaskWizards tab.

4. Click a TaskWizard category. We selected Business Management.

    As you can see in Figure 2-1, when a TaskWizard category is opened, its list of TaskWizards becomes visible.

5. Click a TaskWizard. Here we selected Accounts.

    When you click on a TaskWizard, an explanation of what it does appears.

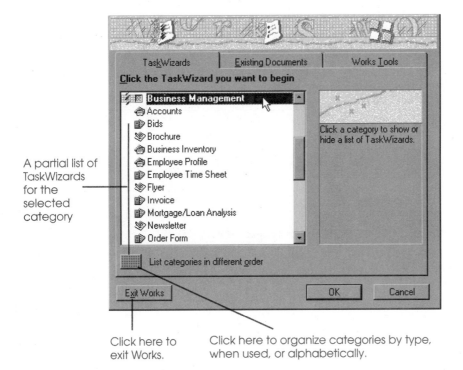

A partial list of TaskWizards for the selected category

Click here to exit Works.

Click here to organize categories by type, when used, or alphabetically.

FIGURE 2-1

Selecting a TaskWizard from the Business Management category

6. Click OK.

Once you begin the TaskWizard process, the Works Task Launcher appears, which gives you the option to create an entirely new document or work with an existing one as you see here:

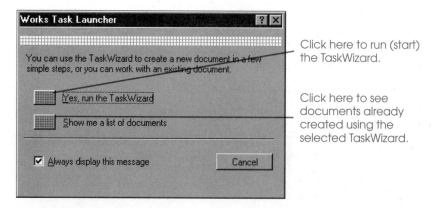

Click here to run (start) the TaskWizard.

Click here to see documents already created using the selected TaskWizard.

7. Click Yes, Run The TaskWizard.

As you can see in Figure 2-2, you are shown the first screen in the selected TaskWizard. This one asks you to select whether you want to create the layout for an Accounts Receivable, an Accounts Payable, or a Checking Account document. Notice also that Works provides a description of the document on the right-hand side of the screen.

The opening screens in all Works' TaskWizards display an Instructions button. You can click on this button to get information on how to use the TaskWizard. You can cancel the TaskWizard by clicking the Cancel button, or run it by clicking Create It!

Creating an Accounts Payable Document

In our example, we'll create a document layout for tracking accounts payable information, as follows:

1. Click a document option button, and then click Create It! We selected Accounts Payable.

The process for creating the database document begins. As you see in Figure 2-3, a database has been created with several different fields (in Form view) into which Mike can enter information about people and companies that owe him money. To let you see more of the document, Help has been hidden.

2. Enter information and print the document.

Document option buttons

A reduced image of the document

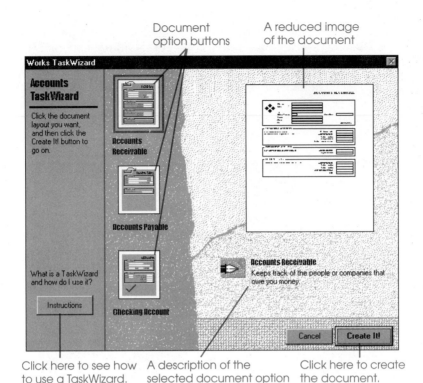

Click here to see how to use a TaskWizard.

A description of the selected document option

Click here to create the document.

FIGURE 2-2
The opening screen for the Accounts TaskWizard

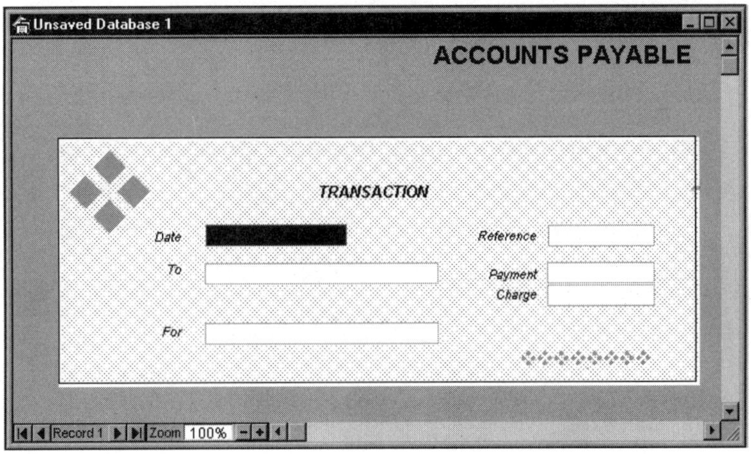

FIGURE 2-3
The Accounts Payable document window

Now Mike must enter the information that the database requires, including date, a reference number to whom the invoice is to be sent, any payments and charges, and what the invoice is for. Enough information was entered to provide a summary of the payments and charges for the database, as you can see in the document shown in Figure 2-4.

FIGURE 2-4

The completed
Accounts Payable
document

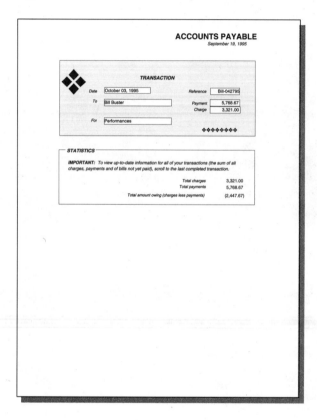

3.   Click the Close button for the Unsaved Database 1 window.

4.   Click No to clear the window without without saving the document.

Starting the Statements TaskWizard

The Statements TaskWizard lets you prepare a monthly overdue notice for customers, showing purchases, payments, credits, and how much the customer owes. We'll continue our example by creating a statement document, as follows:

1. If the Task Launcher is not already present on the screen, click File, and then click New.

2. Click the TaskWizards tab.

3. Click a TaskWizard category. Here we again selected Business Management.

4. Click a TaskWizard. Here we selected Statements. Then click OK, and click Yes, Run The TaskWizard.

    The Statements TaskWizard screen, shown in Figure 2-5, provides you with two options: creating a monthly statement or creating a collection letter.

Document option buttons

A reduced image of the document

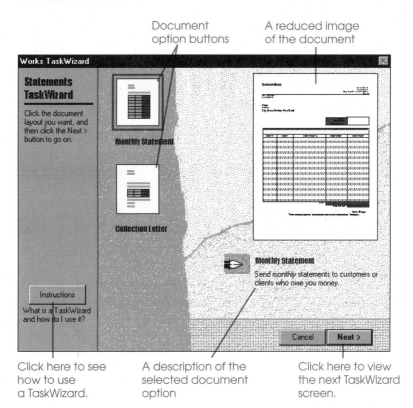

FIGURE 2-5

The Statements TaskWizard opening screen

Click here to see how to use a TaskWizard.

A description of the selected document option

Click here to view the next TaskWizard screen.

Creating a Monthly Statement Document

A monthly statement is a document you send to customers as a courtesy showing overdue balances, purchases, payments, and credits.

1. Click a document option button, and then click Next. We chose the Monthly Statement option button.

   The next Statements TaskWizard screen appears, as shown in Figure 2-6.

FIGURE 2-6
The next
Statements
TaskWizard screen

Click any of these options to customize selected document elements.

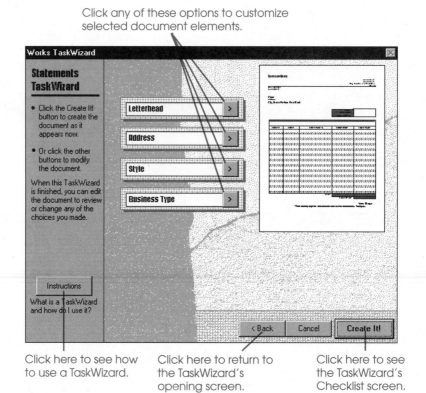

Click here to see how to use a TaskWizard.

Click here to return to the TaskWizard's opening screen.

Click here to see the TaskWizard's Checklist screen.

Different TaskWizards require different types and amounts of information. Within the Statements TaskWizard you need to provide information such as the type of letterhead you want to use, how you want the statement addressed, and more. You can accept the default settings by clicking the Create It! button, which we will do here in our example.

2. Click Create It!

   A Checklist screen listing items to be included on the monthly statement document appears, as shown in Figure 2-7. If you need to

View the options the TaskWizard will
use to create the document.

FIGURE 2-7
The Statements
TaskWizard's
Checklist screen

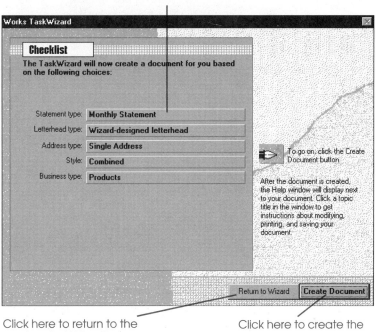

Click here to return to the
previous TaskWizard screen.

Click here to create the
selected document.

change any of these settings, you can click the Return To Wizard
button.

TIP When you're in the middle of a TaskWizard step,
you can always go back and review what you've done
by clicking the Back button or the Return To Wizard
button.

3. Click Create Document.

    Works creates the monthly statement document, without the
specific information that you will want to enter, as shown in Figure
2-8 on the following page.

    Using the word processor, Mike edits the document accordingly,
to produce the document shown in Figure 2-9 on the next page. As

FIGURE 2-8

The unmodified
Monthly Statement
document

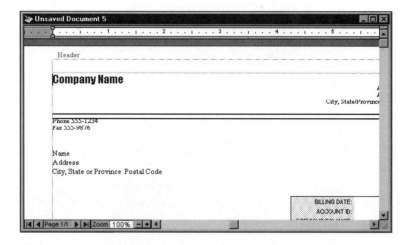

with any other document created with the word processor, the monthly statement can be edited and saved.

4. Click the Close button to close the document window without saving the document.

FIGURE 2-9

The modified
Monthly Statement
document

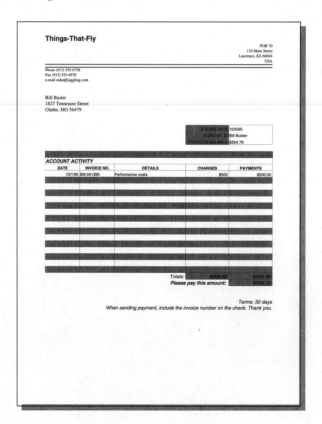

Starting the Price List TaskWizard

The Price List TaskWizard provides an automated procedure for creating a price list document. We'll use this TaskWizard to create the final document in our first scenario example.

1. If the Task Launcher is not already present on the screen, click File, and then click New.

2. Click the TaskWizards tab.

3. Click a TaskWizard category. Here again we selected Business Management.

4. Scroll the list, if necessary, and click a TaskWizard. Then click OK, and click Yes, Run The TaskWizard. Here we selected the Price List TaskWizard.

   The Price List TaskWizard screen, shown in Figure 2-10, provides Mike with three options: Standard Price List, Combination Price List, and Sales Price List. Mike wants to produce a sales price list.

Document option buttons

A reduced image of the selected document

FIGURE 2-10
The Price List TaskWizard options

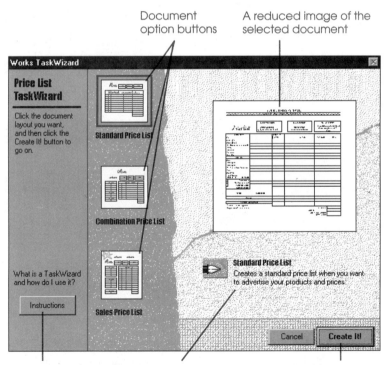

Click here to see how to use a TaskWizard.

A description of the selected document option

Click here to create the selected document.

Creating a Price List Document

Price lists are used to inform customers of prices of products. As with other TaskWizards, it is based on a specific Works module. In this case it's the spreadsheet.

1. Click a document option button, and then click Create It! Here we selected the Sale Price List button

   As you can see in Figure 2-11, a document based on the Works spreadsheet is created and is ready for editing. In Figure 2-12, you

FIGURE 2-11
The unmodified
Price List document

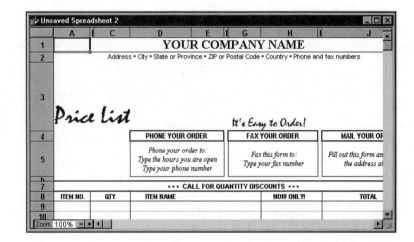

FIGURE 2-12
The modified Price
List document

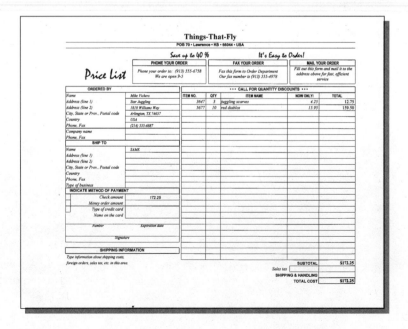

can see what a modified version of the spreadsheet document looks like.

2. Click the Close button for the open document window, and click No to clear the window without saving the document.

Using TaskWizards at Home

Sara wanted only one integrated package to handle all her personal office needs, and that's why she selected Works. Using the Letter TaskWizard, the Loan Analysis TaskWizard, and the Address Book, she can make a good start on creating the documents she needs to manage almost everything. All the TaskWizards that Sara needs are available in the Household Management category.

Starting the Letter TaskWizard

Sara's first order of business is to create a letterhead with a professional layout that she can use for her correspondence. As you will see, the Letter TaskWizard provides her with many attractive choices. We'll use this TaskWizard to demonstrate, as follows:

1. If the Task Launcher is not already present on the screen, click File, and then click New.

2. Click the TaskWizards tab.

3. Click a TaskWizard category. Here we selected Household Management.

4. Click a TaskWizard, click OK, and then click Yes, Run The TaskWizard. Here we selected Letter.

    As you can see in Figure 2-13 on the next page, Sara has a choice of formats, including Professional, Simple, and Formal layout.

Creating a Professional Letter Document

The professional letter document layout provides a simple, business letter arrangement for the letterhead, salutation, body, and closing in the word processor module. We'll create the professional letter document, as follows:

1. Click a document option button, and then click Next. We selected Professional.

FIGURE 2-13
The Letter
TaskWizard

Document
option buttons

A reduced view of the
selected document

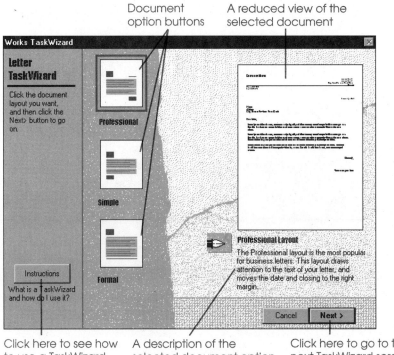

Click here to see how
to use a TaskWizard.

A description of the
selected document option

Click here to go to the
next TaskWizard screen.

Sara can now customize the letter and specify options, as shown in Figure 2-14, for the type of letterhead, address format, content, text style, and extras, such as to whom the letter should be copied, the typist's initials, and more.

2. Click Create It!

The Letter TaskWizard's Checklist screen appears, as shown in Figure 2-15.

3. Click Create Document.

Works begins creating the letter, using the default settings, and the professional letter appears in a document window, as shown in Figure 2-16 on page 64. Sara can now use Works' word processing tools to change the letter's appearance to her liking, as shown in Figure 2-17 on page 64.

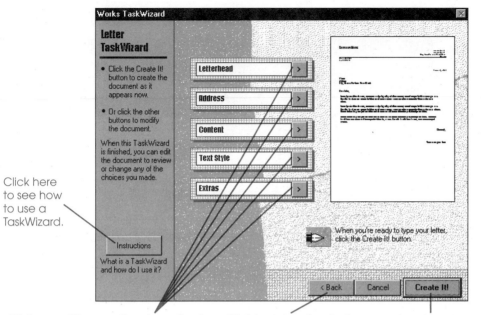

FIGURE 2-14
The next Letter
TaskWizard screen

Click here
to see how
to use a
TaskWizard.

Click any of these options to customize   Click here to return to the   Click here to see the
selected document elements.   TaskWizard's opening screen.   TaskWizard's Checklist screen.

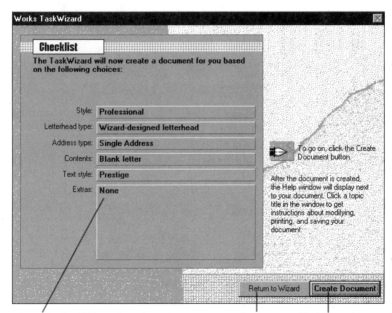

FIGURE 2-15
The Letter
TaskWizard's
Checklist screen

View the options the TaskWizard   Click here to return to the   Click here to create the
will use to create the document.   previous TaskWizard screen.   selected document.

FIGURE 2-16

The professional
letter created by
the TaskWizard

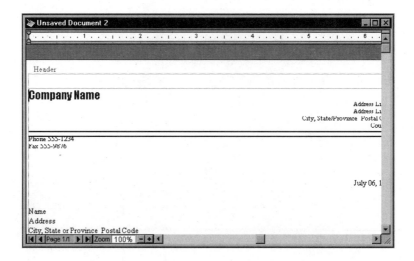

FIGURE 2-17

A completed letter

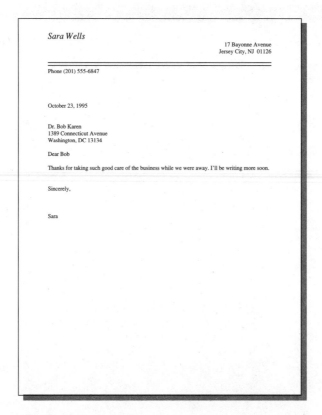

4.   Close the unsaved document window without saving the letter.

Starting the Mortgage/ Loan Analysis TaskWizard

Writing well-designed letters is just one of the tasks that Sara needs to undertake. Another is evaluating a loan that she's planning to take out. She needs to borrow $10,000 for 3 years at an interest rate of 7.5 percent but wants to run the analysis several times with different interest rates. Using the Mortgage/Loan Analysis TaskWizard, she can create a spreadsheet that calculates the alternatives so that she can make an informed decision. We'll demonstrate, as follows:

1.   If the Task Launcher is not already present on the screen, click File, and then click New.

2.   Click the TaskWizards tab.

3.   Click a TaskWizard category. Here we again selected Household Management.

4.   Click a TaskWizard, click OK, and then click Yes, Run The TaskWizard. Here we selected Mortgage/Loan Analysis.

   As you can see in Figure 2-18 on the following page, Sara has a choice of different types of analyses, including Standard Loan, Extra Payments, and Qualification Worksheet.

Creating a Standard Mortgage and Loan Analysis Document

The document for analyzing a standard mortgage or loan is created within the spreadsheet module. This allows you to plug in different variables, such as rates of interest or lengths of term, to evaluate an affordable monthly payment. We'll continue the example by creating a standard loan analysis, as follows:

1.   Click a document option button. We selected Standard Loan.

2.   Click Create It!

   Works creates the Mortgage and Loan Analysis document in the spreadsheet window, as you can see in Figure 2-19 on the next page.

FIGURE 2-18
Selecting the type
of loan from the
Loan/Mortgage
Analysis
TaskWizard

Document
option buttons

A reduced image of the
selected document

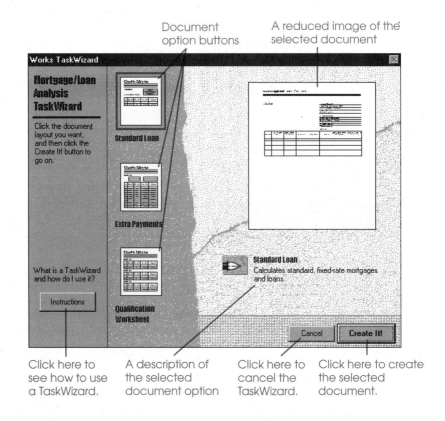

Click here to
see how to use
a TaskWizard.

A description of
the selected
document option

Click here to
cancel the
TaskWizard.

Click here to create
the selected
document.

FIGURE 2-19
The Mortgage and
Loan Analysis
document in a
spreadsheet
window

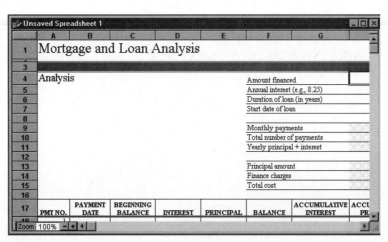

An example of a completed Loan Analysis document is shown in
Figure 2-20.

3. Close the document window without saving the spreadsheet.

FIGURE 2-20
A completed loan
analysis
spreadsheet
document

Mortgage and Loan Analysis

Analysis

	Amount financed	10,000.00
	Annual interest (e.g., 8.25)	7.500
	Duration of loan (in years)	3
	Start date of loan	October 1995
	Monthly payments	311.06
	Total number of payments	36
	Yearly principal + interest	3,732.75
	Principal amount	10,000.00
To display each month's calculations,	Finance charges	1,198.24
extend the table below to row 53	Total cost	11,198.24

PMT NO.	PAYMENT DATE	BEGINNING BALANCE	INTEREST	PRINCIPAL	BALANCE	ACCUMULATIVE INTEREST	ACCUMULATIVE PRINCIPAL
1	10/1/95	10,000.00	62.50	248.56	9,751.44	62.50	248.56
2	11/1/95	9,751.44	60.95	250.12	9,501.32	123.45	498.68
3	12/1/95	9,501.32	59.38	251.68	9,249.64	182.83	750.36
4	1/1/96	9,249.64	57.81	253.25	8,996.39	240.64	1,003.61

Starting the Address Book TaskWizard

This TaskWizard can be used to create the standard Address Book that you can use in all the Works modules. In fact, you can run this TaskWizard from any module to create an Address Book, if there is not a default one already set up.

Sara wants to keep track of her friends by names and addresses, and to organize these in such a way as to be able to find them quickly and even have Works dial their phone numbers! We'll demonstrate using this TaskWizard, as follows:

1. If the Task Launcher is not already present on the screen, click File, and then click New.

2. Click the TaskWizards tab.

3. Click a TaskWizard category. We again selected Household Management.

4. Click a TaskWizard, click OK, and then click Yes, Run The TaskWizard. Here we selected Address Book.

   As you can see in Figure 2-21, you have a choice of six different types of address books: Personal, Business, Customers or Clients, Suppliers and Vendors, Sales Contacts, and Employees.

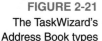

FIGURE 2-21
The TaskWizard's
Address Book types

Option
buttons for
types of
address books

Click here
to see how
to use a
TaskWizard.

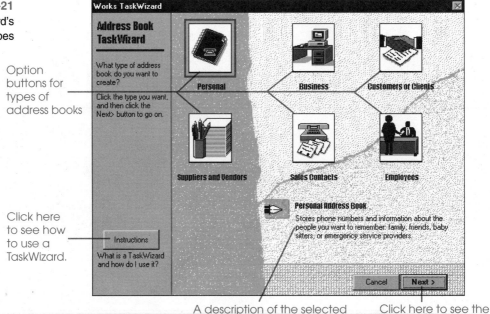

A description of the selected
address book option

Click here to see the
TaskWizard's next screen.

Creating a Personal Address Book

The personal Address Book is a database document where you store names, addresses, and phone numbers of family and friends. We'll create this one, as follows:

1. Click a document option button, and then click Next. We selected Personal.

   The next Address Book TaskWizard screen appears with information about the Personal type of Address Book.

2. Click Next, and then click Create It!

   The TaskWizard's Checklist screen appears, as shown in Figure 2-22.

3. Click Create Document.

   The personal Address Book document appears in a database window, as shown in Figure 2-23.

View the options the TaskWizard will
use to create the address book.

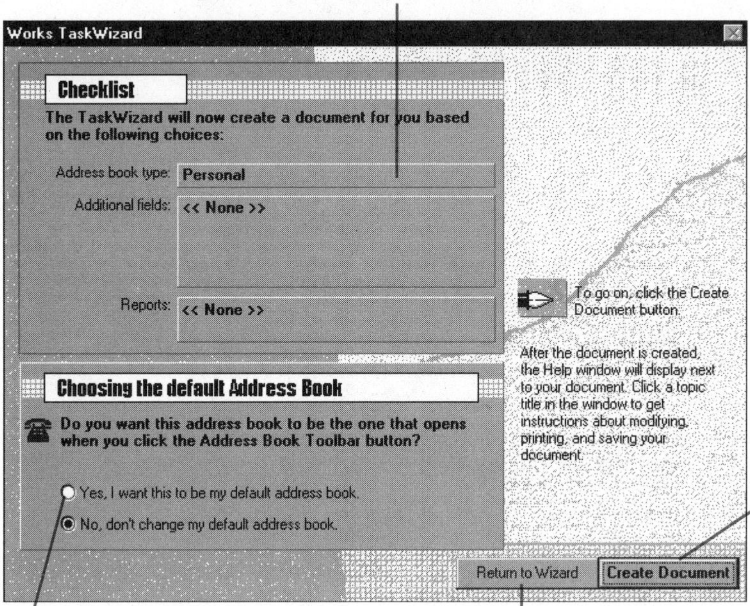

FIGURE 2-22
The Address Book
TaskWizard's
Checklist screen

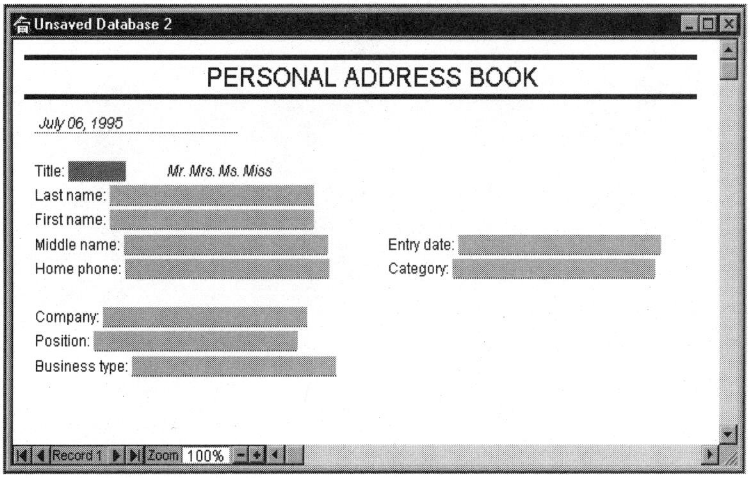

Click here to
create the
selected
address book.

Click here to set up the selected
address book as the default.

Click here to return to the
previous TaskWizard screen.

FIGURE 2-23
The personal
Address Book
document in a
database window
with Form
view active

After entering information in its fields, you can search through
the Address Book to find information and sort the records into a
particular order.

4. Close the database window without saving the document.

Using TaskWizards at School

Sam, a teacher at an elementary school, relies on Works to help him run his classroom. He creates tests using a word processor-based TaskWizard, keeps track of grades using a spreadsheet-based TaskWizard, and keeps track of students and information about them using a database-based TaskWizard. All the TaskWizards that Sam is using are available in the general category titled Students and Teachers.

Starting the Tests TaskWizard

The Tests TaskWizard provides a preformatted layout for generating a true/false, multiple choice, or essay test. We'll demonstrate using TaskWizards within this scenario example by creating a true/false test, as follows:

1. If the Task Launcher is not already present on the screen, click File, and then click New.

2. Click the TaskWizards tab.

3. Click a TaskWizard category. Here we selected Students and Teachers.

4. Click a TaskWizard, click OK, and then click Yes, Run The TaskWizard. Here we selected Tests.

    The Tests TaskWizard provides options for creating a True or False, Multiple Choice, or Essay test as you see in Figure 2-24. In this example, Sam will create a 10-question True or False test.

Creating a True or False Test Form

The True or False Test document is a word-processed form that contains 10 True or False type questions. We'll continue our example by creating it, as follows:

1. Click a document option button, and then click Create It! Here we selected True or False

    The True or False test appears in a document window, as you see in Figure 2-25, with appropriate spaces for Sam to enter the information necessary to personalize the test, including the name of the test, the instructor's name, and the questions themselves. An example of a finished test form is shown in Figure 2-26 on page 72.

2. Close the document window without saving the test form.

Document
option buttons

A reduced image of the
selected document

FIGURE 2-24
The opening Tests
TaskWizard screen

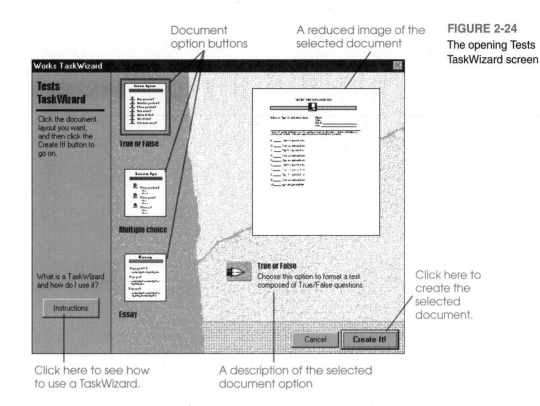

Click here to see how
to use a TaskWizard.

A description of the selected
document option

Click here to
create the
selected
document.

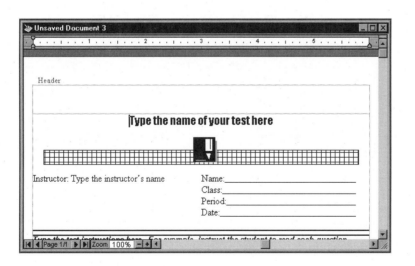

FIGURE 2-25
The True or False
test form in a
document window

FIGURE 2-26
A completed True
or False test form

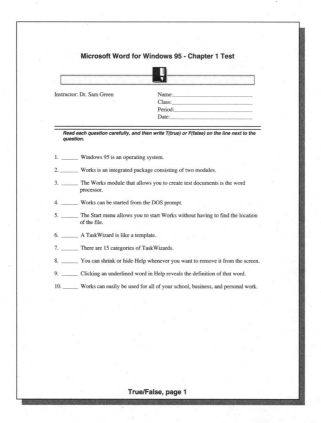

Microsoft Word for Windows 95 - Chapter 1 Test

Instructor: Dr. Sam Green   Name:_____
                                   Class:_____
                                   Period:_____
                                   Date:_____

Read each question carefully, and then write T(true) or F(false) on the line next to the question.

1. _____ Windows 95 is an operating system.

2. _____ Works is an integrated package consisting of two modules.

3. _____ The Works module that allows you to create test documents is the word processor.

4. _____ Works can be started from the DOS prompt.

5. _____ The Start menu allows you to start Works without having to find the location of the file.

6. _____ A TaskWizard is like a template.

7. _____ There are 15 categories of TaskWizards.

8. _____ You can shrink or hide Help whenever you want to remove it from the screen.

9. _____ Clicking an underlined word in Help reveals the definition of that word.

10. _____ Works can easily be used for all of your school, business, and personal work.

True/False, page 1

Starting the Grade Book TaskWizard

The Grade Book is a spreadsheet-based TaskWizard for creating grade book documents. We'll demonstrate by creating one, as follows:

1. If the Task Launcher is not already present on the screen, click File, and then click New.

2. Click the TaskWizards tab.

3. Click a TaskWizard category. Here again we selected Students and Teachers.

4. Click a TaskWizard, click OK, and then click Yes, Run The TaskWizard. Here we selected Grade Book.

   Using the Grade Book TaskWizard, you can create a Standard, Modified, or Weighted Average Grade Book, as you see in Figure 2-27. In this example, Sam will create a standard grade book.

Document option buttons

A reduced image of the selected document

FIGURE 2-27
The opening Grade Book TaskWizard screen

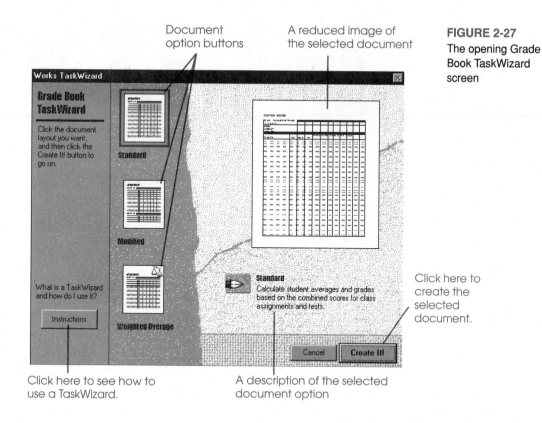

Click here to create the selected document.

Click here to see how to use a TaskWizard.

A description of the selected document option

Creating a Standard Grade Book Spreadsheet

The standard Grade Book is a spreadsheet document that calculates averages for test grades and assignments. We'll continue our example by creating one, as follows:

1. Click a document option button, and then click Create It! We selected Standard.

   The standard Grade Book appears in a spreadsheet window, as you see in Figure 2-28 on the next page. Sam can enter the information necessary to personalize the grade book, including the class and students' names, their grades, and the names of their assignments. An example of a completed grade book is shown in Figure 2-29 on the following page.

2. Close the spreadsheet window without saving the grade book.

FIGURE 2-28

The grade book document in a spreadsheet window

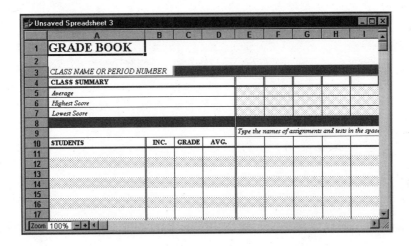

FIGURE 2-29

A completed grade book document

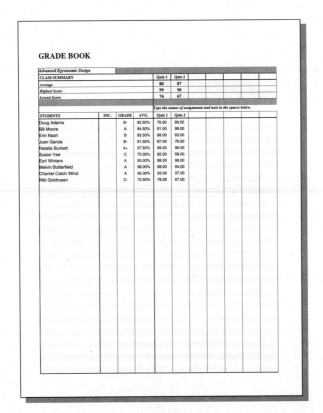

Starting the Student and Membership Information TaskWizard

This TaskWizard creates a database that allows Sam to record names, addresses, and phone numbers for his students or club members. This document also allows you to maintain information on other groups. We'll demonstrate creating one, as follows:

1. If the Task Launcher is not already present on the screen, click File, and then click New.

2. Click the TaskWizards tab.

3. Click a TaskWizard category. Here again we selected Students and Teachers.

4. Click a TaskWizard, click OK, and then click Yes, Run The TaskWizard. Here we selected Students & Membership Information.

    Notice that the Student and Membership Information TaskWizard allows you to create a database of student information, a club roster, or a team roster, as you see in Figure 2-30. In this example, Sam will use the Student Information TaskWizard.

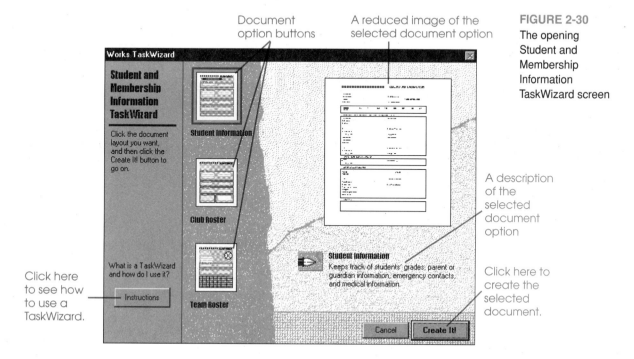

Document option buttons

A reduced image of the selected document option

FIGURE 2-30
The opening Student and Membership Information TaskWizard screen

A description of the selected document option

Click here to create the selected document.

Click here to see how to use a TaskWizard.

Creating a Student Information Database

The student information document is a database for tracking information on students, including their names, addresses, and contacts in case of an emergency. We'll demonstrate by creating one, as follows:

1. Click a document option button, and then click Create It! We selected Student Information.

   The Student Information document appears in a database window, as you see in Figure 2-31. In this document Sam can enter the data necessary to maintain detailed information on each student. A completed record from the Student Information database is shown in Figure 2-32.

FIGURE 2-31
The Student
Information
database

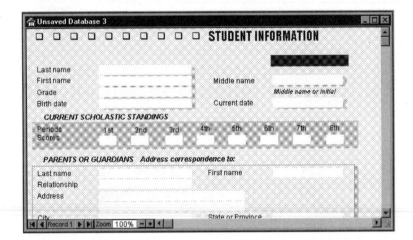

2. Close the database window without saving the document.

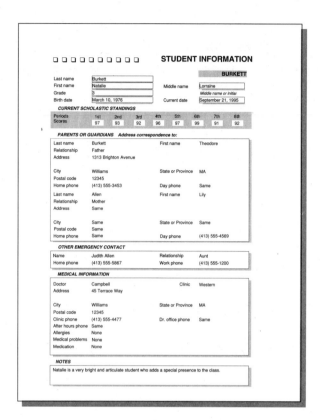

FIGURE 2-32

An example of a record in the Student Information database

The Start from Scratch TaskWizard

OK. You've seen several of the available TaskWizards and observed what they can do, but perhaps you still have trouble deciding where to begin. That's where the Start from Scratch TaskWizard, in the Common Task category, comes in. All you need to know is whether you want to create a text document, a spreadsheet, or a database—Works will take you from there to the finished document. Works accomplishes this by prompting you for various types of information about the document you want to create.

In Table 2-3 on the next page you can see the choices you have when you invoke the Start from Scratch TaskWizard. The contents of your document depend on the module you select and what you want to do.

TABLE 2-3
The options
available in the
Start from Scratch
TaskWizard

Word Processor	Spreadsheet	Database
Text Style	Page Header & Footer	Fields
Page Border	Text Style	Text Style
	Page Orientation	

Using Existing Documents

The Existing Documents option in the Works Task Launcher lets you open
and work with a file that has already been created and saved. You can see
a list of some of the files that have been created throughout these first two
chapters in Figure 2-33.

Works lists the recently opened files in the order in which they were
opened, with the last opened appearing first on the list. To open any
document, just double-click on the name of the file you want to open.

Two other important options are available in the Task Launcher.
These deal with opening existing documents.

The first is the *Open A Document Not Listed Here* button. Works shows
only those documents opened recently—and only those created using any

FIGURE 2-33
The list of existing
documents in the
Task Launcher

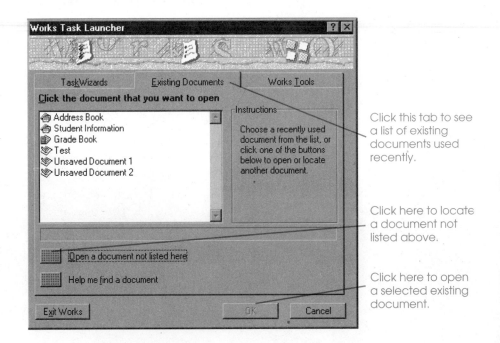

Click this tab to see
a list of existing
documents used
recently.

Click here to locate
a document not
listed above.

Click here to open
a selected existing
document.

of the three Works modules that use documents (communications doesn't use documents). You are certain to have files on your computer created with an application other than Works, including files that Works might be able to read. For example, the Works word processor can read documents created with Microsoft Word or Novell WordPerfect or many other applications. When you click the *Open A Document Not Listed Here* button in the Task Launcher, you will see all the documents in the current folder, not just those created with Works.

TIP Windows 95 allows for filenames up to 255 characters including spaces, so you are no longer stuck with the old eight-character filename and three-character extension from previous versions of Windows. Use these character names to be sufficiently descriptive that you can easily distinguish one similar file from the other. But keep in mind that the longer the filename, the more memory is used. So make your names descriptive, consistent in form, and easy to remember and find—but avoid using more characters than necessary.

The second important button is labeled *Help Me Find A Document*. The more you work with your computer and the more documents you create, the more likely it is that you will misplace a file and not be able to find it as quickly or as easily as you need. That's where this option comes in handy. Clicking this button reveals a Find Files tool exactly like the one found on the opening Start menu in Windows 95. You provide as much information as you can, including the name of the file or even some text from the file, click OK, and Works will do its best to find the file that you are trying to locate.

Creating a New Document

Now and then you may find that a TaskWizard doesn't fit your needs and yet you haven't created a document that you can modify to accomplish the task you've set for yourself and Works. No problem! This means that you need to start a task from the Works Tools tab in the Task Launcher and create a new document. As you see in Figure 2-34 on the following page, you can select from one of four modules: the Word Processor, the Spreadsheet, the Database, and the Communications module. Clicking on any one of these will produce a blank opening screen for that module. You can also exit Works by clicking the Exit Works button, or click Cancel and the Task Launcher dialog box disappears, returning you to the Works desktop and the File, Tools, and Help menus. The remaining chapters in *Running Works for Windows 95* will focus on the use of these modules.

FIGURE 2-34

The Works Tools tab in the Works Task Launcher

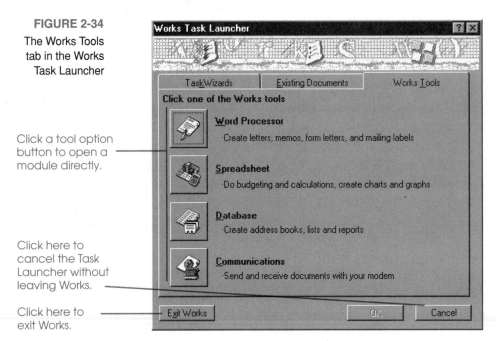

Click a tool option button to open a module directly.

Click here to cancel the Task Launcher without leaving Works.

Click here to exit Works.

Getting Started

In this chapter we've provided you with examples to try on your computer, but we've asked you to discard the unsaved documents. Usually, however, you'll want to save your work, and as you do, you'll accumulate a great number of Works documents. To keep your hard disk tidy, take the time to create one or more folders where you can keep your documents. Later on, you'll be able to delete them easily, if you wish, without worrying about deleting valuable files or leaving a stray file in a folder. Here's how to create a folder using Windows Explorer.

1. Click Start, point to Programs, and then click Windows Explorer.

2. From the toolbar's drop-down menu, select the location where you want the folder created.

Consider creating most folders on the C drive. If the toolbar is not visible, click View, and then click Toolbar or click the device icon for drive C in the All Folders (left) pane.

3. Place the mouse pointer in the right pane.

4. Click the right mouse button and point to New.

5. Click Folder.

6. Type a name for the folder.

7. Press Enter.

▦ Deleting Folders and Files

Deleting folders (directories) and files is just as easy as creating them. Locate the folder or file in the Explorer window, highlight it and point to it, click the right mouse button, and then click Delete.

Coming Next

Now that you have a good foundation as to how to start Works, get help when necessary, and create a variety of documents with TaskWizards, it's now time to turn your attention to an in-depth review of the features each Works module offers. We'll begin in Chapter 3, with the most popular of all the modules—the Works Word Processor.

Part 2

SELECT EDITION

Using the
Word Processor

In This Part Here you get started with the most often used computer application, the word processor. And while you might think you need one of the "Big Boys," the word processor and its features that come with Works for Windows 95 might be all you need to run your business, do your cool work, or write that long-awaited novel.

In Chapter 3, we'll show you how to get started with the word processor, including entering simple text and saving the file that you create, to use later in another Works session. Then we'll introduce you to navigating around a Works document, editing by replacing and deleting text, some special Windows 95 tools like drag-and-drop, and how Works for Windows 95 lets you view a document in draft or page layout (where it looks on the screen like it will when printed).

Chapter 4 focuses on how to format a document: taking words and making them more attractive, including working with the layout of the page, how the margins are set, the use of columns, and printing your masterpiece. You'll learn about two features that speed up almost all your formatting activities: the toolbar and ruler, where just a click of a button corresponds to many menu selections. You can set tabs, bold a sentence, cut and copy text, and even start checking the spelling from the toolbar.

Chapter 5 focuses on teaching you the most advanced word processing techniques that Works has available. Here you'll find out how to make a bookmark, create footnotes, verify your spelling, insert a footer or a header in a document, and create handy tables.

Chapter 3

Getting Started with the Word Processor

I f Works is your first word processor, you'll soon find out that one of the pleasures of using a word processor is the ability it gives you to concentrate on what you want to say—without giving a thought to how those words appear on your screen. Just close your eyes and start typing. Microsoft Works for Windows 95 will faithfully remember every key you press, without ever breaking into your thoughts by stopping at the end of a line with that nasty typewriter bell or blindly running your words off the paper and onto the platen when you reach the end of a page!

If you've used a word processor before, you'll be pleasantly surprised at what this module of Works can do. Unlike other integrated packages, none of the modules in Works, and especially not the word processor, is an add-on. Rather, they are all fully featured applications that are well connected to one another. For example, with the Works word processor you can create columns, insert graphics, count words, dial a phone number, and print envelopes.

This chapter introduces you to the basic skills involved in word processing, including the creation and revision of a document. Now, a word processor can't help you think, nor can it make the words flow when the creative pipeline is clogged. You have to do that yourself. But a good word processor can automate the mechanical tasks required to produce well-organized and thoughtful text.

WYSIWYG: Getting What You See

You're seeing correctly. WYSIWYG (pronounced "wizzywig") stands for What You See Is What You Get. It also describes an important and attractive feature of the Works word processor. Unlike some non-Windows programs, Works shows on the screen what your document will look like when printed—what you see is literally what you get. If you set narrow margins, for example, that's how your document will appear on screen and when it is printed.

WYSIWYG might not seem like a big deal right now, but you'll find that, in addition to making your screen a friendlier place to work, it helps you envision what your documents will look like when you print them. Thanks to WYSIWYG, you can see what a heading like the following will look like *before you print* your document:

A Heading in Bold Underlined Type

You can also see what will happen if you combine different styles of type. Although Works can't help your sense of style and proportion, its

WYSIWYG capability will, at the least, help you see what you're doing and avoid wasting paper on unsuccessful printouts.

Starting the Works Word Processor

In the last chapter, you saw how Works' TaskWizards can help you create a variety of different documents quickly and easily. Even though one of these documents may be just what you need, Wizards are not for every occasion. Many times, you'll need to create a document for which no Wizard is available. Such may be the case when you need to use the word processor.

To start the Works word processor, follow these steps:

1. Start Works. You should see the Task Launcher.

2. Click the Works Tools tab.

3. Click Word Processor.

   You should see the opening screen as shown in Figure 3-1. In subsequent figures you won't see Help. We hide it so that there is more room to show text.

You may want to maximize both the application and document windows to give yourself plenty of room. (The *application window* is the window containing Works. The *document window* is the Works word processing window.)

FIGURE 3-1
The word processor module's opening screen

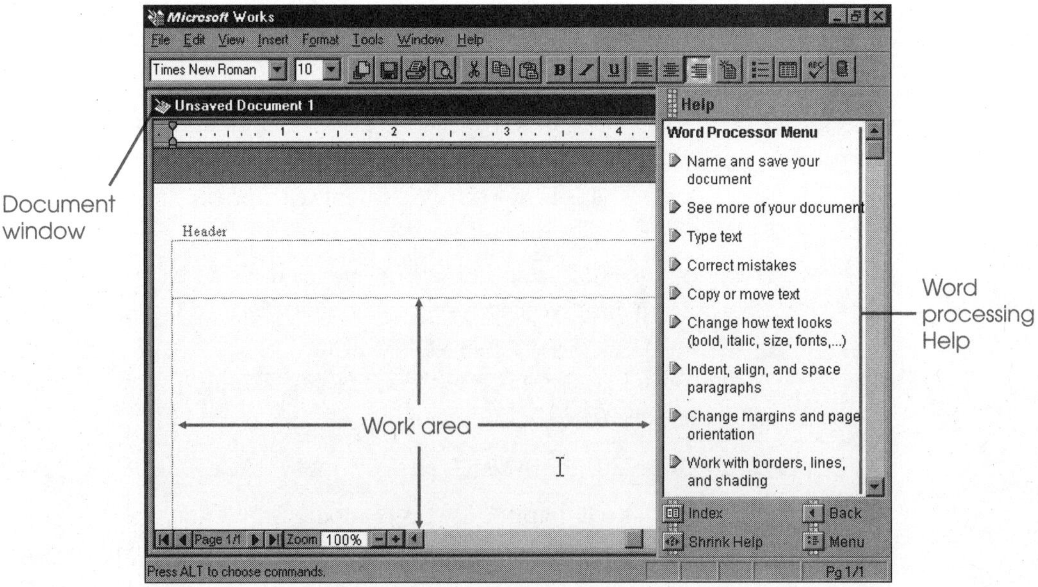

Two Ways to View Your Documents

Here's one more Works word processing feature that's good to know about before you move on to learning how to enter text and format a document.

The Works word processor offers you two viewing options on the View menu. One is Normal view, where the entry and appearance of text and objects offer no page-layout features. In other words, you see words and images on the page, but not how the document will appear when printed. The second is Page Layout view, where layout features like headers, footers, and columns can be seen on screen. In this WYSIWYG view, you see exactly how a document will appear when printed. To change from one view to the other, just select your choice from the View menu. Throughout our discussion of word processing, examples will be shown in Page Layout view, which is the default view (the one that is automatically selected when you start a new session).

An advantage of using the Page Layout view option is that you can actually edit a header or a footer—or any other document element—in Page Layout view. You can also move objects in Page Layout view by dragging them to a new location.

Normal view shows you all the text in a document but only in a single font and a single font size, with none of the Works goodies such as columns and footnotes. The Normal view option might be less convenient to use, but it's faster because Works has to use less memory to get the job done. Especially with a large document, Normal view lets you scroll more quickly through the document. To use this option, simply open the View menu, and then choose Normal.

 TIP Create your documents in Normal view and then when you are ready to format and print, switch to Page Layout view. That way you can save time during the drafting stage—and still get to see how your document will look as you mold it into a polished, finished product.

Entering Text in Your Document

Starting with a blank word processing window, you can type any text you like to create a document. As you type, press Enter only where you want to start a new paragraph. For demonstration purposes, we typed the following paragraphs.

```
To all our friends: [Enter]
You're invited to help us celebrate our 10th anniversary
as a business here in beautiful, rainy Western
Washington. [Enter]
We're having the biggest, best blowout in our history -
a real sales extravaganza. Stock up on all your rain
gear needs: umbrellas, ponchos, waterproof boots,
slickers, hats, and more. At prices you won't believe:
fifty percent off regular prices, and fifty percent more
off the last marked sticker price on all sales items.
Come see us now and save! [Enter]
It's summer now, but remember, fall is right around the
corner. [Enter]
```

On screen they look similar to the document you see in Figure 3-2.

Works tailors itself to the capabilities of your computer and printer, so lines may break differently on different computers. The examples in this book show Works running on a computer connected to a Hewlett-Packard LaserJet printer equipped with several fonts (which determine the look of the characters on the screen). If you have a different printer and you were to type these paragraphs, your lines may be shorter or longer on the screen.

FIGURE 3-2
Text entered in the Works word processor

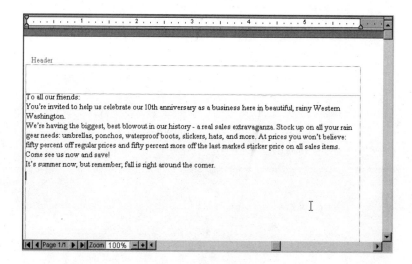

Understanding Word Wrap

As you type in the word processor, you might notice how Works moves the insertion point to a new line whenever your words came close to the right edge of the screen. This Works feature, typical of word processors, is known as *word wrap*. One of the first differences you notice between using a typewriter and using a word processor is that word wrap eliminates the need to press the Enter key (equivalent to the carriage return) to keep lines from extending into the margin. To prevent strange formats from being created in your Works documents, don't press Enter after typing each line of a paragraph. Press Enter only at the *end* of each paragraph.

Wrapping Text in the Word Processor Window

If you are typing with Normal view turned on, you may notice that the text in your document window is no longer completely visible. It extends beyond the right border of the document window. You could use the scroll bars to view the rest of the text, but that would become tedious if you were working with a long document. Works provides an easy way to view all your text in Normal view. If you ever need to turn this feature on, use the following procedure:

1. Click Tools, and then click Options.

2. Click the Wrap For Window check box.

When you do this, Works knows to "wrap" the text of your document and fit it into the window area so that all words are visible, as you see in Figure 3-3 on the following page.

You can easily check to see if the Wrap For Window option is on or off. Simply click Tools, then Options, and look to see if the box is checked. Should a check mark not be there, the option is off. This is purely a matter of preference, and you decide how you want to work with your document windows.

 TIP The Wrap For Window option is only available in Normal view (on the View menu) and not in Layout view. Text wraps automatically in Layout view.

FIGURE 3-3
Wrapping words to
fit a window

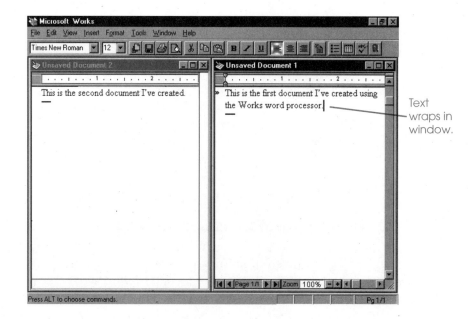

Text
wraps in
window.

Recognizing and Using Special Characters

Works uses its default format for paragraphs: single-spaced with no extra spacing above or below, and with no indent for the first line. It might be difficult to tell where one paragraph ends and the second begins. Even if you opt for a format like this, you can tell exactly where your paragraphs begin and end by opening the View menu, and then choosing All Characters. When this feature is turned on, our sample document window looks like the one below:

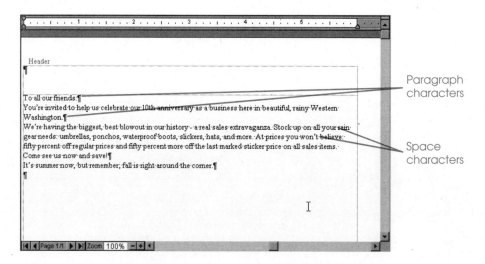

Paragraph
characters

Space
characters

The word processor can display several special characters: tabs, paragraph marks, and spaces are the most common ones you'll see on the screen. You can see two of the characters in the document window shown above. The small dot between words is the Works symbol for a character space, which is entered whenever you press the Spacebar. At the end of each paragraph, you can see a paragraph mark (¶), which appears wherever you press the Enter key while typing.

> **TIP** Here's one good reason to work with the special characters visible: when you select text, you can easily see where to select the spaces surrounding characters and words.

Works doesn't print these characters (or other special characters you'll encounter later), but displaying them while you're writing helps you see exactly what you're doing. With some fonts and certain styles (such as italics), it may be difficult to locate the spacing between words. After you're comfortable with the word processor, you might want to turn off the display (by choosing All Characters again) to simplify the screen's appearance.

Creating Paragraphs

Paragraphs are the building blocks of any document. You're probably accustomed to thinking of a paragraph in the traditional sense: a unified block of text that presents a single idea or part of a topic. When using a word processor, however, you have to extend this definition. Think of a paragraph as any amount of text you want to present in a particular way on a page, with indentation, for example, or in boldface type, or with extra spacing above and below it. In word processing a paragraph is any text—such as a character, a word, several words, a sentence, or many sentences—that ends with a paragraph mark, which is added to your document each time you press Enter.

As you type, Works uses the same format for each paragraph. Whenever you press Enter, Works "clones" a new paragraph, giving it the same spacing and indentation as the previous paragraph. If you start out with a double-spaced paragraph, Works double-spaces all the ones that follow.

Revising Text

No surprise here—it takes lots of work to turn a first draft into a final draft. Most writing, in fact, boils down to the tedium of revising and rewriting—processes that include lots of inserting and deleting text as well as copying and moving text. Works can't help with the actual rewriting, but it can make the revision process easier and cleaner than it is with a pen, pencil, or typewriter.

Moving the Insertion Point Around Your Document

As you revise a document, you'll often need to move the insertion point, select text, or do both to produce the effect you want. To move the insertion point with a mouse, all you do is point to the new location and click.

You might want to use the keyboard for moving the insertion point too, especially if you're really comfortable with a keyboard and decide to fix a typographical error or change a sentence or paragraph as you're writing. Here are some quick ways to move around in a document with the keyboard.

To Move	Press
Left or right one character	Left arrow (←) or Right arrow (→)
Left or right one word	Ctrl+Left arrow (Ctrl+←) or Ctrl+Right arrow (Ctrl+→)
Up or down one line	Up arrow (↑) or Down arrow (↓)

To Move	Press
Up or down one paragraph	Ctrl+Up arrow (Ctrl+↑) or Ctrl+Down arrow (Ctrl+↓)
Beginning of line	Home
End of line	End
Start of document	Ctrl+Home
End of document	Ctrl+End
Top of document window	Ctrl+Page Up
Bottom of document window	Ctrl+Page Down
Up one window	Page Up
Down one window	Page Down

Using the Navigation Buttons

There's another handy way to move around a Works word processor window—using the Navigation buttons you see here:

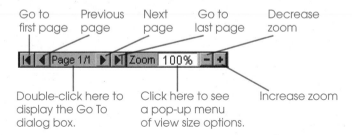

These buttons are located in the lower left corner of the document window. The first five buttons take you in the direction you want to go: to the beginning or end of a document, or to a specific page. The last three allow you to zoom in and enlarge a particular part of a document or zoom out to reduce the document's display size. If you click the Zoom indicator, a pop-up menu appears. From this menu you can select a display magnification.

As you can see, the Navigation button bar tells you how many pages are in the entire document as well as what number the current page you see happens to be. For example, if you see 5/6 on the indicator, you know that you're viewing page five of a six-page document. If you double-click this indicator, the Go To dialog box appears. This allows you to type a specific page number to move directly to that page.

Selecting Text

Revising text requires that you first either move the insertion point or select a block of text, depending on what it is you want to do. For example, to insert a word or sentence or delete a character, you need to move the insertion point to where you want to make the insertion or the deletion. Likewise, to replace a phrase with new text or delete an entire sentence or paragraph, you need first select (highlight) the text block to be replaced or deleted. Both moving the insertion point and selecting text can be accomplished with either the mouse or keyboard. The list on the following page shows you how to use the mouse and the keyboard to select various amounts of text.

Mouse Selection Actions

To Select	Use the Mouse to
A word	Double-click the word.
A line	Click in the document's left margin beside the line.
A sentence	Drag over the sentence (or press Ctrl and click the sentence).
Several lines	Drag the pointer up or down in the left margin.
A paragraph	Double-click in the left margin beside the paragraph.
Entire document	Press and hold Ctrl, and then click in the left margin.

Keystroke Selection Actions

To	Press
Extend a selection	F8+Arrow key
Quit extending	Esc
Collapse a selection	Shift+F8

To Highlight	Press
A word	F8 twice
A sentence	F8 three times
A paragraph	F8 four times
A document	F8 five times
The previous character	Shift+Left arrow (←)
The next character	Shift+Right arrow (→)
The previous word	Ctrl+Shift+Left arrow (←)
The next word	Ctrl+Shift+Right arrow (→)
To the beginning of line	Shift+Home
To the end of line	Shift+End
To the beginning of document	Ctrl+Shift+Home
To the end of document	Ctrl+Shift+End

TIP You can always deselect highlighted text at any time. If the text block was highlighted with the mouse or any keyboard combination with Ctrl or Shift, simply press an arrow key by itself. This moves the insertion point and removes highlighting at the same time. If you used the F8 key to apply highlighting, you can deselect the text by pressing Esc and then an arrow key.

Practice moving the insertion point and selecting various amounts of text in your first Works document. When selecting text becomes almost instinctive, you'll begin to feel more at home with word processing techniques.

Adding and Removing Paragraphs

After you've typed a document, you're not stuck with the paragraphs you created. You can break one paragraph into two, combine two into one, and add new paragraphs wherever you want. We'll demonstrate this with the sample document we showed you earlier:

1. Place the insertion point where you want to insert a paragraph mark. We put it before the word *umbrellas* in our example.

2. Press Enter to create a new paragraph.

   We'll continue by doing the same with the insertion point before the words *ponchos, waterproof boots, slickers,* and in front of the word *At.*

The first two paragraphs are pretty short now, so we'll combine them as follows:

1. Place the insertion point where you want to combine paragraphs. We put ours before the paragraph mark after the period at the end of the first sentence.

2. Press Del. (Press the Spacebar to insert a character space, if there isn't one following a period.)

> **TIP** Remove a paragraph mark to join paragraphs. When you press the Spacebar, a space will be added after the period and before the next sentence.

That's better. Our document appears as shown in Figure 3-4 on the following page.

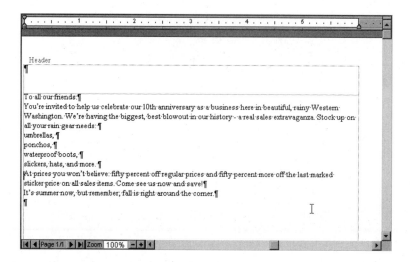

FIGURE 3-4
The document with
paragraphs
rearranged

Adding New Text

The easiest type of revision you can make with Works is adding new text. Suppose, for example, we want to add a new sentence to our practice document, as follows:

1. Use the mouse or the keyboard to place the insertion point where you want to insert text. We put it at the beginning of the sentence *Come see us now and save!*

2. Type the new text. We typed *Sizes for children and adults are now in stock,* and pressed the Spacebar to add space after the new sentence.

When you insert new characters, Works normally moves the existing text to the right to make room for the new text, so adding text to a document doesn't write over the existing text. Works does not automatically overtype or destroy any text when you are adding or inserting additional words.

Using Easy Text for Quick Inserts

Now here's a new Works feature that, as its name reflects, is really easy to use. You can take frequently used phrases, such as greetings and salutations, assign them to a one- or two-character code or word, and insert them automatically in a document. In our example, we will assign the words *Troy Reynolds, General Manager* to the name *Troy.* When we want the words *Troy Reynolds, General Manager* entered in a document, we can just use the Easy Text word *Troy.* Here's how to do it.

1. Place the insertion point where you want to insert an Easy Text entry. We put it at the end of the document (following the period after the word *corner*).

2. Click Insert, point to Easy Text, and click New Easy Text. When you do this, you will see the New Easy Text dialog box.

3. Type a name for the Easy Text entry and press Tab. We typed *Troy.*

4. Type the text for the Easy Text entry in the Easy Text Contents box. We typed *Troy Reynolds, General Manager.*
   The New Easy Text dialog box looks like the one in Figure 3-5.

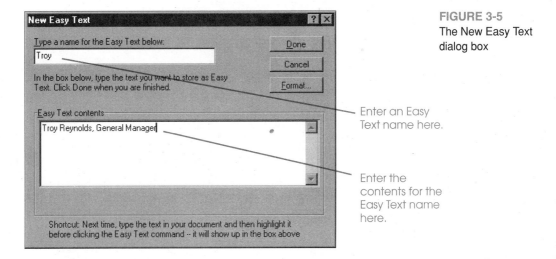

FIGURE 3-5
The New Easy Text dialog box

Enter an Easy Text name here.

Enter the contents for the Easy Text name here.

5. Click Done. Troy is now entered in Easy Text to represent the sample document's closing.

To use Easy Text, follow these steps.

1. Click Insert, and then point to Easy Text.
   The Easy Text options you create will appear on the Easy Text menu, as shown in Figure 3-6 on the next page.

2. Click the one you want to use, and Works will insert the Easy Text entry into your document.

TIP A fast way to enter Easy Text after it's been created is to type the Easy Text word, such as *Troy,* and then press the F3 function key. The full word or phrase will pop out.

FIGURE 3-6

The Easy Text
menu with Easy
Text entries

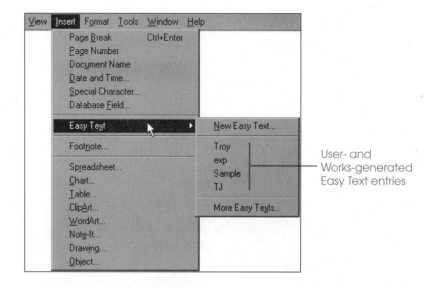

User- and
Works-generated
Easy Text entries

Replacing Existing Text

You may at times want to replace, rather than add, text to a document.
There are two ways to do this. You can set up the word processor to
replace text by selecting Options from the Tools menu and then selecting
either the Overtype option or the Typing Replaces Selection option, as you
can see in Figure 3-7.

The Typing Replaces Selection Option

You can replace selected text with new text as you enter it. For example,
you want to replace an entire paragraph. Rather than select and cut it and

FIGURE 3-7

The Options
dialog box

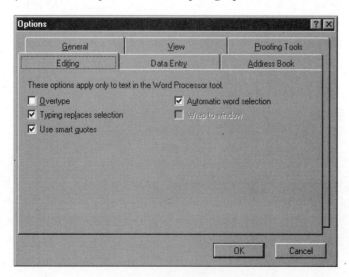

then type in what you want, you can just select the text you no longer want and then start typing. The new text will replace the old text, but only if you have the Typing Replaces Selection option checked on the Editing tab you see in Figure 3-7. Works deletes the selected text as soon as you begin typing new text to replace it. Because Works adjusts the spacing to fit, it doesn't matter whether the deleted text is longer or shorter than the new text. For example: If we select the words *the last marked sticker price on all sale items.* and type *everything in the store.*, the selected text is replaced with the text that we just entered. Now our document example appears as you see in Figure 3-8.

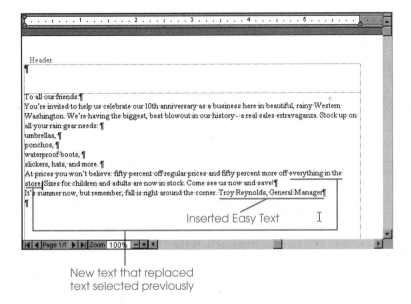

Inserted Easy Text

New text that replaced
text selected previously

FIGURE 3-8
Replacing
selected text

The Overtype Option

In contrast, if you select the Overtype option in the Options dialog box, Works replaces existing characters with new ones as you type. You can tell this option is turned on when you see the OVR indicator on the status bar. We'll demonstrate it, as follows:

1. Place the insertion point where you want to overtype text. We put it before *won't* in the phrase *At prices you won't believe.*

2. Turn on the Overtype option either by pressing the Ins key or by selecting Overtype in the Options dialog box. Notice that the letters OVR appear on the status bar to show that Overtype is turned on.

3. Type over the text you want to replace with the same amount of text. We typed *ca* over *wo* in the word *won't*.

    The word *won't* turns into the word *can't* with just a few keystrokes.

4. Turn off Overtype either by pressing Ins again or by clicking Tools, clicking Options, and clicking Overtype.

Be careful when using Overtype! When you turn on the Overtype option, you must remember that length matters. Works deletes one character of existing text for each new character you type. Suppose, for example, you wanted to change the sentence *The canary ate the cat.* Turning on Overtype and replacing *canary* with *parrot* would produce *The parrot ate the cat.* But replacing *parrot* with *duck* would produce *The duckot ate the cat.* When you toggle Works to turn on Overtype, remember that you've done so. If you're a touch typist accustomed to working from drafts on paper, it can be extremely frustrating to glance at the screen and find you've overtyped an entire sentence or paragraph when you meant to insert text.

TIP You can toggle the Overtype command on and off by pressing the Ins key. This also toggles the display of the OVR indicator on the status bar. When you see OVR, Overtype mode is on; if you don't see it, Overtype mode is off.

Deleting Text

Professional writers have professional editors who find and delete unnecessary words, sentences, and even whole sections of an article or book. If you're working with Works on your own, you'll probably have to be your own editor—a thankless task when you've struggled with creating a document. Often, however, careful editing pays off in clearer, more understandable prose that has greater impact on the intended reader.

For example, our practice document doesn't really need the words *a real sales extravaganza*, so we'll delete them, as follows:

1. Select the text to delete. We selected - *a real sales extravaganza* (including the hyphen).

CAUTION If a single character begins the text you want to select (such as a hyphen), begin the selection with the character, not the space before it. If you try to include the space before the character in the selection, Works will select the preceding word (in our example, *history*) automatically because, by default, the Automatic Word Selection option is turned on in the Options dialog box.

2. Press the Del key or open the Edit menu, and then choose Clear. (You can also choose the Cut command or click the Cut button on the toolbar, which will place the deleted text on the Windows Clipboard.)

 TIP You can also press Backspace to delete highlighted text. If you think you might want to use the text later, choose the Cut button on the toolbar.

Using Undo to Reverse an Edit

Oops! Want to get back that text you just deleted? Although deleting your words seems final, it doesn't have to be. You can undelete text if you change your mind, as long as you haven't made any other changes to your document in the meantime. Suppose we decide we do like the upbeat sound of *a real sales extravaganza*.

You can restore text by opening the Edit menu and then choosing Undo Editing, or, for a quicker method, press Ctrl+Z. (The Alt+Backspace key combination works as well.) The words return to the document, exactly where they were before you deleted them.

As you'll see in other examples, the Undo Editing command reverses more than just deletions. Essentially, Undo Editing reverses the effect of any editing operation that alters the appearance or content of a document. Use Undo Editing when your fingers outpace your thoughts, when you've changed fonts and styles, or when you want to undo any text change.

Remember, though, that you can't undo selectively. You can reverse only your *last* change, so if you do make an error, stop immediately and try Undo Editing.

TIP This is serious stuff. Undo Editing will only undo your last action. If you make an error, don't try anything else. Select Undo Editing immediately! Undo Editing, as its name suggests, undoes editing; it can't retrieve lost files or retrieve earlier versions of a file. And, don't get confused about Cut, Copy, Paste, Clear, and Undo Editing. The Cut, Copy, and Paste commands allow you to delete, copy, and retrieve text in any Windows application. Clear and Undo Editing are used only in Works. What you delete is not placed on the Windows Clipboard. Deleted text can be retrieved immediately only with the Undo Editing command.

Moving Text to the Clipboard

You learned in Chapter 1 about the Windows Clipboard and the concept of cutting and pasting. You'll soon get a chance to see how Cut and Paste can be used to reorganize text by cutting it from the document and then pasting it somewhere else.

See Also For more information on *placing text on the Windows Clipboard*, see "About the Clipboard" in Chapter 1, page 40.

When you click the Edit menu, notice that the Cut, Copy, and Paste commands are displayed in dimmed letters. When a command is dimmed, it is not available for use. Since nothing is selected, no text can be cut or copied. Paste is dimmed because if you haven't cut or copied any text yet, the Clipboard is empty and Works has nothing to paste into your document. We'll demonstrate pasting text in our sample document, as follows:

1. Select the text you want to move. We selected the sentence *Come see us now and save!* We didn't include the special ¶ character in our selection.

2. Click Edit, and then click Cut (or, as a shortcut, use the Ctrl+X key combination).

    The text disappears as if it were deleted. The text you've cut is now stored on the Windows Clipboard. From the Clipboard you can paste text back into any part of a document.

 TIP There are two other ways to cut text. You can click the right mouse button and then click the Cut command that appears on the pop-up menu. Or, you can select the Cut button on the Works toolbar.

---

3. Move the insertion point to where you want to paste the text. We put it near the end of the document, after the phrase *fall is right around the corner.*

4. Click Edit, and then click Paste (or, as a shortcut, use the Ctrl+V key combination).

    The text we cut is inserted at the insertion point location. The edited document looks as shown in Figure 3-9. Notice that we also inserted a space character between the period and the word *Come* at the beginning of the sentence we just pasted.

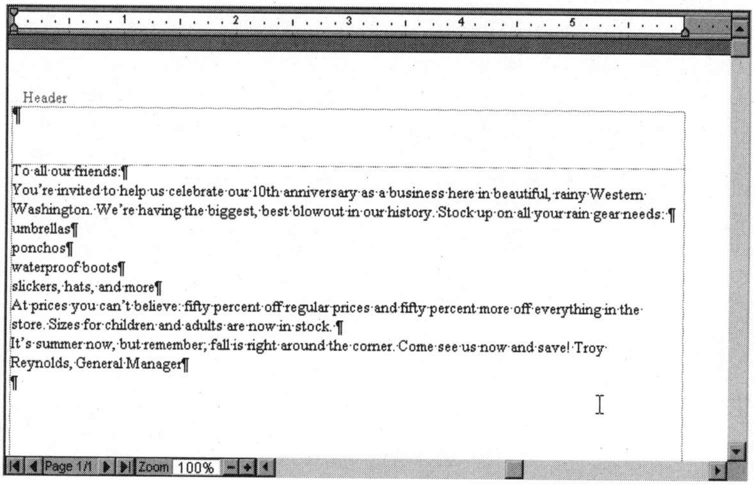

Header

To all our friends:¶
You're invited to help us celebrate our 10th anniversary as a business here in beautiful, rainy Western
Washington. We're having the biggest, best blowout in our history. Stock up on all your rain gear needs:¶
umbrellas¶
ponchos¶
waterproof boots¶
slickers, hats, and more¶
At prices you can't believe: fifty percent off regular prices and fifty percent more off everything in the
store. Sizes for children and adults are now in stock.¶
It's summer now, but remember; fall is right around the corner. Come see us now and save! Troy
Reynolds, General Manager¶
¶

Page 1/1 Zoom 100%

FIGURE 3-9
The edited document after cutting and pasting text

105

TIP There are two other ways to paste text. You can click the right mouse button and then click the Paste command that appears on the pop-up menu. Or, you can select the Paste button on the Works toolbar.

Cut and paste is that simple. Bear in mind, however, that the Clipboard holds only one item at a time. Thus, if you cut text and then go on to cut (or copy) another selection of text, the second block of text replaces the first on the Clipboard. The first block of text is gone and can't be retrieved.

TIP You can cut, copy, and paste from a Works document to any other Works document, or any other Windows application, and you can paste the same information in as many times as you want to, just by repeating the paste task.

Moving Text with Drag-and-Drop

Drag-and-drop might sound like the name of a new dance, but it's actually the name of a terrific feature of Works and Windows 95. With drag-and-drop, you simply drag the selected text wherever you want it to appear. No more cut and paste. Here are the exact steps for dragging and dropping text. We'll demonstrate by moving the word *ponchos* to another line.

1. Select the text you want to move. We selected the word *ponchos* as shown in Figure 3-10. Notice that we selected the special paragraph character (¶) that follows it.

    Notice also that when you place the mouse pointer over the selected text, the indicator DRAG appears beneath the pointer, as you see in Figure 3-10.

Select text to drag and drop.

Mouse pointer with DRAG indicator

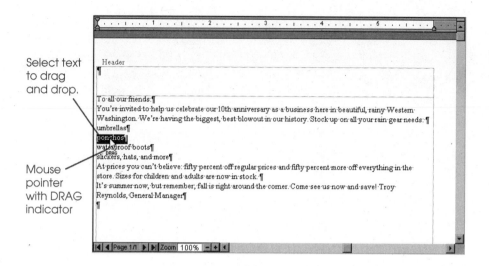

FIGURE 3-10
Selected text

2. Drag the selected text to where you want it moved. We dragged the selected word to below the line containing *waterproof boots*. Now our sample document appears as shown here:

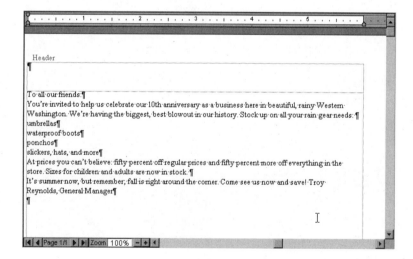

As you drag the mouse, the insertion point moves with it, allowing you to place the text precisely. When you release the mouse button, the text will disappear from its original location and will appear in the new location. Keep in mind that this procedure is not the same as cutting or copying text because the moved text is not stored temporarily on the Clipboard.

Not only can you use the mouse to move text within your Works word processing document, but you can also copy text or other information by dragging it to a new location. You can drag and drop information within the same word processing document, between different Works documents, or (sometimes) between a Works document and a document created in another Windows-based application.

To copy or move information from or within Works using the mouse, open the documents you want to change. Tile the document windows. Always make sure the location where you want to drop the text is visible in the destination document. (Use the scroll bars if necessary.)

After selecting the text you want to copy or move, follow these steps:

To	Destination	Do this
Move	To another Works document or to a document created in another Windows-based application	Select the text, click within the selection, and then hold Shift as you drag.
Copy	Within a single Works document or to another Works document or a document created in another Windows-based application	Select the text, click within the selection, and then hold Ctrl as as you drag.

TIP Remember that you can click the right mouse button to Cut, Copy, and Paste text, by selecting the appropriate commands from the pop-up menu that appears.

You might see a message or a cursor indicating the text can't be dropped. If this occurs, it means the application you're dragging the selected text to doesn't support the drag-and-drop editing feature.

Works always inserts the information at the location of the insertion point. If you make an error, simply undo the drag and drop action by opening the Edit menu, and then choosing the Undo Drag and Drop command. If you want to cancel a drag and drop operation in progress, simply press Esc.

Copying Text

Information gets onto the Clipboard in one of two ways: you cut it with the Cut command on the Edit menu, or you copy it with the Copy command on the Edit menu. Although both commands do very similar tasks, one important difference should be noted. When you cut information, you remove it from the document. When you copy information, you duplicate that information, keeping the text in its original location.

Suppose we have some ideas about revising the first paragraph of our document, but we'd like to keep the original to compare the two versions. You can copy a paragraph to the Clipboard, paste it back into the existing document (or create a new one and paste it there), and then make revisions to one copy while leaving the other intact. We'll demonstrate this, as follows:

1. Select the paragraph you want to copy. We selected the one beginning with *You're invited*.

2. Click the Copy button on the toolbar.

3. Place the insertion point where you want to insert the copied text. We put it in front of *umbrellas*.

4. Click the Paste button on the toolbar.

The copied paragraph is pasted into the document below the original as shown here:

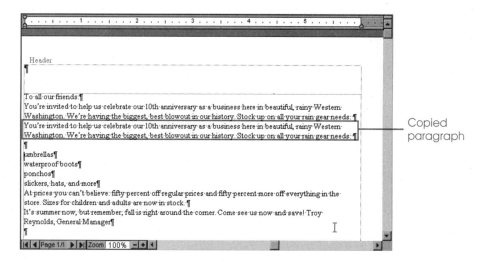

Copied paragraph

Saving a File

Saving your documents is very important. You should save them often so that you protect your work in case of a sudden power failure or other occurrence that threatens data. The first time you save a document you must give it a name. We'll demonstrate this, as follows.

1. Click File, and then click Save. You'll see the Save As dialog box shown in Figure 3-11.

FIGURE 3-11

The Save As dialog box

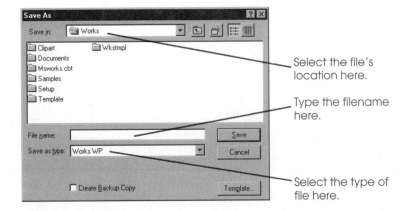

Select the file's location here.

Type the filename here.

Select the type of file here.

2. Use the Save In drop-down list to locate the folder in which you want the file saved.

3. Type a name for the file. We named our sample document *Sales Note 6-15-95* in the File Name text box.

    Note that with Works for Windows 95, you're not restricted to the eight-character filename limit that earlier versions of Works imposed. You can use up to 255 characters, but you still can't use the special characters \ / : * ? " < > |. So, the filename *Sales Notes for June 15, 1995* is perfectly valid (although probably longer than necessary), while a filename like *Sales Notes/Today* would not be valid because the / (slash) character is not allowed in filenames.

4. Click OK.

    Works saves the document in a file named *Sales Note 6-15-95*. Works always attaches the .WPS extension to any word processing document file it saves, but you can see it only if you use the Properties command in the Windows Explorer, when the file is selected.

Saving Works for Later

There's a good chance that you won't always have the time to complete your work in a single session, so here's how to save your work and return to the same place later on.

1. Click Tools, and then click Options.

2. When you see the Options dialog box, click the View tab.

3. Click the Use Saved Workspace At Startup option.

4. Click the Save Workspace command button.

5. Click OK.

The next time you start Works, it will restore your screen, document and all, exactly as you left it.

 TIP If you follow the previous steps, Works will start you where you left off, but only if your original document was saved at least once. The Save Workspace feature just defines which files to open, yet doesn't save them.

Making Automatic Backups

When you're busy, it's sometimes easy to make a mistake. To protect your work, Works will automatically make a backup copy of a document. This takes place if you check the Create Backup Copy check box in the Save As dialog box. Works will then make an extra copy of the document each time you save your file, placing the copy in the same folder where the original is saved. The only difference is that Works will use a different extension attached to the backup file. When you save a word processed document and have a backup created, it will be saved as filename.bps, or, in our example, Sales Note 6-15-95.bps. Here's a small list showing you what the extensions are when backups for the different modules are made.

Module	Backup Extension
Word Processor	.BPS
Spreadsheet	.BKS
Database	.BDB
Communications	.BCM

As you can see, when Works creates a backup file, the backup copy keeps the same filename, except its filename extension begins with B instead of W. When you do create a backup, it means that the two files take up twice as much space because there are two files stored on disk (the original and the backup). If you need to conserve space on your disk, then you can make a backup and transfer it to a floppy disk.

> **TIP** Always make backup files. If something happens to the original file, you can open the backup file and recover a recent copy of your document.

Each time you select the Save command, Works saves the current version you see on screen in the original document file (the one with the WPS extension). At the same time, Works replaces the contents of the backup file (the one with the BPS extension) with the next most recent version of the document. To summarize, the following three actions take place each time you select the Save command with the automatic backup feature turned on:

- The current version of the document is stored in the original file with the WPS extension.

- The version of the document at the time of the prior save is stored in the backup copy with the BPS extension.

- The version of the document that existed two saves ago (stored in the backup file prior to the current save) is replaced and permanently gone.

Coming Next

Even though the word processing skills you learned in this chapter are the most basic, they may well be the most important. You need a good foundation to build on to tackle the more advanced and complex word processing features that make Works so powerful. Let's move on to some of those now and focus on formatting a document.

Chapter 4

Formatting a Document

No matter how well your document is written, its appearance can make the difference between a bunch of sentences and a persuasive, attractive presentation. That's why Works has so many different options available for formatting words, paragraphs, and pages. And, most of these changes are as close as a few clicks away. We'll begin exploring them with a general overview of how to format a document, with lots of hints about using the toolbar and the ruler as you write, edit, and print your documents.

Formatting Characters and Paragraphs

What a document says is always important, yet the way it looks can increase the impact of what you say and ensure that you effectively communicate your message. Good formatting can mean the difference between a document that is read carefully . . . and one that is tossed aside. This chapter is all about how to format your text.

Changing the Way Characters Look

The toolbar is your shortcut to the most common commands the Works word processor offers. You'll use the toolbar a great deal when you format, revise, and print documents. Now is a good time to become familiar with how the various boxes and buttons appear on the toolbar you see here, and to get an idea of what they do.

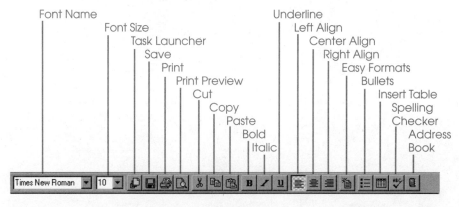

In the following sections you'll see how you can use the toolbar buttons to quickly format a document instead of the menu commands they represent.

You'll probably want to take the toolbar for a test run, so open a new word processor document using the New command on the File menu (if the Task Launcher is not open), and then click the button representing the Word Processor.

Selecting a Font

At the left end of the toolbar you'll see a box for font names. Each font is a different design of type; each has a name, such as Courier, Helvetica, Script, or Times Roman, and each creates characters with a particular look and style. Your printer's capabilities determine which fonts are available. Your Works screen might not look exactly like the illustrations in this chapter, but don't worry. All the basic procedures are the same.

Font characteristics, including type, size, and style, can be used in two ways. After text is entered, the text can be highlighted and then changed. Or, before the text is entered, the font and size options can be selected so that text you enter will appear formatted just as you specified. Which method will work for you? It's up to you to decide. Many find it more effective to enter text first and get the content down, and then go back and format. That way, what you want to get across can be clarified before you make any changes to the text's physical appearance.

 TIP If you can't see the toolbar or the ruler, it's because you have those options turned off on the View menu. Click View, and then click Toolbar or Ruler so that a check mark appears next to each to show the option is turned on.

The Font Name box on the toolbar displays the name of the font you're currently using. Try out your fonts by following these steps:

1. Click the button to the right of the Font Name box to see a list of available fonts, as shown here.

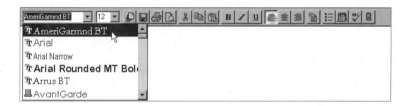

2. Click a font name other than the one that is highlighted. That becomes the active font.

Or you can change the font *after* text is entered by highlighting the text and then selecting the font you want to use.

Selecting a Font Size

The second box from the left end of the toolbar indicates the size of the font at the insertion point position. You can use the Size drop-down list to change the size of a font. Font sizes are measured in units called points. There are 72 points to an inch. Standard documents are often printed in either 10-point or 12-point type, the latter being larger and easier to read.

The Font Size box on the toolbar displays the current font size. You can change font size by following these steps:

1. Click the button to the right of the Font Size box to see other available sizes.

2. Click the size you want.

 TIP If a size you want isn't listed, click the current size indicator to "collapse" the list while the current size remains highlighted. Then type the size you want and press Enter.

Here's a sample of different font sizes.

This is Bookman 8 point

This is Bookman 12 point

This is Bookman 16 point

This is Bookman 20 point

This is Bookman 24 point

Selecting a Character Style

The portion of the toolbar shown below consists of three buttons grouped by function. From left to right they are labeled B (for **bold**), I (for *italic*), and U (for <u>underline</u>). Each assigns a special appearance, or attribute, to selected characters.

These buttons can be used as follows:

1. Using the mouse, select one word by double-clicking it.

2. Click the Bold button on the toolbar.
    The text's style or appearance will change to **bold**.

3. Using the mouse, select another word by double-clicking it.

4. Click the Italic button on the toolbar.
    The text's style or appearance will change to *italic*.

5. Using the mouse, select a third word by double-clicking it.

6. Click the Underline button on the toolbar.
    The text will be <u>underlined</u>.

Any of these attributes can be combined. Just click more than one. Also, any of these attributes can be turned off. The toolbar buttons act as toggle switches. Clicking once turns it on (notice it looks pushed in); when it is turned on, clicking it again turns it off.

TIP You can also bold, italicize, or underline existing text by selecting it first and then using the Ctrl+B, Ctrl+I, or Ctrl+U key combinations.

Another Way to Work with Fonts and Styles

Fonts, font sizes, and character styles are also accessible through the Font and Style command on the Format menu. When you select the Font and Style command, you will see the Format Font and Style dialog box shown in Figure 4-1 on the following page.

Using this dialog box, you can select the font, size, and style; you can also see what the font will look like before you make the actual selection. In Figure 4-1 you can see how 16-point Wide Latin italic will appear. Works offers a neat preview box so that you can see how a font will appear while you're still trying out different attributes. Note that you can only preview

FIGURE 4-1
The Format Font
and Style
dialog box

Select font here.

Select font size here.

Select font style here.

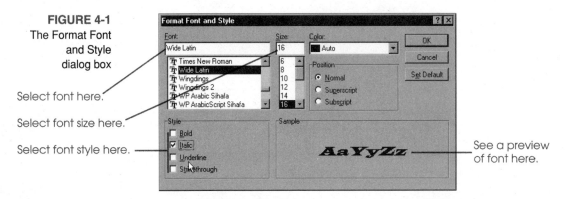

See a preview
of font here.

a font in the Format Font and Style dialog box, and not through any of the commands on the toolbar.

You can also use the options in this dialog box to create superscript and subscript characters, such as $a^2=b^2+c^2$ and $R_{profit*fun}$. Click the Cancel button to exit the Format Font and Style dialog box without making any changes.

Beware of Font Junk

You can mix and match fonts, sizes, and styles. As long as the selected text remains selected, you can underline it, make it bold, and italicize it as well. But, as you can see here, you can also end up with font junk like this . . .

<u>where</u> *the message* ***becomes the medium***

(instead of the other way around). What you want to say is obscured by the way it looks. Be careful. Often the simplest combinations of fonts, sizes, and styles are the best, especially when used consistently for like elements.

Keep the following points in mind when you work with fonts, sizes, and attributes.

Underline and bold are both used for emphasis, to make certain words or phrases stand out. You can use both interchangeably. However, if you use either underline or boldface too much, they will lose their power to make the reader notice what you want to emphasize. In <u>other</u> words, <u>don't</u> underline <u>every</u> other <u>word!</u> Also, underlining sometimes means to italicize. When manuscripts are professionally printed, the underlined words are usually set in italics. If you want your words printed in italics, underline them in the draft copy; they'll be easier for an editor or desktop publisher to spot.

Finally, the bold feature is generally used to highlight a section heading, as in an outline. The underlining feature is more often used for emphasizing text.

Afraid that you might be a victim of font junk? Then use a TaskWizard. The document the TaskWizard creates has predesigned formatting— designers have made sure that there will be no visual conflicts. For example, in Figure 4-2, you can see the first page of a newsletter created by one of Works' Wizards. While the content is nonsense and Works requires you to provide your own, you can get a sense of how fonts are supposed to go together. For example, the headline is 100-point Times Condensed, and the text is 10-point Arial, with bold for the article titles and page numbers in the contents box.

FIGURE 4-2
A TaskWizard-generated news-letter showing how nicely fonts can work together

Changing Text Alignment

The three buttons on the toolbar that display lines of "text," as you see here, affect the way selected text (be it a paragraph, a word, or a single character) is aligned (or justified) on the page. Figure 4-3 on the following page illustrates text aligned with the three styles.

Left Align — Center Align — Right Align

FIGURE 4-3

The three text
alignment styles

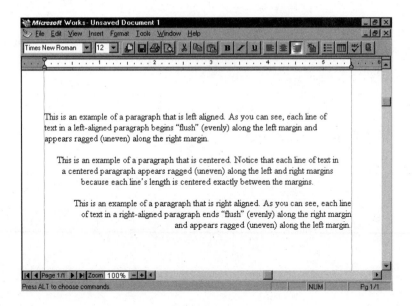

To use any of these styles, follow these steps:

1. Place the insertion point anywhere in the text you want to align.

2. Click the Left Align, Center Align, or Right Align button.

The Left Align button aligns each line of text flush on the left margin. The Center Align button centers text between the left and right margins of the page. The Right Align button right-aligns text, in which the left edges are ragged but the right edges line up flush down the right margin. Right justification is often used for quote attributions or for separating information on one line like this:

Volume 1, Number 1   October, 1995

TIP Full justification, where the lines of text align flush on both the left and right margins, is available by opening the Format menu, choosing Paragraph, and selecting Justified from the Indents and Alignment tab. Most books, including this one, use full justification.

Formatting a Document Chapter 4

Changing the Way Paragraphs Look

You'll find that using the toolbar is the fastest way to carry out many commands, though not the only way. With the toolbar's handy Font Name and Font Size boxes, plus the six formatting buttons, you can do a lot quickly. But there are many other available options for changing the appearance of a document. Here we'll explore some of the other possibilities, available under the Paragraph command on the Format menu.

When you choose this option, you see the Format Paragraph dialog box shown in Figure 4-4. This dialog box includes two tabs, one labeled Indents and Alignment, and one labeled Spacing.

Select indentation here.

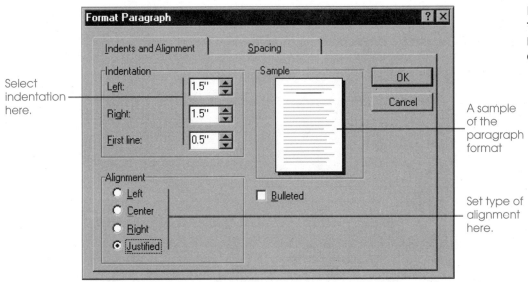

A sample of the paragraph format

Set type of alignment here.

FIGURE 4-4
The Format Paragraph dialog box

Adding Indents and Aligning Text

You can change the appearance of paragraphs with the Indents and Alignment options by clicking that tab in the Format Paragraph dialog box (Figure 4-4). The Indents and Alignment options let you set the amount and type of alignment and whether a bullet character (•) precedes the selected paragraph.

To use the Indents and Alignment tab, follow these steps:

1. Place the insertion point in an existing paragraph, or select several consecutive paragraphs.

2. Click Format, and then click Paragraph.

3. Click the Indents and Alignment tab.

4. Set the attributes you want by clicking the appropriate option buttons.

5. Click OK.

In the Sample area shown in Figure 4-4 on the preceding page, you can see how a paragraph looks with left and right margins of 1.5 inches, a first-line indent of .5 inches, and justified text.

Changing Line Spacing in a Paragraph

The Spacing tab displays a group of options that allows you to set spacing between lines and before and after paragraphs, as shown in Figure 4-5.

FIGURE 4-5
The Format dialog box's Spacing tab

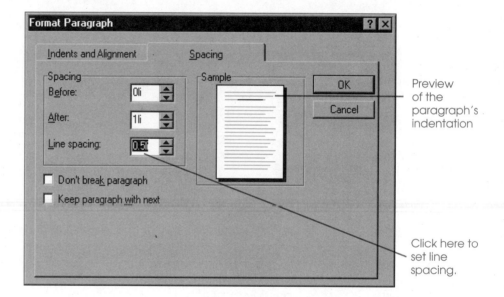

Preview of the paragraph's indentation

Click here to set line spacing.

For example, if you want to change line spacing from single to double spacing, follow these steps:

1. Place the mouse pointer anywhere in the paragraph that you want to double-space.

2. Click Format, and then click Paragraph.

3. Click the Spacing tab.

4. Click the up arrow for the Line Spacing option until you see 2li.

5. Click OK.

You might notice an interesting relationship between the Spacing tab and the Indents and Alignment tab in the Format Paragraph dialog box. You can switch back and forth from one to the other, and the current sample area will reflect all previous settings. For example, if you select certain options under the Indents and Alignment tab, those settings will be in force when you switch to the Spacing tab. It's quick, easy, and efficient to set line spacing, alignment, and other options using these two tabs.

> **TIP** You can also add bullets to paragraphs through the Indents and Alignment tab by clicking on the Bulleted check box. Bullets are useful in setting off lists.

Formatting Documents with Easy Formats

The Easy Formats option on the Format menu allows you to specify a format that can be quickly applied to paragraphs. In the earlier versions of Works, this was called Quick Format. You can specify a particular paragraph style from many options and apply it as needed to new text. To use this option, follow these steps:

1. Place the insertion point in an existing paragraph, or select two or more consecutive paragraphs.

2. Click Format, and then click Easy Format.

   When you do this, you'll see the Easy Format dialog box as shown in Figure 4-6 on the following page. Each predefined paragraph style on the left contains multiple format settings that appear in the Description box. The Sample box presents a small (thumbnail) image of the paragraph's layout in relation to the page and an example of its font setting.

   Figure 4-7 on the following page shows you how a paragraph looks in a document window when you apply the Flyer Text Easy Format option to it. Notice that its text appears in 24-point Arial bold, with centered alignment, with specific spacing measurements, and special borders.

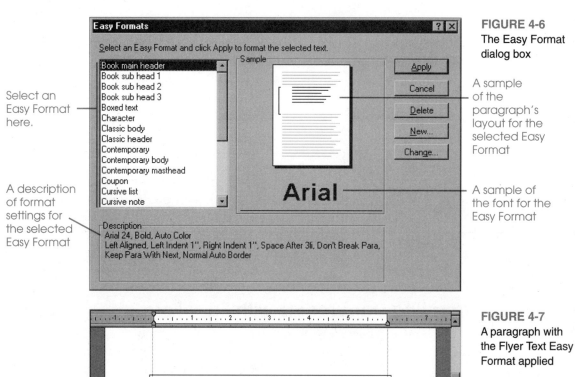

Select an
Easy Format
here.

A description
of format
settings for
the selected
Easy Format

FIGURE 4-6
The Easy Format
dialog box

A sample
of the
paragraph's
layout for the
selected Easy
Format

A sample of
the font for the
Easy Format

FIGURE 4-7
A paragraph with
the Flyer Text Easy
Format applied

Changing Indents and Margins with the Ruler

Just below the toolbar, at the top of the document window, you can see
an on-screen ruler that looks like this:

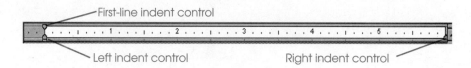

First-line indent control

Left indent control

Right indent control

By default, the ruler shows measurements in inches. If you want, you can use the Options command on the Tools menu to change the measurement unit to centimeters, picas (sixths of an inch), points (12 points to a pica), or millimeters.

The three triangles on the ruler allow you to control a paragraph's first-line indent, right indent, and left indent.

Like the toolbar, the ruler lets you change settings for one or more paragraphs without using menu commands. What's more, you can double-click on the ruler to display the Format Tabs dialog box, which allows you to set tab positions, alignment, and leader characters. Tab settings will be discussed later in this chapter.

First-Line Indentation

A first-line indent is the amount, typically .5 inch, that the first line of a paragraph is indented, relative to the other lines. To indent the first line of one or more selected paragraphs, you can use either the ruler or the Indents and Alignment tab in the Format Paragraph dialog box.

With the ruler, you can use the mouse to drag the first-line indent control (the top triangle at the left end of the ruler).

To indent the first line in a paragraph, follow these steps:

1. Place the insertion point anywhere within the paragraph.

2. Drag the first-line indent control right to the .5-inch mark on the ruler. It might take some practice to position the control precisely on the .5-inch mark. As you can see in Figure 4-8 on the following page, a vertical line in the document window moves with the control as you drag it to help you align the text in the document. When you release the mouse button, the first-line indent is set.

Paragraph Indentation

Left and right paragraph indents determine how far an entire paragraph is indented, relative to the margins of the page. When you use left and right indentation, you are adding to the amount of white space at the edges of the page. With the ruler, you drag the left indent control (the lower triangle at the left end of the ruler) and the right indent control to set the left and right indents, respectively. You can also use the Indents and Alignment tab in the Format Paragraph dialog box.

For example, you can see in Figure 4-9 on the following page that the left indent control is set at 1 inch and the right indent control is set at 5 inches.

FIGURE 4-8

Moving the first-line indent control

Dragging the first-line indent control one-half inch

Vertical line moves with control to show the indent in the document.

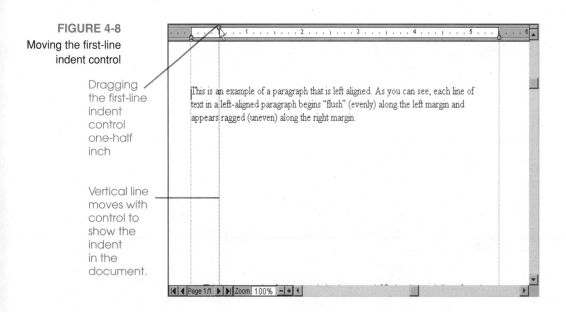

FIGURE 4-9

Indentation settings on the ruler

Left margin   New indentation   Right margin

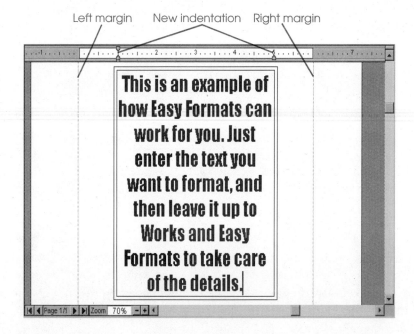

Formatting a Short Memo

To demonstrate formatting a document we will create a short memo by typing the following text. On screen the document appears as shown in Figure 4-10 after we have applied some simple, but impressive, formatting changes. To see the entire memo in the figure, we reduced the document view to 70 percent.

```
Memo
Dear good friends of ACME Widgets:
Fun for you! The Bored of Directors theater group will
be producing their annual review on November 14 at 8:30
PM. If you remember last year we had tons of fun, lots
of laughs, junk food galore, and a good time.
Tickets usually go fast for this event, so get yours as
soon as possible. See you there!
Jackson H. Jordan
VP for Fun & Games
```

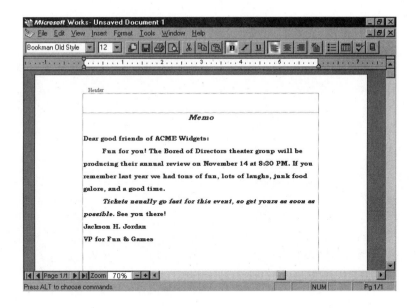

FIGURE 4-10
A formatted memo

Here's how to format the memo as you see in the figure.

1. Select the entire document by pressing Ctrl and clicking in the left margin, and then select the Bookman font. (If this font is not available on your system, select a different font.) Then select 12 for the font size.

2. Select the word *Memo*, click the Center Align button on the toolbar, click 14 for the font size, click the Italic button, and click the Bold button.

3. Select the two body paragraphs beginning with the words *Fun* and *Tickets*. Click Format, click Paragraph, and set the first-line indent to .5 inch on the Indents and Alignment tab. (You could also drag the first-line indent control on the ruler to do this.)

4. While the Format Paragraph dialog box is open, click the Spacing tab, set the line spacing option to 2li, and click OK.

5. Select the sentence *Tickets usually go fast for this event, so get yours as soon as possible*, and click the Italic button on the toolbar.

Now, that wasn't so bad, was it? In fact, it was pretty easy—and it certainly made the document more attractive. Let's now try other types of formatting tools that Works offers.

Setting Tabs with the Ruler

Tabs are predefined stops along the ruler that make it a cinch to align text and create lists like this:

Here are the enrollment steps as I see them.
1. Get an enrollment form.
2. Contact your advisor.
3. Determine what course you want to take.
4. Enroll.
5. Pay fees.

You can set tabs using the ruler, or using the Format Tabs dialog box. Works lets you set several types of tabs: left-aligned, centered, right-aligned, and aligned on a decimal point. You can see examples of how text aligns around tab stops in Figure 4-11.

When a left tab is set, text that you enter moves to the right of the left-aligned tab setting. As you can see in Figure 4-11, the text aligns to the right of the tab stop. Works places a ∟ on the ruler for a left tab.

Setting a center tab centers text on the position of the tab setting. Figure 4-11 shows the text extending an equal distance to the left and right of the tab stop. Works places a ⊥ on the ruler for a center-aligned tab.

When a right tab is set, text that you enter moves to the left of the right-aligned tab setting. As you can see in Figure 4-11, the text aligns to the left of the tab stop. Works places a ⌐ on the ruler for a right tab.

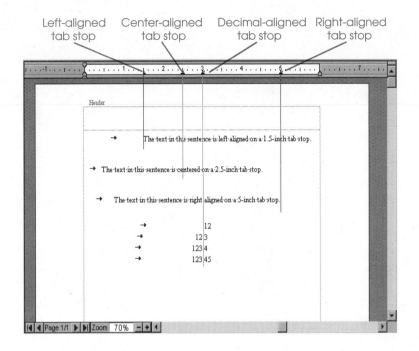

FIGURE 4-11
Text alignment
around tab stops

Finally, when a decimal tab is set, text that you enter moves to the left of the decimal tab setting until you press the decimal point (type a period). Then the text moves to the right. This is the ideal tab stop alignment to use when you enter numbers that contain decimals. Works places a ⊥ on the ruler for a decimal tab.

If you don't set any tabs, Works uses default left-aligned tabs set at every .5-inch position.

Setting Tabs with the Format Tabs Dialog Box

You can also set tabs in the Format Tabs dialog box, which appears when you select the Tabs command on the Format menu. The Format Tabs dialog box looks like this:

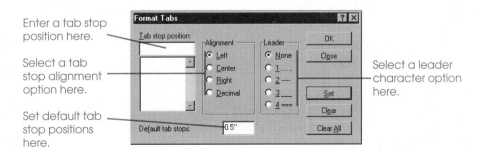

This might be the simplest and most direct way to set tabs. Here's how.

1. Click Format, and then click Tabs.

2. Click Clear All to clear all the previously set tabs.

3. In the Tab Stop Position box, enter the position (in default units) of the first tab.

4. Click an Alignment option button.

5. Click Set to store the settings and set another tab stop, or click OK to return to the document.

 TIP You can display the Format Tabs dialog box by double-clicking on the ruler. Then set any number of tabs you wish for the selected paragraph.

When you set tabs, you can also specify a type of leader character. These are repeating characters that fill the tab spacing. For example, here's how a tab dot leader appears.

Chapter I. History of Juggling...2
Chapter II. Why You Should Juggle...............................6
Chapter III. Different Types of Juggling.......................8
    A. Balls..10
    B. Clubs...12
    C. Diablos...14
    D. Spears (ouch!)..17

To use leader characters, just click on the Leader option you want, and Works will insert the characters automatically when you press Tab.

Now we will demonstrate using the ruler to set tabs in a sample document. We'll create the following list of items; press Tab once and type the word for each line:

```
hammer
nails
shingles
tape
cement
```

Now we can use the ruler to set tabs, as follows:

1. Select the lines to be formatted.

2. Move the mouse pointer to the ruler, just below the 1.5-inch mark, and click.

Works inserts a left-aligned tab stop (the only kind you can set with the ruler) at that position. The list appears as you see in Figure 4-12. Notice that we turned on All Characters (on the View menu) so that you can see the special tab characters.

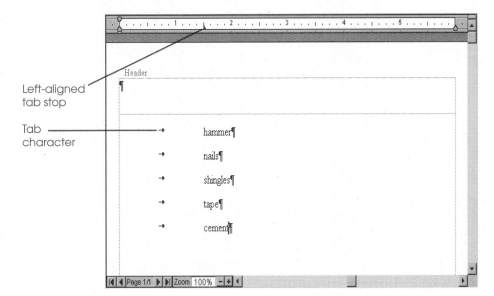

Left-aligned tab stop

Tab character

FIGURE 4-12
Left-aligning a list with a single click on the ruler

Header

hammer¶

nails¶

shingles¶

tape¶

cement¶

TIP Works can create what's called a hanging indent, where each line but the first in a paragraph is indented. You can do this by placing the insertion point in the paragraph and then using the Ctrl+H key combination to have Works create this format for you.

Using Tables in a Word-Processed Document

You can also use tabs to create tables, which have more than one column, but it's cumbersome and inefficient. For example, the table you see here was created using tabs.

	Democrats	Republicans	Total
Males	32	45	77
Females	28	27	55
Total	60	72	132

While it looks acceptable, you can't add lines, insert a new column, or easily format a table set up with tab stops.

Instead, you can use Works' special table feature, which provides a variety of built-in formats that insert a table directly into a word processing document. For example, in Figure 4-13, you can see a four-column table.

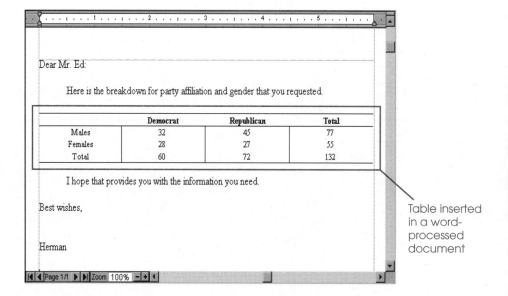

Table inserted
in a word-
processed
document

To create a table, follow these steps:

1. Place the insertion point in the location where you want the table.

2. Click Insert, and then click Table.

   When you do this, you'll see the Insert Table dialog box as shown in Figure 4-14.

3. Enter the number of rows you want in the table.

4. Enter the number of columns you want in the table.

5. Select one of the many different formats you want to use. You can see an example of the selected table format in the Example box.

6. Click OK.

7. Enter the table's data.

The table is now part of the word-processed document. If you need to edit it, just click anywhere in the table where the edit is to take place, make the change, and then click outside of the table.

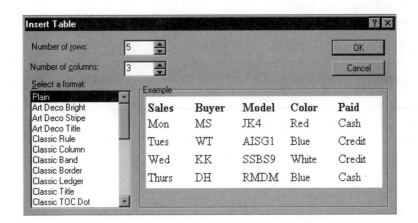

FIGURE 4-14
The Insert Table
dialog box

Setting Up a Document's Page Layout

The layout of a printed page is governed by more than the alignment, spacing, and indentation of the paragraphs. You've no doubt encountered form letters or handouts on which the text literally covered the paper, marching down the page in rank after closely spaced rank of small, dark blots of ink.

Such printing might initially save a few dollars, but the money saved can actually be money wasted if no one wants to read what the writer has to say. Conventional wisdom maintains that adequate margins, indents, and paragraph spacing enhance the readability of any document. So do such elements as page numbers, running heads that appear at the top of each page, and controlled breaks that avoid awkward interruptions in words, lines, and paragraphs.

You've already seen how to control spacing in paragraphs. Now you'll learn how to adjust a document's top, bottom, left, and right margins. You'll also find out how to:

- Select a page size and orientation
- Number pages
- Print footnotes
- Set columns
- Break lines and pages at a specified place

■ Keep certain words together on the same line

■ Keep all lines of a particular paragraph on the same page

Setting Margins

Works automatically sets reasonable margins for a printed page. To check the margins, choose the Page Setup command from the File menu. When you do this, the Page Setup dialog box appears with the Margins tab in view, as shown in Figure 4-15.

FIGURE 4-15
The Page Setup
dialog box

Set
margins
here.

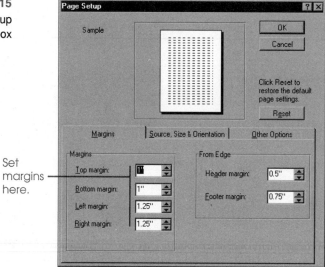

The four options in the Margins box show the current settings for the top, bottom, left, and right margins. They appear in the unit of measurement you specify in the Options dialog box. If your setting is in inches, you see top and bottom margins of 1 inch and left and right margins of 1.25 inches, by default. To change any of these, type a new measurement (whole or decimal number). You can omit the unit of measure unless you want to specify a different one. For example, you can type *5 cm* even though Works displays all other measurements in inches. However, Works will convert the setting to default units. For instance, the next time you open the Page Setup dialog box the 5 cm setting would appear as 1.97 inches.

Left and right margins of 1.25 inches are standard for letters and similar documents, but you might want to change one or both to suit a particular layout. For example, if you're planning to print and bind a report, increase the left margin to 1.5 inches, or more, to allow space for the binding. If you're preparing a manuscript or a draft document for review, increase both side margins to allow adequate room for editing or review notes.

The default top and bottom margins, on the other hand, might be a little tight for your purposes. Business documents, especially letters, tend to leave plenty of space at the top and a bit less at the bottom, so a top margin of 1.5 inches might be more appropriate.

You can also set the margins, or positions, of the header or footer. A header is text that appears on the top of each page. A footer is text that appears on the bottom of each page. This book uses headers, which is the text that you see at the top of this page.

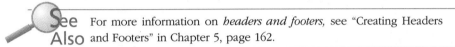

See Also For more information on *headers and footers,* see "Creating Headers and Footers" in Chapter 5, page 162.

To set margins, simply click on the margin you want to change and enter the new value. You can increase or decrease the measurements in increments of .10 inch by clicking on the option's up or down arrow button. Look to the Sample area at the top of the dialog box to see the effect of the change.

TIP You can use the Tab key to move from one margin setting to another. Press Shift+Tab to move back to the previous setting.

Selecting a Page Size and Orientation

In the Page Setup dialog box, the Source, Size & Orientation tab shown in Figure 4-16 on the following page offers options for changing page size and orientation. These options are especially useful if you need to print on larger paper or smaller stock (such as postcards). The Orientation option can be used to select Landscape if you have a very wide document (such as a table).

To work with Source, Size & Orientation options, follow these steps:

1. Click File, and then click Page Setup.

2. Click the Source, Size & Orientation tab.

FIGURE 4-16
The Source, Size &
Orientation options

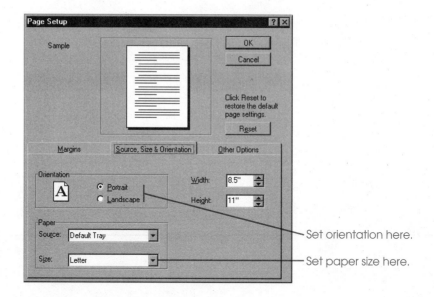

3. Select the paper size you want to use.

4. Select the document's orientation.

   In Portrait orientation, the page's width is the shorter dimension (like any standard page); in Landscape orientation, the page's width is the larger dimension.

5. Check the Sample area to see whether it shows the size and orientation you want.

TIP If your printer has more than one paper source—such as both a regular paper tray and an envelope feed—you can select your printer's paper source on the Source, Size & Orientation tab.

Numbering Pages

The Other Options tab in the Page Setup dialog box, as you see in Figure 4-17, is where you can enter the page number with which you want Works to start numbering the document (be it 1 or 1000).

The page numbering will begin on the document's first page. If you want to begin the document with a page number other than one (1), enter the page number you want to begin with in the Start Page Number box.

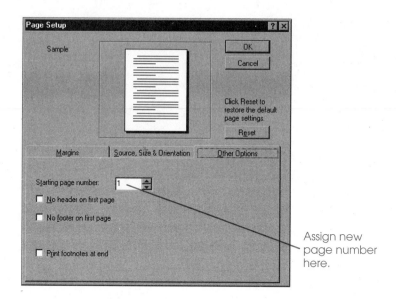

FIGURE 4-17

Entering a new
page number in
a document

When might you want to begin a document with a page number other than
one? One example might be creating a new document file for each chapter
in a manuscript. You would begin the new chapter with a page number
that follows consecutively the last page number of the previous chapter.

Formatting Text in Columns

Columns enhance the appearance of a document and take just a click to
create. You can set up single or multiple columns, making good writing
into a very attractive and readable document.

You can create columns by following these steps:

1. Click Format, and then click Columns.

    You will see the Format Columns dialog box shown here.

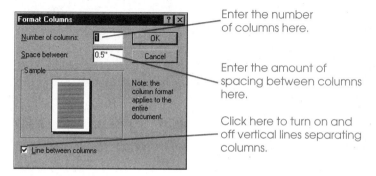

137

The width of a column is determined by the number of columns on a page, the page margins, and the space between columns (with .5 inch as the default).

2. Enter the number of columns you want to appear.

3. Press the Tab key to move to the Space Between box and to see in the Sample area what the columns look like.

4. Enter the space you want between columns.

5. Click off the Line Between Columns check box if you don't want a line between columns.

TIP It's best to leave the Space Between setting alone if you're working with only two or three columns. Generally, you don't need to worry about the space between columns, unless you have so many columns that the space between them becomes wider than the columns themselves! Keep in mind that you want your reader's eye drawn to the text, not to the spaces between columns.

You can see how columns were used in the Print Preview window, shown in Figure 4-18, where three columns were used to format the

FIGURE 4-18
A three-column page layout, as seen in a Print Preview window

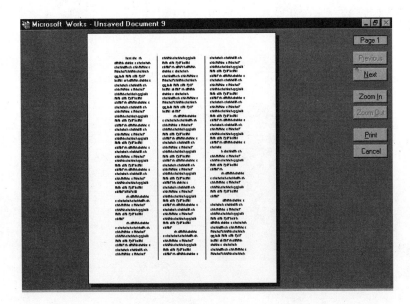

document. You can select only one column setting for any document, and that selection can be made any place in the document. The column format applies to the entire document. In earlier versions of Works, columns would not appear on screen. Now they do, but only in Page Layout (not Normal) view, so you can see exactly how your document should look.

Working with Text from Page to Page

Sometimes you may want to begin a new page without having to completely fill the previous page. For example, suppose you want to begin Chapter 2 on a new page, but the last page of Chapter 1 only fills up half the sheet. The answer? A page break. In other situations you might want to keep text together. If a quotation appears at the bottom of a page, for example, you certainly don't want the first line to appear on one page and the remaining lines on subsequent pages. Let's look at how you can deal with these and other text management issues.

Working with Page Breaks

When you create a multiple-page document, Works keeps track of the document's length. Works also shows you where page breaks occur as you're typing by displaying a new page character (>>) at the left edge of the screen in Normal view. (This symbol appears at the top of a new word-processed document as well.) In Page Layout view, Works actually shows you the edge of the page, graphically.

Sometimes, pages will break where you don't want them to (for example, at the end of a letter, between the closing and your signature). To correct this, you can either insert a manual page break or tell Works that certain paragraphs must stay together on the same page. Here's how you do both.

Inserting a Manual Page Break

To insert a manual page break, follow these steps:

1. Move the insertion point to the place you want a new page to begin.

2. Click Insert, and then click Page Break (or press the Ctrl+Enter key combination).

Works then displays a dotted line showing the page break, plus the >> character, as you can see here.

....
>>

After you insert a manual page break, choose Paginate Now on the Tools menu (or press the F9 function key) so that any adjustments in page length are made automatically. To see how other pages might have been affected by the insertion of the page break, view them in Print Preview. If you later decide you don't want a manual page break you inserted, place the insertion point in front of the first character following the page break, and then press the Backspace key.

Keeping Paragraphs Together

You might want to ensure that two paragraphs stay together on the same page. There are two ways to do this and keep a Works-initiated page break from interrupting paragraphs in a document. You can do this by having Works keep a line paragraph, such as in a list, on one page, or by keeping related paragraphs together on a single page. In either situation, you use the Spacing tab in the Format Paragraph dialog box (see Figure 4-5 on page 122).

To keep all lines of a paragraph on the same page, click the check box next to Don't Break Paragraph. To keep related paragraphs together, click the check box next to Keep Paragraph With Next.

TIP Be careful with the commands that keep text together. If, for example, the closing in a letter is the only thing that carries over to an additional page, go up a few lines and press the Enter key until there are a few lines of text along with the closing. If you elect to keep the closing as part of the last paragraph, the previous page will have a significant amount of blank space at the bottom.

Viewing and Printing Documents

You'll be glad to know that, because Works is an integrated program, the printing process is consistent throughout the Works modules. Once you've defined the margins, formatting, running heads, and other elements of a document, the only steps remaining are previewing and printing. We'll cover both of those here. Any special printing functions or operations particular to a module will be addressed in our discussion of each module.

Using Print Preview

You've learned about Print Preview and its Zoom feature, so neither needs much additional explanation. Print Preview is great for examining format changes before you print and saving paper.

One preview aspect you haven't seen, however, is the Previous and Next buttons in the Preview window. So far, you've previewed single-page documents, where these buttons are inactive. On a multiple-page document, you use the Previous and Next buttons to move from page to page. Previous takes you back one page (if there is one), and Next takes you forward one page.

Previewing a document saves time and paper. More important, it can also reduce your frustration when a printout doesn't look as you thought it would. For example, you might use several page breaks and keep other text together to create a certain effect. The only way to check whether these tools served their purpose (without printing) is to preview the document.

Setting Up for Printing

Before you can print a document, Works has to know that there is a printer available and what kind it is. In most cases, you needn't worry about this because Windows 95 helps you set up for printing when you install it. And, because Works is a Windows application, it can use the printer setup you have already defined. Once you tell Windows about your printer, printing becomes a simple matter of choosing the Print command from the File menu, where it appears in Works and many other Windows applications.

If you choose the Print command on the File menu, the Print dialog box appears, where you can select a printer from a list of printers that have already been installed. Why install more than one printer? Some people print drafts on one printer (such as a low-resolution printer), and then print the final versions using a high-resolution printer (say, a laser printer).

To add a new printer to the list or to add or remove fonts, you'll have to use the appropriate Windows 95 utility program.

Using Win95 to Install Printers and Manage Fonts

Adding printers and adding and removing fonts takes place through the Control Panel in Windows 95. To install a printer, click the Start button, point to Settings, click Control Panel, and then double-click the Printers folder. Double-click the Add Printer object and follow the instructions in the Add Printer Wizard. To add or remove a font, click the Start button, point to Settings, click Control Panel, double-click the Fonts folder, and then click File and the Install New Font command. In the Add Fonts dialog box you will need to locate the font you want to add and then click OK.

Printing

After your document looks exactly the way you want it to and you've set up your printer, printing is a snap. All you need to do is choose Print from the File menu, and you'll see this dialog box:

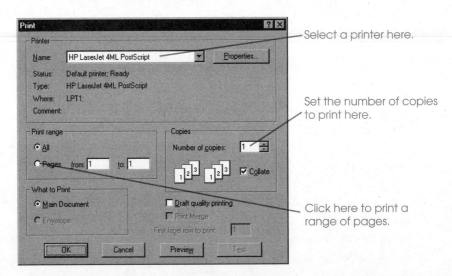

Select a printer here.

Set the number of copies to print here.

Click here to print a range of pages.

Works will print one copy of the current document. If you want more, type the number you want in the Number Of Copies box.

▓▟ Drag-and-Drop Printing with Windows 95

It's easy to print documents in Windows 95, whether the application used to create the document is open (or is not even running). Just open the My Computer or Windows Explorer window, locate the file icon for the document you want to print, and drag it to the shortcut icon for the printer connected to your system. This icon should be on the desktop. If not, you can create one by opening the My Computer window, opening the Printers folder, selecting the printer, clicking the right mouse button, and selecting the Create Shortcut command on the pop-up menu.

Dragging a file icon to the printer's shortcut icon opens the application associated with the type of file you want to print, opens the document you want to print, and, in some cases, opens the application's Print dialog box. Then all you have to do is click the OK button to send the data to the printer.

If you drag a file icon to the printer's icon and a box appears with an error message, you will probably need to create an association between the file and an appropriate application. To do this, do the following:

1. Open the My Computer window, locate the file, and select it.

2. Select View, select the Options command, and select the File Types tab in the Options dialog box.

3. Select the icon for the file's type in the Registered File Types scroll box, and select the Edit command button.

4. Select the New command button, type *print* in the Action text box, and press Tab.

5. Enter the path to the application's program file that starts (opens) the application, and select OK. Then close all open windows.

If you wish to print part of a multiple-page document, click Pages in the Print Range box and fill in the From and To boxes with the starting and ending page numbers. For example, to print only page 43 of a document, enter the number *43* in the From box and *43* in the To box, and then click OK. If you want to print from a certain page to the end of a document, enter the page you want to start with in the From box and a page number greater than the last page (such as *999*) in the To box.

TIP   Want to save toner when printing on a laser printer? Click the check box for the Draft Quality Printing option in the Print dialog box. You'll get perfectly readable output, only not as dark as usual.

Coming Next

With text entry, editing, and formatting basics covered, let's now turn to some advanced word processing features in Works. You can ask Works to check spelling, supply synonyms, locate specific text items, and mark places in a document as well as generate footnotes, headers, and footers.

Chapter 5

Getting the Most from the Word Processor

Besides its formatting, graphics, and layout capabilities, Microsoft Works for Windows 95's word processor offers a number of options that are bound to make your word processing tasks easier. To finish coverage of this application, we'll take a look at some of these features that are powerful yet not necessarily difficult to use. Some, such as the spelling checker or the Find feature, will likely become regular parts of your word processing routine. Others, such as using special characters or creating bookmarks, might become occasional assistants you'll appreciate in special circumstances.

Using Bookmarks to Save Your Place

Unless you've got a photographic memory, you'll probably find yourself scrolling long documents up and down, searching for information you want to refer to as you write about another topic. But scrolling can be very time consuming and tedious. One way to save yourself some time when you're working on a long document is to insert bookmarks at appropriate sections of the document. Works' *bookmarks* can be used as special hidden markers for a document's selected locations, which can be scrolled into view instantly. For example, you might insert a bookmark at each heading in a proposal or a report, at the beginning of a price list, or at the locations of inserted graphics. Or you might simply want to mark the place where you stopped reading a lengthy document on screen.

Marking a Specific Location with a Bookmark

Bookmarks are the computer equivalent of ordinary bookmarks, including paper clips, dog-eared pages, marking pens, and highlighters. You simply move the insertion point to the place in the document that you want to mark, and then insert the bookmark. To demonstrate using this feature, we'll insert bookmarks in the sample document you see in Figure 5-1 on the next page. Although this document isn't very long, we can use it to demonstrate how easily you can create and use a bookmark.

1. Place the insertion point where you want to insert the bookmark. We placed ours in front of the word *umbrellas*.

   You can place bookmarks anywhere in a document. Usually the best place is at or near the beginning of a topic.

FIGURE 5-1
The document we'll
use to demonstrate
inserting a
bookmark

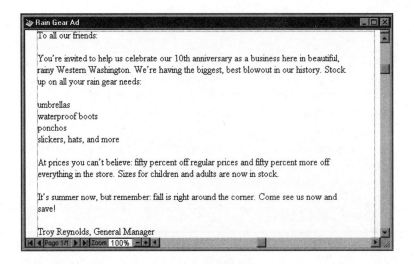

To all our friends:

You're invited to help us celebrate our 10th anniversary as a business here in beautiful, rainy Western Washington. We're having the biggest, best blowout in our history. Stock up on all your rain gear needs:

umbrellas
waterproof boots
ponchos
slickers, hats, and more

At prices you can't believe: fifty percent off regular prices and fifty percent more off everything in the store. Sizes for children and adults are now in stock.

It's summer now, but remember: fall is right around the corner. Come see us now and save!

Troy Reynolds, General Manager

2. Click Edit, and then click Bookmark.

You'll see this Bookmark Name dialog box:

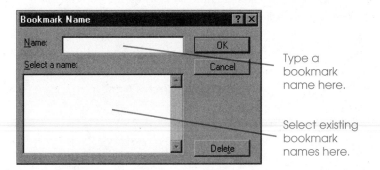

Type a bookmark name here.

Select existing bookmark names here.

Here you can assign a name to the bookmark. After you have done so, Works will associate the name with the location you've marked, and you can return to that exact part of the document whenever you want.

3. Type a name for the bookmark in the Name box, and click OK. We typed *products*.

Works displays the names of all the document's assigned bookmarks in the Select A Name box of the Bookmark Name dialog box, so when you assign names, try to make them descriptive and distinct. You can include spaces in a bookmark name, but if it's longer than 15 characters, Works will truncate (shorten) the name. Even so, you can still use it to jump to the part of the document you marked.

Jumping to a Bookmark

Bookmarks are not visible in the document window, but they're there. To use one, follow these steps:

1. Scroll to the top of a document.

2. Click Edit, and then click Go To.
    You'll see this Go To dialog box:

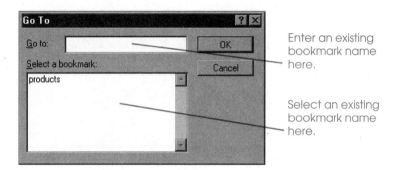

Enter an existing bookmark name here.

Select an existing bookmark name here.

The Go To dialog box also lists the names of all bookmarks you've assigned to a particular document. They appear in the Select A Bookmark scroll box.

TIP   You can press F5 to display the Go To dialog box. But, you can only set a bookmark, field name, or range name in the Go To box.

3. Double-click on the bookmark name that you want to go to.
    For example, to go to the bookmark *products* that we defined in the last section, we simply double-clicked it. Almost instantly, Works jumps to the location in the document that's associated with the bookmark.

If you create a bookmark and later decide you no longer need it, choose Bookmark from the Edit menu, select the bookmark name in the dialog box, click Delete, and then click Close. If you decide to rename a bookmark, go to the bookmark's place in the document, choose Bookmark from the Edit menu, and type a new name. When Works asks if you want to replace the existing bookmark, click OK. Once you've assigned a bookmark name, you can't use that name again in the same document.

Creating Footnotes

Footnotes are an important part of professional papers and academic and business publications, and they can often be useful in other documents, too. You can easily create footnotes to present amplifying statistics in a report, to give citations from other sources, and to note facts that you want to document outside the body of your text.

Typing and numbering footnotes can be a chore without a computer. Works makes the process a breeze by taking over the drudgery of referencing them. Works places all the footnotes neatly at the end of the document—even though it doesn't look that way on the screen. Footnotes are more easily seen than described, so we'll create one.

1. Open an existing word processor document or enter text in a new one.

2. To add a footnote at the insertion point location, click Insert, and then click Footnote. You'll see this Insert Footnote dialog box:

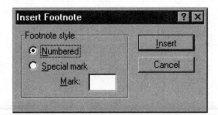

Notice that Works lets you mark footnotes with either numbers or special marks (you can choose your own).

3. Click Insert to accept the Numbered option, which is the default footnote type, and to insert a footnote reference.

The document immediately scrolls to the bottom of the current page, as shown in Figure 5-2, where a footnote reference has been inserted near the bottom of the window.

Notice that Works inserts a two-inch horizontal rule and a footnote superscript (raised) 1 near the bottom of the page, just above the area reserved for the document's footer. This helps keep the footnote's text completely separate from the document's text. If you scroll up to where the insertion point was located when the Insert Footnote command was

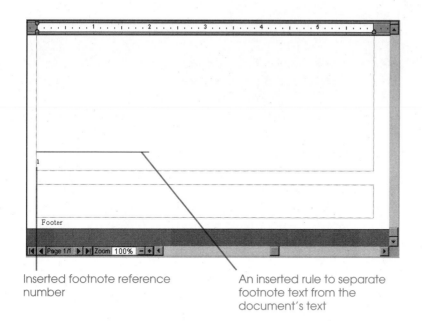

FIGURE 5-2
The footnote area
in a document
window

Inserted footnote reference
number

An inserted rule to separate
footnote text from the
document's text

selected, you'll see that a superscript 1 appears in that location, as
you see here:

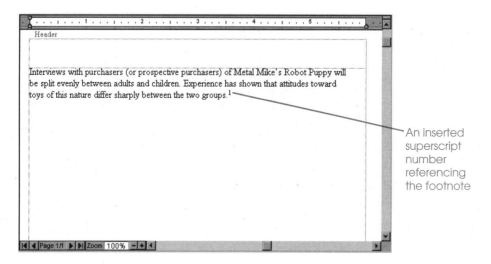

An inserted
superscript
number
referencing
the footnote

NOTE Be aware of a clear distinction between footnotes and
footers. Footnotes, whether one or many, traditionally appear
only at the bottom of the page on which they're referenced.
Footers appear on each page of the document, and there can
be only one per page.

Works keeps track of footnote numbers, so if you had already inserted four footnotes, a superscript 5 would have appeared here.

Works applies the font and font size you've chosen for the body of your document to both footnote reference numbers and footnote text. To conserve space and to minimize the visual impact of footnote reference numbers in the text, you might want to print all footnote-related material in a smaller size. You can format footnote text using the same toolbar buttons and menu commands that you use for the document's text. After you insert the footnote reference, you need to enter the footnote's text, as follows. When you insert a footnote, your cursor moves to the bottom of the page and appears next to the footnote reference number. Step 1 is automatic. You would only have to manually move the cursor if you decided not to enter footnote text at the time you inserted the footnote.

1. Click to the right of the footnote reference number that is inserted near the bottom of the page (you might have to scroll to get there).

2. Type the text you want to appear in the footnote.

After you've created footnotes, you can edit them and move reference numbers by cutting and pasting, just as you do with normal text. If you add or delete footnote references in the body of your text, Works renumbers the remaining footnotes for you—so they'll never be out of order.

Printing Footnotes at the End of a Document

Footnotes are used to cite quotations or summaries, or to make comments that supplement the information in the body of your document. Microsoft Works is preset to print your footnotes at the bottom of each page that contains a footnote reference, although you can choose to print all the footnotes at the end of the document. There they're called endnotes.

To specify that Works prints footnotes at the end of your document, follow these steps:

1. Click File, click Page Setup, and then click the Other Options tab.

2. Click the Print Footnotes At End check box.

3. Click OK.

With this option turned on, all footnotes will print at the end of the document, rather than on the pages where they were inserted.

Checking Your Spelling

The tasks of creating, formatting, and laying out a document are yours alone, yet Works can help you save time when you're grasping for a word that's just out of reach . . . or want to check your spelling . . . or need to find or replace specific text . . . or wish to save formats to avoid duplicating your efforts. We'll start with spelling.

Most people have trouble spelling certain words. Does *parallel* have one *r* or two? Is *embarrassment* really spelled with all those double letters? Is it *wierd* or *weird?* Does *broccoli* have one *c* and two *l*'s, or the other way around?

Works has an online dictionary of 120,000 words that it uses to check the spelling in your documents, and you can add words to that dictionary as well. Sometimes it's necessary to add words to the dictionary so that Works doesn't stop on words that are spelled correctly, but unrecognized, such as your first name or technical terms, like *psychoanalytic, quark,* and *gluon.* You can check spelling in an entire document, or you can limit the operation by selecting only a specific section you want to check.

To demonstrate, we typed the following sentence in a new word processor window. Notice that the sentence contains several misspelled words.

```
Let us go nww, you and eye, where the sunlight drapes
the sky. All the way to microsoft.
```

Now we'll check the spelling, as follows:

1. Place the insertion point at the beginning of the document.

2. Click Tools, and then click Spelling (or press F7).

   Works begins checking the document's spelling. If Works encounters an unrecognized word, it selects the word and displays the Spelling dialog box, shown in Figure 5-3 on the next page.

   Now, you can do a variety of things when Works stops on a word that it doesn't recognize. To begin, check that the unrecognized word is, in fact, a misspelling. If so, look at the list of words in the Suggestions box. In this box Works displays those words that might work as replacements for the unrecognized word. In our example, Works stopped on the first word it couldn't recognize, *nww.* To

FIGURE 5-3
A selected
unrecognized word
and the Spelling
dialog box

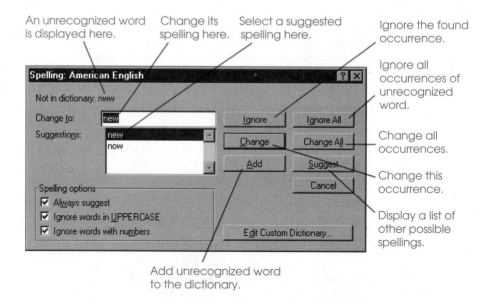

An unrecognized word
is displayed here.

Change its
spelling here.

Select a suggested
spelling here.

Ignore the found
occurrence.

Ignore all
occurrences of
unrecognized
word.

Change all
occurrences.

Change this
occurrence.

Display a list of
other possible
spellings.

Add unrecognized word
to the dictionary.

substitute a listed word for *nww*, just double-click on the correct spelling.

3.   To correct a misspelling in a document, highlight the word you want in the Suggestions box and click the Change button. Here we selected *now*.

If you'd rather see a list of additional possible spellings, click the Suggest button, and a list of possible other word choices appears. If the unrecognized word happens to be spelled correctly (but it just happens not to be in the Works dictionary), you can click the Ignore button to leave the unrecognized word as it is and continue checking the document.

After you take action on an unrecognized word, the spelling checker then moves to the next word it doesn't recognize. In this case, Works found irregular capitalization in the word *microsoft*. Works knows this word should be capitalized because it's an entry in the Works dictionary. (The inclusion of *Microsoft* in Works' dictionary isn't rampant boosterism. You'll find *IBM*, *WordPerfect*, and *Macintosh* there, too.)

Notice that Works' spelling tool skipped over the word *eye*, even though it should have been *I*. Works can't check for correct word usage, so remember always to proofread your documents carefully for mistakes like this one. It's easy to mistakenly use homonyms—words that sound alike but mean something different, such as *eye* and *I*, *cent* and *scent*, or *too* and *to*. Spelling checkers actually check your typing, rather than your spelling and usage. Sound-alike words, or words spelled the same but of different meanings, won't be flagged by the spelling checker.

The occurrence of *microsoft* is the last misspelling in our sample document, but before we correct it, let's look at the remainder of the Spelling dialog box. See Figure 5-3 to learn what each command button does.

As you can see, the spelling checker is both powerful and flexible. To finish up our example, we'll complete the spell-checking process as follows:

1. Click the Change button to accept the correct spelling. In this case we'll accept the capitalization *Microsoft*.

2. Click OK in the dialog box that appears to tell you that the spelling check is complete.

 CAUTION Be careful with the Add button. If the spelling checker stops on a word and you want to add it to the dictionary, be absolutely certain that it's spelled correctly before you click Add. If you mistakenly add a word that's spelled incorrectly, Works will never identify the word as being unrecognized or spelled incorrectly. If you do accidentally add a word that's misspelled, click the Edit Custom Dictionary command button in the Spelling dialog box and make the correction in that file.

Finding Synonyms with the Thesaurus

The Works Thesaurus consists of a large and nicely cross-referenced collection of synonyms for most common (and even some uncommon) words. To demonstrate, we typed the following text in an open area of the document window, and then we used the Thesaurus, as follows:

```
Don't desert me now, luck. Serendipity is my middle name.
```

1. Place the insertion point on the word for which you want to look up a synonym. We placed it on the word *desert*.

2. Click Tools, and then click Thesaurus (or press Shift+F7).
   You'll see this dialog box:

The selected word appears here

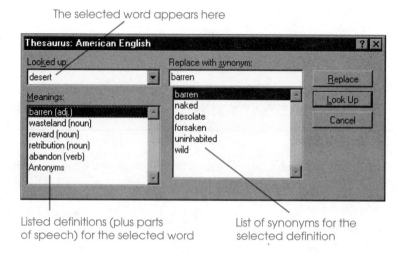

Listed definitions (plus parts of speech) for the selected word

List of synonyms for the selected definition

In the upper left corner of the Thesaurus dialog box you can see the word that was looked up. The box titled Meanings contains a list of various definitions for *desert*, along with the part of speech—such as noun, verb, and adjective (adj.)—that each definition represents. The highlighted definition in the Meanings box corresponds to the list of words (in this case, *barren, naked, desolate, forsaken*, and so on) displayed in the Replace With Synonym box. In other words, they all mean *barren*, with differences in tone. Now we'll look at another list of synonyms.

3. Click an entry in the Meanings box. We selected *abandon (verb)*.
   The list of synonyms (words of the same or nearly the same meaning) changes immediately.
   To the right of the list of synonyms are three buttons labeled Replace, Look Up, and Cancel. These buttons perform the following functions:

   ■ Replace: Replaces the selected word in your document with the selected word in the Replace With Synonym list

- Look Up: Displays a new list of synonyms for the selected word in the Replace With Synonym list

- Cancel: Closes the Thesaurus dialog box and leaves the original word unchanged in the document

    Now you can complete your practice with the Thesaurus.

4. Select a synonym in the Replace With Synonym list. We selected *forsake*.

5. Click Replace.

    The word in our document changes from *desert* to *forsake*.

NOTE Even though the Thesaurus can be quite helpful, it has its limits. If Works can't find a synonym for a word you select, it will tell you so through a simple dialog box showing the word along with the message *No synonyms found.*

Finding Text and Replacing It

Works has two search commands: Find and Replace. Like bookmarks, Find can be useful when you need to search a document for specific text or for special characters, such as Tabs and page breaks. Replace works like the Find command, except that it both finds text plus special characters *and* replaces them with other text or special characters that you specify.

When you use Find, Works scrolls the document, if necessary, and selects the first occurrence of the text you specify that follows the current position of the insertion point. If it isn't the occurrence you seek, you can click the Find Next button to continue the search.

When you use Replace, Works also finds the first occurrence of the text you specify following the insertion point. It then asks if you want to replace the text and, after following your instructions, goes on to the next occurrence, and the next, until it reaches the end of the document.

TIP   Replace can also be used to speed up your typing. If you constantly use a particular word or term, such as *psychological* or *federal* or *Plato*, you can enter *psy* or *fdl* or *plt* and then replace that abbreviation with the complete text. It can even be faster than using Easy Text.

Unlike Spelling, which asks if you want to continue checking from the beginning when it reaches the end of the document, Find and Replace goes to the end of the document and then stops. To search an entire document, be sure to first place the insertion point at the beginning of the document. It's a small matter, but one that can mean the difference between a complete and an incomplete search and replace operation. If you want to search just part of a document, select the portion to be searched *before* choosing the command. To demonstrate using the Find command, we opened a new document and entered the following text:

```
Works is a great tool. It consists of a wp, a ss, and a
db. All of these applications have a great deal in
common. The wp is especially easy to use and has as much
power as you may need.
```

To use the Find command, we did the following:

1. Place the insertion point at the beginning of the document.

2. Click Edit, and then click Find.
   You'll see this Find dialog box:

Type the characters you want to find here.

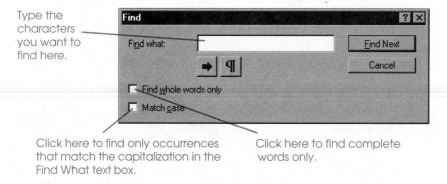

Click here to find only occurrences that match the capitalization in the Find What text box.

Click here to find complete words only.

The Find What text box is where you type the text you want to find.

3. Type the text you want to find. We entered *wp*.
   Even though the box is relatively small on your screen, you can type more than it appears to hold. Find searches for the entire set of characters you enter.

4. Click the Find Next button.

As you can see in Figure 5-4, Works highlights the first occurrence of the characters that were typed in the Find What text box.

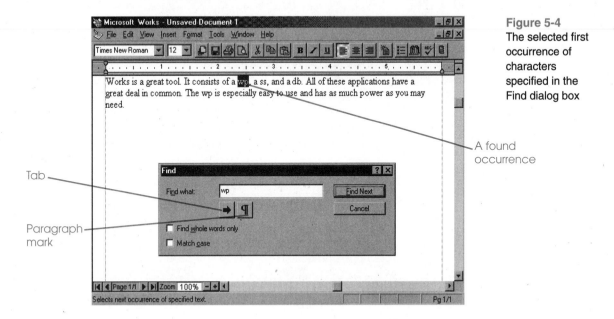

Tab

Paragraph
mark

Figure 5-4
The selected first
occurrence of
characters
specified in the
Find dialog box

A found
occurrence

If you want to limit a search to whole words, check the Find Whole Words Only check box. Doing this will eliminate those occurrences in which your text is part of a larger word—for example, the *works* in *fireworks* and *gasworks*. To search only for exact matches of uppercase and lowercase letters, click the Match Case check box. For example, doing this finds *Works* (if you typed it that way), but not *WORKS* or *works*.

Now we'll demonstrate using the Replace command.

1. Move the insertion point to the beginning of the document.

2. Click Edit, and then click Replace.

The Replace dialog box, which is almost identical to the Find dialog box, appears as shown on the following page.

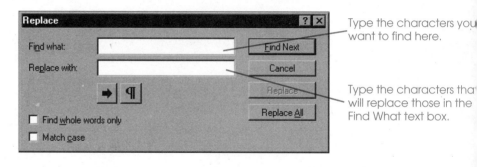

Type the characters you want to find here.

Type the characters that will replace those in the Find What text box.

The Replace dialog box, however, includes a Replace With text box where you type the text that is to replace the text in the Find What text box. It also includes a Replace All button that you can click to replace, in one step, every occurrence of the Find What text in the document. Use this option with care because all replacements happen quickly. You can reverse all changes with the Undo command, but that will take you right back to where you started.

3.   In the Find What text box, enter the text you want to replace. We'll use the already entered text *wp*. Because Works remembers the last Find What entry, it automatically fills in the Find What box.

4.   Type the text you want to replace the Find What text in the Replace With text box. We entered *word processing*.

5.   Click Replace All.

Works replaces all occurrences of *wp* with the words *word processing* in our example.

CAUTION   Here's a warning well worth heeding. When you replace text, provide as much information for Works to search for as possible. For example, if you want to find the word *in* and replace it with *on*, don't search for the letter *i* and replace it with the letter *o*. In that case, the words *into*, *find*, and *fiction* would become *onto*, *fond*, and *foctoon*! If you do search for words that can be part of larger words (such as *in* or *on*), search for the entire word by selecting the Find Whole Words Only check box.

See Also For more information on *using Easy Text entries,* see "Using Easy Text for Quick Inserts" in Chapter 3, page 98.

Using Wildcard Characters to Find Text

If you're not certain about the spelling of a word you want to find, you can use the question mark (?) as a wildcard character to take the place of any other single character. For example, to find *pin, pan,* and *pun,* you can type *p?n* in the Find box. Similarly, to find both *soon* and *seen,* you can type the search text as *s??n.*

To search for or replace special characters, use the following codes in the Find and Replace dialog boxes.

Use This Code	To Find or Replace
^t	Tabs
^p	Paragraph marks
^n	End-of-line characters
^d	Manual page breaks
^s	Nonbreaking spaces
^^	Caret marks
^?	Question marks
^w	White space (combination of Tabs, spaces, and nonbreaking spaces; or nonbreaking spaces alone)

As you can see in Figure 5-4 on page 159, Works includes two buttons in the Find dialog box that insert the codes for the common Tab and paragraph characters. You can put these special characters to good use when jumping from page to page of a document. You can also use them to clean up files (such as those that are converted from another application) that contain unneeded paragraph marks or that contain blank spaces instead of Tabs. For example, a document might contain two paragraph marks between paragraphs, but you want only one. To replace all occurrences, type *^p^p* in the Find What text box, type *^p* in the Replace With text box, and click the Replace All button.

TIP You can use the Replace dialog box to delete unwanted characters. Just type the characters in the Find What text box, but leave the Replace With text box blank (or delete its previous entry). Then click the Replace or Replace All button.

Although the Find and Replace features may take some time to learn, they can really be worth the investment. Just think how easy it will be to find extra spaces placed after periods in a 100-page document and change them all to only one space.

TIP Before using Replace, especially the Replace All button, save your document. Should you make an error, close the document *(don't save it!)*, and then open the previous version and try again.

Creating Headers and Footers

A header is any text that repeats at the top of the pages in your document, such as a chapter title or a subject line in a report. Likewise, a footer is text that repeats at the bottom of the pages, such as a page number or the date of printing. Whether you're in Normal or Page Layout view, headers and footers might be the easiest of all the Works features to use.

You can practice creating a header or a footer by following these steps:

1. If you are in Page Layout view, simply click in the header or footer area on the page where you want the header or footer to appear.

   The header area is at the top of the page, and the footer area is at the bottom of the page. They're clearly designated in Page Layout view.

2. If you're in Normal view, the top of the first page in the document contains an H and an F, as you see in Figure 5-5. Enter the header and the footer in those locations. Figure 5-5 shows an example of a two-line header and a two-line footer.

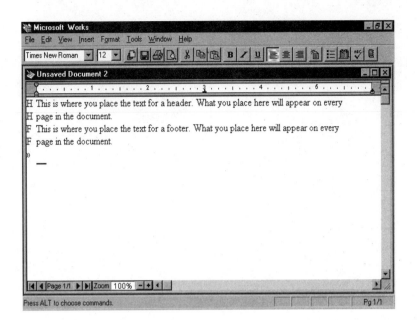

FIGURE 5-5
Entering a header
and a footer in
Normal view

The header or footer that you place in the appropriate area in the document in Normal view or Page Layout view will appear on every page in the document, unless you replace it with another header or footer.

NOTE You can only have one header and one footer in a document, and, once they are entered, they will appear on every page.

Setting Margins for Headers and Footers

Increasing the default values for the top and bottom page margins can be especially important if you plan to include a header or footer in a document. Works prints headers and footers within the top and bottom margins. If you use the default Page Setup settings, it will print a top running head, or header, .5 inch from the top edge of the page and a bottom running footer .75 inch from the bottom edge.

To change the spacing between the header and the text, click File, click Page Setup, and then click the Margins tab. Set a larger or smaller value for the header margin so that it prints closer to or further from the top of the page. The footer margin is adjusted the same way.

TIP On some printers, such as the Hewlett-Packard LaserJet, headers and footers don't print exactly where the margin settings indicate because the printer has small "unprintable" regions at the top and bottom (as well as the sides) of the page. Check your printer manual or experiment a little to determine how close your printer comes to the actual edge of the page.

Adding Special Characters to Your Documents

Page numbers, the date, the time, and filenames are useful items of information for a running head (or for other parts of a document, for that matter). Using the Insert menu, you can insert the name of the document, a page number, or today's date.

For example, to create the following header, you would enter the filename (Chapter 5), the date (10/26/95), and the page number (1), using options on the Insert menu.

```
Chapter 5 completed on 10/26/95 - Page 1
```

We'll demonstrate creating this header, as follows:

1. Click Insert, and then click Document Name (which is Chapter 5 in our example).

2. Type any additional text, if appropriate. In this case, we typed *completed on.*

3. Click Insert, and then click Date and Time.

4. Click the 10/26/95 format. (The format options on your screen will reflect the current date.)

5. Type any additional text or characters, if appropriate. In this case, we pressed the Spacebar, typed a hyphen, pressed the Spacebar, typed *Page,* and pressed the Spacebar again.

6. Click Insert, and then click Page Number.

The way the header actually appears in the document is

```
*filename* completed on October 26, 1995 - Page *page*
```

The *filename* and *page* entries are special codes Works inserts that tell it to insert the correct information in the header when the document is printed.

Inserting Other Special Codes

On occasion you might need to insert other characters as well. The following table lists important special characters you can insert in your text, and what they do.

Character	Action
Optional hyphen	Hyphenates a word if it must be broken at the end of a line; displays as a hyphen with a 90-degree bend on its right end; appears if All Characters is on (Keyboard: Press Ctrl+Hyphen)
Nonbreaking hyphen	Prevents a hyphenated word from breaking at the end of a line; appears as a hyphen (Keyboard: Press Ctrl+Shift+Hyphen)
Nonbreaking space	Prevents related words, separated by a space, from being broken at the end of a line; appears as a small, superscript o (Keyboard: Press Ctrl+Shift+Spacebar)
End-of-line mark	Starts a new line; displayed if All Characters is on; appears as a left-pointing horizontal arrow with a 90-degree bend on its right end (Keyboard: Press Shift+Enter)

These special codes can be used to dress up or add detail to your documents. For example, a letter might contain the special character for inserting a date. That way, whenever you print the letter, the date of the printing (not of the *writing* of the letter) will be inserted. The time and date in a header can help readers distinguish between different drafts of a document.

Working with Hyphens and Spaces

You know about word wrap, that wonderful feature that automatically places on the next line full words that can't fit at the end of the previous line. But not all lines end conveniently. For example, an especially long word that can't fit on one line will have to go to the next, and, depending on the justification you select, the initial line might look quite odd. A fully justified line consisting of a few long words will have extra space between the words and letters.

Normally, if Works can't fit an entire word at the end of a line, it simply wraps the word to the next line. Sometimes, however, you want to hyphenate words at the end of a line to make the line endings less ragged or to decrease extra space between words in a justified paragraph. Chances are you won't need to do this type of fine-tuning very often, because most documents look fine without such niceties. A little tinkering, however, can be useful when an important letter, proposal, business plan, or prospectus must look as good as possible.

Hyphens

A hyphen by any name might seem like a hyphen, but, as you can see from the list of special characters shown previously, Works actually recognizes three different types of hyphens:

- Those you normally type (as in *left-aligned tab*).

- Those you want to use only if a word can't fit at the end of a line

- Those you want to use at all times to prevent a hyphenated word or name from being broken at the end of a line

To demonstrate how these hyphens work, we set our current font and font size to Times New Roman 12, made sure that the right margin was at 6 inches, and verified that All Characters on the View menu was turned on. Then we typed the text shown below:

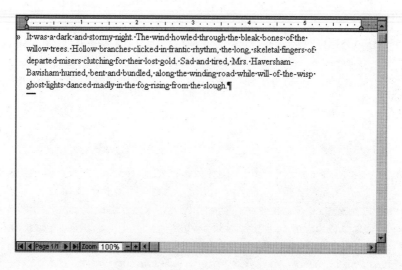

166

Now we'll fiddle with the line endings. Suppose we decide that Haversham-Bavisham, a hyphenated name, shouldn't break at the end of a line, as it does now. Here's how we fixed it.

1. We selected the hyphen that appears in the name.

2. We deleted it.

3. Then we replaced it by inserting a nonbreaking hyphen from the Insert Special Character dialog box.

    The nonbreaking hyphen tells Works to keep the name together, which it does by moving the entire name to the next line.

However, this operation created a considerable gap to fill at the end of one line. We can fix this is by inserting an optional end-of-line mark. Here's how to do that.

1. Move the insertion point before the word where you want to insert the end-of-line mark. We placed it before the word *fingers*.

2. Insert an optional end-of-line mark from the Insert Special Character dialog box.

Displaying special characters can produce inaccurate line breaks on screen because more space is needed to display them. If you insert a lot of optional hyphens in a document, check the finished layout before printing by turning off All Characters or by using Print Preview or Page Layout view.

Coming Next

Good work! We're done with the word processor module. Now you should know enough to create a stunning wedding invitation, that final term paper, or the growth report your boss has been hounding you about. It's time to move on to the Works spreadsheet, where you'll learn how to manipulate and organize numbers to produce show-stopping graphs.

Part 3

Using the Spreadsheet

In This Part Here you're introduced to the electronic ledger we call a spreadsheet: a set of rows and columns. In them you place numerical data (mostly) as well as text, and then manipulate it to achieve the goal you want, whether it's a budget or a stocks analysis or a record of car expenses.

In Chapter 6, we introduce you to the basics: important terms, understanding what a cell is, the formula bar, and using a cell range to greatly facilitate the use of the spreadsheet. The chapter also includes the nitty-gritty of entering spreadsheet data and editing it, sorting data, and finding and replacing information in a spreadsheet, much like you did with the word processor.

As always, Works for Windows 95 contains goodies galore, such as the AutoFormat feature, for instantly attractive spreadsheets, and AutoSum, to quickly add a row or column of numbers.

Chapter 7 shows you the true power of Works in using formulas and predesigned functions to save yourself hours of work and ensure accuracy of results.

Chapter 8 focuses on bringing to life the numbers in your spreadsheet through the creation of charts. With the click of one button, you can create over a dozen types of standard charts, and then go off to create your own design. If you never thought that a picture was worth a thousand words, try one of these dazzling charts at your next business meeting!

Chapter 6

Getting Started with the Spreadsheet

column and row titles to keep them visible as you scroll the spreadsheet, insert and delete columns and rows, and hide and protect cells.

Even though a spreadsheet is primarily a tool for manipulating numbers, you'll find that the appearance of its text is important as well, because text entries in a spreadsheet identify and clarify the meaning of the numeric data for anyone who reads the spreadsheet. Here you'll learn about working with fonts, sizes, and styles to make your text entries more attractive and more informative.

In spreadsheets, numbers are the main attraction. Just as with text, you can change the way numbers appear (for the better, we hope), using any one of several formats. Each format displays numbers in a particular way, depending on what the numbers in a spreadsheet represent.

You will explore ways to organize rows and columns of information and find text or numbers that need to be modified. You'll also look at using borders and shading to improve the appearance of your spreadsheets.

Organization of spreadsheet data is very important, and Works allows you to sort spreadsheet information in a variety of ways.

Just like working with long documents in the word processor, finding information quickly is often necessary in large spreadsheets. And just like the word processor, the spreadsheet module provides a feature for searching a spreadsheet to find the text or numbers you want to locate—and you can replace selected occurrences too!

Finally, you'll find out how to fine-tune and then print all or part of your spreadsheets.

From the time you were small you constantly used numbers to communicate. Eventually, words become your primary vehicle for communicating thoughts and ideas, while numbers satisfied your need to organize, understand, and communicate data. In business, at home, and at school, the Works spreadsheet can help you manage the ever-growing quantity of numbers that sometimes seem to dominate our everyday activities. With the Works spreadsheet, *you* are in control of the *numbers*!

What Can You Do with a Spreadsheet?

This chapter takes you into the world of the spreadsheet—an electronic ledger sheet that you can use to build, organize, and print numerical information without resorting to pencils and erasers. You'll find the basics here—entering, editing, and printing data (which can be both text and numbers). In the next two chapters you'll learn how to work with formulas and functions and see how to turn spreadsheet data into charts.

See Also For more information on *formulas and functions*, see Chapter 7, "Working with Formulas and Functions," page 215; for more information on *creating charts for spreadsheet data*, see Chapter 8, "Creating Charts," page 255.

The Works spreadsheet module is used for creating documents that store, manipulate, and track all kinds of information. Here are a few of the tasks you can use the spreadsheet for:

- Create and maintain budgets that track income and expenses for your home, office, or social organization.

- Prepare and maintain salary information, including years of service and volume of sales produced.

- Build an amortization schedule of monthly payments of a loan, based on the principal, annual interest, and term (time period).

- Perform a "what-if" analysis that allows you to examine a new set of calculated results by changing one or more variables.

- Design an accounts receivable form.

- Make a bar graph chart that visually represents information about sales and bonuses.

Many of the TaskWizards that you read about in Chapter 2 make use of the spreadsheet module to create these and other types of documents. For example, the Grade Book and Loan Analysis documents, both of which you saw in Chapter 2, are Wizard-generated spreadsheets that have been designed for specific purposes.

See Also   For more information on *using TaskWizards*, see Chapter 2, "What Do You Want to Do?," page 43.

Say Hello to the Spreadsheet

Because Works is a Windows application, many of the procedures you learned in the word processing module, such as copying and moving data, are carried out in nearly the same way in the spreadsheet module. The best way to learn is by doing, so let's start right now with some illustrative examples of building spreadsheets. To open the spreadsheet module, you do the following:

1. If necessary, start Works.

2. Click the Works Tools tab in the Works Task Launcher.

3. Click the Spreadsheet button to start the spreadsheet module with a blank spreadsheet.

4. Maximize both the application and document windows.

Works displays a blank spreadsheet like the one shown in Figure 6-1. (In the figure's example, notice that Help has been hidden from view.)

As you can see in Figure 6-1, Works assigns the name Unsaved Spreadsheet 1 to the as-yet-unsaved spreadsheet document.

The Spreadsheet Cell

At first glance, the spreadsheet window appears a lot busier than a word processor window, primarily because the spreadsheet displays a grid of cells. Each *cell* is capable of holding text, a numeric value, a date, or a formula used to calculate new values.

Each cell in a spreadsheet has a unique address, composed of its column letter and row number (for example, A1, A2, B1, B2, and so on). Altogether, a single Works spreadsheet contains 256 columns and 16,384 rows, for a total of 4,194,304 cells. The first 26 columns are lettered A

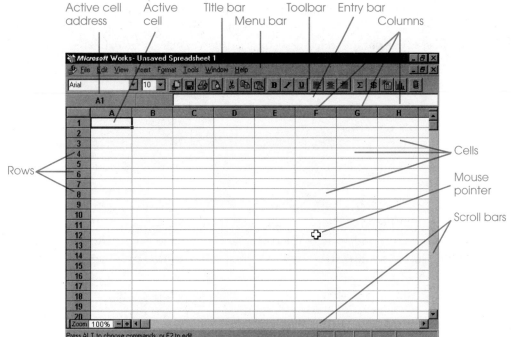

Active cell address · Active cell · Title bar · Menu bar · Toolbar · Entry bar · Columns

Rows · Cells · Mouse pointer · Scroll bars

FIGURE 6-1

The spreadsheet module's opening window

through Z; succeeding columns are lettered AA through AZ, BA through BZ, and so on, ending with column IV at the extreme right edge of the spreadsheet. Rows are numbered sequentially; the last row is 16384. The address for the last cell in a spreadsheet, in the bottom right corner, is IV16384, which represents the junction of column IV and row 16384.

Think about it. The number of rows and columns in a Works spreadsheet allows for the entry of data into more than 4 million cells (4,194,304, to be exact)! That's a lot of information. You may never use all these cells, but some people do. The size of a spreadsheet alone will give you some idea of the capabilities the Works spreadsheet module offers.

If you look at Figure 6-1 on your screen, notice that cell A1 appears to be outlined with a thick, dark border. This border is actually the cell pointer. The *cell pointer* is used to activate a cell, which is necessary to enter data in the cell. There can only be one active cell in a spreadsheet document.

Using the Toolbar

Many window elements in the spreadsheet window—scroll bars, the title bar, control buttons, and the status bar at the bottom of the window—are identical to the window elements in the word processor window.

175

The toolbar in the spreadsheet window also is similar to the toolbar in the word processor window. But, four of the buttons differ to give you easy access to often-used spreadsheet features. These spreadsheet-specific buttons are shown on the toolbar here:

Specifically, the four toolbar buttons to the left of the Address Book button are different. The AutoSum button adds the values in the rows or columns that are adjacent to the current cell pointer location. The Currency button formats values in currency. The Easy Calc button provides you with the tools to perform simple calculations. The New Chart button creates a visual image of selected spreadsheet data. Remember that, as with any toolbar, you can remove existing buttons, or add new ones.

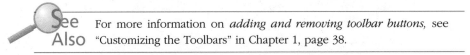

See Also   For more information on *adding and removing toolbar buttons,* see "Customizing the Toolbars" in Chapter 1, page 38.

Using the Entry Bar

Another important element in the spreadsheet window is the entry bar, located below the toolbar. The entry bar consists primarily of a space where Works displays the text, value, or mathematical formula you are entering in the active cell. You can both view and edit cell contents on the entry bar.

To the left of the entry bar are several related elements. The Cancel button and the Enter button become visible only after you type letters or numbers that appear on the entry bar, as you see here:

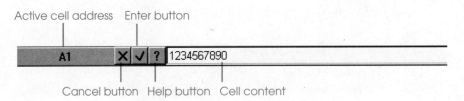

The cell reference area displays the address of the active cell. The Cancel and Enter buttons let you use the mouse in place of the Esc or Enter keys to cancel or accept what you've typed into the cell, although you can use Esc or Enter if that's more natural for you.

We'll demonstrate how the entry bar and the Cancel and Enter buttons work, as follows:

1. Click any blank cell.

2. Type a series of numbers. For example, we typed *1234567890.*

   As you type, notice that the characters in the cell "scroll" to make room for new numbers. Works will remember everything you type and assign it to the proper cell, even if the cell is too narrow to display all you type at once. The entry bar, however, displays all the cell's contents.

3. Click the Cancel button to cancel the entry.

   The text disappears. (You can also cancel the entry by pressing the Esc key.)

Now we'll demonstrate using the Enter button and, at the same time, see what happens to an entry that's too long to display in a cell.

1. Type text that's more than nine characters long in any cell. We typed *Pepperoni Pizza.*

2. Click the Enter button to complete the entry.

   The text appears on the entry bar and in the active cell. (You can also complete the entry by pressing Enter or Tab.)

Works displays text in both the active cell and the cell to its right. You can see all of a cell's contents if the adjacent cell is vacant. Now we'll try something else.

1. Click in the cell to the right of a cell that contains text.

2. Type some text or numbers and click the Enter button. We entered *12345.*

   Part of the original text now appears only in its own cell. We haven't lost any text, even though the cell displays only a portion of it.

3. Click the cell to the left of the cell you just placed an entry in.

   As you can see, the entry bar displays the entire contents of the cell when you highlight it. In our example, the entry bar displays *Pepperoni Pizza.*

In general, you can enter data in a spreadsheet cell by using the following steps:

1. Place the mouse pointer over the cell where you want to enter data.

2. Click once to make the cell active. It will appear with a dark border.

3. Enter the data.

4. Click the Enter button (the entry bar button with the check mark), or press the Enter key.

Editing Cell Contents

When you use the spreadsheet, you edit the content of a cell on the entry bar, usually. You can clear, replace, or edit the contents of a cell by following these procedures.

- To clear a cell, select it and press the Del key. Or, point to the cell, click the right mouse button, and select the Clear command on the pop-up menu.

- To replace the contents of a cell, select it, type the new entry, and press Enter.

- To edit the contents of a cell, select the cell and click on any character on the entry bar. When you do this, an insertion point appears where you clicked (which puts you in EDIT mode, as the status bar at the bottom of the window will show). You can also press F2 to switch to EDIT mode. When you do this, the insertion point appears in the current cell, where you can edit the entry.

When you're editing cell contents, you can position the insertion point simply by pointing to the location you want and clicking. The procedure is just like the one you learned when you tried your hand at editing text in the word processor. You can drag the mouse to highlight one or more characters for deletion or replacement. You can also use any of the following keys to control the insertion point and to highlight characters on the entry bar.

Key	Effect
Home	Move to beginning of entry
End	Move to end of entry
Left and Right arrow keys	Move the insertion point one character left or right
Ctrl+Left arrow and Ctrl+Right arrow	Move the insertion point to the beginning or end of a word

Key	Effect
Shift+Left arrow and Shift+Right arrow	Extend highlight over one or more characters
Del	Delete selected characters or (if no characters are selected) delete the next character to the right

TIP When you enter more characters in a cell than will fit the width of the entry bar, the entry bar's text display area drops down so that you see all of the characters you are typing. When editing long entries, you can jump back and forth on the entry bar using the Home and End keys, plus the Left and Right arrow keys.

If you ever need to clear existing spreadsheet entries and start over, follow these steps:

1. Highlight all the cells containing what you've typed so far by dragging the highlight over them.

2. Position the mouse pointer anywhere over the highlighted cells, click the right mouse button, and then click Clear.

Working with Cell Ranges

Building a spreadsheet lets you organize data so that you can easily compare, contrast, summarize, and calculate information. You often work with values in a group of one or more cells, called a range. A *range* refers to any rectangular group of cells, including a single cell, several cells, or all the cells in the spreadsheet.

To select all the cells in a spreadsheet, click Edit, and then click Select All. (When you want to deselect, you click anywhere in the spreadsheet.)

TIP To select all the cells in a spreadsheet, you can also click in the box located in the upper left corner of the spreadsheet window where the row of column headings and the column of row headings meet.

Notice that when you select all cells in a worksheet, the entry bar displays the range address A1:IV16384, as you see here:

A1:IV16384	

Range address (for selected entire spreadsheet)

When a range is selected, Works identifies the range by displaying its address, which is composed of the address of the range's top left cell, a colon, and the address of its bottom right cell. For example, the range address A1:C5 encompasses the 15 cells that form the rectangular group that spans columns A, B, and C and rows 1 through 5.

A range is any group of cells that forms a rectangle. Each cell in the range must share at least one border with another cell. You can't highlight cells in a diamond shape, an L shape, or any other nonrectangular shape. Nor can you select more than one range at once. If you try to do this, the first range of cells you have selected will be deselected as soon as you start to select the second range.

You'll use ranges for many tasks, including adding columns of numbers, applying formatting, and choosing values to chart. You'll especially want to use ranges to create formulas that perform calculations using values in one or more ranges.

To demonstrate the Works spreadsheet module, we'll work with a sample spreadsheet by entering the headings and numbers shown in Figure 6-2 and then save it under the name *pizza*. When entering data in a spreadsheet, you can use the Tab and arrow keys to move easily from cell to cell.

FIGURE 6-2
Enter the text and numbers as you see them in this sample spreadsheet if you want to work through the examples.

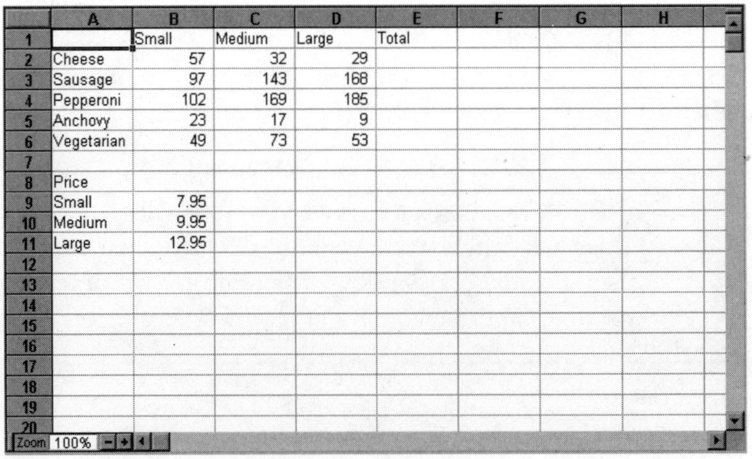

	A	B	C	D	E	F	G	H
1		Small	Medium	Large	Total			
2	Cheese	57	32	29				
3	Sausage	97	143	168				
4	Pepperoni	102	169	185				
5	Anchovy	23	17	9				
6	Vegetarian	49	73	53				
7								
8	Price							
9	Small	7.95						
10	Medium	9.95						
11	Large	12.95						

Zoom 100%

Works attaches the extension .WKS to a spreadsheet when it saves it for the first time (but you'll only see the extension when you are viewing a filename in either the My Computer or Explorer window).

Checking Your Spreadsheet's Spelling

Just like the word processor, the spreadsheet offers the spelling check feature. You can start it by selecting the Spelling command on the Tools menu. To use the spelling checker, follow these steps:

1. Click Tools, and then click Spelling (or press the F7 key).

2. Respond to any unrecognized words found by the spelling checker.

3. Click OK when the spelling check is complete.

Working with Data

There's a lot to learn about using a spreadsheet. Let's begin with how to move around. Then we'll look at how to copy and move data, which can be both text and numbers. We will finish with some ideas about working with cells, columns, and rows.

Moving Around

Many spreadsheets are too large to display on a single screen. One easy way to move from place to place in a large spreadsheet is to use the Go To command, located on the Edit menu. Using this command (or the F5 key), you can move directly to a cell. The Go To command can be used to jump to specific cells or the first cell in a range address. Works highlights the cell or range you specify.

As you work with a spreadsheet, you'll find that you need to scroll or move from place to place frequently. As in the word processing window, the scroll bars can be used to move quickly to different areas of the spreadsheet. You can also use the keyboard. The following keys are useful for moving around in a spreadsheet. Notice that these keys are available only if you aren't currently editing on the entry bar.

Key	Result
Left arrow or Right arrow	Left or right one cell
Up arrow or Down arrow	Up or down one row

Key	Result
Home	First cell in current row
End	Last column containing data in any row
Ctrl+Home	Top left corner of the spreadsheet
Ctrl+End	Last cell in the bottom right corner (this cell is in the last row and the last column that contain data or formatting; the cell itself doesn't necessarily contain data or formatting)
PgUp or PgDn	Up or down one screen
Ctrl+PgUp or Ctrl+PgDn	Left or right one screen
Ctrl+Left arrow or Ctrl+Right arrow	Left or right to the beginning or end of the current or next block of cells containing data
Ctrl+Up arrow or Ctrl+Down arrow	Up or down to the beginning or end of the current or next block of cells containing data

Entering Identical Data in Multiple Cells

Works lets you fill a range with identical information in a variety of ways, including across a row, down a column, or across multiple rows and columns. To fill every cell in a selected range with the same entry that exists in the range's upper left cell, simply press the keyboard shortcut Ctrl+Enter. You can use this key combination to enter data or formulas. Works copies the information in the selected range's upper left cell to the highlighted cells to the right and below it. For example, suppose we want to fill a range with the number 123. The steps to do this are as follows:

1. Select a range of cells. We selected cells A1 through D7.

2. Type the text you want to fill the range with, but don't click the Enter button or press a key. We typed *123*.

3. Press Ctrl+Enter.

   Works immediately fills the selected range with the same data entered in its upper left cell, as you can see in Figure 6-3.

   In a similar fashion you can use the mouse to fill a range of cells in a row or in a column with the entry in the active cell. You can do this with an existing entry or as you are entering a cell's content. Just point to the

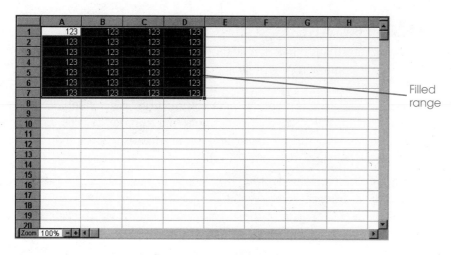

FIGURE 6-3
Filling cells with the same information

tiny square in the lower right corner of the cell pointer to change the mouse pointer to a small, dark cross labeled FILL, like this:

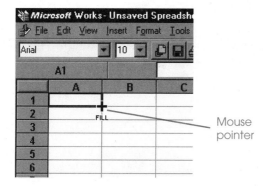

Mouse pointer

With the mouse pointer in this shape, it's easy to drag the highlight down the active cell's column or across its row to fill the range with the active cell's data. Here's how to do it:

1. Select a cell.

2. Type an entry (like *123*).

3. Position the mouse pointer over the tiny square in the lower right corner of the cell pointer.

   The mouse pointer changes to a small, dark cross with the label FILL.

4. Drag the highlight down to select a range of cells down the column below the active cell or across the row to the right of the active cell. Then release the mouse button.

   The selected cells contain the same data as the active cell.

Moving and Copying Data

Moving information in a spreadsheet is generally synonymous with organizing or reorganizing a spreadsheet. Although copying information is as easy as moving it, "copying" is a little harder to define because there are several ways to copy spreadsheet information. For example, you might want to enter the same data or formula in a number of cells, or to copy a cell's contents to another part of the same spreadsheet, or even to copy all or part of one spreadsheet to another.

You can also move and copy values to any area in the same spreadsheet or a different spreadsheet. It doesn't matter if the values are those you've entered as data or those you've calculated with formulas.

To move or copy data to the Windows Clipboard, you use the Cut and Copy commands or toolbar buttons, which work exactly as they do in the word processor. You can copy cells or ranges in either rows or columns, but you can't alter the orientation of a range. If the cells you copy are in a column, you can't duplicate them in a row, nor can you reorient a row to become a column. In other words, the *target* range, which is the destination where the copied data will be pasted, will be the same shape as the *source* range, which contains the data you want to copy. We'll demonstrate copying values by using the spreadsheet in which we entered the 123 data.

1. Select the range of data you want to copy. We selected the range A1:A7 in our example.

2. Click the Copy button on the toolbar to copy the selected cells to the Clipboard.

3. Select a cell that you want to be the upper left corner cell of the target range. We selected cell F1.

4. Click the Paste button on the toolbar.

    Works copies the contents of the Clipboard to the selected target range, placing the first of the copied cells in the selected cell as you see in Figure 6-4.

When you copy or move a range of cells, Works uses the selected destination cell as the upper left corner of the target range. Be sure that there are no cells containing data or formulas within the target range. If cells in this area *do* contain data or formulas, the information they hold will be overwritten by the contents of the copied cells.

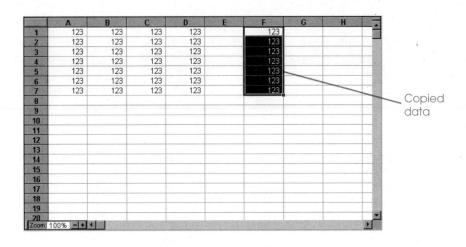

FIGURE 6-4
Copying
information in a
spreadsheet

Copied
data

Working with Cells, Columns, and Rows

You can control the appearance, display, and behavior of your spreadsheets in several ways. By default, Works displays the toolbar; it also displays gridlines on the screen, although it doesn't print them unless you choose to do so with the Other Options tab in the Page Setup dialog box, which appears when you select the Page Setup command on the File menu. The following sections describe the commands you use to control Works' appearance when using the spreadsheet module.

Toggling Gridlines On and Off

If you find that the gridlines on the screen get in your way, you can turn them off and on at will. Here's how we turned off the gridlines in the pizza spreadsheet you see here:

	A	B	C	D	E	F	G	H
1		Small	Medium	Large	Total			
2	Cheese	57	32	29				
3	Sausage	97	143	168				
4	Pepperoni	102	169	185				
5	Anchovy	23	17	9				
6	Vegetarian	49	73	53				
7								
8	Price							
9	Small	7.95						
10	Medium	9.95						
11	Large	12.95						
12								
13								
14								
15								
16								
17								
18								
19								
20								

Zoom 100%

185

1. Click View, and then click Gridlines.

    Even though the gridlines are turned off, the rectangular cell pointer encloses the active cell and jumps from cell to cell when you move it, as it does when gridlines are turned on.

2. Click View, and then click Gridlines when you want to turn them back on.

Freezing Row and Column Titles

When you're working on or printing a large spreadsheet, you can freeze row and column titles. Doing this keeps the titles—text that identifies the data in the rest of the spreadsheet—on screen at all times and causes Works to print them on each page of a multiple-page spreadsheet. If you work with large spreadsheets without freezing the titles, understanding the significance of the data as you scroll the titles out of view can be difficult.

To freeze column titles, follow these steps:

1. Select a cell in column A, below the titles you want to freeze.

2. Click Format, and then click Freeze Titles.

    No matter how far down the spreadsheet you scroll, the frozen column titles will remain on screen.

To freeze row titles, follow these steps:

1. Select a cell in row 1 to the right of the last title you want to freeze.

2. Click Format, and then click Freeze Titles.

    No matter how far to the right you scroll, the frozen row titles will always be displayed.

To freeze both row and column titles, follow these steps.

1. Select a cell below and to the right of the last column and row title you want to freeze.

2. Click Format, and then click Freeze Titles.

    No matter how far down you scroll, the column titles remain on screen, or no matter how far to the right you scroll, the row titles remain on screen.

Freezing titles provides a terrific way to view both the spreadsheet's titles and the corresponding data in a separate area of the spreadsheet. Here's how we froze titles in our example pizza spreadsheet:

1. Select cell C2.

2. Click Format, and then click Freeze Titles (it's turned on when there is a check mark beside it).

3. Click on the right scroll arrow on the horizontal scroll bar.

    Column B isn't shown because it's scrolled behind the frozen column A, as illustrated in Figure 6-5.

Column B scrolled   Row titles   Column titles
behind frozen titles   frozen   frozen

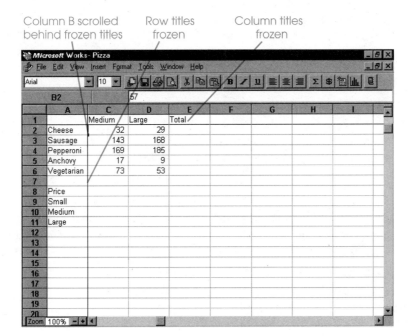

FIGURE 6-5
Freezing both row
and column titles

4. Turn off the Freeze Titles command, when you want to unfreeze titles.

Another way to view different parts of a large spreadsheet is to split the window and scroll to the areas you want to view in each pane, as we've done in Figure 6-6 on the next page. (We also turned the gridlines back on.) You've already seen how to split a document window and scroll different parts of the document into view in the word processor module. It works the same way in the spreadsheet module. Simply drag the split bar (the mouse pointer changes to a bar labeled ADJUST) until you create the approximate size of the second spreadsheet window. You can work in either pane.

FIGURE 6-6
Splitting a window
to view different
spreadsheet areas

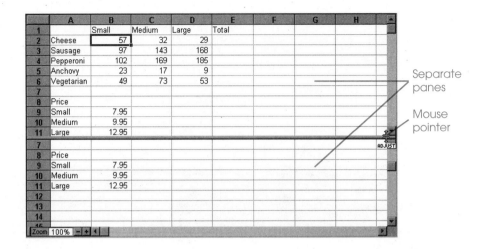

Separate
panes

Mouse
pointer

Protecting Spreadsheet Information

Protecting information is vital in certain spreadsheets, such as a spread-sheet used to manage and calculate payroll information. When you protect a cell, a range, or an entire spreadsheet, you are ensuring that accidental changes or deletions to valuable data and formulas can't be made by you or others. Essentially, protected cells become what is known as read-only cells, whose contents can't be changed.

To protect information, you use the Protection command on the Format menu. This displays the Format Protection dialog box, which contains two check box options, as you see here:

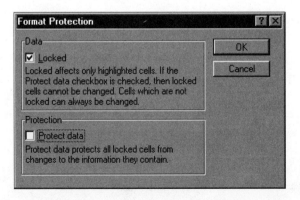

The first option, Locked, is on by default for every cell in the spreadsheet. Despite this option's name, however, the cells are not locked, in the sense that you can enter, modify, and delete data. When you turn on the Protect Data option, though, all cells that have the Locked option turned on can't be modified. Because every cell's Locked option is on, by default, turning on the Protect Data option essentially protects the entire spreadsheet—you can't modify any cell.

In some cases, you might build a spreadsheet that other users will have access to for entering data. The spreadsheet might contain a series of formulas that you've set up that will use the data entered by others to calculate results. Because you want to ensure that these formulas won't be modified while others have access to the spreadsheet, you can turn on the Protect Data option to protect the entire spreadsheet, and then turn *off* the Locked option for only those cells that others will enter data (numbers) in. The protected-formula cells will operate on these unlocked cells.

To demonstrate how protection works, we'll use the pizza spreadsheet as follows:

1. Click Format, and then click Protection.

2. Click the Protect Data check box and click OK.
   Now the entire spreadsheet is secure from change.

To test the spreadsheet's protection status, we'll do the following:

1. Select any locked cell. We selected cell B2.

2. Type an entry and click the Enter button on the entry bar. We typed *32*.
   Instead of changing the value as it normally would, Works displays the dialog box you see here:

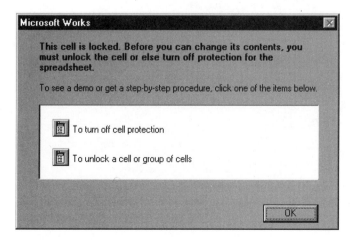

189

Notice that you can click on either of the options in this dialog box and get instructions on unprotecting either selected cells or the whole spreadsheet.

Now to unprotect a selected cell, do the following.

1. Click OK to cancel the dialog box.

2. Select a protected cell.

3. Click Format, and then click Protection.

4. Click the Locked check box to deselect it.

5. Click OK.

As you can see, you can unprotect some data while protecting other data.

TIP Don't use cell protection unless you need it, because there is no way to tell what cells are locked once that process is complete. If you're in doubt, select all the cells in the spreadsheet, open the Format Protection dialog box, and then select the Protect Data option to turn it off.

Hiding Cells

Another way to protect data and formulas, or at least remove them from open view, is to actually hide the columns in which the data or formulas appear. Although this approach is less effective than using the Protect Data option, it's useful when you want to temporarily eliminate columns that intervene between two or more sections of a spreadsheet where you want to work. Even when columns are hidden, Works remains aware of their contents and accurately calculates any formulas.

To hide columns using the mouse, simply reduce their width to nothing. We'll demonstrate this as follows:

1. Point to the boundary between any two columns.

   The mouse pointer changes to a bar with a two-headed arrow running through it labeled ADJUST, as you see on the following page.

ADJUST

Mouse pointer when
adjusting column width

2. Drag the boundary left, all the way to the next column's boundary, and then release the mouse button. The column disappears.

When you "hide" columns, Works doesn't change the remaining column letters. For example, if you hide column C, it will be missing from the column labels. Because of this, hidden columns shouldn't be considered a true security measure. Anyone who knows how to use Works (or how to use any spreadsheet application, for that matter) will detect that a column is hidden and will know how to redisplay the missing column.

To hide more than a single column, follow these steps:

1. Select more than one column by dragging across the column headings.

2. Click Format, and then click the Column Width command.
   Works displays this Column Width dialog box:

You use this dialog box not only to hide columns, but also to change their widths. Simply type the width (in number of characters) and click OK. To hide the selected columns, you reduce their widths to nothing, which we'll do now.

3. Type *0* (zero), and click OK.

To redisplay the columns once they've been hidden, follow these steps:

1. Drag across the column headings for the two columns between which there are hidden columns.

2. Click Format, and then click Column Width.

3. Either click OK to accept the default width of 10 or type a new width and then click OK.
   The hidden columns return to view.

You can also adjust the height of a row in such a way that zero height, in effect, results in a hidden row. To change the height of a row, you can either adjust it using the mouse pointer, or click Format, click Row Height, and then enter a value that's different from the default 12-point size.

Inserting and Deleting Rows and Columns

Despite Works' assistance, a spreadsheet doesn't spring into being, perfectly formed, at the click of a mouse button. It takes time, patience, and experimentation before you get it right. Suppose you've been entering data and you suddenly realize you forgot to allow an extra column or row for a needed element.

Chances are, this will happen to you more than once because you'll be concentrating on what you want the spreadsheet to do, rather than on how you want it to look. As the spreadsheet takes shape, you'll find places where you could use an extra row or column for displaying information you hadn't originally thought of including. Conversely, you'll sometimes want to delete extra rows or columns that you allowed for but now don't need. You might also want to select and delete rows or columns to "erase" information or cell formatting.

When you need to add or delete rows or columns, you can do so with the Insert Row and Delete Row commands and the Insert Column and Delete Column commands on the Insert menu. You can use these commands at any time.

To insert or delete a row or a column, you must first tell Works where you want the insertion or deletion to be. You do this by selecting a row or column. To select an entire row or column, point to the row number or column letter and click. Works highlights the entire row or column. To demonstrate inserting and deleting columns, we'll return to our favorite pizza spreadsheet example.

We'll insert a new column to the left of the column named Total as follows:

1. Point to the column that you want to appear to the right of the new column and highlight it by clicking once on the column heading. In our example we selected column E.

2. Click Insert, and then click Insert Column.

   As you see in Figure 6-7, Works inserts the new column to the left of what was column E (now column F), and it relabels the columns to the right to avoid any break in the lettering sequence.

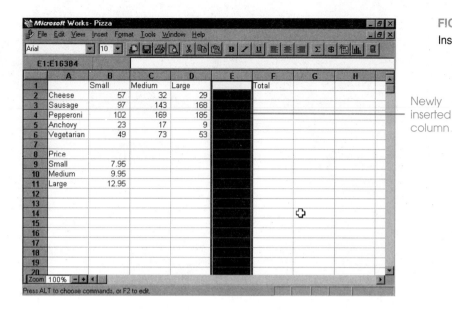

FIGURE 6-7

Inserting a column

Newly inserted column

While we're at it, we'll add an Onion pizza right after the Anchovy pizza by inserting a new row. Here's how to do it.

1. Point to the row you want to appear below the row that will be inserted and highlight it with a click on the row heading. In our example we selected row 6.

2. Click Insert, and then click Insert Row.

TIP Another way to insert a single column or row is by pointing to the column or row heading where you want to insert it and clicking the right mouse button, instead of the left. This action both highlights the entire column or row and displays a pop-up menu, which contains the Insert Column command or the Insert Row command, depending on what you've selected. Select the Insert Column command or the Insert Row command to insert the column or row.

If you want to add more than one column or row, just select the number of columns or rows you want to add and then use the same commands as shown above. For example, to add two new columns, select the two columns that you want to follow the new one, Click Format, and then click Insert Columns.

Deleting rows follows the same exact steps as those shown on the preceding page. Rather than select Insert Columns or Insert Rows, however, you select Delete Columns or Delete Rows. For practice, delete the column (E) you just inserted.

Working with Text

The spreadsheet we've been working with, like most others, includes two types of information: text and values. The distinction between the two is simple: text is nonnumeric information that can't be used in calculations; values are numeric data and always begin with a numeral (0 through 9), a plus sign (+), a minus sign (–), or a currency symbol ($). Cells containing dates and times actually contain numeric values, but they can be displayed in standard date or time formats.

Most text is easily distinguished from numbers, but on occasion you might include numeric information, such as years (1995, 1996, and so on) or ID numbers, as headings or descriptive text. If the spreadsheet is complex, you can ensure that Works treats these numbers as text by beginning each entry with a quotation mark (such as "*1991*, or "*123 Main Street*). Because Works treats a number preceded by a quotation mark as text, the number won't accidentally be calculated.

Formatting Text

To format text in a spreadsheet, you follow the same steps as in the word processor. The only real differences are that (1) you select cells instead of words or paragraphs and (2) when you choose to align text, you do so in relation to the cell borders, not the margins of the page. To demonstrate how this works, we'll boldface and underline the column titles in cells B1 through E1 in the pizza spreadsheet example by doing the following:

1. Drag the mouse to select the cells you want to format. We selected cells B1 through E1.

2. Click the Bold and Italic buttons on the toolbar.

Works aligns text at the left edge of a cell by default. You can change this with the alignment buttons on the toolbar. We'll demonstrate this in the pizza spreadsheet example.

1. Select the cells you want to format. We used the cells already selected.

2. Click the Center Align button on the toolbar.

The newly formatted cells in our pizza spreadsheet example are shown in Figure 6-8.

To "unformat" a cell, select it and remove the formatting by clicking on the appropriate buttons on the toolbar.

	A	B	C	D	E	F	G	H
1		*Small*	*Medium*	*Large*	*Total*			
2	Cheese	57	32	29				
3	Sausage	97	143	168				
4	Pepperoni	102	169	185				
5	Anchovy	23	17	9				
6	Onion							
7	Vegetarian	49	73	53				
8								
9	Price							
10	Small	7.95						
11	Medium	9.95						
12	Large	12.95						
13								
14								
15								
16								
17								
18								
19								
20								

Zoom 100%

FIGURE 6-8

Formatting and aligning column titles

Using the Format Cells Dialog Box

You can do a good deal of formatting with toolbar buttons, but much more with the Font tab in the Format Cells dialog box you see here:

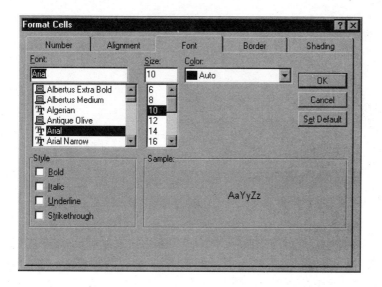

In this dialog box you see a variety of tabs. For now we'll look at options available on the Font and Alignment tabs. We'll deal with the Number, Border, and Shading tabs later in this chapter.

For selected cells you can use the Font tab to select the font you want to use, its size and style, and its color, plus you can see a preview of how the characters will appear. This dialog box provides one-stop shopping. Just select the Font and Style command from the Format menu, make the changes you want in the Format Cells dialog box, and click OK.

TIP You can access the Format Cells dialog box by placing the mouse pointer inside any cell, clicking the right mouse button, and selecting Format.

Aligning Text

You saw above how you can use one of three toolbar buttons to align text horizontally (left, center, and right). But you also have a series of alternatives that add power to these simple alignment buttons. If you click on the Alignment tab in the Format Cells dialog box, you'll see the alignment options shown here:

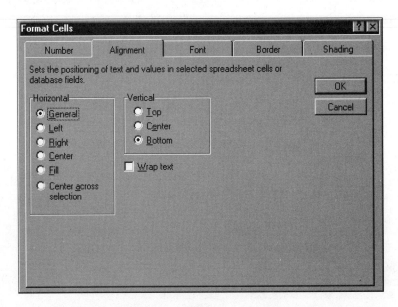

Here, you can align entries not only horizontally, but vertically (top, center, and bottom) as well. In Figure 6-9, you can see where we've aligned the column titles both horizontally and vertically in the center of the cells in row 1, which has a larger row height setting than the other rows.

	A	B	C	D	E	F	G	H
1		*Small*	*Medium*	*Large*	*Total*			
2	Cheese	57	32	29				
3	Sausage	97	143	168				
4	Pepperoni	102	169	185				
5	Anchovy	23	17	9				
6	Onion							
7	Vegetarian	49	73	53				
8								
9	Price							
10	Small	7.95						
11	Medium	9.95						
12	Large	12.95						
13								
14								
15								
16								
17								
18								
19								

Zoom 100%

FIGURE 6-9

Aligning text horizontally and vertically in a range

Working with Numbers

Numbers are at the heart of any spreadsheet. You can type numbers with the row of keys at the top of the keyboard (not the function keys) or, when the Num Lock key is turned on, you can use the numeric keypad at the right of the keyboard. Works always right-aligns numbers in cells, unless you specify otherwise, and normally displays partial values as decimals if the cell is wide enough (up to eight decimal places).

TIP Remember the wonderful Undo feature from the word processor module? It's alive and well in the spreadsheet module (and in the database module too). Use it *immediately* after the operation you want to undo.

You can type and calculate both positive and negative values. You indicate negative numbers either by preceding them with a minus sign (–) or by enclosing them in parentheses—for example, ($500.00). Works displays negative values in both forms, depending on the format option you prefer to use.

Using Number Formats

Because numbers can represent so many different types of values, such as quantities, currencies, and percentages, Works offers many different formats for numbers. When you apply number formats, you don't format the number itself. Rather, as with text, you format one or more selected cells to display numbers in a specific format. Formatting "sticks" to a cell even after you've changed or deleted the number it contains.

To demonstrate the available number formats, we'll open a new spreadsheet example with the New command on the File menu and type in the headings and numbers shown in Figure 6-10.

FIGURE 6-10

Some sample data for working with number formats

	A	B	C	D	E	F	G	H	
1	General	1.1	-1.1	1234	0.95				
2	Fixed								
3	Currency								
4	Comma								
5	Percent								
6	Exponential								
7	Leading Zeros								
8	Fraction								
9	True/False								
10	Date								
11	Time								
12	Text								
13									
14									
15									
16									
17									
18									
19									
20									

Zoom 100%

Each row label in column A represents a different number format option. Next, we'll select cells B1 through E12, and then click Edit and click Fill Down to copy the numbers you see in row 1 to the selected range.

The Fill Down command duplicates information by copying it into selected cells that appear below the cells to be copied. You'll find the Fill Down command and the complementary Fill Right command particularly useful in repeating formulas for calculating similar values.

Let's look at the number formats. The first two, next to General, in Figure 6-10, show the default format (the format Works uses unless you specify otherwise) for positive and negative numbers. Works always tries to display any number as precisely as possible. This is what the General format will do for you.

TIP Type a currency symbol ($) before a number and Works will recognize the Currency format. You can also type a percent symbol (%) and Works will recognize the Percent format.

To select other number formats, use the Number command on the Format menu, or click the right mouse button, select Format, and then select the Number tab from the Format Cells dialog box. In both cases, you'll see the Number tab options shown here:

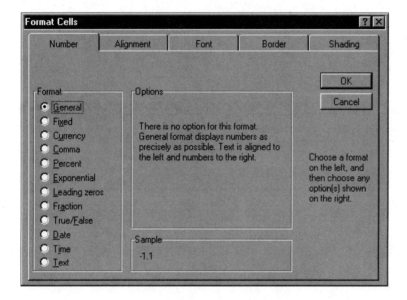

Here's how to select the Fixed format, for example.

1. Select the range of cells you want to format. In our example we selected the range B2:E2.

2. Click the right mouse button, and then click Format.

3. Click the Number tab.

4. Click a Format option button. We selected the Fixed option.

5. In the Options box on the Number tab, select the number of decimal places, if you want to change the default (2) setting. We left 2 as the number of decimals to use.

6. Click OK.

Now we'll format the next row of values as currency.

7. Select the cells you want to format. We selected the range B3:E3 in our example, and used the Currency button on the toolbar to apply the Currency format.

As you can see in Figure 6-11, we continued using the Number tab in the Format Cells dialog box to apply the formats described in column A to the corresponding values. Some data is meaningless in certain formats (such as a negative time value), and a label appears in those cells telling you the value is invalid in that format. Notice also that pound signs (########) appear in column D for a formatted entry that is too wide to fit in the cell. We'll discuss how to address this situation later in this chapter.

FIGURE 6-11

Different number formats applied to sample data

	A	B	C	D	E	F	G	H
1	General	1.1	-1.1	1234	0.95			
2	Fixed	1.10	-1.10	1234.00	0.95			
3	Currency	$1.10	($1.10)	$1,234.00	$0.95			
4	Comma	1.10	(1.10)	1,234.00	0.95			
5	Percent	110.00%	-110.00%	########	95.00%			
6	Exponential	1.10E+00	-1.10E+00	1.23E+03	9.50E-01			
7	Leading Zeros	00001	-00001	01234	00001			
8	Fraction	1 1/10	-1 1/10	1234	0 19/20			
9	True/False	TRUE	TRUE	TRUE	TRUE			
10	Date	1/1/00	Invalid Date	5/18/03	Invalid Date			
11	Time	2:24 AM	Invalid Time	12:00 AM	10:48 PM			
12	Text	1.1	-1.1	1234	0.95			
13								
14								
15								
16								
17								
18								
19								
20								

Zoom 100%

NOTE If you format a row or a column in a specific number format, Works will remember the format. Even if you extend beyond the range of entered values, that format will "stick."

Here is a brief list describing number format options.

General format displays numbers as integers (whole numbers) or as decimals. If a number is too long to be displayed in a cell, Works uses the exponential notation format (the scientific notation described later in this section). A minus sign indicates a negative number.

Fixed format displays numbers with the number of decimal places you specify. If a number must be truncated, this format rounds the decimal portion up or down accordingly, but Works remembers the actual value. For example, the value 3.456 in a cell formatted for two decimal places would be displayed as 3.46, whereas 3.454 would be displayed as 3.45. A minus sign indicates a negative number.

Currency format displays numbers as currency values, which includes dollar signs and commas to separate thousands, if necessary. If you type a currency symbol with the number, Works automatically assumes the Currency format. Negative amounts are enclosed in parentheses.

Comma format displays numbers with comma separators. For example, 111111 would be displayed as 111,111. As with the Currency format, negative numbers are enclosed in parentheses.

Percent format displays numbers as percents. This format multiplies a number by 100 and displays it as a percentage with the number of decimals you specify. When you type values into cells formatted for displaying percents, type the decimal equivalent of the percentage. The spreadsheet multiplies the value by 100. Thus, 70 becomes 7000.00%, whereas .7 becomes 70.00%. A minus sign indicates a negative percentage.

Exponential notation format, often used in science and engineering, displays numbers as a "root," such as 1.10, plus the power of 10 by which the number is multiplied to create its "long" form. In Figure 6-11, the E indicates exponential notation, 1.10 is the number to two decimals, and +00 shows that the number (originally 1.1) is not multiplied by any power of 10.

Leading Zeros format pads numbers with zeros on the left to fill them out to the required number of digits (five in the example). If the number already consists of the required number of digits, no leading zeros are added.

Fraction format displays values as fractions with a 0 in front so that .2 becomes 0 1/5 and .78 becomes 39/50. You can also round fractions by selecting an option in the Round To list that appears in the Fraction box in the Format Cells dialog box.

True/False format displays numbers as logical values in which any nonzero number produces TRUE and 0 produces FALSE. The True/False format is useful when you want to check spreadsheet cells for 0 and nonzero values, without regard to the actual values. For example, you would use the True/False format to see whether calculations that depend on other calculations work as expected.

Date and Time formats display numbers as dates or times in any of the forms listed in the Date box or the Time box in the Format Cells dialog box. The Date box is shown here:

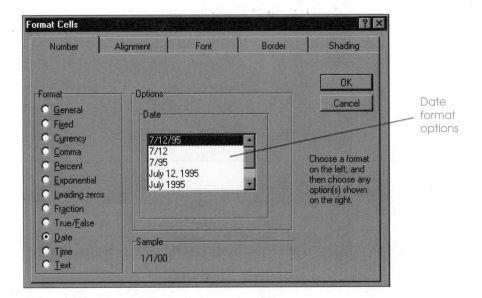

Date format options

Choose a format on the left, and then choose any option(s) shown on the right.

The Date and Time formats are useful in several different situations. You can use them to display entries for a series of dates or times and to "stamp" spreadsheets with the date and time they were created. You can also use the formatted date and time values to calculate elapsed time periods. Works can calculate with date values representing January 1, 1900, to June 3, 2079. Date values outside this range are displayed as text.

Text format sorts entries, including those with numbers or special characters. "Special characters" can include hyphens, such as the ones that occur in postal codes and phone numbers. To display values as text, apply the Text format to blank cells before entering values into them.

The Too-Small Cell

If after formatting a range of values you see a set of pound signs (########) in the cell, Works is telling you that a formatted number is too large to be completely displayed in a cell (see Figure 6-11 on page 200). The solution to this is simple. Widen the column with the mouse (the easy way) by dragging its right column border, or use the Column Width command on the Format menu. To widen a column with the mouse, do the following:

1. Select a cell in which the pound signs appear because the entry is too wide to fit within the standard column width.

2. Place the mouse pointer on the right border of the header for the column that contains the cell pointer.

    The mouse pointer turns into a vertical bar with a double-headed arrow through the middle labeled ADJUST.

3. Drag the border to the right approximately one-half inch.

    The column's width increases. The formatted value should appear. If it doesn't, widen the column a little more until you can see the value.

 TIP If you want to adjust a column's width so that the column will be just wide enough to display the widest entry in a range of entries, click the Best Fit button in the Column Width dialog box.

Advanced Formatting

You can enhance or clarify a spreadsheet by using formatting. As in the word processor, Works gives you a variety of options: fonts, font sizes, alignments, and borders. All of these options might be familiar to you from your work with the word processor. You can apply different fonts, styles, and sizes to different parts of the spreadsheet. As you prefer, you can use the toolbar to make font and size selections, or you can use the Font and Style command on the Format menu.

When it's time to print your spreadsheet, be sure to use the Print Preview command to see how the information fits on the page and how the data will appear. To improve the overall layout, remember that you can adjust column widths and row heights, fonts, and font sizes to open up a cramped spreadsheet or condense one that sprawls too much.

Simple as it sounds, a small change in font or font size may make a dramatic difference in your printed documents. This is especially true when you change from a monospace font such as Courier, in which a lowercase i requires as much space as a capital W, to a proportional font such as

Helvetica, in which characters take up only as much linear space as they need. You might want to try using different fonts, font sizes, alignments, and borders on one of your sample spreadsheets to see their effects.

You also have an assortment of other format changes you can make, including shading and borders.

Using Shading for Emphasis

We'll demonstrate some more with the pizza spreadsheet to see how to use shading to highlight a range of cells. With a few clicks, you can use shading to emphasize particular areas of a spreadsheet. We'll be working on the pizza spreadsheet example shown in Figure 6-9 on page 197.

1. Highlight the range you want to format with shading. We selected the range B1:E1 in our example.

2. With the mouse pointer on the selected cells, click the right mouse button, and then click Format.

3. Click the Shading tab and you will see the set of options shown here:

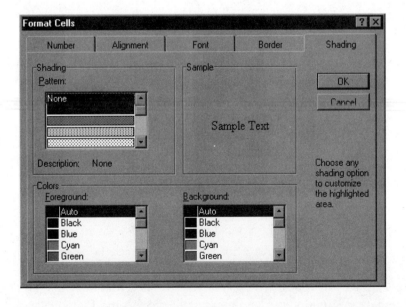

The Foreground option (in the Colors group) refers to the color of the dots or the pattern that you are creating. The Background option refers to the solid color on which the dots or pattern appears. For example, if you select white background with red foreground, you would see red dots on a white background.

TIP If you're lucky enough to have a color printer, it's in the Shading tab of the Format Cells dialog box that you can specify the foreground and background color in which your spreadsheets will print. You can accomplish some stunning effects this way. And don't forget: you can preview them in this dialog box before you make the final selection.

4. Select a shading pattern option. We selected the fifth shading pattern option down (the widely spaced dots).

5. Click OK.

6. We applied the same shading option to the range of pizza types and sizes in column A (range A2:A12) to make the pizza spreadsheet appear as you see in Figure 6-12.

	A	B	C	D	E	F	G	H
1		Small	Medium	Large	Total			
2	Cheese	57	32	29				
3	Sausage	97	143	168				
4	Pepperoni	102	169	185				
5	Anchovy	23	17	9				
6	Onion							
7	Vegetarian	49	73	53				
8								
9	Price							
10	Small	7.95						
11	Medium	9.95						
12	Large	12.95						
13								
14								
15								
16								
17								
18								
19								
20								

Zoom 100%

FIGURE 6-12

Shading applied to the range of column titles in a spreadsheet

Using Borders for Outlining

Here's another formatting option for outlining particular cells or ranges. You can apply a border to help emphasize a cell or range of cells. We'll continue with the pizza spreadsheet. Here, we'll enter a thick line to more clearly demarcate row and column headings, as follows:

1. Select the cells you want to format. We selected the range B1:E1.

2. Click the right mouse button with the mouse pointer pointing anywhere in the selected range, and then click Format.

3. Click the Border tab.

   You'll see this set of Border options:

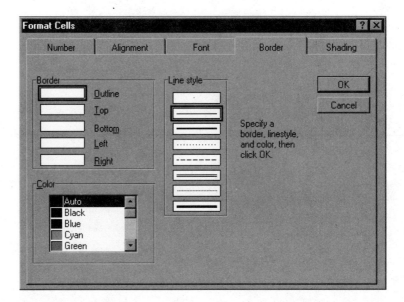

4. Click a border option in the Border box. We selected the Bottom option.

5. Click a style option in the Line Style box, and then click OK. We selected the thickest line option (at the bottom of the list).

   The column headings now have thick lines as the bottom border of the cells. We did the same to the range of pizza and size labels in the range A2:A12, as you can see in Figure 6-13.

Applying Multiple Format Options with the AutoFormat Command

The AutoFormat command makes formatting tabled information in Works spreadsheets a snap. It allows you to select a range and then choose from one of 22 different predesigned formats. In Figure 6-14, you can see two

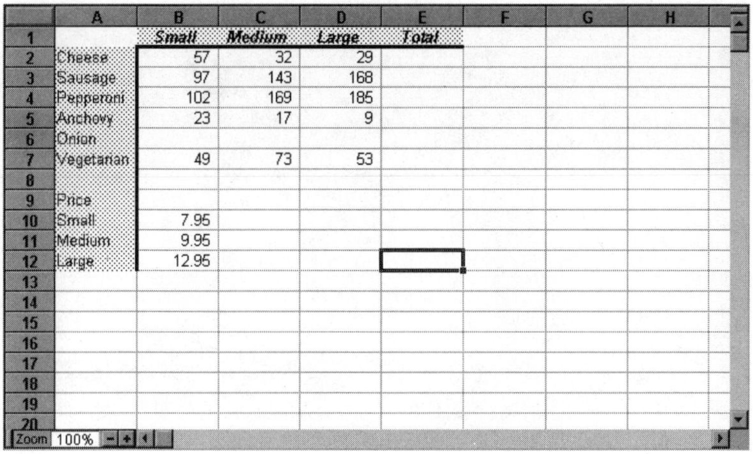

FIGURE 6-13

Using borders to make a spreadsheet more attractive

examples of formatting applied with the AutoFormat command: Classic Columns (on the left) and Classic Rule (on the right).

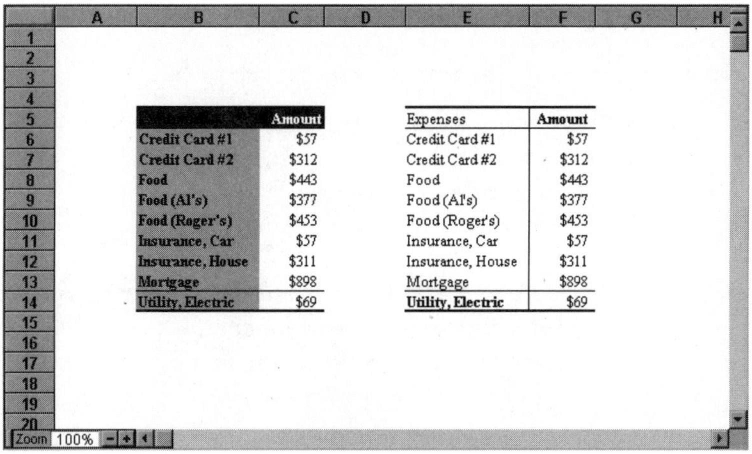

FIGURE 6-14

Two formatting examples applied with the AutoFormat command

Here's how to use the AutoFormat command.

1. Select the range of cells containing tabled information you want to Format.

2. Click Format, and then click AutoFormat.

    When you do this, you'll see the AutoFormat dialog box shown on the next page.

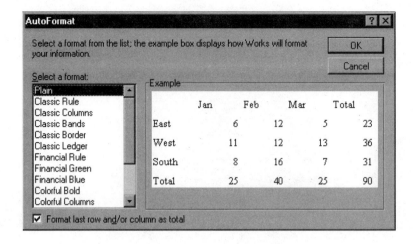

You can see a partial list of all the different available formats.

3. Select the format option you want to use.

    You can view what it will look like in the Example area before you click OK.

4. Once you find the one you want to use, click OK.

The AutoFormat command gives you a very convenient method for applying multiple format options to a range of data in a single operation. The process is easy, neat, and impressive.

TIP After you apply a formatting option to a selected range with the AutoFormat command, you are free to customize it to your liking by changing selected format elements. For example, you can increase the thickness of a border, change a shading pattern or color, or modify a font for selected data.

Sorting Rows

The Works spreadsheet can sort information, arranging selected rows of data in alphabetic or numeric order. Works sorts based on the information in a column (A, B, C, and so on); you can specify up to three columns, in order of importance, for it to consider. During the sort, Works checks the contents of the first column and arranges the rows to match the sort you specified (ascending or descending). An *ascending* sort organizes informa-tion alphabetically (a, b, c . . .) and numerically (1, 2, 3 . . .); a *descending* sort organizes information in reverse alphabetically (z, y, x . . .) and numer-ically (9, 8, 7 . . .).

If you specify a second and, possibly, a third column, Works turns to them to refine the result by sorting entries that are duplicated in the previous column(s). We'll demonstrate how this works by sorting a list of expenses alphabetically in column A along with their amounts in col-umn B, as you se in Figure 6-15.

	A	B	C	D	E	F	G	H
1	Expenses	Amount						
2	Insurance, House	$311						
3	Credit Card #1	$57						
4	Mortgage	$898						
5	Food (Roger's)	$453						
6	Insurance, Car	$57						
7	Food (Al's)	$377						
8	Utility, Electric	$69						
9	Credit Card #2	$312						
10	Food	$443						
11								
12								
13								
14								
15								
16								
17								
18								
19								
20								

Zoom 100%

FIGURE 6-15
Some data for practicing sorting

1. Select the range of rows you want to sort. We selected the range A2:B10 in our example.

    Because you don't want to include the column titles in a sort, be sure they are not included in the selected range.

2. Click Tools, and then click Sort.

    You will then see two dialog boxes that will ask you to decide the following questions.

    ❑ Do you want to sort the highlighted information or all of the information in the spreadsheet?

    ❑ Which column do you want to sort on (in this case the choices being column A or column B)?

    ❑ Do you want the sort to be in ascending or descending order?

3. Click OK in the first dialog box.

4. Click the Sort button.

The data you see in Figure 6-16 was sorted in ascending order using column A.

FIGURE 6-16
Sorted data

Newly sorted
data range

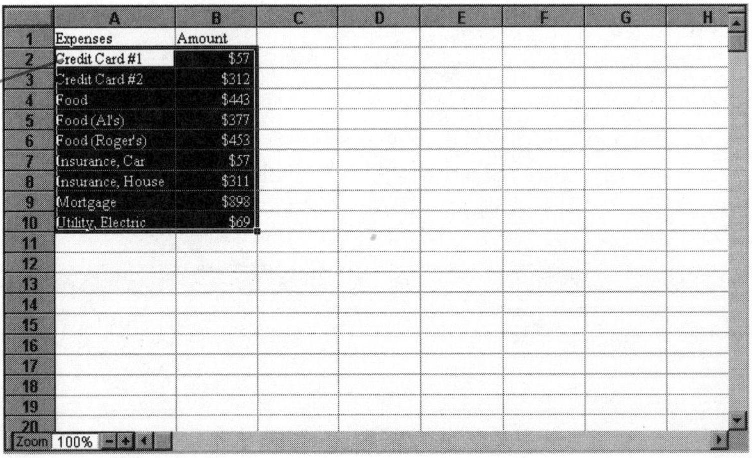

	A	B	C	D	E	F	G	H
1	Expenses	Amount						
2	Credit Card #1	$57						
3	Credit Card #2	$312						
4	Food	$443						
5	Food (Al's)	$377						
6	Food (Roger's)	$453						
7	Insurance, Car	$57						
8	Insurance, House	$311						
9	Mortgage	$898						
10	Utility, Electric	$69						
11								
12								
13								
14								
15								
16								
17								
18								
19								
20								

Zoom 100%

Works sorts the entries and modifies the spreadsheet. Here you can see how categories in column A (such as the two Credit Card entries) were sorted in alphabetical order.

Sorting is fast and useful for arranging any type of alphabetic or numeric information. If you want to preserve both the original and the sorted versions, save the original under one name and the sorted spreadsheet under another.

TIP You can use the Advanced button in the second Sort dialog box to control sorting *within* sorting when the primary column contains duplicate entries. For example, if the first column contains three *Smith* entries, you can set up the second column to sort the *Smith* rows alphabetically by the data in the second column. The Advanced button expands the Sort dialog box so that you can select a second and third column, if necessary, as well as the sort order (ascending or descending) for each.

Finding Data with the Find Command

The Go To command provides a quick way to jump to a specific cell, regardless of what it contains. But what do you do if you know the value you want, but don't know which cell it's in? You use the Find command on the Edit menu.

The Find command in the spreadsheet works much like Find does in the word processor, with one exception. The word processor lets you refine a document search by limiting the command to whole words or uppercase and lowercase, but the spreadsheet lets you refine a search by specifying direction (left to right by row, or top to bottom by column). If you're searching a large spreadsheet, specifying a horizontal or vertical scan can speed the process by tailoring the search to the orientation of the spreadsheet.

You can select columns, rows, or cell ranges to limit the search to a particular part of the spreadsheet, or you can select any cell and have Works search the entire spreadsheet. To demonstrate how simple it is, we'll use the pizza spreadsheet (see Figure 6-12 on page 205) example as follows:

1. Click Edit, and then click Find.

2. Type the text you want to find in the Find What box. We typed *7.95*.

3. Works proposes to search by rows, rather than columns. The example spreadsheet is small enough that the search direction doesn't matter, so we clicked OK.

    Almost immediately, Works selects cell B10, which contains the value 7.95.

Changing Data with the Replace Command

Remember how, with the word processor, you could search for occurrences of text and then change each with new text? You can do the same with the spreadsheet. This is a great tool for changing a simple value or a set of incorrectly entered ones.

To use this option, click Edit, and then click Replace. You'll see this Replace dialog box:

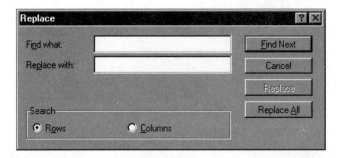

Just as with the word processor, Works will ask you for both the string of characters you are searching for and those that will replace them. Click Find Next and Works will search for the occurrence. Then click Replace to replace the occurrence. Or, click Replace All to replace all occurrences.

Printing a Spreadsheet

Because printing in Works is uniform throughout the three applications, this section deals only with features unique to the spreadsheet. If you need more information about headers, footers, or other topics, see Chapter 5, "Getting the Most from the Word Processor," page 145.

When it comes to printing, a spreadsheet can differ from a word-processed document in one important way. Although it's a single document, the spreadsheet can be either too wide or too long to fit on a single page. This means you might find yourself doing some fine-tuning before you print.

If you create a document that's both too wide and too long to print on one page, Works breaks up the spreadsheet and prints it on separate pages. It does this in the following order: upper left section first, lower left second, upper right third, and lower left fourth.

To control page breaks at the bottom, you can use the Page Break command on the Insert menu. To control page breaks from side to side, you can insert a page break between columns with the Page Break command, or you can adjust column widths or insert a blank column wide enough to force the column to its right onto a new page.

As in the word processor, you can add headers, footers, and page numbers to a printed spreadsheet. You can also adjust page and header margins and, of course, preview the spreadsheet before printing. (This is always a good idea.)

If your printer can print landscape (wide) orientation, you can reverse page length and width in the Page Setup dialog box. In the Page Setup dialog box you can change margins and page orientation, just as you can for word-processed documents. When you select the Other Options tab in the Page Setup dialog box, you can select whether to print the gridlines that are visible on the screen version of the spreadsheet. As you can see here, you can also direct Works to print (or not print) the row and column headings.

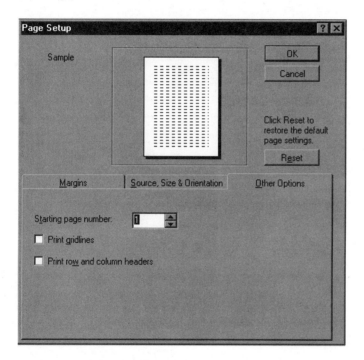

Printing Part of a Spreadsheet

You can choose to print all or part of a spreadsheet. This is one area in which the spreadsheet differs significantly from the word processor. To print part of a word-processed document, you select the starting and ending pages in the Print dialog box. By contrast, to print part of a spreadsheet, you specify the area to print with the Set Print Area command on the Format menu. Using the command is simple.

To print a range of cells, follow these steps:

1. Select the cells you want to print.

2. Click Format, and then click Set Print Area.

3. Click OK in response to Works' confirmation that you want to select a range to print.

TIP To see the cells before printing, click the Print Preview button on the toolbar. Only the print area you selected appears.

To deselect a print area, select the entire spreadsheet and choose Set Print Area again.

TIP To quickly select the entire spreadsheet, either choose Select All on the Edit menu, or click on the unlabeled, rectangular box above the row 1 header and to the left of the column A header.

Coming Next

You've merely scratched the surface of what the spreadsheet module can do for you. In the next chapter you'll learn about creating formulas and using the powerful set of built-in functions that accompanies Works for Windows 95. Let's turn to that chapter now.

Chapter 7

Working with Formulas and Functions

The Microsoft Works for Windows 95 spreadsheet contains lots of handy tools that make working with numbers easy. Among its most powerful features are the ability to instantly calculate formulas you create and its set of built-in formulas, called functions. Using formulas, you can develop your own calculations based on the relationship between different variables. To use a function, you simply select the one you want from a Works menu and click it into your worksheet. Do you want to know when that loan will come due? The mean and standard deviation of a set of numbers? How much you owe on the house? You'll find out how to use functions that answer these questions.

Working with Functions

You know about formulas. They compute such things as the area of a square (l^2, or the length of one side squared) or the amount of time it takes for an investment to double ($S=P(1+I)^n$) or the semi-interquartile range ($Q=(Q1–Q3)/2$). A *formula* is a set of values, variables, and operators that perform calculations on existing values to provide new values. No matter what your task, using Works to compute formulas can be a great help.

There are two types of formulas: those you create yourself, and those that are built into the Works application. You use the first type to create custom calculations designed for a very specific purpose. The second type, called *functions*, are built-in equations that perform useful tasks, such as calculating averages, depreciation, and loan payments. Works comes with 76 functions that are simple to use.

When referring to cells in formulas, you can enter a single cell or a range of cells. Even better, you can refer to a cell by its address, or you can give it a descriptive name and use that name in your formulas. We'll talk about naming ranges of cells later in this chapter. For now, let's create a sample formula to demonstrate how spreadsheets perform calculations.

Building a Formula

You tell Works that you're about to build a formula by first typing an equal sign (=) in the cell where you want the formula to reside. If you don't type an equal sign, Works will consider the entry to be text, plain and simple.

We'll use the pizza spreadsheet example to demonstrate how to create several types of formulas. The spreadsheet is shown in Figure 7-1.

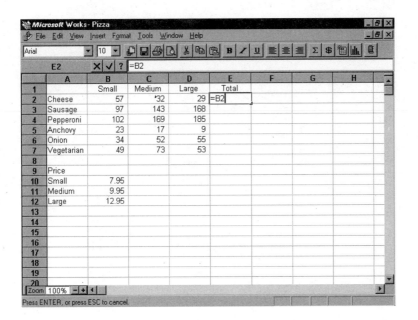

FIGURE 7-1
Entering a cell
reference in a
formula

The pizza spreadsheet includes values for numbers of pizzas sold that
will provide useful data to calculate totals. We'll start by building a simple
formula that adds the number of small, medium, and large cheese pizzas.
This will help to show the basics of entering a formula as well as to
demonstrate, by contrast, how useful Works' built-in functions can be.

We're going to calculate the total number of pizzas sold by type of
pizza, beginning with cheese. The values we want to add first are in cells
B2, C2, and D2 (the range B2:D2). Here's how to build the formula.

1. Click the cell in which you want to enter the formula. We clicked
    cell E2.

2. Type = (an equal sign) to let Works know you're starting a formula.

3. Type (or click) a cell that contains the first value you want to
    include in the formula. We typed *B2*.

    As you can see in Figure 7-1, Works immediately displays the
    cell reference on the entry bar and in the cell, indicating that it will
    use the value in cell B2 in the calculation.

4. Type an operator. We typed + (a plus sign).

    The plus sign appears on the entry bar.

5. Click the next cell to include in the formula. Type another operator,
    and continue to enter the rest of the cell references for the values

you want calculated and the appropriate operators. We entered *C2+D2*.

> **TIP** At this stage, notice the POINT indicator on the status bar. This tells you that you're free to select (point to) any cell or range you want included in the formula.

6. Click the Enter button (or press Enter) to complete the formula.

   When we enter the formula, the total for cells B2 through D2 (118) appears in cell E2. Whenever you want to refer to cells in a formula, simply point and click those cells. Works does the rest.

Automatically Updating Results

Suppose we try this: change the value in cell C2 from 32 to 12 and press Enter. What happens? The formula's calculated result in cell E2 changes from 118 to 98 in our example spreadsheet. The result appearing in cell E2 depends on the values in cells B2, C2, and D2. When one of the three is changed, the total must change as well.

This is no small deal. Imagine working with a complex spreadsheet in which hundreds of values are interconnected, and wanting to see how changing this or that value affects the final outcome. This "what-if" feature, which we'll explore later in this chapter, is one of the primary reasons why spreadsheet programs are so popular in the business world. They allow you to play out several different scenarios and examine the impact on one variable of changing one or more other variables.

It's easy to check the contents of a cell by selecting it and reviewing the entry bar. Notice in Figure 7-2 that the result appears in cell E2, but the cell's content is the formula, which you see on the entry bar.

> **TIP** Formulas and functions can be edited like any other cell entry. Use the F2 function key, or click on the entry bar and move the insertion point to the location where you want to make the edit.

When building related formulas in a spreadsheet, be careful not to create a circular reference. A *circular reference* is a reference to a cell or

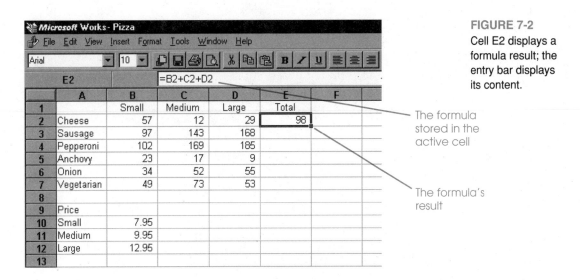

FIGURE 7-2
Cell E2 displays a formula result; the entry bar displays its content.

The formula stored in the active cell

The formula's result

range in a formula that refers to (includes) a cell that will display the formula's result. A circular reference has no start and no end, so Works can't calculate it correctly. If you see the CIRC indicator on the status bar at the bottom of the screen, check your formulas for a reference that refers to a cell that is supposed to display the formula's result, like the example shown in Figure 7-3.

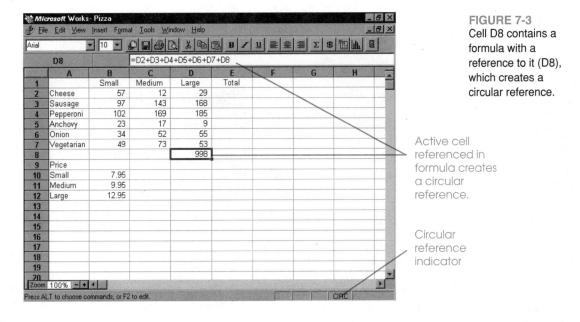

FIGURE 7-3
Cell D8 contains a formula with a reference to it (D8), which creates a circular reference.

Active cell referenced in formula creates a circular reference.

Circular reference indicator

Using Operators

When you build a formula, you use mathematical operators, such as the plus sign (+) and the minus sign (–), to tell Works how to operate on the numbers. You can use these operators, shown in the following table, in formulas in both the spreadsheet and the database.

Operator	Meaning
^	Exponent, as in 2^3 for 2^3
+ and –	Positive and negative
* and /	Multiplication and division, as in 2*3 and 6/2
+ and –	Addition, as in 2+2, and subtraction, as in 2–1
= and < >	Equal, as in PROFIT = INCOME, and not equal, as in PROFIT < > LOSS
< and >	Less than, as in COST < PRICE, and greater than, as in PRICE > COST
<= and >=	Less than or equal to, as in SUPPLIES <= BUDGET, and greater than or equal to, as in INCOME >= EXPENSE
~	Not, as in ~(PROFIT < INCOME)
|	Or, as in FIXED COST | VARIABLE COST
&	And, as in ADS & BROCHURES

Some of these operators perform arithmetic calculations and are equally applicable to both the spreadsheet and the database modules. Others, such as the tilde (~), the pipe (|), and the ampersand (&), are known as *logical operators* because they help with comparisons and searches.

Controlling When Works Calculates Formulas

In our pizza spreadsheet example, we showed you how Works automatically calculates formulas again whenever you change a value in the spreadsheet that's referenced in the formula. Sometimes, however, you might want to put off using this recalculation feature until you've made a series of changes. In other words, you might want to change more than one value and *then* examine the impact of all the changes at once, rather than one at a time. You might also find that the constant recalculation on large spreadsheets can cause time-consuming delays in your editing.

You can control when Works calculates formulas, either by having Works automatically calculate the result of a formula (or function), or by manually directing Works to recalculate when you're ready. Manual calculation tells Works not to update the spreadsheet each time you make a change that affects a formula, but rather to wait until you're ready to have all the calculations occur. Automatic calculation gives Works the go-ahead to recalculate all the formulas in a spreadsheet as soon as any change is made that impacts a formula. Automatic calculation is the default.

To change to manual calculation, follow these steps:

1. Click Tools, and then click Options.

2. Click the Data Entry tab and click the Use Manual Calculation option you see here:

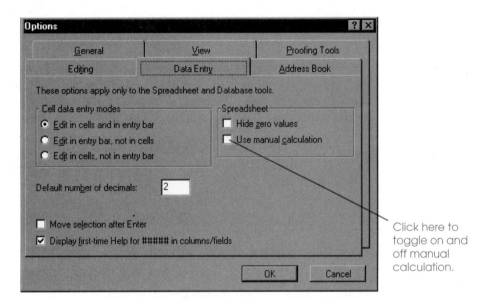

Click here to toggle on and off manual calculation.

In a small spreadsheet like the one we've been working with, whether manual calculation is on or off won't make much difference in the way you work with the results you get. However, if you're using many formulas of increasing complexity, this feature can be a time-saver. You needn't wait for one formula to finish its work before you create another one.

Controlling the Order of Calculation

Formulas often perform several calculations to achieve a result. Calculating an average, for example, requires totaling a group of items and then dividing by the number of items. Many formulas include more than one operator; Works performs each calculation in a specific order, depending on the operator.

The standard order of calculation is:

Order	Operator
First	^
Second	+ and – (positive and negative)
Third	* and /
Fourth	+ and – (addition and subtraction)
Fifth	= and < >, < and >, <= and >=
Sixth	~
Seventh	| and &

If more than one operator with the same "rank" appears in a formula, Works evaluates each operator from left to right and performs calculations in order, according to the ranking shown above.

To see how this order of evaluation can affect a formula, we can select an empty cell in our spreadsheet and follow these steps:

1. Type = (an equal sign) to start a formula.

2. Type a formula using any values and a variety of operators, and click the Enter button. We entered $8+8/4*3^3$ for this demonstration.

Works calculates the result of our formula, 62, because it follows its internal rules for evaluating mathematical operators. To summarize, Works does the following with our formula:

- First, it evaluates the exponent 3^3 (or 3^3) and calculates 27.

- Second, it evaluates the division and multiplication operators from left to right $8/4*27$ (or $2*27$) and calculates 54.

- Third, it evaluates the addition operator $8+54$ and calculates 62, the result.

Sometimes you might want Works to perform the calculations in a different order. In such cases, Works needs to know which order of operations to follow to get the desired outcome. To override the normal order of calculation, use sets of parentheses to enclose those portions of the formula you want Works to calculate first before performing the rest of the calculations. If you want to control more than one calculation in a formula, you can nest one set of parentheses within another to control the order in which the enclosed calculations are performed.

Using the same formula as before, we can produce an entirely different result by enclosing certain values and operators in parentheses. For instance, suppose we try this in another cell in a practice spreadsheet:

■ Type =*(8+(8/4)*3)^3* and click the Enter button.

This time the parentheses control the order of evaluation, so the result is 2744. Works evaluates the inner set of parentheses first, which contains the division operator (8/4) and calculates 2. Because the multiplication operator takes precedence over the addition operator in the outer set of parentheses, Works next evaluates 2*3 to calculate 6, and then adds 8 (6+8) to calculate 14. Finally, Works evaluates the exponent operator (14^3) and calculates 2744, the result.

Using a Built-In Function

Now for shortcuts—and the fun. You can create formulas galore, but why go to all that trouble when you can use one of the built-in functions or predefined formulas that comes with Works?

As we said earlier, Works offers 76 built-in functions. It's unlikely that you'll use all of these functions in your spreadsheets. Rather, you're more likely to use just a few, based on the type of work you do. Of course, all the functions are ready for your use at any time.

Functions save time and work. They're also a necessity in some spreadsheets. Consider this problem: suppose you have 100 employees, and you want to total the weekly payroll. If your spreadsheet starts at cell A1 with the employee's name, and cell B1 shows the employee's salary, the spreadsheet would look something like this:

	A	B
1	Maria Sandoval	$335.00
2	John Jones	$287.50
3	Pam Chung	$380.00
...	...	...
99	Madhu Ghandi	$500.00
100	Fred Buchner	$325.00

To add the total salaries, you'd probably think that you should move to cell B101, and begin typing the following formula:

```
=B1+B2+B3+B4 ... +B99+B100
```

But, consider how much work this would be. It would take a lot of time and effort, and because of all the typing, you could easily make a typo, which would give you an error.

The solution, of course, is to use a Works function. By using the function, you need only type a few characters. A function saves time and eliminates mistakes. Functions might seem confusing at first, but they'll save you a lot of work and make the Works spreadsheet much easier to use. You can type a function directly into any cell.

In the payroll spreadsheet example, you can total the column of weekly salaries by entering the built-in SUM function, which totals values in one or more cells or ranges. All you need to do is to move to cell B101, type *=SUM(B1:B100)*, and click the Enter button. Works automatically sums or totals all of the values in each referenced cell (the range B1:B100) and displays the result in cell B101.

You can use the SUM function to total not only columns, but also rows. Sometimes, however, you'll want to add values from cells scattered around the spreadsheet. In this case, type in the SUM function and type or point to the exact cells, separating each with a comma like this: *=SUM(B2,D3,C1)*. You can also sum more than one range, such as *=SUM(B2:B7,C1:C4)*.

Totaling a Range with the AutoSum Button

Because the SUM function is one you're likely to use often, Works includes an AutoSum button on the toolbar. By using this button, you can total columns or rows automatically. Just select a cell adjacent to the column or row of values you want to sum, and double-click the AutoSum button. Works enters a SUM function in the selected cell, and the sum for the row or column will appear.

The AutoSum button is a great tool when you've built a spreadsheet and the cells you want to total are grouped in a range, either down a column or across a row. Be aware, though, that the AutoSum button gives precedence to columns over rows. This means that if you double-click the AutoSum button to total an intended range of values in a row but there is also a range of values in the column above the active cell, you'll get a total for the column range instead. To avoid this situation, position the cell pointer and click (a single click) the AutoSum button. Works inserts the SUM function along with a suggested range reference, which is highlighted, as you see in Figure 7-4. Then all you have to do is type the correct range, if the suggested one isn't the one you want to total.

Using the pizza spreadsheet example once again, we can compute the total number of cheese pizzas in a different way, by replacing the formula we entered earlier with the SUM function. We'll use the easiest method first, the AutoSum button.

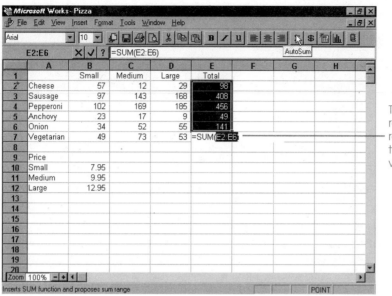

FIGURE 7-4

A SUM function and a suggested value range

Type a new range reference to total the row values.

1. Click the cell in which you want to enter a SUM function. We clicked cell E2.

2. Double-click the AutoSum button.

   Works automatically enters the SUM function along with the range of cells (B2:D2) that will be summed, and then displays the result, as you see in Figure 7-5. That's all there is to it.

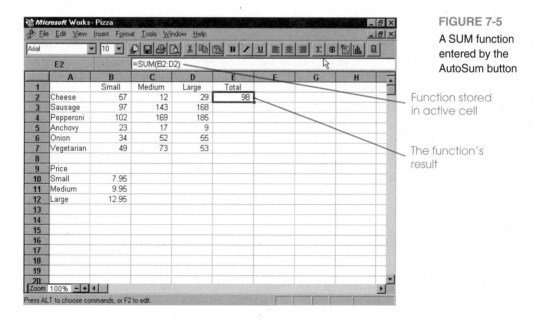

FIGURE 7-5

A SUM function entered by the AutoSum button

Function stored in active cell

The function's result

TIP Clicking the AutoSum button caused a number of sophisticated operations to take place very quickly. Works entered the equal sign and function name, scanned the spreadsheet and looked for cells to be summed, highlighted those cells, completed the function, calculated the total, and displayed the result before you could say, "AutoSum this, please."

Let's look at the function shown on the entry bar in Figure 7-5 on the preceding page. Although the results of the formula (=B2+C2+D2) and the function (=SUM(B2:D2)) are the same, each reaches its result in a different way. Built-in functions follow the same basic design, regardless of the calculations they perform. The SUM function, as an example, can be broken down as follows:

- The function starts with an equal sign, as do all Works formulas.

- The word SUM names the function. Other functions have other names. When you type functions on your own, remember to always start them with the function name.

- A set of parentheses surrounds the cells that Works proposes to total. Whenever you use a function, you must enclose values—or cell or range references—within parentheses.

Now we'll demonstrate calculating a total for sausage pizzas by typing a SUM function.

1. Click the cell in which you want to enter a SUM function. We clicked cell E3.

2. Type =sum(

3. Highlight the range that contains the values you want to sum with the mouse or arrow keys. We selected the range B3:D3.

4. Type) (a closing parenthesis) and click the Enter button (or press Enter.

    The result in our example, 408, appears in the cell, and the SUM function appears on the entry bar.

Selecting Built-In Functions

You can find a list of all the Works functions in Appendix A, "Built-In Spreadsheet and Database Functions" (page 497). You can also see them in the Insert Function dialog box you see here:

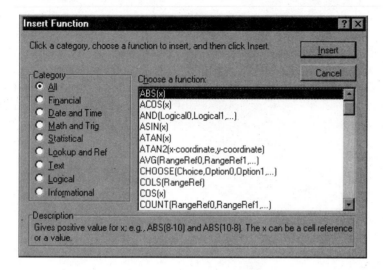

This dialog box helps you choose and enter functions by displaying a list of all the built-in functions available in Works. You can also display only certain functions, such as those used for statistical calculations or for Date and Time, by clicking the appropriate category (there are eight).

Each of the categories available in the Insert Function dialog box contains a set of functions. For example, to use the SUM function using the Insert Function command, follow these steps:

1. Place the insertion point in the cell where you want the results of the function to be located.

2. Click Insert, and then click Function to display the Insert Function dialog box.

3. Click the Statistical category.

4. Click SUM(RangeRef0,RangeRef1,...).

5. Click the Insert button.

6. Enter the range of cells between the parentheses on the entry bar.

7. Press Enter.

In step 6, you're advised to enter the range of cells you want SUM to add together to give you the total of the values. This range of cells is actually called the *argument*. This is a computer term for the values the function needs to perform its task.

The big advantage to using the list of functions from the Insert Function dialog box is that you can review all the available functions and also look at the structure of the argument you'll have to provide. You can also read an explanation of the function in the Description box at the bottom of the dialog box. With functions that you use often, you probably don't need any additional information; but for rarely used (but important) functions, the list and descriptions can be indispensable. Another advantage with the Insert Function command is that you'll minimize typing errors (and impress your colleagues) since the syntax of the function is automatically entered.

Using Functions and Formulas

You know that functions are predesigned formulas. And if you can use a function, rather than a formula, that's exactly what you should do. Functions are already written and can be more accurate. But formulas allow for very special applications. And, using a function along with a formula provides you with even greater power. For instance, you might want to take the average of a set of numbers (using the AVG function) and multiply it by a certain factor (such as .8) to produce a result that's 80 percent of the average of a set of scores. The combinations of using a function as part of a formula are endless and will come up again and again as you use these powerful tools.

Using Easy Calc

Works contains other easy-to-use tools for working with numbers that take advantage of the built-in functions. The Easy Calc command on the Tools menu is one such tool. You tell Easy Calc what you want to do (sum, multiply, subtract, divide, average, or any other operation available with the other functions) and Easy Calc will walk you through the operation. The Easy Calc command presents the Easy Calc dialog box you see here:

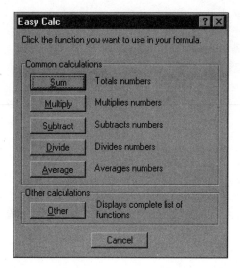

To use Easy Calc, follow these steps:

1. Click the cell where you want the formula to be created.

2. Click Tools, and then click Easy Calc.

3. Click whatever function you want to use such as Sum or Divide or Multiply.

4. Click or highlight the cells you want to perform the operation on.

5. Click Next.

6. Confirm the cell where you want the results of the formula entered.

7. Click Finish.

TIP You can bypass the Tools menu by selecting the Easy Calc button on the toolbar. Like the Easy Calc command, the Easy Calc button displays the Easy Calc dialog box.

Copying and Moving Formulas and Functions

When you work with spreadsheets, you'll often need to perform the same calculation on different groups of cells. In the pizza spreadsheet, for example, we need totals for the other types of pizza; and totals for the different sizes, too, would be helpful. We'll start by using the AutoSum button to total (in cell B8) the column of small pizzas sold.

1. Select the cell where you want to enter a SUM function. In this case, we selected cell B8.

2. Double-click the AutoSum button.

   The total number of small pizzas (362) appears in the selected cell.

Now we'll copy the formulas. In Chapter 6 we showed you the Works feature for filling a range with the active cell's contents by dragging the little box in the lower right corner of the cell pointer. We also showed you how to use the Fill Down command to copy information to a selected range down the column containing the active cell. You can use either of these methods to copy formulas as well. To demonstrate the results more clearly, we'll turn on the Works feature for viewing formulas in cells and then fill a range to copy the SUM function, as follows:

1. Click View, and then choose Formulas.

   The Formulas command tells Works to display formulas in those cells that contain them. To accommodate their display, this command causes the columns to expand suddenly, which in turn moves your Total column almost out of view.

   NOTE You can select all the cells in the spreadsheet and resize the columns using the Column Width command on the Format menu, or you can scroll to the right so that you can see the columns.

2. Click the cell containing the SUM function to be copied. We selected cell E3.

3. Point to the little box in the lower right corner of the cell pointer.

   When the mouse pointer is positioned properly, it changes to a cross labeled FILL.

4. Drag the cell pointer's border down to the last cell in the range where you want to copy the function, and release the mouse button. We dragged down to cell E8.

The selected function copies down the column. The range E3:E8 in our example contains SUM functions that total ranges in the rows to the left. Now we'll copy another SUM function, using the Fill Right command on the Edit menu.

5. Select the range of functions to be copied. We selected the range B8:D8.

6. Click Edit, and then click Fill Right.

7. Click View, and then click Formulas when you want to turn off the display of formulas.

The copied formulas appear in the ranges B8:D8 and E2:E8 in our example, as you can see in Figure 7-6. Notice in each that Works has adjusted the range references so that they refer not to the cells in the original formula, but to *cells in the same position* relative to the new formula. For instance, the SUM function in cell E4 references the range B4:D4, the function in cell E5 references the range B5:D5, and the function in cell C8 references C2:C7. Works modifies cell references in this way, so you don't have to adjust them manually (possibly introducing errors).

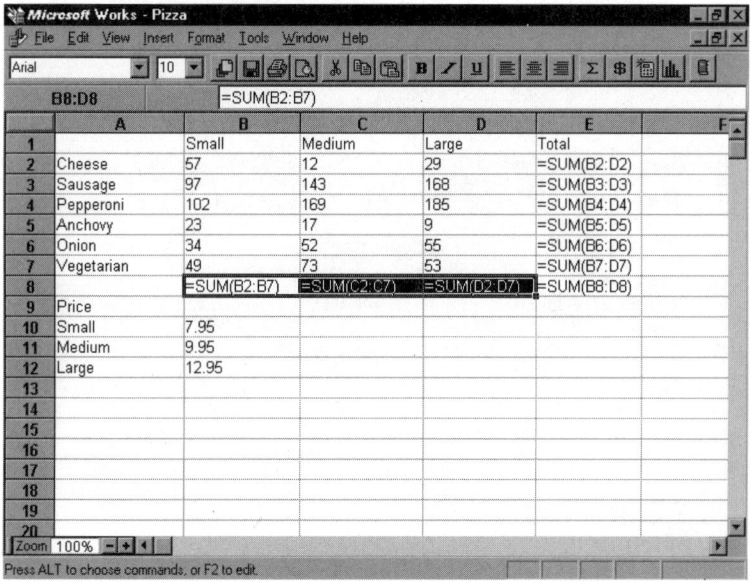

FIGURE 7-6

Copied functions with relative references

Cell or range references that change when you copy formulas or functions are called *relative references*. You might not always want cell references to change, however. Say you want copied formulas or functions to refer to a value in one particular cell or one particular row or column. You do this by using absolute or mixed references, rather than the relative references. We'll discuss these different types of cell references shortly.

 CAUTION Proceed with care when you move and copy formulas. Works does the best it can, but both moving and copying formulas can produce unexpected and even bizarre results. Save your work frequently for added insurance.

In general, when you move or copy a range of cells containing one or more formulas that refer to cells outside the range, Works does the following:

- When moving, Works keeps the original references to nonmoved cells. The references to moved cells reflect their new locations.

- When copying, either within the same spreadsheet or from one spreadsheet to another, Works alters all relative references to reflect the new locations of the copied cells.

To get an idea of how relative references can give you some surprising results, we'll demonstrate the following in our pizza spreadsheet example:

1. Select the range of SUM functions. We selected the range E2:E8.

2. Click the Copy button on the toolbar.

3. Click any blank cell. We selected cell G10.

4. Click the Paste button on the toolbar.

The selected functions copy to the range G10:G16 in our example, as shown in Figure 7-7. Notice that the entry bar displays =SUM(D10:F10). The relative references to the ranges changed; they now refer to ranges in the same relative positions from where you placed the copied functions, which don't contain any values. That's why the results of the copied functions all display zero.

The logistics of moving and copying formulas, especially within or between spreadsheets that contain other formulas and data, can make you feel like Hannibal taking elephants across the Alps. Wherever possible,

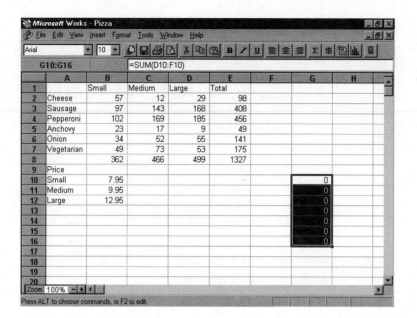

FIGURE 7-7
One effect of
copying functions
with relative
references

your best bet is to try to copy or move data *first*, before resorting to moving or copying formulas. Such precautions are particularly important in spreadsheets with sensitive information, like your income taxes or your fourth-quarter profits. Sometimes reinventing your formulas is preferable to untangling masses of relative cell references.

TIP You can minimize the chance of introducing errors when moving or copying formulas and functions. Use the Cut and Copy commands or buttons to begin the procedure, but then use the Paste Special command to insert the contents of the Clipboard. The Paste Special command lets you insert values from cut or copied cells that contain formulas. You can choose to insert the values (with the Values Only option), or add the incoming values to those already in the selected cells (Add Values), or subtract the incoming values (Subtract Values).

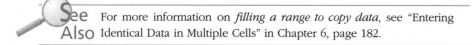

See Also For more information on *filling a range to copy data*, see "Entering Identical Data in Multiple Cells" in Chapter 6, page 182.

Working with Relative, Absolute, and Mixed References

Relative cell references give a cell's position relative to another cell. A relative reference is comparable to saying, "Go one block east and three blocks north" from wherever you happen to be. When you build a formula using relative references, you're telling Works to use the value in the cell that is X columns and Y rows away from the current cell. That's what happened when Works created the SUM functions with the Fill Down and Fill Right tasks you performed in the pizza spreadsheet. The copied functions refer to ranges in the same relative positions from the cell where the results of the functions are to appear. The references in the functions change as the cells where the results will appear change.

Absolute cell references refer to a specific cell in a spreadsheet. An absolute reference is comparable to saying, "Go to the intersection of State and Main." No matter what the starting point, there is only one intersection of State and Main.

To distinguish an absolute cell reference from a relative cell reference, insert a dollar sign ($) before the column letter and row number in a formula's reference. For example, the reference $A$5 in a formula would tell Works to use the value in cell A5, regardless of that cell's location relative to the formula's cell. If cell A5 were entered as an absolute reference in a formula that was moved, the cell reference would remain $A$5. Typing dollar signs is tedious, even if a spreadsheet isn't large. Luckily, Works provides a simple alternative: press the F4 key to change any cell reference from relative to absolute.

Absolute cell references are particularly useful in spreadsheets where a single value, such as an hourly wage or a loan rate, is used in multiple formulas scattered throughout the spreadsheet, or when you move or copy formulas to new locations but want to retain a reference to a particular cell. For example, in Figure 7-8 you can see how Larry, Moe, and Sam all worked different hours, but the hourly rate (in cell C3) remains the same.

Look at the formulas in cells C7, C8, and C9. Because Pay is computed as the number of hours worked times the hourly rate, and because we want to keep the hourly rate constant, the hourly rate is represented by $C$3 in each formula in each cell. Now we'll demonstrate using an absolute cell reference to calculate gross income on small pizzas in our pizza spreadsheet example.

1. Click the cell where you want to enter a formula. We selected cell F2.

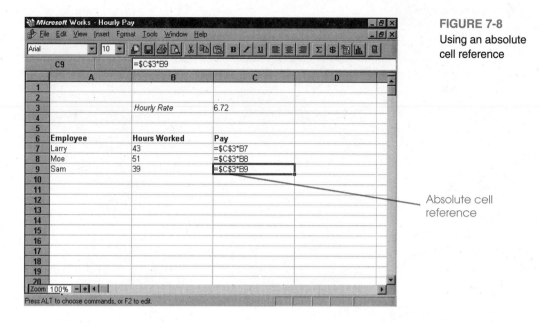

FIGURE 7-8

Using an absolute
cell reference

Absolute cell
reference

2. Type = and click the cell that contains the value you want to use as a constant. We selected cell B10, which contains the price for small pizzas.

   The relative cell reference for the selected cell appears on the entry bar.

3. Press the F4 key.

   Notice that dollar signs ($) appear before the column reference and the row reference on the entry bar.

4. Enter the rest of the formula. We typed * (an asterisk), clicked cell B2, and clicked the Enter button.

   The formula calculates the result 453.15 in our example. Now we will copy the formula down the column to see how the absolute reference stays the same in copied formulas.

5. Click the cell that contains the formula with an absolute cell reference. We selected cell F2.

6. Position the mouse pointer over the small box in the lower right corner of the cell pointer.

7. Drag the cell pointer's border down to the last cell in the range to be filled and release the mouse button. We dragged down to cell F7.

The formula copies (fills) down the selected range. As you can see in Figure 7-9, we turned on the Formulas view to show the range of copied formulas. Notice that each formula contains the absolute reference to cell B10.

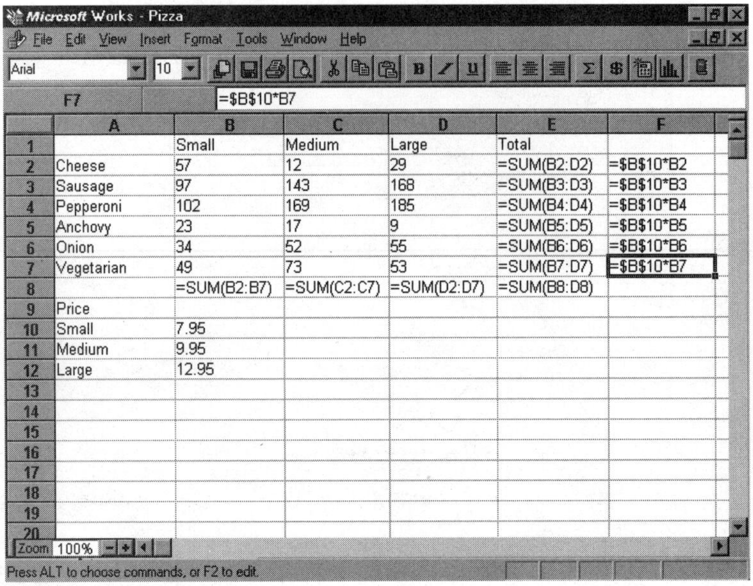
Microsoft Works - Pizza

F7 =$B$10*B7

	A	B	C	D	E	F
1		Small	Medium	Large	Total	
2	Cheese	57	12	29	=SUM(B2:D2)	=$B$10*B2
3	Sausage	97	143	168	=SUM(B3:D3)	=$B$10*B3
4	Pepperoni	102	169	185	=SUM(B4:D4)	=$B$10*B4
5	Anchovy	23	17	9	=SUM(B5:D5)	=$B$10*B5
6	Onion	34	52	55	=SUM(B6:D6)	=$B$10*B6
7	Vegetarian	49	73	53	=SUM(B7:D7)	=$B$10*B7
8		=SUM(B2:B7)	=SUM(C2:C7)	=SUM(D2:D7)	=SUM(B8:D8)	
9	Price					
10	Small	7.95				
11	Medium	9.95				
12	Large	12.95				

Press ALT to choose commands, or F2 to edit.

FIGURE 7-9
A formula with an absolute reference ($B$10) copied down a column to produce multiple calculations

Naming Cell Ranges

Now let's look at some advantages with naming cells and ranges. Even though cell references become second nature and are easier to interpret after you gain a little experience with Works, they're still somewhat cryptic at first glance. Names, which you can assign to any cell or range of cells, are much easier to decipher than numbers, if only because they're closer to "real" language and can more clearly describe cell contents. For example, instead of referring to the range B10:B12, why not refer to the range *Prices* instead?

Cell and range names are especially useful in the following types of spreadsheets:

- Large or complex spreadsheets containing specific information to which you want to refer
- Spreadsheets from which you want to extract or link information for use in another document, such as a word-processed document
- Spreadsheets in which descriptive formulas would be a real help

Naming cells and ranges is easy and one of the more entertaining features of the spreadsheet. We'll use the pizza spreadsheet example to show you some of the ways you can assign a name to a range of cells.

1. Highlight the range you want to name. We selected cells A2 through D7, the pizza names and sales figures by size.

2. Click Insert, and then click Range Name.
   You will see this Range Name dialog box:

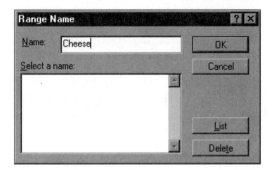

   Notice in our example that Works proposes the name Cheese, which corresponds to the text in the top left corner of the selected range. That's not terribly appropriate.

3. Highlight the text you want to change in the Name box.

4. Type a new name and click OK. We entered *Pizza Sales*.

5. Click any cell outside the range you just named.

6. Click Edit, and then click Go To (or press the F5 function key).
   Works displays a new dialog box similar to the one it uses for assigning names, with the range name you just assigned listed in the Names box.

7. Double-click the desired range name.
   Works highlights the range you named. In our example, this procedure highlights the range named Pizza Sales.

 TIP You can name an individual cell as easily as a range; simply select that one cell and go through the steps listed above.

Even though we've assigned a name to cells A2 through D7 in our example, those cells are not off-limits as far as other names are concerned. You can assign different names to sets of cells within the named range, as well as to sets of cells partly in and partly out of the range. We'll demonstrate, as follows:

- We named the range B2:B7 *Small*.

- We assigned the name *Medium* to the range C2:C7, and assigned the name *Large* to the range D2:D7.

- We assigned the name *Price-Small* to the price in cell B10, *Price-Medium* to the price in cell B11, and *Price-Large* to the price in cell B12.

- We assigned the name *Total-Small* to the total in cell B8, *Total-Medium* to the total in cell C8, and *Total-Large* in cell D8.

All these names are overkill for such a small spreadsheet, yet there's a point to be made. Even in large spreadsheets that you create, you might find that you've named so many groups of cells that you're beginning to lose track of what's what. To refresh your memory, you can use the List button in the Range Name dialog box, as follows:

1. Find an empty group of cells below or to the right of any cells containing text or data. In this case, we selected cell G11.

2. Click Insert, and then click Range Name.

3. Click the List button in the dialog box.

Works inserts a list of names and the cells they represent, beginning with the list in the cell you selected before choosing the command. Notice that Works requires two adjoining columns and the number of rows that correspond to the number of names you've assigned. If you started the list where there was insufficient room, Works would overwrite existing data with the list of names. This is why it's so important to find a vacant area of the spreadsheet large enough for listing names.

If you want to insert the list well away from your working area, and yet you want to be able to consult it freely, scroll to an empty part of the spreadsheet, select a cell, and insert the list. Next, select the list and assign it a name before scrolling back to your workspace. When you want to consult the list, use the Go To command from the Edit menu. Before you print the spreadsheet, however, be sure to check for the list and either delete it (with the Clear command) or omit it from the print area.

Range Names and Formulas

Now that you know about cells and cell ranges, you can see how helpful descriptive formulas can be. To make things a bit clearer in our spreadsheet example, we made some titles bold, added a new row title in cell A8 and a column title in cell F1, and added an empty row above Price as shown in Figure 7-10.

	A	B	C	D	E	F	G	H
1		Small	Medium	Large	Total	Small Sales		
2	Cheese	57	12	29	98	453		
3	Sausage	97	143	168	408	771		
4	Pepperoni	102	169	185	456	811		
5	Anchovy	23	17	9	49	183		
6	Onion	34	52	55	141	270		
7	Vegetarian	49	73	53	175	390		
8	Total Sales	362	466	499	1327			
9								
10	Price		Total Cost					
11	Small	7.95						
12	Medium	9.95						
13	Large	12.95						
14								
15								
16								
17								
18								
19								
20								

Zoom 100%

FIGURE 7-10

Formatting adjustments to the pizza spreadsheet prior to naming ranges

To start, select a cell that contains a formula that totals the cells in a range you named. Notice the formula on the entry bar. Without prompting, Works has replaced the original range argument in the formula with the name you assigned those cells. In our example the function =SUM(B3:B7) changed to =SUM(Small). You'll see this happen whenever you assign a name to a cell or a range of cells incorporated in a formula.

We can use assigned names in our spreadsheet example to create formulas as follows:

1. Select a cell in which you want to enter a formula and type = (an equal sign) to begin the formula. We selected cell C11.

2. Click a named cell to include in the formula. We selected cell B8 (named Total-Small) to tell Works we want that cell in the formula.

3. Enter any appropriate operators and other cell or range references to complete the formula. Here we typed * (an asterisk) and clicked cell B11 (the price).

   If you were to look at the formula on the entry bar at this point, you would see how range names were substituted for cell addresses.

4. Click the Enter button to complete the formula. You can see the result of our example in Figure 7-11.

If we hadn't assigned names to these cells, our formula would be =B8*B11. Useful, but not very descriptive. Instead, the entry bar reads

    ='Total-Small'*'Price-Small'

Much better. (Works adds the single quotation marks enclosing the names.)

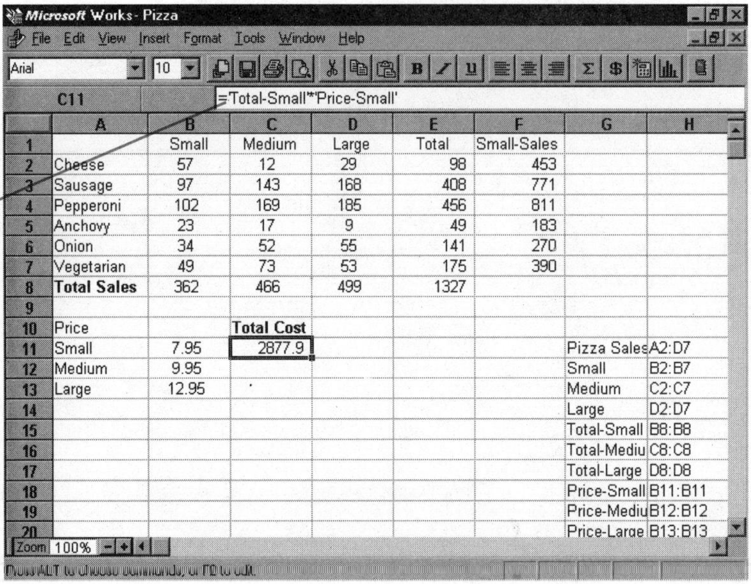

FIGURE 7-11
Creating a formula
with descriptive
range names

Range name
references in
formula

Now we'll create similar formulas for medium and large pizzas by selecting cells C11 through C13, opening the Edit menu, and then choosing the Fill Down command. The result is shown on the next page.

If it looks as though we've made a mistake, we have. Works displays 0 as the totals for medium and large pizzas. If you were to select cell C12 and look at the entry bar, you would see that Works treats names as relative references. It found the prices for each size pizza because the original formula simply referenced the cell directly to the left of the formula cell. However, Works expected to find the total sales for medium pizzas in cell B9 (one cell below the original formula's relative reference), and the total sales for large pizzas in cell B10 (two cells below the original formula's relative reference). To correct this we can edit the formulas as follows:

1. Select the cell containing the first copied formula. We selected cell C12.

	A	B	C	D
1		Small	Medium	Large
2	Cheese	57	12	29
3	Sausage	97	143	168
4	Pepperoni	102	169	185
5	Anchovy	23	17	9
6	Onion	34	52	55
7	Vegetarian	49	73	53
8	**Total Sales**	362	466	499
9				
10	Price		**Total Cost**	
11	Small	7.95	2877.9	
12	Medium	9.95	0	
13	Large	12.95	0	
14				
15				

2. Select the cell reference you want to change on the entry bar. We selected cell B9.

3. Click the correct cell to include in the formula. We selected cell C8, which contains the total sales for medium pizzas.

   Works replaces the highlighted cell reference in the formula with the name assigned to the cell you clicked. The formula is now correct, so we can continue:

4. Click the Enter button.

5. We can edit the formula for totaling large pizzas in the same way.

   Now we can create a formula to calculate a grand total, as follows:

1. We select cell C14 and use the AutoSum button to total the sales of pizzas in cells C11 through C13.

2. Then we format the range of total costs (C11:C14) as Currency using 2 decimal places.

   You can see our final pizza spreadsheet example in Figure 7-12 on the next page.

Creating a Series

One element common to many, if not most, spreadsheets is that values and formulas repeat (and even text does too). Because of its columnar format, a spreadsheet is ideal for laying out sequential sets of data such as sales by month, salaries by week, operating expenses by quarter, and so on.

We know that it's easy to fill cells either to the right or down. It's also easy to have Works generate a sequence of entries, such as 4 months in a

FIGURE 7-12
The completed
pizza spreadsheet

	A	B	C	D	E	F	G	H
1		Small	Medium	Large	Total	Small-Sales		
2	Cheese	57	12	29	98	453		
3	Sausage	97	143	168	408	771		
4	Pepperoni	102	169	185	456	811		
5	Anchovy	23	17	9	49	183		
6	Onion	34	52	55	141	270		
7	Vegetarian	49	73	53	175	390		
8	Total Sales	362	466	499	1327			
9								
10	Price		Total Cost					
11	Small	7.95	$2,877.90					
12	Medium	9.95	$4,636.70					
13	Large	12.95	$6,462.05					
14			$13,976.65					

Zoom 100%

row, 12 years, or 30 days. This can save you a great deal of time entering data.

The Fill Series command on the Edit menu is particularly useful in creating column and row titles. It can take a starting value and generate a series of numbers or dates in selected cells, increasing them by the interval you select. To demonstrate how this works we can set up a new spreadsheet as shown in Figure 7-13, which we'll call Daily Sales. Then we'll enter data by filling series, as follows:

1. Select the range of cells you want to fill with a series. We selected the range A5:A12.

   In this example, we must include cell A5 in the selection. Works needs a "seed" number to start the series. Without a starting point, Works can't carry out the Fill Series command.

FIGURE 7-13
A new spreadsheet
document in which
series of numbers
can be entered

	A	B	C	D	E	F	G	H
1	Venue Dinner Daily Sales, week of July 10, 1995							
2								
3		July 10, 1995						
4	Dinner #							
5	1							

Zoom 100%

2. Click Edit, and then click Fill Series.

When you do this, you see this dialog box:

You use this dialog box to create a series (such as 1, 2, 3) or a series of dates (such as 11/1/95, 11/2/95, 11/3/95) or even a series of days (Monday, Tuesday, Wednesday). The Step By box lets you choose the intervals within the series. For example, stepping by 2 creates the series 1, 3, 5, 7, and so on.

For this example, the series choices available are Number and Autofill. Number is an option because your starting value, 1, can only be part of a numeric series. Autofill bases the sequence on the nature of the first entry in the column. For example, filling a series beginning with Quarter 1 would produce Quarter 2, Quarter 3, and so on.

3. Click OK to create the series.

Now we'll create a second series—the days of the week—across the top of this small spreadsheet by doing the following:

4. Select the range you want to fill with a series. We selected the range B3:H3.

5. Click Edit, and then click Fill Series.

This time, Works suggests Day, which is the logical choice.

6. Click OK. Our spreadsheet example appears as shown in Figure 7-14 on the following page.

Notice that we increased the width of columns to see the series entries.

FIGURE 7-14
A spreadsheet with
two filled-in series

	A	B	C	D	E	F	G
1	Venue Dinner Daily Sales, week of July 10, 1995						
2							
3		July 10, 1995	July 11, 1995	July 12, 1995	July 13, 1995	July 14, 1995	July 15, 1995
4	Dinner #						
5	1						
6	2						
7	3						
8	4		Filled series				
9	5						
10	6						
11	7						
12	8						
13							
14							
15							
16							
17							
18							
19							
20							

Zoom 100%

You can choose Weekday if you want to skip Saturdays and Sundays. The other possible choices for a date are Month, which fills the series with monthly intervals, and Year, which steps through the series by year.

TIP For Works to know how to extend a series, it uses the first value and determines what it should be (Date, Day, Month, and so on). If you use a date as the "seed," be sure that it appears in Works' Date format, otherwise Works won't know what to do with it.

We'll continue building on this example by filling more series.

1. Type a range of numbers for the first column of data. We entered the numbers *5, 12, 9, 15, 22, 3, 11,* and *7* in the range B5:B12.

2. Working row by row, we can now fill the range C5:H12 with series of numbers by using the Fill Series command. For rows 5–7 we'll use a step interval of 3; for rows 8, 11, and 12, we'll use a step interval of 1; and for rows 9 and 10, we'll use a step interval of 2.

   Next, we entered the label *Total* in cell A14. Then we selected cell B14, and used the AutoSum button to total the numbers in column B. Finally, we used the Fill Right command to copy the formula from cell B14 to the range C14:H14.

To complete this example, we applied formatting, such as borders, bold, and italics, and turned off gridlines to create the final spreadsheet shown in the Print Preview window you see in Figure 7-15.

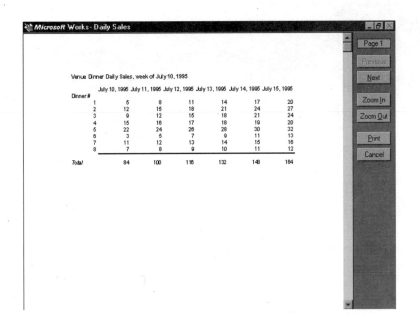

FIGURE 7-15
A spreadsheet
created by filling
cells shown in the
Print Preview
window

What If?

Far and away, the most valued feature of a spreadsheet is its ability to test different values to see the effect they'll have on your calculations. You can use many ways to set up a spreadsheet to do this. For example, you can create a table to evaluate the effects on various monthly loan payments for a series of principal amounts and rates of interest based on varying loan terms. As you can see in Figure 7-16 on the following page, each formula that calculates a monthly payment in the table can include an absolute cell reference to a cell that stores a value for the loan's term. To look at varying payment options, simply plug in different values for the term value. Each formula recalculates instantly to tell you *what* payments will be *if* a term is *x* number of months.

Using built-in logical functions is another common way to apply what-if analyses to spreadsheets. The built-in IF function can be used to create a formula that tailors the result to conditions you define. For example, IF we sell 10,000 gizmos, THEN our profit will be X, ELSE our profit will be Y. The IF function produces one of two results, depending on whether the condition you set up (*If we sell 10,000 gizmos*) is true (*our profit will be X*) or false (*our profit will be Y*). The following examples show you the basics of using the IF function. Experiment with this function. You'll learn how to use it quickly and find its use invaluable.

FIGURE 7-16
A table set up for
what-if analyses

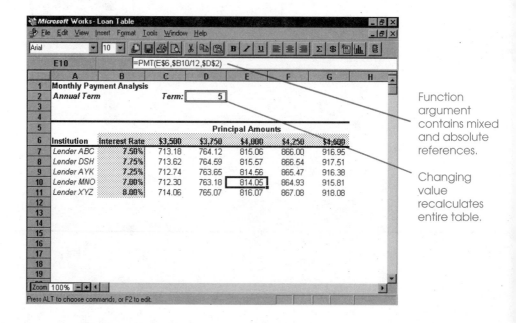

Function
argument
contains mixed
and absolute
references.

Changing
value
recalculates
entire table.

The format of the IF function is as follows:

`IF(Condition,TrueValue,FalseValue)`

In this function's argument, Condition represents a value, a comparison formula (for example, =D12<=360), or the result of a calculation. TrueValue represents the result produced if the condition is true, and FalseValue represents the result if the condition is false.

The following example (see Figure 7-17) uses the sales from four Gizmo, Inc. stores to determine how much of each month's total represents profit. The example assumes that gizmos sell for $0.99 each and that Gizmo, Inc. makes 18 percent per gizmo on sales over $10,000 and 14 percent per gizmo on sales of $10,000 or less.

We can use an IF function to carry out this logical calculation, as follows:

1. Select the cell where you want to enter the function. We selected cell B12.

2. Type =*if(* or select the IF function from the Function list discussed earlier.

3. Enter the Condition argument. To do this in our example, we clicked cell B9, and typed *>10000,* (always be sure to type the comma between arguments).

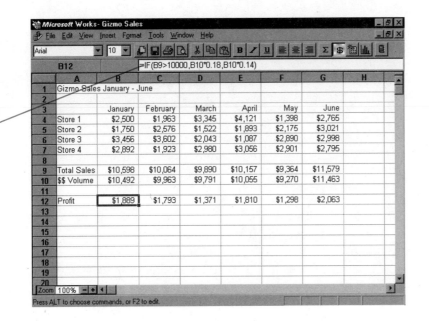

Logical IF function

FIGURE 7-17
Entering an IF
function in a cell

4. Enter the TrueValue argument. For our example we clicked cell B10 and typed *18%,*

5. Enter the FalseValue argument. For our example we clicked cell B10, typed *14%),* and pressed Enter.

    The formula is complete; as you see in Figure 7-17, it looks like this:

    ```
    =IF(B9>10000,B10*18%,B10*14%)
    ```

6. Use the Fill Right command to copy the formula and calculate additional profits. We copied it to the range C12:G12.

    Notice that on the entry bar Works converts the numbers typed as percentages into their decimal equivalents: 0.18 for 18 percent and 0.14 for 14 percent.

What Does IF Mean?

An IF function isn't the easiest set of characters to interpret. This is what your formula means, piece by piece.

=IF(B9>10000 is the conditional part of the formula. This is the part Works evaluates to check whether the condition is true or false. In other words, *Is the result in cell B9 greater than 10 thousand dollars?*

B10*0.18 is the result if the condition is true. If sales are greater than $10,000 for the month, Gizmo, Inc., makes a profit of 18 percent per gizmo.

If the condition is true, Works calculates 18 percent of the income shown in cell B10.

B10*0.14 is the result if the condition is not true. If sales are $10,000 or less for the month, Gizmo, Inc., makes only 14 percent profit. If the condition is false, Works calculates 14 percent of the income shown in cell B10.

It's a series of contingencies where you define what happens, should one or another value (either numbers or words) be met.

IFs Within IFs

Sometimes you'll want to evaluate conditions that can have more than one true/false outcome. When this happens, you can place one IF function inside another, in the same way you can nest sets of parentheses inside others when controlling the order of calculation in a formula.

In this example, for instance, Gizmo, Inc., might find that profits are 18 percent for sales over $10,500, 14 percent for sales between $10,001 and $10,500, and 12 percent for sales of $10,000 and less. To calculate profits for all three situations, we have to expand the formula. We can do that by entering this formula:

```
=IF(B9>10500,B10*.18,IF(B9>10000,B10*.14,B10*.12))
```

Here's what this IF function does. If the value in cell B9 is greater than $10,500, Works multiplies the income in cell B10 by 0.18. If the condition is false, but the value in cell B9 is greater than $10,000, multiply the income in cell B10 by 0.14. Otherwise, multiply the value in cell B9 (now down to any value of $10,000 or less) by 0.12.

TIP If you enter information incorrectly on the entry bar, Works will try to point out the error and give you a chance to fix the entry.

Functions like IF are very powerful, *if* a bit intimidating at first sight. Be patient and practice. You'll find that these functions will become everyday tools.

Calculating with Dates and Times

Although numeric values are the most common entries in spreadsheets, using calculations with dates and times can be quite common, too. Date and time values can be used for "stamping" spreadsheets, tracking progress, and calculating elapsed times.

Works gives you two ways to use dates and times. The first is as a fixed value, the second is as an entry that's updated when you open the spreadsheet.

To display the date or time, Works starts with a serial number based on your computer's internal clock and calculates the appropriate result. Dates are formatted in long or short form, and times are formatted on the basis of a 12-hour or a 24-hour clock. Here's how Works presents each of these formats.

Time	12-Hour	24-Hour
Hour, minute, second	02:26:31 P.M.	14:26:31
Hour, minute	02:26 P.M.	14:26

Date	Long Format	Short Format
Month, day, year	December 1, 1995	12/1/95
Month, year	December 1995	12/95
Month, day	December 1	12/1
Month only	December	No short form

Open a new spreadsheet and try entering the time and date in each of these formats.

Entering Any Date or Time

One way to enter times and dates is to simply type them. Use this method when you want one or more entries that don't represent the current time or date. You can follow one of the formats shown in the preceding table, or you can type the time or date in one form and then use the Number command on the Format menu to change the format, as follows:

1. Select a cell and widen it to accommodate about 15 characters.

2. Type a date in short form and click the Enter button. We typed *12/1/95.*

    Now we can change the date's format to the long form.

3. Click Format, and then click Number.

4. Click Date in the Format Cells dialog box's Format box.

5. Click a Date format option in the Date box, like the one shown here.

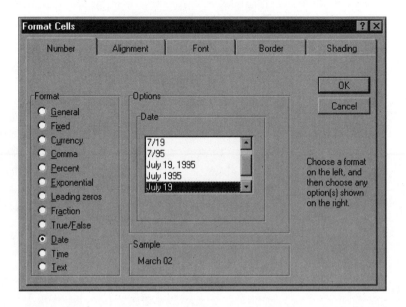

6. Click OK.

   The date's display changes to the selected format, such as December 1, 1995.

Entering the Current Date or Time

You can use two other methods to enter the current date or time. One method, which makes use of the NOW function, inserts a serial number in the cell. This number consists of an integer and a decimal. The integer part represents the number of days that have elapsed since January 1, 1900; the decimal part represents the portion of the current day (24 hours) that has elapsed. When you use the NOW function, Works updates the serial number whenever you reopen the spreadsheet and, in doing so, recalculates and updates the time or date as well.

After you use the NOW function, you can use the Format Cells dialog box to convert the serial number to either a time or a date, in whatever format you want. You can also switch the format from time to date, or vice versa. We'll demonstrate the NOW function, as follows:

1. Select an empty cell, and type *=NOW()*

2. Works inserts a number in the cell, such as 34886.94306, which corresponds to July 7, 1995, and 10:38 PM.

3. Click the date or time format you prefer, and then click OK.

 TIP Another way to format the current date or time, without having to click in the Format dialog box is to use the keyboard shortcuts Ctrl+; for the date and Ctrl+Shift+; for the time. When you use this method, Works inserts the date or time as a fixed entry that won't be updated, unless you specifically change it.

Using Dates and Times in Formulas

The Works spreadsheet can even stretch its wings a bit and pretend to be a project-management program of sorts. Because Works can use dates and times in calculations, you can use the spreadsheet to track elapsed times.

When you use dates and times as part of a formula, either you can refer to the cells that contain them, or you can type the dates or times as part of the formula. If you choose the latter approach, however, enter dates in short form. Also, be sure to enclose the date or time in single quotation marks (for example, '12/1/95'). If you don't, Works won't recognize the entry as a valid date or time. Figure 7-18 on the next page shows an example of a simple tracking spreadsheet that uses time and date information.

If you want to create this spreadsheet or a similar one, keep the following points in mind:

- The formula for calculating days elapsed subtracts the start date from the end date, not vice versa. Because Works doesn't compute weekends and holidays in its calculations, column C gives the number of weekends and holidays to subtract from the total. (The complete formula is shown on the entry bar.)

- A SUM function totals the number of vacation and sick days in columns D and H. The AutoSum button could have been used instead.

- Extra cells are left blank for additional entries. Entering additional formulas is a simple matter of filling the extra cells. If you want,

FIGURE 7-18
A spreadsheet that
tracks elapsed
days in time periods

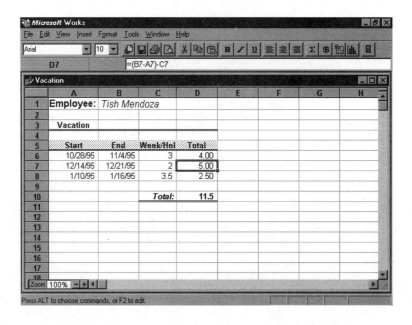

you can omit the extra columns and add new ones as needed with the Insert Row/Column command.

All other parts of this spreadsheet should be old news, now that you're an accomplished Works worker.

TIP To determine the number of days between two dates, just create a formula that subtracts one serial value from the other (for example, 35054–35047). Be sure to format the cell in which the result appears so that it's a single number of days.

Using Templates

Chances are that your spreadsheets will tend to follow certain forms and patterns. When you find yourself repeating layouts and formatting, remember that Works allows you to set up and save templates. A *spreadsheet template* is a file that's generally set up with text (titles) and formulas but little or no data. You can use a template to create a spreadsheet by opening the template; entering data, which causes the preset formulas to calculate results; and saving the document in a new file with a different name. This preserves the template file and saves the data in a new spreadsheet file. To create a single spreadsheet template that opens whenever you start the Works spreadsheet, do the following:

1. Create the layout you want.

2. To save it as a template, open the File menu, and then choose the Save As command. The Save As dialog box appears.

3. Select Template. The Save As Template dialog box appears.

4. Type a name for the template file, and click OK.

 TIP Always check to make sure that WORKS SS is displayed in the Save File As Type box. If it isn't displayed, select it.

Coming Next

A picture is often worth much more than a thousand words. Much of the data that you work with in a spreadsheet can convey information more effectively if it's presented in a chart. Chapter 8 shows you how to create and enhance those charts.

Chapter 8

Creating Charts

Would you like to have someone read the following two series of numbers to you: 5, 7, 11, and 17, versus 1, 4, 9, and 16? Or, would you rather look at the chart you see below? From which presentation of information do you learn more?

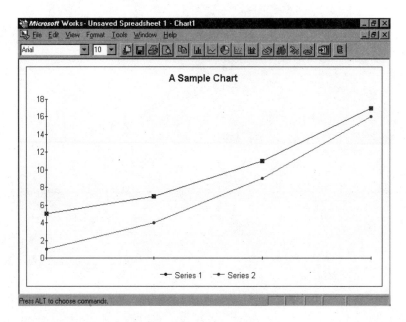

The corresponding numbers in these two series differ by 4, 3, 2, and 1, with succeeding pairs of numbers coming closer and closer together. You probably saw the pattern more quickly in the chart than you did when hearing the numbers recited. Patterns are easier to recognize in graphics than they are in independent sets of numbers, letters, symbols, or other characters. A picture is still worth a thousand words.

When you work with numbers, charts can be invaluable in helping to visualize patterns of any type, including trends, comparisons, ranges, or fluctuations. Look at business or academic documents and you'll find that they're often filled with impressive charts.

One scatter chart can be clearer than pages of data to the scientist trying to figure out how many starfish are on the bottom of the sea as a function of sea depth. A set of bar charts or line charts can be more useful than piles of printouts in helping an economist interpret the effects of gasoline prices on the cost of fruit and vegetables.

Because of the importance of charts, we'll devote an entire chapter to their creation and modification. Besides, many people feel that creating and working with charts is the most enjoyable aspect of using Works.

Creating a Chart

Works can chart spreadsheet data with a click of the mouse button when you point to the New Chart button on the toolbar. All you need to do is use a spreadsheet to provide the values you want charted. We'll use the pizza spreadsheet example below to demonstrate charting data.

	A	B	C	D	E	F	G	H	
1		Small	Medium	Large	Total				
2	Cheese	57	12	29	98				
3	Sausage	97	143	168	408				
4	Pepperoni	102	169	185	456				
5	Anchovy	23	17	9	49				
6	Onion	34	52	55	141				
7	Vegetarian	49	73	53	175				
8	**Total Sales**	362	466	499	1327				
9									
10	Price		**Total Cost**						
11	Small	7.95	$2,877.90						
12	Medium	9.95	$4,636.70						
13	Large	12.95	$6,462.05						
14			$13,976.65						
15									
16									
17									
18									
19									
20									

Zoom 100%

To create a chart, you begin by selecting the range of cells containing the data you want charted. A range can consist of as many as six consecutive rows or columns. Although you can include blank rows or columns of cells in the range, it's best not to—because Works will plot the "values" of those empty cells or treat text differently from the way you might expect. At best, the chart might look unprofessional. At worst, it could be misleading.

In the pizza spreadsheet example, we have a made-to-order range of cells to chart (A2:D7), which lists sales of six types of pizza in three sizes. We can easily turn this data into a chart, as follows:

1. Select the range of data to chart. We selected the range A1:D7.

2. Click the New Chart button on the toolbar.

   Works shows you the New Chart dialog box on the following page, where you can select the type of chart you want to use and make adjustments.

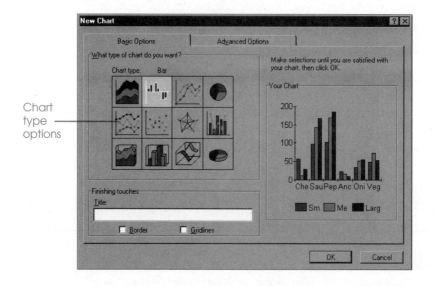

Chart
type
options

The default chart type Works uses when you click the New Chart button is a bar chart. We'll stick with the bar chart for now.

3. Click OK.

Almost immediately, Works opens a new window, named Pizza - Chart1, and displays a bar chart, as shown in Figure 8-1.

The bar chart is the default chart type Works uses when you click the New Chart button. Notice that Works has turned text into labels along the

FIGURE 8-1

The default bar chart for the pizza spreadsheet

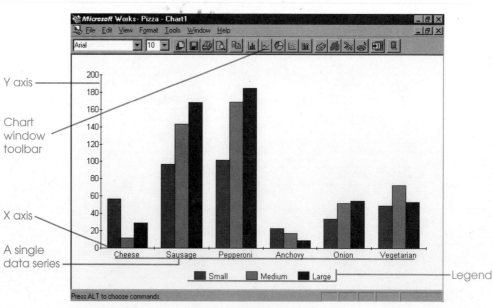

Y axis

Chart window toolbar

X axis

A single data series

Legend

horizontal axis of the chart. When the first column or top row of a range of cells contains text, Works turns the text into labels, as shown in the illustration.

The New Chart dialog box allows you to select from 12 different types of charts; add a title, a border, and gridlines; and provide information so that Works charts the data in the proper direction. Best of all, you can see everything you have specified (in the Sample area) and make changes before you click OK to get the final chart.

Some Charting Terminology

Even though charting is easy, knowing how Works "views" a chart and the data in it can help you create a chart easily and quickly. The best way to develop a feel for the charting process is to examine both the chart and the spreadsheet.

When you compare the cells you selected with the chart Works produced, you can see that Works rotated the spreadsheet cells 90 degrees. This happens when the selection includes more rows than columns. When the selection includes more columns than rows, Works keeps the original orientation. Works was designed to make data as visually informative as possible.

Except for circular pie charts, all charts (such as the one you see in Figure 8-1) have both a horizontal, or X, axis and a vertical, or Y, axis. Works refers to the X axis as the category axis (the type of pizza in Figure 8-1) and the Y axis as the value axis (the number of pizzas sold in Figure 8-1). The category axis identifies the values being charted. The value axis is the measure against which values in a line, bar, or scatter chart are plotted.

The value axis of the chart is divided into units against which Works plots the values in the cells you selected for charting. Works determines the lowest and highest values for you, depending on the smallest and largest values in the range. As you will learn later in this chapter, you can change these values to modify the way the charted data appears.

See Also For more information on *changing data to modify a chart*, see "Modifying a Chart" on page 287 of this chapter.

When you chart more than one set of data, as we did in Figure 8-1 with small, medium, and large pizzas, Works uses a different color or pattern to represent the values in each set. And if you don't have a color printer, Works automatically uses a pattern to represent colors. You'll discover more about this feature later in the chapter.

Finally, note that each series of values is given its own color (or pattern). A series (such as small, medium, or large) is a related group of values from a single row or column in the range selected for charting. The number of small pizzas forms one series in the chart, just as Glop, Son of Glop, and Return of Son of Glop would form a recognizable (if uninspiring) series of films.

TIP   You can easily tell which cell range is included in each series. In the chart window, choose Go To from the Edit menu. Then if you double-click on any range, you'll return to the spreadsheet and that range.

Saving a Chart

The process of saving a chart can be so simple that you literally don't have to think about it. Works links charts to the spreadsheets from which they're created, so saving one or more charts is merely a matter of saving the spreadsheet file through a standard Save dialog box. Even if you forget about a new or changed chart and proceed to close the spreadsheet, Works reminds you when you choose the Close command. Because the chart is part of the spreadsheet, when you open one, you also open the other. To select a chart once it's been saved and closed, just select the corresponding spreadsheet and the chart will be available on the Window menu.

The Chart Toolbar

The chart toolbar that appears at the top of the work area is shown on the next page. Like any other toolbar, it contains a set of buttons that makes working with charts fast and efficient.

You'll find many of the same features on this toolbar that you've seen on the word processor and spreadsheet toolbars, but here you will also find a set of buttons, each representing a particular type of chart. Keep these in mind as we now discuss changing chart types and the different kinds of charts available for each type.

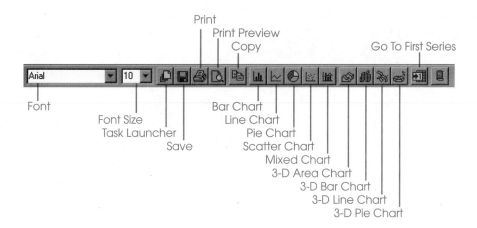

Changing Chart Types

Although Works creates a bar chart by default, you can choose from several other types of charts, all of which are available through the New Chart dialog box or on buttons on the chart toolbar.

The last chart button on the right (the Go To 1st Series button) is used to modify a series in the spreadsheet from which the chart was generated.

All the chart types are available through the New Chart dialog box, but not all of these options are available on the toolbar. If you can't find the particular type of chart you want on the toolbar, open the New Chart dialog box by choosing the Create New Chart command from the Tools menu.

After you've created a basic bar chart for spreadsheet data, you can change chart types at any time to see which type best suits the data you're charting. Before you get more involved in the whys and wherefores of creating charts, you might like to see what your chart looks like in other formats.

Now we'll demonstrate what the pizza data looks like as a line chart, as follows.

1. Click the Line Chart button on the toolbar.

   As with all chart type buttons, the Chart Type dialog box appears. This dialog box expands your choices even further, showing you both the basic types and variations of the chart you selected.

   In the following sections, we'll transform our chart several times to see how the same data is represented in some of the different chart types. For now, we'll change our chart to a line chart.

2. Click OK to see a line chart.

TIP You already know about "font junk," where different fonts, sizes, and styles are mixed beyond repair (or understanding!). The same thing can happen with charts. Not all data is compatible with all types of charts; certain data must be illustrated using only one type of chart. Be careful, and be sure your chart says what the data says, not just what you want it to say.

3. Now, click the Bar Chart button, and then click OK.

Bar Charts and When to Use Them

Bar charts are often used for comparing values such as the following examples:

- Total sales of Arbor Shoes, by region, for the last four quarters

- The U.S. national deficit compared to tax revenues for the years 1980 through 1990

- Consumption of electricity by your household for each of the last 12 months

Works produces six types of bar charts. To see them, follow these steps:

1. Click the Bar Chart button and you'll see the Chart Type dialog box as shown in Figure 8-2.

2. Click the Variations tab to see the six types of bar-chart variations that Works offers, as shown in Figure 8-3.

Notice from the examples in the dialog box that Works charts positive values above the X axis and negative values below it. To make values easier to interpret, the bar chart can include horizontal gridlines (option 4) or it can print the actual value above or below each bar (option 5).

The stacked bar charts in options 2 and 3 "add" series values to produce a single bar for each category on the X axis. We can see how this works, as follows:

1. Double-click option 2 to stack the series values.

   This creates a bar equivalent to the sum of its parts for each category.

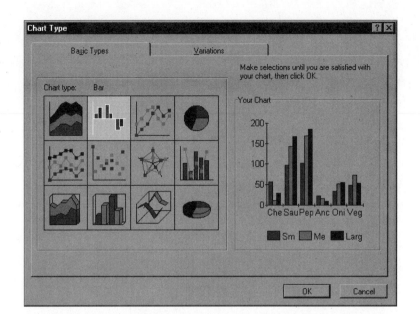

FIGURE 8-2
The Chart Type
dialog box

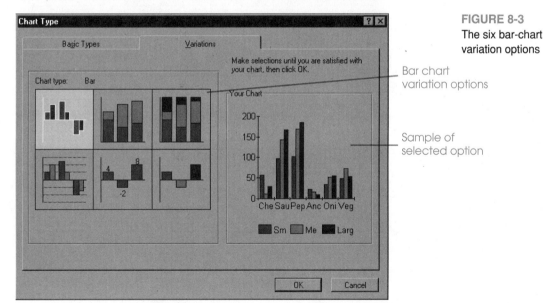

FIGURE 8-3
The six bar-chart
variation options

Bar chart
variation options

Sample of
selected option

2. Click the Bar Chart button again, click the Variations tab, and double-click option 3.

  This selection represents the parts of each bar as a percentage of the total for each category.

Line Charts and When to Use Them

Line charts are useful for showing trends and fluctuations over time, such as:

■ Atlantic and Pacific tuna catches over the last decade

■ Number of travelers per month on three major airlines

■ Ice cream sales in Phoenix and Minneapolis from January through December

Six line-chart variation options are available, as shown in Figure 8-4. To see them on your screen, click the Line Chart button on the toolbar and then click the Variations tab. Most of the line charts use markers to indicate individual values and to distinguish one series from another by color or shape. Works uses different-colored circles on a color screen and solid shapes, such as circles, squares, and diamonds, on a black-and-white screen. If you want, you can change the markers with the Shading and Color command on the Format menu.

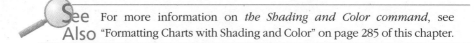

See Also For more information on *the Shading and Color command*, see "Formatting Charts with Shading and Color" on page 285 of this chapter.

If markers aren't important to your chart, you can choose option 2 to display lines alone. Conversely, if the lines aren't important, you can choose option 3 and display markers only. Options 4 and 5 are standard

FIGURE 8-4

The six line-chart variation options

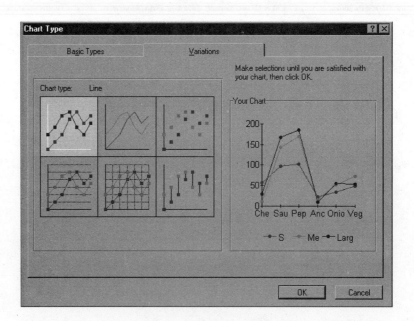

line charts, but with either horizontal or both horizontal and vertical gridlines.

Option 6 looks a bit odd for a line chart, but it's well suited for stock prices and similar values in which highs and lows are as important as trends over time, or even more so. This variation differs from the others because it uses markers and vertical lines, instead of continuous lines, to show the range between the lowest and highest values in each set. If you have intermediate values, Works adds markers on the line to show the position of each intermediate value, relative to the lowest and highest positions.

To turn the pizza chart example into a line chart, we can double-click on any available option.

Whole and Sliced Pies and When to Use Them

Both eye-catching and easy to interpret, pie charts are useful in any situation in which the parts need to be seen in relation to the whole, such as poll results, census findings, federal spending, state budgets, city taxes, and personal income and expenses.

Pie charts show a single set of values as ratios or as slices of an entire pie. Pie charts are commonly used for demographic reports such as:

- Percentage of households in various income ranges that have one or more computers

- Proportion of Republicans who voted

- Percentage of total time spent with clients

Creating a pie chart is straightforward. To demonstrate we'll use the pizza spreadsheet and its highlighted range A1:D7, so the pizza types (cheese, onion, and so on) will appear as labels on the chart.

1. Click the Pie Chart button.

   You'll see the now-familiar Chart Type dialog box with the pie chart type highlighted.

2. Click the Variations tab.

   The six pie-chart variations appear in the dialog box shown in Figure 8-5 on the following page. Notice that you can create a pie chart with category labels, percentages, or labels *and* percentages.

3. Double-click option 5 to create a pie chart that shows the percentage each slice represents.

265

FIGURE 8-5

The pie-chart
variation options

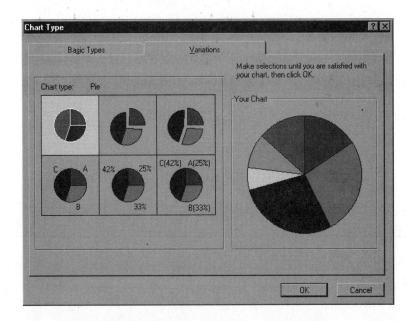

Aside from whether to add labels, your biggest decision when creating pie charts is whether and what part or parts to explode, or separate, from the rest. If you choose option 2, Works explodes the first value outward. Choose option 3, and Works simulates the Big Bang and explodes the entire pie.

If you don't want to explode the entire pie, but you do want to explode a slice other than the first, create a standard pie chart and do the following:

1. Click Format, and then click Shading and Color.

2. Click the slice you want to explode.

3. Click Explode Slice.

4. Click Format.

5. Click Close.

You can also select the pattern and color you'd like applied to each slice. You can repeat this procedure to explode additional slices. When you've finished, click the Close button. You can also use the Shading and Color command to create an exploded pie chart with labels, percentages, or both—something you can't do directly from the set of pie-chart variation options. In Figure 8-6, we've changed patterns, altered colors,

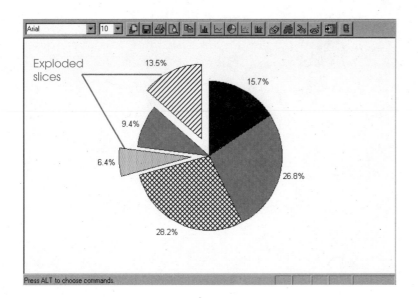

FIGURE 8-6
Exploding slices
and applying colors
and patterns

and exploded two slices from the pie chart representing pizza spreadsheet data.

TIP You can double-click on any slice to display the
Shading and Color dialog box. No need to make a trip
to the menu.

NOTE Works allows you to create only eight charts without
saving and closing one. To delete a chart once you've reached
that limit of eight, click Tools, and then click Delete Chart. Works
will list the charts already created. Select the one you want to
delete, and click Delete. Click OK when you're finished.

Stacked Line Charts and When to Use Them

Stacked line charts are line charts with a dash of stacked bar chart tossed
in. Instead of plotting values independently, stacked line charts add or
subtract the values in each series so that the marker in the topmost line
reflects the combined total.

We can take a look at a stacked line chart for our pizza spreadsheet
data by doing the following:

1. Click Tools, and then click the Create New Chart command.

2. Click the Stacked Line chart option.

   This chart type must be selected in the New Chart dialog box. (There's no Stacked Line Chart button on the toolbar.)

3. Click the Gridlines check box in the Finishing Touches box.

4. Click OK.

   Now the pizza spreadsheet data is represented in a stacked line chart with horizontal and vertical gridlines that make it easier to read, as you see in Figure 8-7.

FIGURE 8-7
A stacked line chart with gridlines turned on

Top markers reflect totals

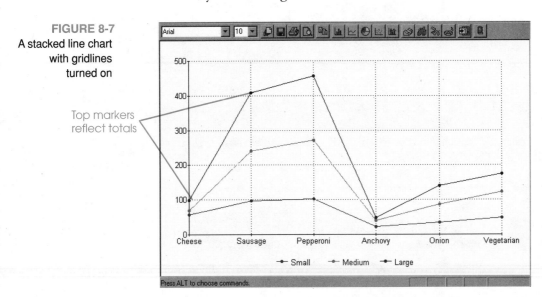

5. Click in the spreadsheet window or select its name from the Window menu.

   By comparing the chart with the totals for each type (category) of pizza, we can see that Works has added the values for each series (small, medium, and large) in constructing the line chart. Note that the markers in the topmost line correspond to the combined total for each category. In contrast, a regular line chart for the same range of cells would plot values (and lines) independently.

X-Y (Scatter) Charts and When to Use Them

Scatter charts show relationships between sets of data by plotting values against both the horizontal and vertical axes of the chart. Bar, line, and stacked line charts use the X axis for categories, whereas scatter charts use both the X and Y axes as scales for numeric values. Each corresponding X and Y point is graphed.

Typical examples of data used in scatter charts show the relationship between the following items:

- Height and weight

- Education and income

- Amount of ice cream consumed and daily temperature

Other charts might compare age with auto accidents or sick time reported against overtime worked. If you're a scientist, you might use scatter charts to see if a relationship exists between hours of light and flower production for geraniums.

You can see the options for scatter charts in the dialog box shown in Figure 8-8.

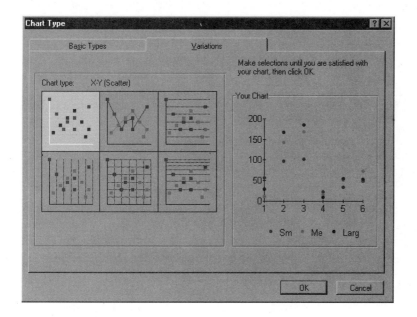

FIGURE 8-8
Scatter plot chart variations

> **TIP** Scatter plots are very useful for tracking the change that occurs in one variable while another changes as well. These changes don't reflect a causal relationship (where one change causes another), but rather only an association between the two variables.

Combination Charts and When to Use Them

A combination chart is, as its name indicates, a combination of a bar and a line chart. Because you can include a second vertical axis on the right of a chart, the combination chart is especially useful when you want to chart two differently scaled series. Combination charts are also valuable when you want to draw a clear distinction between two series of values. You might, for example, choose this type of chart when plotting

- The asking and selling prices for houses
- Sales volumes for new and used cars
- Average loan amounts during periods of different interest rates

As you can see in the Chart Type dialog box shown in Figure 8-9, there are four types of combination charts.

FIGURE 8-9
The combination chart variations

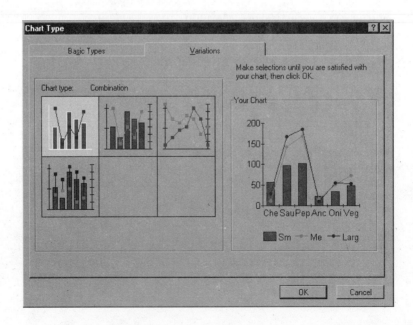

TIP On the toolbar, combination charts are labeled Mixed Chart in the tool tip box that appears when you point to the button.

Options 2 and 3 are useful for displaying differently scaled values. Option 4 is a likely candidate for financial data—for example, bars showing stock volumes and range lines showing high, low, and closing prices.

We'll demonstrate creating a combination chart, using a spreadsheet containing average new and used car prices over a five-year period, as shown in Figure 8-10.

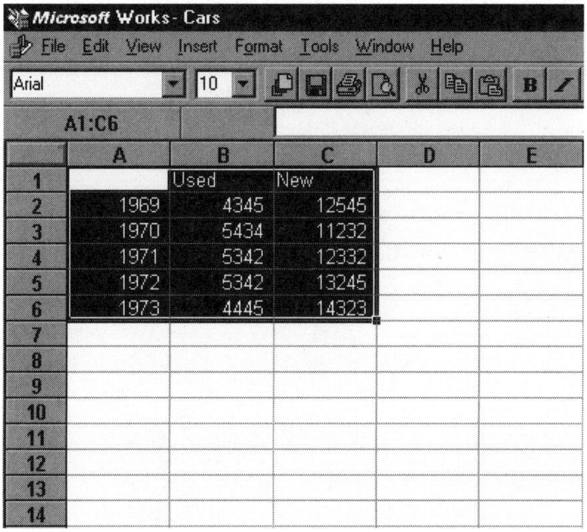

FIGURE 8-10
A spreadsheet of new and used car prices

The steps are as follows:

1. Select the range to be charted. We selected the range A1:C6 in this example.

2. Click the New Chart button.

3. Click the Combination chart type.

4. Click OK.

    The resulting chart is shown in Figure 8-11 on the next page.

FIGURE 8-11
A simple
combination chart

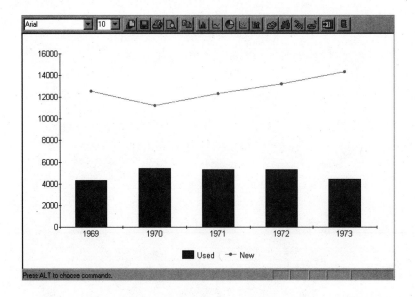

FIGURE 8-11
A simple
combination chart

Dressing Up a Chart

Works creates great charts, as you've discovered. But your own personal imprint on them makes them even more attractive and informative. After you've created a chart, you can do many things to change its appearance and add emphasis to the information it conveys. You can add titles, include legends that identify series within categories, and insert labels that clarify some or all of the data points in the chart. You can also add a second Y axis, as well as define or change the intervals and scales that Works uses for both axes. To enhance a chart's appearance, you can also change fonts, add boldface and other character styles, and apply or change colors and patterns.

We'll deal with all these features in the remainder of this chapter.

Adding Titles to Your Charts

Titles might be your best bet for making a chart more informative. Works lets you add a main title, a subtitle, and titles for the X axis, the Y axis, and (if you include one) the right vertical axis.

To include any or all of these on a chart, use the Titles command on the chart window's Edit menu. Remember that you're working in the chart window when you make these modifications.

To demonstrate adding titles to a chart, we'll use the pizza spreadsheet example. First we'll create a default bar chart by selecting the range A1:D7. Then we can add a chart title and a subtitle, as follows:

1. Click Edit, and then click Titles.

    You'll see this Edit Titles dialog box:

2. Enter the chart's title and subtitle. We entered the text shown above.

3. Click OK.

As easily as that, you can add titles to your charts, without worrying about spacing or alignment. You simply type the title you want. To delete a title, reverse the command: click the Titles command, highlight the title you don't want, press the Del key, and then click OK.

Take a look at the chart in Figure 8-12 on the following page to see how the titles look and how much more informative the chart is.

Creating a Title from Existing Text

You can also add a title to a chart without having to enter any new text, merely by using text that already exists on the spreadsheet. Instead of typing the title in the Edit Titles dialog box, type the address of the cell containing the text you want. Then, when Works carries out the Titles command, it will use the text in the cell you selected as a title on your chart.

You can also use range names instead of cell references. If a name refers to more than a single cell, however, Works will use the contents of the first cell in the range as the title. Recall that in the pizza spreadsheet example we assigned the range name *Small* to the range B2:B7. If we were to type *Small* in the Edit Titles dialog box, Works would use the first value, 57, as the title of the chart.

FIGURE 8-12
A chart with titles

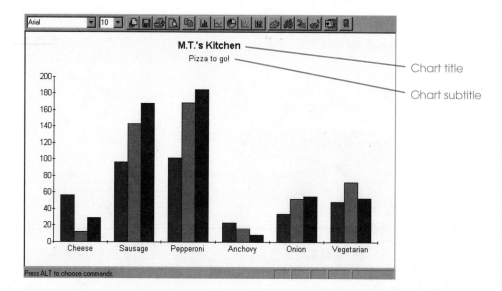

If you're going to use range names, keep in mind that Works treats them as references to cells. If you want to use a range name as text, rather than as a cell reference, precede the name with a double quotation mark (").

For example, the name Pizza Sales refers to the range A1:D7 in the spreadsheet. To use this range name as the title for the vertical axis, you would type *"Pizza Sales* in the Edit Titles dialog box. The double quotation mark tells Works to treat the name as text. This situation is comparable to typing a double quotation mark in front of a number when you want to enter the number in a cell as text, not as a value.

Adding a Legend to Your Chart

A legend is the key to the color, pattern, or marker used for each series in a category. In the pizza spreadsheet example, the three different series (small, medium, and large) are each represented with different colors. They could just as well be indicated by different textures or patterns.

Like the marks, symbols, and colors on a map, a blueprint, or a diagram, legends help the reader interpret the material correctly and with the least amount of effort. You can include legends on all but pie charts. (You identify slices on pie charts by choosing the chart option that includes percentages, categories, or both when you create the pie chart.) Works automatically assigns legends to a chart if no legends were selected when the chart was created. It uses the names Series 1, Series 2, and so on.

When you select a range to represent in a bar, line, or scatter chart, Works creates the appropriate legends for you if the range includes row or column titles for each series being plotted. Note that this isn't the same as creating category labels on the X axis. Category labels (such as Cheese and Anchovy in the pizza chart) identify the categories Works is charting.

On the other hand, legends identify the values (such as small, medium, and large) that are plotted. To see the difference, we'll demonstrate creating some legends, as follows:

1. Click Edit, and then click Legend/Series Labels.

    When you do this, you'll see this Edit Legend/Series Labels dialog box.

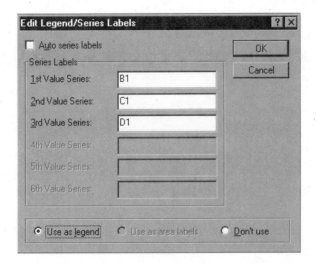

    You can see above that the information in cell B1 is being used as the label for the legend for series #1, the information in cell C1 as the label for the legend for series #2, and the information in cell D1 to label the legend in series #3. You should also notice—and this is important—that the Use As Legend option button at the bottom of the dialog box is checked. This means that Works will use these labels as legend labels.

2. Type the cell references for the cells containing the text you want to use as legend entries in the Edit Legend/Series Labels dialog box. We used those you see above.

TIP If the Auto Series Labels check box at the top left of the Edit Legend/Series Labels dialog box is checked, Works will automatically insert Series 1, Series 2, and so on as part of the Auto Legend feature. To enter different legends, be sure this box is not checked. As in creating titles, you can use cell references to spreadsheet text, rather than typing the text yourself. To use text that's also a range name, insert a double quotation mark before the range name to indicate that the name is to be treated as text, not as a cell reference.

3. Click OK to create the legend.

At the bottom of the chart, below the category labels, Works creates three legend entries next to three small boxes showing the color or pattern used for the values plotted for small, medium, and large pizzas. If this were a line chart, Works would display markers, rather than colors or patterns, yet the result would be the same—more information to help you and your audience better understand the contents of the chart.

Adding Labels to Your Charts

Titles, legends, and labels form a descending sequence for identifying chart elements. Titles identify all or part of the chart. Legends identify key elements. Labels identify actual values. You can label values on a bar or line chart, but not on a pie chart. For a pie chart, select the chart option (4, 5, or 6) that includes labels.

The easiest and most common way to label data is to include the actual value for each data point. You can also label data with text or other information by using existing entries from the spreadsheet or by typing new entries for use as labels. In some stand-alone spreadsheets like Microsoft Excel, you can insert such labels directly on the chart, but you can't do that in Works. To create labels, follow these steps:

1. With a chart window active, click Edit, and then click Data Labels.

This Edit Data Labels dialog box appears:

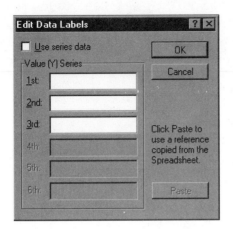

The Use Series Data check box at the top is all you need to label a chart with the actual values plotted.

2. Click the Use Series Data check box.

3. Click OK.

You'll see the chart's series labeled, as shown in Figure 8-13. Choosing this label option overrides any others you specify in the rest of the dialog box.

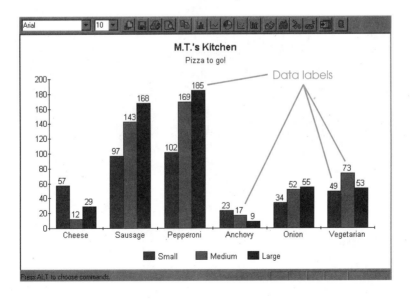

FIGURE 8-13
Labeling series in a chart

The Value (Y) Series box is where you enter the references of cells containing the labels you want to use. To ensure that values are labeled correctly, be sure you understand which values are included in the first, second, and subsequent Y series. If you need to check, cancel this command and choose Go To from the Edit menu. Works will display the cell ranges for each series in the Go To dialog box.

The OK, Cancel, and Help buttons in the dialog box work as you'd expect, but the Paste button is new. When you want to use cell contents other than plotted values as data labels, you can copy the information from the spreadsheet to the Clipboard and then use the Paste button to insert the copy in one of the Value (Y) Series boxes.

Now we'll return to the pizza spreadsheet example and assign a different type of label.

1. Type the text you want to use for data labels in the appropriate cells. We entered *S* in cell B1, *M* in cell C1, and *L* in cell D1.

2. Return to the chart. (Select it from the Window menu.)

3. Click Edit, and then click Data Labels.

4. Click the Use Series Data check box to turn the option off.

5. Type the appropriate cell references. We entered *B1* for the 1st Value (Y) Series, *C1* for the 2nd, and *D1* for the 3rd.

6. Click OK.

    The value labels disappear and are replaced by S, M, and L at the top of the three series bars in the first chart category, as you see in Figure 8-14.

Now go back to the previous Small, Medium, and Large series labels.

Adding a Second Vertical Axis

In bar, line, and scatter charts, Works displays a single Y axis by default. You can add a second vertical axis at the right edge of the chart when it's needed to improve readability or to show two different scales.

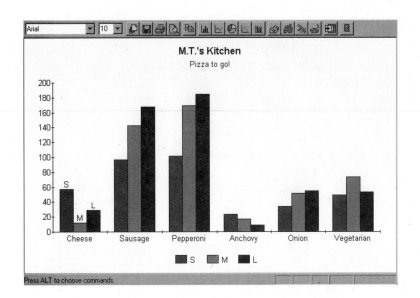

FIGURE 8-14
New value labels in
the pizza chart

To add a second vertical axis, you use the Two Vertical (Y) Axes command on the Format menu. We can use this command to create a second vertical axis on the pizza chart, as follows:

1. Click Format, and then click Two Vertical (Y) Axes.

2. You'll see this Format Two Vertical Axes dialog box:

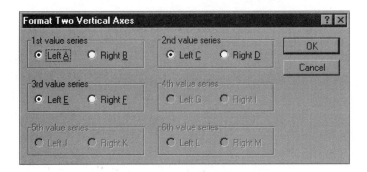

The dialog box might seem a bit cluttered at first, but the contents are easy to interpret. There are boxes for six series—the most Works can handle in a single chart. For each series, you can choose an axis on the left or on the right. (The letters A through M represent the keys you press to choose each of the options if you prefer using the keyboard rather than the mouse.) Notice that only the first three boxes are active, because there are only three series in the pizza chart example.

When you have a single vertical axis, Works automatically turns on the Left option for each plotted series. To create a right vertical axis scaled to the values in a particular series, click the Right option in that series box, as follows:

1. Click the Right option in the 1st Value Series box.

2. Click OK to create the right vertical axis.

    The new chart with a right axis added is shown in Figure 8-15.

FIGURE 8-15

Adding another Y axis to a chart

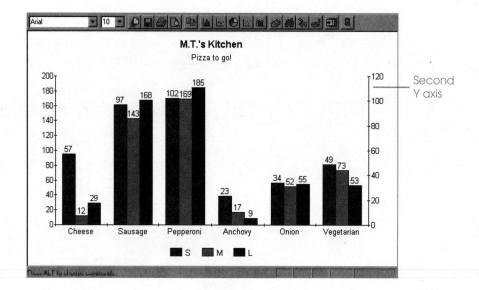

Notice in our example that the new axis has a different maximum value (120), even though it defaults to the same 20-pizza intervals used on the left axis. This happened because Works used the maximum and minimum values in the first value series to create the scale. This series, which contains the number of small pizzas sold, has a smaller range (23 to 102) than do the other series; thus, Works has created a "smaller" scale.

Notice, too, that creating a right axis that's scaled differently from the left one can create some potentially confusing results. The bars for the first value series are no longer proportional to the bars in the other series, even though they all represent the same basic information. That's because Works has to fit the same amount of information in an even smaller space (with the new axis on the right).

A better approach would be to create a right axis that's identical to the left one. You follow the same steps as before, with one minor change: you click the Right option in all three series boxes. You'll end up with two identical axes because Works will fit the largest range for a series.

Changing the Scale of an Axis

Even though Works excels at figuring out an appropriate scale for the values it plots, you'll sometimes want to change an aspect of the scale.

For example, you might want to unclutter the Y axis by leaving larger intervals between units, or to change the proportions of the bars in a chart by using a logarithmic scale based on a multiplication factor, rather than on a set of equal values.

By changing the extreme values on the Y axis, you can artificially increase or decrease differences represented by lines. In Figure 8-16 you can see two charts that plot the same information. The one on the left has a range of 30 to 70, and the one on the right has a range of 0 to 70. You can see how the differences on the chart with the larger range appear to be larger than those shown on the other chart, even though they're actually the same.

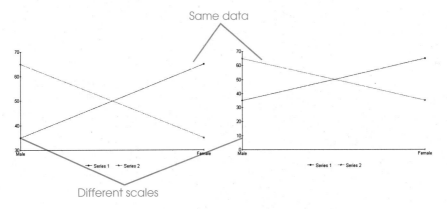

FIGURE 8-16

The same charted data using a shorter scale (left) and a longer scale (right)

The Vertical (Y) Axis, the Right Vertical Axis (if you've added a second axis), and the Horizontal (X) Axis commands on the Format menu let you change the scale of the left and right Y axes on a bar, line, or scatter chart. Each command displays the following Format Vertical Axis dialog box.

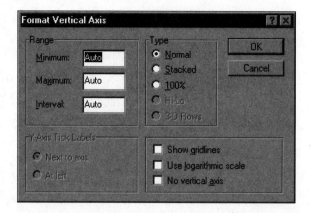

Note the following aspects of the Format Vertical Axis dialog box:

■ The Minimum and Maximum boxes let you set the smallest and largest values on the scale. The Auto setting lets Works determine these values.

■ Interval lets you specify how large the steps between units should be. Again, the Auto setting lets Works do the work.

■ The entries in the Type box set the type of scale:

❑ Normal for charts like the current one.

❑ Stacked for stacked bar or stacked line charts in which each value contributes to a total.

❑ 100% for stacked bar charts in which each value is represented as a proportion of 100 percent.

❑ Hi-Lo for line charts in which you display high and low ranges, as in stock values.

❑ 3-D Rows for rows in which a three-dimensional element is created within the chart.

■ Show Gridlines is another way (besides chart-type options) of displaying gridlines.

■ Use Logarithmic Scale sets the scale to a logarithmic rather than linear measure.

■ No Vertical Axis deletes any vertical axis in the chart. (Why would you want to do this? Sometimes you can increase clarity by reducing clutter.)

Suppose we want to simplify the scale on the vertical axes of our pizza chart. And, we've added data labels, so we really don't need the closely spaced intervals Works has provided. Here's what we can do:

1. Click Format, and then click Vertical (Y) Axis.

2. Type another interval in the Interval box. We typed *50.*

3. Click the Show Gridlines check box.

4. Click OK.

5. Click Format, and then click Right Vertical (Y) Axis.

6. Type another interval in the Interval box. We typed *50.*

7. Click OK.

Works changes both scales. If you have different scales, use the Vertical (Y) Axis command to change the left axis and the Right Vertical Axis command to change the right one.

Formatting Chart Text with Fonts

With the Works charting feature, you can now use many fonts, in any style and size that you choose. You simply select the title element in the chart you want to change by clicking once, and then select the Font and Style command on the Format menu. This displays the Format Font and Style dialog box (which you've already used in Chapter 6 to change the fonts and style of spreadsheet data), where you can make changes to fonts in chart labels and titles.

As in the other Works applications, however, the actual fonts and font sizes available to you depend on your computer and, even more so, on your printer, its capabilities, and the way you've defined it to Windows.

So far, our chart looks pretty good, but it could use a little sprucing up. We'll change the title's font to 14-point, italic, bold, as follows.

TIP Click the right mouse button while pointing to any text in a chart and then click the Font and Style command to quickly make changes. You can also click the right mouse button to gain access to the Edit Titles dialog box as well.

1. Click the chart's title.

   A small rectangle with handles will appear around the title's text, like this:

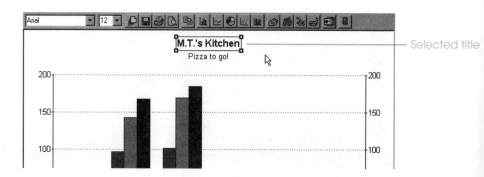

2. Click Format, and then click Font and Style.

3. Click the Bold and Italic options in the Style box.

4. Click the 14 point option in the Size scroll list.

5. Click OK, and then click anywhere outside the selected title.

   The modified chart example appears as shown in Figure 8-17.

FIGURE 8-17

Changing the style
and size of
chart text

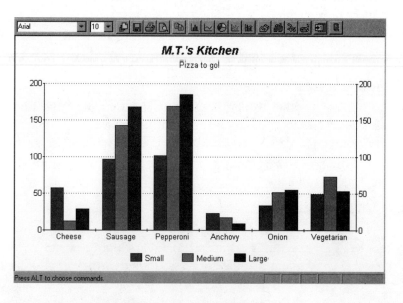

We encourage you to try all the charting options that Works provides, to gain experience working with the software.

TIP You can add a border, make the chart a one-series chart, or make your chart 3-D with a click by using the options at the bottom of the Format menu.

Formatting Charts with Shading and Color

The Shading and Color command on the Format menu can provide more fun than any one chart maker deserves—but don't go overboard by using too much of a good thing.

With this command, you can specify screen and print colors (the latter only if you have a color printer), patterns for different series in bar and pie charts, and markers for data values in line charts. As mentioned earlier, you can also use this command to explode the slice of your choice in a pie chart.

When you choose the Shading and Color command from the Format menu, Works displays this Format Shading and Color dialog box:

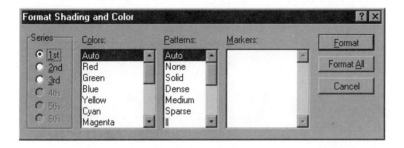

Works tailors the options in the dialog box to suit the type of chart you're working with. For example, this dialog box shows the options available for a bar chart. When you work with a line chart, you see many options in the Markers box because a line chart uses markers. When you work with a combination chart, Works displays a choice of markers if you select a series (in the Series box) represented by a line in the chart.

 TIP To work with shading and/or color for any one series, just double-click on that series and you'll see the same Format Shading and Color dialog box.

Here's a rundown of the options included in the dialog box and their purposes:

- The Series option lets you choose the value series to format.

- The Colors option lets you pick a color for the series. Auto tells Works to use a predefined set of colors (red for the first series, green for the second, and blue for the third).

- The Patterns option lets you choose a pattern for the bar or line representing the selected series. If you work with a color monitor, but print in black-and-white, Auto tells Works which predefined patterns to use in place of color during printing. (You can see these patterns on screen by choosing Display As Printed from the View menu.)

- The Markers option lets you choose the type of marker used for data points in a line chart. Again, Auto sets the markers for you when you display or print the chart in black-and-white.

- The Format button in the dialog box tells Works to apply the choices you've made to the selected series. Use this button if you want to make additional changes to other series.

- The Format All button applies one or more choices you've made to all series in the chart. Use this button, for example, to change all lines in a line chart from solid to dotted, or to change all bars in a bar chart from multicolored to magenta. (In the latter case, Works changes to a different pattern or marker for each series, so you can still distinguish one bar or line from another.)

- The Close button is labeled Cancel until you make a formatting change. Cancel, as usual, cancels the command. Close tells Works you've finished formatting. When you click Close, Works updates the chart with the changes you specified.

Here are the steps to follow in working with the Format Shading and Color dialog box.

1. Click Format, and then click Shading and Color.

2. If you have a color monitor, select a new color for the first series, and then click the Format button. Do the same for the other two series, clicking the Format button for each.

   As you make these changes, you'll see them occur in the chart, located behind the dialog box.

3. Now select a single color, and click Format All. Click Close to make the changes.

   Notice that Works displays different patterns to distinguish one bar in the chart from the next.

4. Return the formatting to Auto unless you prefer the display you've produced.

Modifying a Chart

After you've created a chart, you don't have to worry about updating it whenever you change data in the spreadsheet. Works does that automatically because the two documents are linked. As you remember, when you save the chart on which the spreadsheet is based, you're actually saving both.

You might, however, want to change category labels, alter the definition of a series, or add a new series or delete an old one from a chart. Then, too, you might find that you want to create or change a chart by including one or more series from separate (nonadjacent) locations on the spreadsheet. You can do all this with the Series and Paste Series commands on the Edit menu.

Changing Category Labels

Category labels, like data labels, must already exist on a spreadsheet before you can incorporate them in a chart. After you've entered them on your spreadsheet, however, you can simply select them and copy them into place. The orientation of the copied cells doesn't matter, so you can copy a row of labels into a chart whose categories are based on column titles, and vice versa. For example, suppose M. T. has developed a political consciousness and has decided to name her pizzas. We would accomplish this as follows:

1. Switch to the spreadsheet, and type new names in any range. We made the following entries in cells B17 through G17: *Purist, Conservative, Liberal, Independent, Grassroots*, and *Radical*.

2. Select the titles and copy them to the Clipboard using the Copy button on the toolbar.

3. Return to the chart, click Edit, and then click Paste Series.

   The Paste Series dialog box appears.

4. Click Category, and then click OK.

   The old categories are replaced by the new names.

Changing Series

Changing the Y series is similar to changing category labels. Once again, you use cell references and either the Paste Series or Series command. For example, suppose M. T. adds an X-Large sized pizza to the menu and wants to include it in the chart. We could do so by following these steps:

1. Return to the spreadsheet by choosing it from the Window menu.

2. Insert a new column where you want it. We inserted a new column E to the right of the Large column.

3. Type a new name for the column and enter its data. We entered the label *X-L* and typed *20, 13, 17, 8, 1,* and *15* into cells E2 through E7.

4. Copy the contents of the new column to the Clipboard.

5. Return to the chart.

6. Click Edit, and then click Series.

7. Click the box next to the 4th series.

8. Click the Paste button (in the dialog box).

9. Click OK to add the new series.

10. Now click Format, and then click Two Vertical (Y) Axes.

    Notice that the Left option is turned on in the 4th Value Series box. Because we created two vertical axes, and this is the only Left option selected, the new series controls the left axis.

11. Click the Right I option.

12. Click OK to bring everything into line.

13. Now use the Legend/Series Labels command on the Edit menu to label the fourth series with the column's title.

    The modified chart appears as shown in Figure 8-18.

Charting Nonadjacent Ranges

You can use the Series and Paste Series commands to create a chart using non-adjacent data ranges. Because ranges don't have to be oriented in the

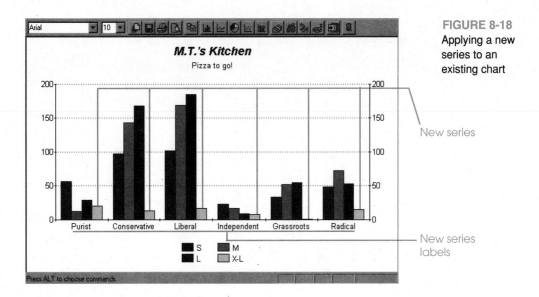

FIGURE 8-18

Applying a new
series to an
existing chart

New series

New series
labels

same directions, these commands can be useful if you want to chart related values that are laid out horizontally in one range, but vertically in another.

The examples we just showed you used these two commands, so here we'll outline this new procedure.

1. If you're creating a new chart, select the first range.

2. Click the spreadsheet's New Chart button on the toolbar to create the chart.

3. Click OK in the New Chart dialog box.

4. From the new chart, return to the spreadsheet and select the second range to chart.

5. Copy it to the Clipboard.

6. Return to the chart.

7. Use the Paste Series or the Series command to turn the references for the copied cells into the second value series.

8. Click OK to update the chart.
   You might need to return to the spreadsheet and repeat the procedure for additional data ranges.

That's it! Horizontal, vertical, close together, or widely spaced—you can turn the cell ranges of your choice into the chart you want to see.

Setting Up and Printing a Chart

The process of setting up and printing a chart is very similar to that in other Works applications. We'll review the differences you need to understand to get the job done right for charts.

Previewing a Chart

If you work with a color monitor but print in black-and-white, the colors you see on screen are replaced by patterns and differently shaped markers in print.

There are several ways to see what the printed chart will look like. The easiest method—and the one designed for this purpose—is to choose the Display As Printed command from the View menu. You'll see the chart as it will appear when printed. For example, in Figure 8-19, you can see what the printed chart would look like when printed in black-and-white. Works replaces color with patterns if you don't have a color printer.

FIGURE 8-19
How the pizza
spreadsheet chart
will appear
when printed

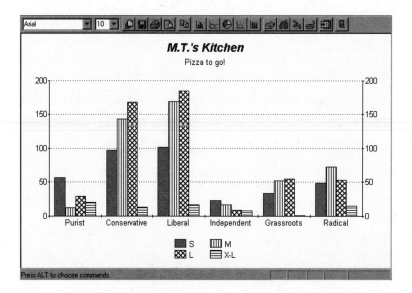

If you don't feel like using this command, click the Print Preview button on the toolbar. You'll see a smaller, but otherwise identical, "printed" version of your chart. If you'd rather not use either of these methods, you can also choose Black as the color for the entire chart in the Shading and Color dialog box. This last approach is pretty roundabout, but it's available.

Page Setup and Printing

When you're ready to finish up and print a chart, you can add running heads, page numbers, and other information with the Headers and Footers command on the View menu. Just enter the text you want to appear on the top (header) and bottom (footer) of each page.

To set up your margins, you use the Page Setup command from the File menu. This is also where you'll specify the orientation of the printing (portrait versus landscape).

Normally, Works sets up a chart so that it prints on a full page. If you select the Other Options tab, Works reduces the chart to the size one screen would occupy, which is about one-quarter of a page. This is a useful option when you're printing small or uncomplicated charts. If you use it, be sure to check all text and labels before printing to verify that they'll be reproduced completely and without appearing too cramped.

Under Other Options, you can also select to print on a full page but keep the chart dimensions proportionate in both height and width.

TIP Keep the original proportions if what the chart "says" is more important than the way it looks. For example, do this if relative heights of bars or relative placement of lines is critical to the chart's impact. Use a full page if the overall appearance of the chart is more important than exact ratios of height to width, and if you don't mind the chart being shortened or widened to accommodate the page size. Use the Full Page, Keep Proportions option, if you want on one page an exact duplicate of what you see on screen.

Printing a chart is, as usual, a simple matter of choosing the Print command and specifying the number of copies you want. If you switch between portrait (high) and landscape (wide) mode for printing, however, Works might tell you that the printer setup description needs to be modified, even if you've switched the page length and width measurements in the Page Setup dialog box.

If you must modify your printer setup, check the dialog box that appears for options that let you toggle between portrait and landscape mode. Be sure to reset the printer when you're finished, to avoid surprises when you try to print your next "normal" document.

Coming Next

That's the end of the spreadsheet discussion. You now have two of the Works modules well in hand and are ready to learn about managing information through the use of a database. So get out your coin collection, comic books, or latest stock report, and let's go to work.

Part 4

SELECT EDITION

Using the Database

In This Part

If you've got lots of things to take care of, or even just a few that you want to keep lots of information on, then the Works for Windows 95 database is what you need. It allows you to create the most simple or complex form to keep track of every piece of information about your book collection, swimming team, or progress in organic chemistry. And you can do all these things with some simple instructions, beginning with Chapter 9.

You'll learn what a database is and how the important elements work together, including files, records, and fields. You'll be introduced to another toolbar, making your database creation and maintenance a snap. Just like a word processor or a spreadsheet, databases can also be edited, so we'll review those techniques as well, plus how to add and delete fields and records easily.

Chapter 10 gives you the essentials of managing a database. While the database is a collection of information, what you *do* with the information is just as important as its collection. For example, sometimes you may want to sort the database on such a field as last name or year of birth, or use the Find feature to turn up that special coin among your treasury of 2,500. You can also use the powerful query language that Works for Windows 95 features, to say, for instance, "Show me all the players who hit better than .250 and who are in the National League." Queries are powerful tools that let you get the information you need to make informed decisions.

Chapter 11 offers a detailed discussion of how to create a report in a variety of different formats, depending on which information you want to use. Once the report is defined and you have selected the rows and columns you want to include, it's only a matter of printing to get the hard copy document that reflects the important information in your database.

Chapter 9

Getting Started with the Database

t is time to turn our attention to the Microsoft Works for Windows 95 database module, a tool for storing and managing information. This chapter and Chapters 10 and 11 describe ways to use the Works database module to create a system to manage information, such as inventories, price lists, catalogs, and collections. Because "data is data," how you work with it makes all the difference in the world. That's where the Works database proves to be a valuable tool in your Works toolkit.

What Is a Database?

A *database* is a collection of information organized according to certain criteria. The phone book is a database; so are a teacher's grade sheet and your collection of baseball cards. A database management system is the tool used to create a database and to manage its information. For our purposes, though, we'll speak of the two functions as the same. Therefore, Works as a whole is a database, and what you organize using Works is a database as well.

Database programs require more structure than most other types of applications because they provide fast access to any fact in a collection of information. Like a librarian who must be able to find any single book in a collection of unrelated books, a database program must be able to find the one record you seek in an entire collection of related, but independent, entries. Neither the librarian nor the database program can anticipate what you'll request, so both must rely on a structure or a form to make searching quick and effective.

Many of the TaskWizards that we listed in Table 2-1 in Chapter 2 (page 45) can be used to create databases that serve a variety of purposes. For example, the Address Book, Phone List, Employee Profile, and Business Inventory are all Wizard-generated documents based on the database management system that Works provides.

Understanding Databases: Forms, Records, Fields, and Files

The Works database module structures information through forms, records, fields, and files. A *form* is the on-screen equivalent of a paper data-entry form. It organizes the display of information for a single record. For example, it could be the form you would use to catalog each individual car for a used car business. A *record* is one completed form or one set of information about a particular entry in the database. For example, record 23 might contain the make, model, year, serial number, and price of a Toyota Celica. A *field* is one item of information within a record, such as the price of the Celica. Finally, a *file* is a collection of records, which can be called a database.

You can see how fields, records, and files relate to one another in this illustration:

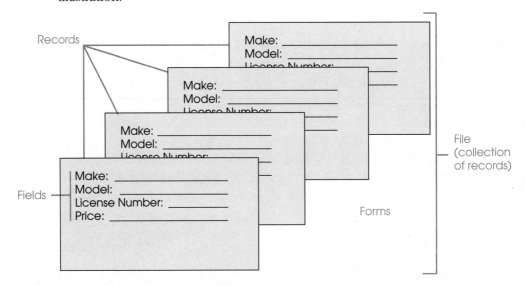

In this chapter, we'll use a database containing an inventory of cars to demonstrate some of the fundamentals of using this module and the powerful features that Works offers. We'll also use a database of stock prices to demonstrate how to perform calculations on numerical data with functions.

Viewing a Database in Different Ways

Before you actually begin creating a database, we need to first discuss two of the views the Works database management module uses to present information: List view and Form view.

Using views is comparable to using different lenses on a camera. If you use a regular lens and look through the camera at a tree, you see one image. If you switch to a wide-angle lens and look through the camera at the same tree, you see something different. One view of the tree can show its entire structure, another can show the leaves in great detail, and yet another can filter the light so that you see one particular aspect of the tree, such as different colors that correspond to warm and cool areas.

It's the same with a database; each view shows your data from one of four different aspects.

In List view you enter, view, and modify database records on a spreadsheet-like grid that shows many entries simultaneously. You generally use List view for scanning and editing a database or for viewing selected records in it. In Figure 9-1, you can see sample database information in List view. List view is the default view, and it's the view that you must use to create the initial database before viewing it in any other mode.

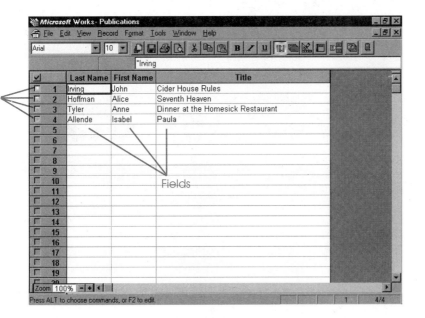

FIGURE 9-1
Database information displayed in List view

In Form view, you enter, view, and modify database records one at a time. You generally use Form view to modify information in a single record. In Figure 9-2 on the following page you can see some sample database information, including author's last name, first name, and book title in Form view.

In Form Design view, you can arrange fields on a form and customize the form by adding borders, color, and shading to fields and field names. You can even add objects such as graphics. The Form Design view appears to be almost identical to the Form view. The only difference, but a major one, is that in Form Design view you can make changes to the form's structure. In Form view you can't.

Finally, Report view shows you just what a hard copy of your database will look like when it's printed. The report feature of Works can provide some powerful customization, organization, and formatting features.

FIGURE 9-2

Database
information in
Form view

Fields

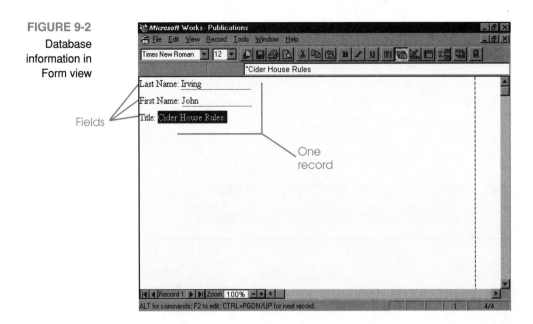

Here's a summary of the four views and the Works tasks for which you will use them.

View	How to Use It
List	View more than one record at the same time
	Duplicate information from record to record
	Enter a series of numbers, dates, and other information
	View the results of sorting
Form	Enter and view information one record at a time
	Print a blank form
Form Design	Modify a form's structure and appearance
	Design a Works on-screen form to match a printed form
Report	Print a report that organizes information into groups
	Perform calculations on fields, such as the average value of a coin collection

Understanding
List View and Form View

When you start the database application with a new "document," Works begins in List view, because it presents database information in a familiar table or gridlike structure.

You can create a database only in List view, but as you'll see, Form view can be easier to work with, especially for data entry, because you can also view all the fields for just one record at a time. Remember, you can modify the form that you create only in Form Design view. Then you can see what it looks like in Form view.

As you work with a database, you'll find the method of working you like best. In general, however, you can assume that Form view is particularly useful when you want to do the following:

- Cut, copy, delete, or insert whole records

- View the structure of the form

- Insert, delete, or modify information in fields

  List view, by contrast, is valuable when you want to do the following:

- View or select multiple records at the same time

- Select a field and all the entries in it

- Copy, clear, or fill fields in multiple entries at the same time

- Format the display of data

List view is the default setting, so we'll start working in that view to create a simple database. After that, you'll switch to Form view to see the difference.

Creating a Database

OK, we're ready to begin. Although Works lets you rearrange fields, add new ones, and delete unnecessary ones with little effort, you should plan ahead to accommodate the information you want in your database. Deleting fields after you've entered data deletes the data in those fields; this can mean extra work to recover or redistribute information in each existing record.

The fields you create will eventually be your means of searching for and sorting your data. Keep this in mind as you create fields for your database. For example, you can create a single field for area code, exchange (prefix), and telephone number, or you can create separate fields for each. If you create a single field, you'll only be able to search for, or sort, entire phone numbers, such as (206) 555-1000. If you create separate fields for each, you'll be able to search your database by area code, exchange, *or* phone number.

TIP It's a good idea to use graph paper and plan your database *before* you begin to use Works; only then should you collect the data that will go in the database. That way, you can see before you start what fields need to go where and what information belongs in each field.

Think about how often you'll want to find only telephone exchanges. In the end, a compromise may be best: the area code in one field, and the exchange and the phone number in a second. Similarly, if you're working with names in some form or other, you almost always need to have the last name in a separate field because virtually every database, at one time or another, sorts on the last name.

Creating a Database in List View

List view is where all databases start, beginning with opening the database module of Works for Windows 95.

1. Click the Database button in the Works Task Launcher dialog box, or click File, click New, and then click the Database button in the Task Launcher dialog box.

   Works displays this Create Database dialog box:

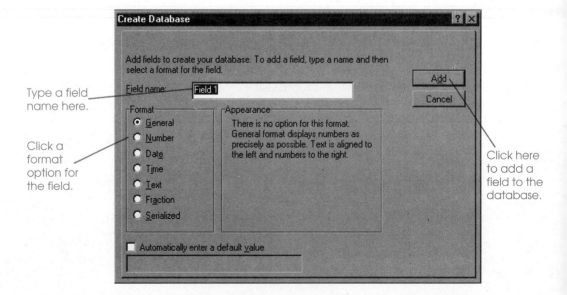

Type a field name here.

Click a format option for the field.

Click here to add a field to the database.

As you can see, Works requires a name for the first field at least, before you can begin working with the database. You can also specify the format of the field as you create it such as Number ($1,234), Date (July 10, 1995), and Time (10:04 P.M.).

Here's a sampling of the different types of formats and how different values appear once you select a format category (such as Time), and then select a specific format (such as 10:57.34).

Format	Example 1	Example 2
General	1234	5678
Number	1,234.56	$1,234.56
Date	7/11	7/95
Time	10:57	10:57.34
Text	Bill	Jill
Fraction	½	1/4

2. Type a field name and click Add (or press Enter) for each field you want to create.

    Be sure to select a format option for any fields that will store numerical, date, or time information.

3. Click Done when you're finished creating fields.

4. Maximize the document window and hide Help to enlarge your workspace.

    The database structure in List view appears as you see in Figure 9-3 on the following page.

5. You can enter data in the database in the same way as you would enter data in a spreadsheet. We entered the 12 records you see in Figure 9-4 on the following page.

    NOTE Works assigns a .WDB extension to the file when you save a database. When we saved this database, Works called it *cars.wdb*. But, because Windows 95 doesn't list extensions, you won't see the .WDB extension unless you look at your list of files through the File Manager or Explorer.

In general, each time you start a new database, you'll be shown the Create Database dialog box and then be asked to define each field in the database, field by field. You'll also be in List view. Finally, the default format is General.

FIGURE 9-3

The database
structure in
List view

Field name

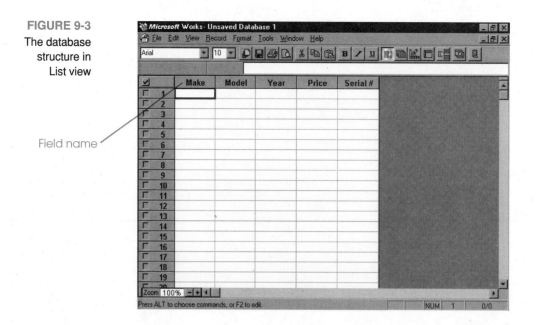

FIGURE 9-4

The database
in List view with
data added

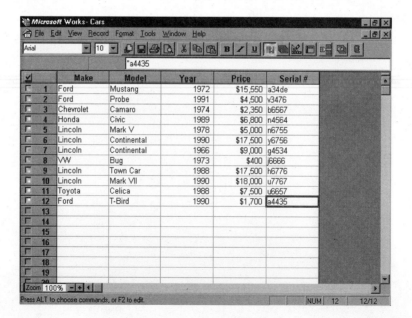

	Make	Model	Year	Price	Serial #
1	Ford	Mustang	1972	$15,550	a34de
2	Ford	Probe	1991	$4,500	v3476
3	Chevrolet	Camaro	1974	$2,350	b6567
4	Honda	Civic	1989	$6,800	n4564
5	Lincoln	Mark V	1978	$5,000	n6755
6	Lincoln	Continental	1990	$17,500	y6756
7	Lincoln	Continental	1966	$9,000	g4534
8	VW	Bug	1973	$400	j6666
9	Lincoln	Town Car	1988	$17,500	h6776
10	Lincoln	Mark VII	1990	$18,000	u7767
11	Toyota	Celica	1988	$7,500	u6657
12	Ford	T-Bird	1990	$1,700	a4435

TIP As you enter data, you'll see many similarities between the spreadsheet and the database. When you enter data in the database, you'll see the familiar Cancel and Enter buttons, just as you did in the spreadsheet module's entry bar.

The Basic List View Window

As you can see, the database window has many things in common with other Works windows, such as the familiar menu bar across the top, the toolbar, and a large work area. There are some different elements as well.

At the bottom of the window, toward the left, are the Navigation buttons you see here, which allow you to move from record to record with a click of the mouse. Here's how they work:

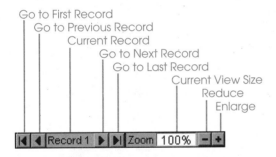

The set of Zoom buttons are to the immediate left of the horizontal scroll bar. You can use this set to zoom in on part of a database by magnifying your perspective. As you can see, the default magnification is 100%, the standard for all new databases. You can zoom up to 200% and down to 50%.

To the right of these buttons are two sets of numbers. The first, 12 in Figure 9-4, is the current page or record (on which the insertion point appears). Next, the fraction in the lower right corner (12/12 in Figure 9-4) represents the current record over the total number of records in the database. For example, the numbers 24/879 would indicate the 24th record of 879. In Figure 9-4, we're on the twelfth of twelve records. These handy numbers can help you keep track of your work in the database.

Below the Navigation buttons on the status bar are tips on commands that you can use in the database.

Using the Toolbar

As with all Works modules, you'll find a toolbar at the top of the screen. What's different about the database toolbar? Six buttons that allow you to switch views, insert records, or use filters to display selected sets of records, as you see here. Filters will be discussed in Chapter 10.

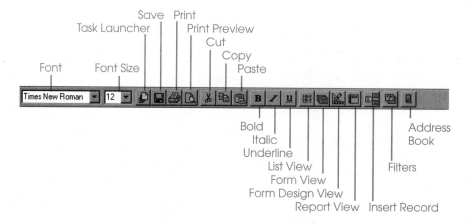

Like the other toolbars, the database toolbar has buttons that save, cut, copy, and offer you help. You can also add or delete buttons as needed to customize your toolbar to fit the way you like to work.

 TIP Remember that Works can check your database spelling, just as it did for your spreadsheet entries. Look for the Spelling command in the same place, on the Tools menu.

 For information about *using filters,* see "Querying a Database to Find Information" in Chapter 10, page 339.

Using the Best Fit Feature

In List view, you have the greatest-of-all-time formatting helpers. To adjust the field to exactly the width that's needed, select the Best Fit button in the Field Width dialog box shown next:

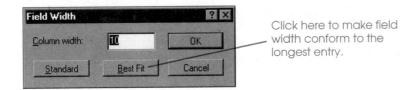

Click here to make field width conform to the longest entry.

Like the Best Fit button in the spreadsheet module's Column Width dialog box, this button adjusts the widths of one or more fields to fit the largest field entry of data. In fact, it might not be a bad idea to select all the records and do this when you're working, to ensure that all the information is visible.

To make things even easier, you can simply double-click on the name of a field or on a row, and Works will adjust the field size and row height to fit the widest or largest entry exactly. Pretty cool.

Changing Views

Many, but not all, of the database features work in both Form view and List view. You can create fields in List view and see them in Form view, although you can't create a database in Form view.

You can look at the database in Form view by doing the following:

1. Click View, and then click Form (or use the F9 function key or click on the Form View button on the toolbar).

Figure 9-5 on the following page shows the sample database in Form view.

When you're in Form view, notice that you see one complete record at a time—the information for the Ford T-Bird, in this case. To see other records, use the navigation buttons to the left of the horizontal scroll bar. You should also notice that the toolbar doesn't change. The same buttons that are available in List view are available in Form view.

You can also format fields for currency, for example, and see the same format in either view. You can't, however, assume that the same field width will carry over into both views, or that the style (such as italic) or size will transfer from one view to another.

Notice the default font and font size in Figure 9-5 (Times New Roman 12) and the field width of 20 characters that Works uses in Form view. If you contrast this with List view by clicking the List View button, you'll see that the defaults change. In List view, the font and size are changed to Arial 10 and the column (field) width is 10 characters.

FIGURE 9-5

The Cars database
in Form view

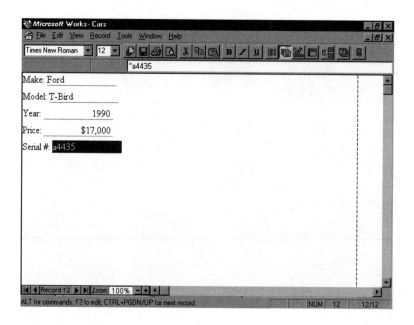

This disparity between List view and Form view occurs since Works tries to trade off the available spaces for greater clarity of the presentation. Here are some general rules about format and views:

- Additions, deletions, and changes that affect the information or structure of the database carry over from one view to the next. Rest assured that a cell containing the value 234 in one view will be a cell containing the value 234 in the other.

- Characteristics that aren't integral to the form or data differ from view to view. Text in 12-point Times New Roman in one view might be shown as 10-point Arial in another.

Splitting the Screen to View Your Data

Just as with the spreadsheet, you can also view the active file in more than one pane simultaneously. Like the spreadsheet, the database lets you split the screen and scroll independently in two or four "panes" to view different parts of a large database.

To split the screen, use the following steps.

1. Be sure you're in List view.

2. Drag the split box at the top of the vertical scroll bar, and release the mouse button when the bar is where you want it on the screen.

3. Drag the split box at the left edge of the horizontal scroll bar, and release the mouse button when the bar is where you want it on the screen.

4. Clicking in one pane and then another, scroll through your database to see different parts of the same "document."

    As you do, notice that the top and bottom panes on each side show the same fields, but they can show different records. The left and right panes can show different fields, but the same records.

> **TIP** If you want to return to a full screen and get rid of extra panes, just double-click on the split bar and all panes will disappear.

5. When you finish viewing the panes, drag the split boxes out of the document window to eliminate the splits, and then scroll to the beginning of the database.

Editing a Database

Databases change. Rarely is one created that you don't add records to, delete records from, change the number and size of its fields, and so on. The databases on your computer will have to be updated periodically—it's in their nature. That's when editing becomes important.

Editing Data in Fields in List View

Replacing data in a field is a breeze. You simply highlight the existing data and start typing. When you select data in a field (not the field name itself) and press a key, Works takes that keystroke as a signal to replace the information currently in that field with the new information that you're entering. To edit data in a field, do the following:

1. Click View, and then click List (or click the List View button), if you are not in List view.

2. Click the data you want to replace.

3. Type the data you want to replace the existing data, and click the Enter button (or press the Enter key).

Just like that, one entry replaces another. If you want to delete the contents of a field without replacing it, select the data, and then choose the Clear command from the Edit menu or point to the entry, click the right mouse button, and click the Clear command.

TIP Another way to delete information from a field is to click the entry to highlight it, and then press the Del key.

You can also edit field contents on the entry bar, much as you learned to do in the spreadsheet. The same steps work in the database as in the spreadsheet, as follows:

- To highlight one or more characters, click the entry and then drag the highlight over it, or press and hold Shift and use an arrow key.

- Click anywhere in an entry to position the insertion point at that location. Using the keyboard, move the insertion point one character at a time with the arrow keys. Move the insertion point to the beginning of the entry by pressing Home, or move it to the end by pressing End.

- Press the F2 key, and the insertion point will be placed at the end of the entry in the cell. Then you'll be able to edit the field contents.

- Press Del to delete characters you've highlighted.

When you need to make changes to different fields in many records, you'll probably find List view preferable to Form view because it lets you see so many records at once.

Adding New Records in List View

Few databases are created and finalized at the same time. Instead, after you've created a database, you'll want to add records. You can add records in List view or Form view.

To add a new record at the end of the database, follow these steps:

1. Click the next open cell in the first column.

2. Using the Tab key to move from field to field, enter the data for the new record.

You don't always want to add records just to the end of the database. To add a record anywhere within the database, you can follow the steps described below. In this example, we'll add a new record following record 7.

1. Position the mouse pointer over the row 8 header and click it to select row 8.

2. Click Record, and then click Insert Record.

3. Enter the data for the new record.

 TIP Works will also insert a new record if you select a single field cell instead of an entire row. Just click in any field in the row after which you want the new record to appear.

Deleting Records in List View

The process of removing whole records is similar to that of adding them. You select the record and then select the Delete Record command.

1. Click in any cell for the record you want to delete.

2. Click Record, and then click Delete Record.
   The record is gone, and the succeeding records are renumbered correctly.

 TIP Fortunately, deleting can be undone. Use the Undo button right after you delete a record. Remember that the Undo function works only when it's invoked *immediately* after the deletion is made.

Adding Fields in List View

When you add a new field, Works always displays (and prints) the new fields to the right of previously existing fields in List view. To add a field in List view, use the following steps.

1. Highlight the field (column) next to where you want to add a new field.

2. Click Record, click Insert Field, and then click Before, if you want the new field added before the highlighted field, or After, if you want the new field added after the highlighted field.

   When you do this, you will see this Insert Field dialog box:

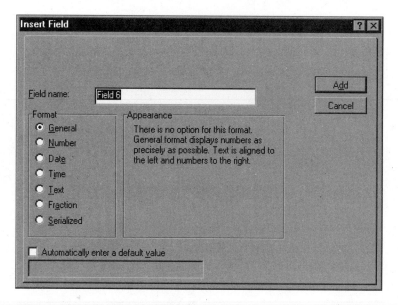

3. Enter the name of the field in the Field Name box.

4. If necessary, select a format.

5. Click Add. The new field will be added.

 CAUTION If you add a field in List view and then switch to Form view, the new field will appear on the top of another field—hardly usable. What you'll have to do is use the Form Design view to rearrange fields.

TIP You can add as many fields as you want, once you see the Insert Field dialog box. Just keep going until finished and then click Done.

We added the following fields to our Cars database example so that it looks as shown in Figure 9-6. The format for each is listed to the right of its name below.

Stock No.	General
Date Sold	Date (7/1/95 form)
Sold For	Currency, 2 decimals
Down	Currency, 2 decimals
Balance	Currency, 2 decimals
Notes	General

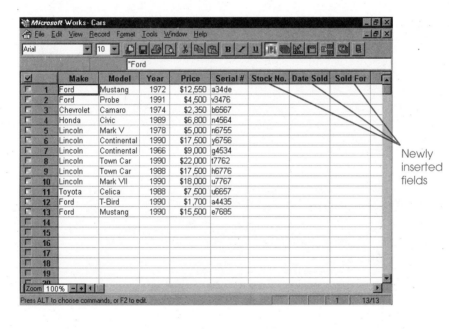

FIGURE 9-6
Adding new fields to the Cars database

Deleting Fields in List View

To delete a field in List view, follow these steps:

1. Highlight the field you want to delete by clicking on the field's name.

2. Click the Cut button on the toolbar.

   Works will warn you that you're about to delete the field from the database and ask you if you wish to continue.

3. Click the appropriate button to complete the operation.

You can add new fields anywhere in the database—at the end, at the beginning, or between existing fields—and then edit the records to include whatever additional information you want.

Using the Fill Command in List View

The database, like the spreadsheet, includes three Fill commands that can save you a lot of time when entering data. These are Fill Right, Fill Down, and Fill Series. These commands are available only in List view, because only there can you make entries to multiple records. The Fill commands work exactly as they do in the spreadsheet. For example, to enter a number or date series in a field, you can do the following:

1. Click on the first cell in the field that you want to fill with a series.

2. Type the first number in the series.

3. Extend the highlight so that it covers the field cells for all the records to which you want to enter the series data.

4. Click Edit, and then click Fill Series.

5. Click OK in the Fill Series dialog box.

Protecting Your Database

After you've gone to the trouble of building a database, you'll want to ensure that your information is protected from damage or inadvertent change. Protection in the database works much the same way it does in the spreadsheet, except that you can apply protection to forms as well as data by using the following procedure to protect a field.

1. Click on any cell in the field, or select the entire field by clicking on the field name.

2. Click Format, and then click Protection.

You will see the this Format Protection dialog box.

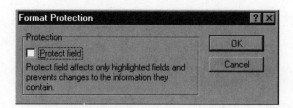

3. Click the Protect Field check box and click OK.

The selected field is protected, meaning that data can't be deleted or added in this field while this option is turned on.

TIP It's a good idea to protect the entire form when you're sure you are finished. That way, you can still change data and even change the form, should you need to later, by removing the protection. Do that by selecting all the records (click Edit, and then click Select All or use the Ctrl+A key combination) and proceeding as above.

To turn off protection, select the protected field or any cell in the field, go to the Format Protection dialog box, and click the Protect Field check box so that the feature is turned off.

See Also For more information about *protecting data* in a spreadsheet, see "Protecting Spreadsheet Information" in Chapter 6, page 188.

Hiding Information

While you work, you can also hide fields and records or temporarily remove sensitive or unneeded parts of your database from view. You hide a field by changing its width to 0, using the Field Width command on the Format menu. When you want to redisplay the field, do the following:

1. Select the fields before and after the hidden field, by dragging across the field names.

2. Click Format, and then click Field Width.

3. Click OK to accept the default width (or change the width if you like).

The hidden field appears.

Hiding Records

In List or Form view, you can hide records by clicking on any cell in the record, clicking Record, and then clicking Hide Record. To redisplay hidden records, choose the Show command from the Record menu, and then click All Records.

TIP Don't hide records or fields unless you are sure you must. It's easy to hide records or fields, forget you've done so, and then panic when it comes time to work with the data later on.

Designing Database Forms in Form Design View

So far in this chapter, you've seen how you can easily create a database form and enter data using a spreadsheet-like list in List view. You can also click the Form View button on the toolbar and see one record at a time, displayed for your convenience.

It's only through the Form Design view, however, that you can change the appearance of the record in the data entry form and modify how its fields are arranged. There's nothing pretty about List view, other than that it works fine. But it's not *supposed* to be pretty, only useful for entering data into the database. The Form Design view is, however, supposed to make things look good, and that's where we'll turn our attention to now.

Adding a New Field in Form Design View

Adding a field in Form Design view is similar to doing so in List view. To add a new field, follow these steps:

1. Click View, and then click Form Design (or click the Form Design button or press Ctrl+F9).

2. Click Insert, and then click Field.
   The same Insert Field dialog box you saw earlier appears.

3. Type a field name for the new field.

4. Click OK.

The new field appears as shown in Figure 9-7, obscuring other fields. When you add fields this way, you'll have to move them to new locations. Remember that Form Design view is a working view in which the form is open to modification. So don't be alarmed at how things look now, for they can be easily changed.

X and Y coordinates

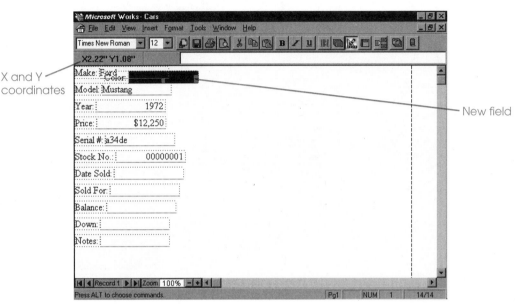

New field

FIGURE 9-7
Adding a new field in Form Design view

When you're working in Form Design view, be aware of the X and Y numbers (actually, coordinates) in the upper left corner below the toolbar (Figure 9-7). This is a set of coordinates used to place objects in the work area. The spreadsheet has a cell reference in this area; for the database, Works displays the current location of the insertion point along X and Y axes that begin at the top left corner of the page. In Form Design view, you can precisely control the placement of database fields. The location of the insertion point can help you move or insert fields with an accuracy of up to .01 inch. Working with the default settings of 1.00 inch for the top margin and 1.25 inches for the left margin, the insertion point in Form Design view starts out slightly below and to the right of the top and left margins. The coordinates "X1.25 Y1.00" appear in a new form.

Reorganizing Fields in Form Design View

You can move one or more fields in Form Design view with the Position Selection command on the Edit menu. A faster way, though, is to use the mouse.

1. Be sure you're in Form Design view.

2. Verify that Snap To Grid is turned on (on the Format menu).

   Works sets up a grid of invisible lines that help you align fields in Form Design view. If you're between lines, then Works will "snap" the field to a line.

3. Click a field name to highlight it.

4. Press and hold the Ctrl key, and click any additional field names you want to move at the same time.

   The fields you want to move are highlighted.

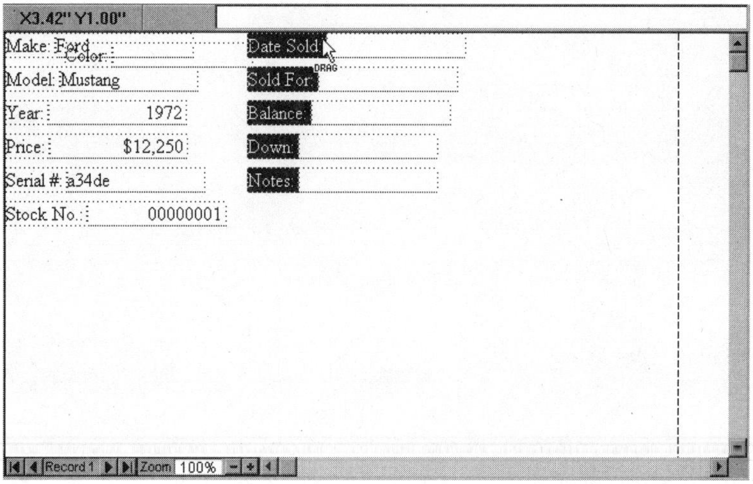

FIGURE 9-8

Dragging several
fields at once in
Form Design view

5. Drag the fields to where you want them placed on the form. We rearranged ours as shown in Figure 9-8. We also dragged the new field to another location, as shown in Figure 9-9.

   As you move the mouse pointer (note that the DRAG indicator becomes a MOVE indicator), the field goes along with it until it can be placed in a more convenient or appropriate location on the database form. If Snap To Grid were not turned on, you could maneuver the outline up, down, and sideways in smaller increments. Here, since we want to align fields in a pattern, Snap To Grid is preferable.

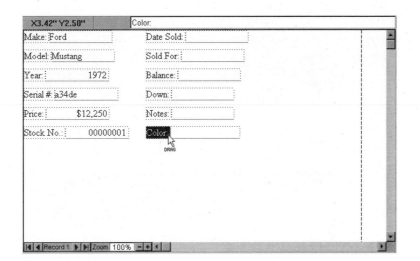

FIGURE 9-9
Repositioning an
inserted field

Changing Field Widths

As you create a new field, Works uses the default value of 10 characters
for its width (in List view). You may need more room (you get one of those
nuisance ######## indicators, meaning that the cell is too small to display
its contents) or less room, depending on the content of the entries. You
may also find that some of the fields are too large, so just for the sake of
appearance you might want to change their size.

There are two ways to change field width.

1. Highlight the field (not its name) that you want to adjust.

2. Click Format, and then click Field Size.

    Works displays this Format Field Size dialog box:

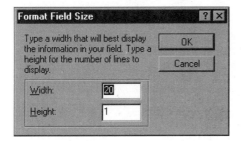

3. Type another width, and click OK.

That's the first and most precise way to change the width of a field.
Or you can try this faster way:

1. Highlight the field (not its name) that you want to adjust.

   Notice that the selected field now contains three sizing handles:
   horizontal, vertical, and diagonal.

2. Point to the diagonal sizing handle in the lower right-hand corner
   of the highlighted field, as shown here:

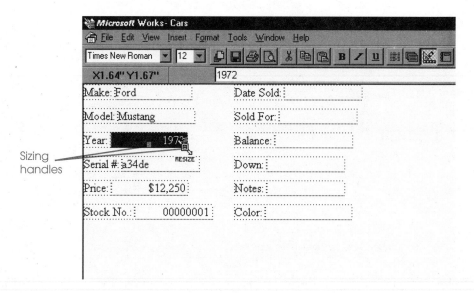

Sizing
handles

Notice that the mouse pointer becomes a diagonal arrow
labeled RESIZE.

You can drag the box left or right to resize the width of a field,
and you can drag it up or down to change the number of lines in a
field.

3. Drag the selected field's sizing handle to adjust the field's width.

   If your hand slips and drags the corner downward, slide the
   mouse pointer up again to keep this a one-line field.

> **TIP**   Keep in mind that when you change the width of
> a particular field on your screen, you're changing the
> width of that field throughout the entire database.

Reorganizing a Form in Form Design View

Where a new field is placed doesn't really matter because you can move it wherever you want. You don't have to worry about aligning the field perfectly before you create it. You can always nudge the field into position after you've named and sized it. Let's align and place fields now and format them so that they're more attractive. As we work in Form Design view, we'll click the Form View button on the toolbar every now and then to see how our form really appears as it's used to enter data.

We moved all the fields around as you see in Figure 9-10 to create space above them for some text we're going to add.

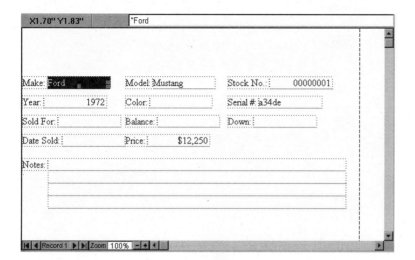

FIGURE 9-10
Reorganizing fields

All the fields were rearranged by simply dragging them (by either their title or the information area), and they were then standardized to be 18 characters in width using the Field Width command on the Format menu. The Notes field was expanded by dragging the diagonal sizing handle down and to the right. Try it.

TIP To format more than one field in Form Design view, click on the first field (not the field name!), and then hold down the Ctrl key as you click on each additional field to select it. Then make the size changes you need.

Aligning Text in Fields

Works, by default, very sensibly right-aligns numbers and left-aligns text. But you can change alignment for any type of data by doing the following:

1. Hold down the Ctrl key, and click any fields in which you want to realign data.

2. Point to one of the selected fields, and click the right mouse button.

3. Click Alignment.

   When you do this, you will see this Format dialog box:

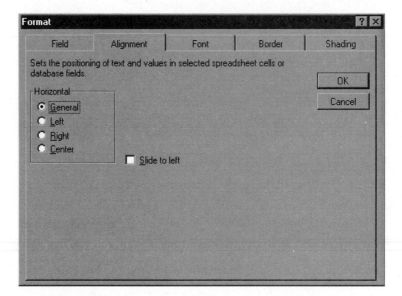

4. Click an alignment option button in the Horizontal box to realign the information in the fields.

5. Click OK.

6. Click the Form View button on the toolbar to check your progress, and then switch back to Form Design view.

Applying Borders to Fields

We can spruce up the information area of the field by adding a border around the entire area.

1. Hold down the Ctrl key and click all the fields (not their names) to select them.

2. Point to a selected field, click the right mouse button, and then click Border.

   When you do this, you'll see this set of options in the Format dialog box:

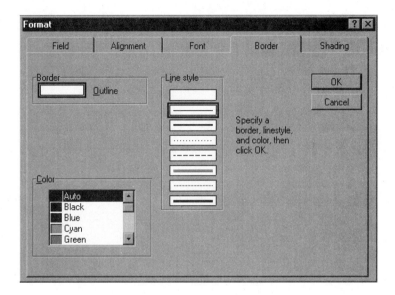

3. As you did with the spreadsheet, select a Line Style option and then click the Outline option in the Border box. We used an unbroken line.

4. Click OK, and then click the Form View button.

   You'll see all the fields formatted with borders, as shown in Figure 9-11 on the following page.

TIP Note that when you point to a field and click the right mouse button, you can take advantage of many different format tools, including those you have seen earlier, such as shading and changing fonts and styles.

FIGURE 9-11

Fields formatted
with borders shown
in Form view

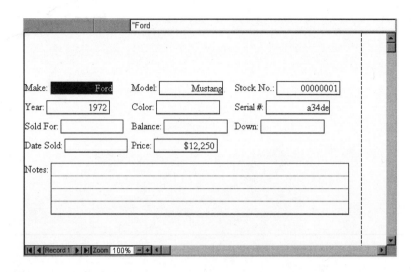

Adding Labels and Descriptions

A label is another way to use text to identify a portion of your database. You don't use labels with field names, but they're great for such things as including instructions or special notes on a form.

1. Be sure you're in Form Design view, and click where you want to begin typing the label.

2. Type the label's text, and then click the Enter button.

    Works accepted the text as a label rather than as a field, because you didn't define it as a field using the Create Database dialog box you've seen several times in this chapter.

When you create labels, Works lets you apply boldface and other character styles to them so that they'll stand out from the remainder of the form. You can also use different fonts and sizes for emphasis.

A label we entered appears in Form view in Figure 9-12. We changed the font to 16-point Arial and applied bold and italics to the label. We also dragged the label to center it.

That's the easy way to add a label. The other way is to choose the Label command from the Insert menu. When you do this, you'll see the Insert Label dialog box. Simply enter the label you want to use, and click OK.

You can use labels for other, more informative text as well. For example, we could add a label to the Notes section of our Cars form to remind the person filling out the form to include mileage, overall condition, and any repair work done to make the car more salable. Or, if you

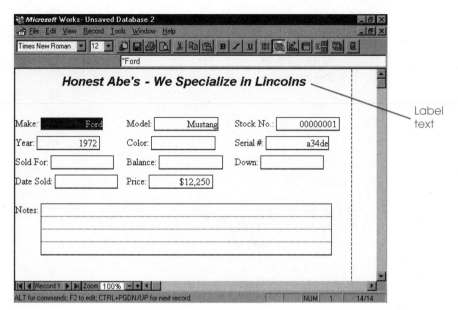

FIGURE 9-12
Adding a label to a database

have an employment application form on screen, you could easily provide instructions such as *Please provide your date of birth* with a field for date of birth following the label.

Labels are moved the same way fields are moved. Simply drag them where you want them to go. And guess what? They're deleted the same way as well. Simply highlight them and press the Del key. Guess what else? You can easily undo the mistaken deletion of a label using the Undo command or the Ctrl+Z key combination.

Entering and Editing Data

To enter some data in a modified form in Form view, click to the right of the field name you want and simply fill out the form for each record you want to create. You don't enter data in Form Design view.

To move to the first field, click in the field. To move to subsequent fields, use the Tab key. To move backward in the form, use the Shift+Tab key combination.

We completed record 1, which appears in Form view as shown in Figure 9-13 on the next page. We left the font as is.

FIGURE 9-13

A completed record
in Form view

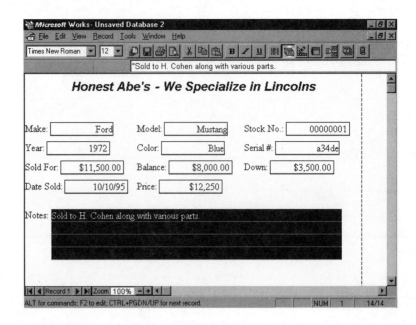

Adding New Records in Form View

Adding records in Form view is similar to doing so in List view. Keep the following notes in mind when adding a record in Form view.

- Click the Last Record button in the Navigation bar to the left of the horizontal scroll bar to move to an empty form at the end of the database.

- Use the Tab key to get to the first field in that blank record. Enter data to add as many records as you want; Works will add them after the existing records.

- Scroll to the record before which you want to add a new record. Click Record, click Insert Record, and Works will insert a blank form at that location. All succeeding records will be renumbered.

In what view should you add records? It really doesn't matter, so use the view that you prefer.

Making Calculations

You're already familiar with how similar the database module's List view is to the document window view you see in the spreadsheet module. These two applications also overlap considerably in their ability to perform calculations. The spreadsheet can use a formula to produce a new value.

The database can also use values from one or more fields to calculate the entry that belongs in another field.

> NOTE The Works database doesn't allow you to paste in a function like the spreadsheet does. You have to enter the function manually by typing it.

For example, in our sample form, we created fields for the selling price of a car, the down payment, and the balance owed. Here's how you can enter a formula in Form view.

1. Go to the first record, if necessary.

2. Click the field where you want to enter a formula.

3. Type a formula and click the Enter button. We entered this one:
   =Sold For-Down

   Note that there are fields in the database named *Sold For* and *Down*. The values in the fields are used to calculate the result, not the field names themselves.

Creating formulas in the database is quite similar to creating them in the spreadsheet. However, you must type database field names to enter them into a formula when working in Form view. In List view, by contrast, you can point to cells to include their references, just as you do in a spreadsheet formula.

The example in Figure 9-14 on the next page shows a simple database of stock prices where we'll incorporate database functions into fields. You must be in List view to use database functions.

Now we can use three Works functions—MAX, MIN, and AVG—to fill in the new fields. MAX finds and displays the highest value in a set of cells or fields you specify. MIN finds and displays the lowest value. AVG calculates the average value. For each of these functions, we'll enter the fields Day 1 through Day 5 as the values for Works to examine. The steps are as follows:

1. In an appropriate field in row 1, type a formula. We entered this one: *=max(day 1, day 2, day 3, day 4, day 5)*

   Type the field names, including spaces, as they appear in the form. If you don't, Works will display a message telling you the formula contains an error.

		Stock	Day 1	Day 2	Day 3	Day 4	Day 5	High	Low	Average
	1	A	$37.50	$38.75	$40.00	$41.25	$42.50			
	2	B	$1.50	$1.25	$1.00	$0.75	$0.50			
	3	C	$28.25	$29.25	$30.25	$31.25	$32.25			
	4	D	$1.40	$2.90	$4.40	$5.90	$7.40			
	5	E	$79.75	$80.25	$80.75	$81.25	$81.75			
	6									
	7									
	8									
	9									
	10									
	11									
	12									
	13									
	14									
	15									
	16									
	17									
	18									
	19									

Zoom 100%

2. Click the Enter button when you're done typing.

    Notice in our example that Works displays the highest stock
    price in this field for each record in the database, as shown in Figure
    9-15.

=MAX(Day 1,Day 2,Day 3,Day 4,Day 5)

		Stock	Day 1	Day 2	Day 3	Day 4	Day 5	High	Low	Average
	1	A	$37.50	$38.75	$40.00	$41.25	$42.50	42.5		
	2	B	$1.50	$1.25	$1.00	$0.75	$0.50	1.5		
	3	C	$28.25	$29.25	$30.25	$31.25	$32.25	32.25		
	4	D	$1.40	$2.90	$4.40	$5.90	$7.40	7.4		
	5	E	$79.75	$80.25	$80.75	$81.25	$81.75	81.75		
	6									
	7									
	8									
	9									
	10									

Entered
function
calculates
a result for
each record.

3. For the Low field, we entered this formula: =min(day 1, day 2, day
    3, day 4, day 5)

    Now Works displays the lowest stock price.

4. For the Average field, we entered this formula: =avg(day 1, day 2,
    day 3, day 4, day 5)

    This time Works calculates the average value for the five days
    and displays the result.

    The results of using the functions are shown in Figure 9-16.

    Even though you enter a function for only one record, Works
    applies it to the same field in all the records. If you were to click the
    Form View button and scroll through the other records in the database,

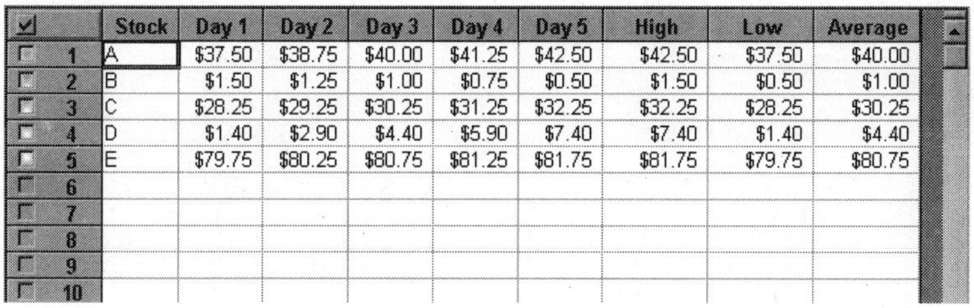

✓		Stock	Day 1	Day 2	Day 3	Day 4	Day 5	High	Low	Average	
□	1	A	$37.50	$38.75	$40.00	$41.25	$42.50	$42.50	$37.50	$40.00	
□	2	B	$1.50	$1.25	$1.00	$0.75	$0.50	$1.50	$0.50	$1.00	
□	3	C	$28.25	$29.25	$30.25	$31.25	$32.25	$32.25	$28.25	$30.25	
□	4	D	$1.40	$2.90	$4.40	$5.90	$7.40	$7.40	$1.40	$4.40	
□	5	E	$79.75	$80.25	$80.75	$81.25	$81.75	$81.75	$79.75	$80.75	
□	6										
□	7										
□	8										
□	9										
□	10										

FIGURE 9-16

Using three functions in a database

you would see that each record now shows the calculation results for the appropriate fields.

Coming Next

Now you have the basics of creating and using a database to manage information effectively. What's left to explore are more advanced techniques for using the Works database to sort records and search for information. Let's turn our attention to those now, and to other database features.

Chapter 10

Using a Database to Locate Information

Organizing and constructing a database requires a fair amount of time and planning, especially if you want to design a complex form or enter hundreds or even thousands of records. But, as you now realize, the planning time is well spent.

Getting the information into a record is only part of using a database effectively. The methods you can use to work with and manage a database are just as important; they are the focus of this chapter.

After the database form is designed, however, you don't have to bother with sorting, alphabetizing, or selecting records, because that's where Works excels. After records are entered, the database is ready for use—whenever and however you need it. How to organize, manage, and locate records efficiently is what this chapter is all about.

Sorting Records

After you create a database, you will want to organize it so that it's easy to reference. You can do this in a variety of ways, including alphabetically, numerically, and chronologically. With Works, sorting database information is a piece of cake. Works can sort on as many as three columns or fields.

Alphabetic and numeric sorting can go either up or down. An upward, or *ascending*, sort order goes from A to Z and from 0 to 9. A downward, or *descending*, sort order moves in the other direction, that is, from Z to A or from 9 to 0.

Sorting on Multiple Fields

You can sort records in either List view or Form view. Of the two, List view gives you a better feel for the results because you can see a number of sorted records at one time. If you sort records in Form view, Works displays only the first record in the sorted database. To see other records, you must scroll using the Navigation buttons.

To demonstrate sorting and other database management features, we'll use the same *Cars* database example we worked with in Chapter 9. The Cars database is shown in List view in Figure 10-1 on the following page. In the examples notice that we have hidden Help and maximized the document window.

		Make	Model	Year	Price	Serial #	Stock No.	Date Sold	Sold For	Down	Balance
	1	Ford	Mustang	1972	$12,550	a34de	1	7/10/95	$11,500	$3,500	$8,000
	2	Ford	Probe	1991	$4,500	v3476	2	8/12/95	$9,876	$2,500	$7,376
	3	Chevrolet	Camaro	1974	$2,350	b6567	3	4/27/95	$13,432	$5,000	$8,432
	4	Honda	Civic	1989	$6,800	n4564	4	7/6/95	$4,656	$2,000	$2,656
	5	Lincoln	Mark V	1978	$5,000	n6755	5	3/4/95	$14,543	$7,500	$11,043
	6	Lincoln	Continental	1990	$17,500	y6756	6	5/4/95	$21,343	$15,000	$6,343
	7	Lincoln	Continental	1966	$9,000	g4534	7	2/23/94	$19,767	$15,000	$4,767
	8	Lincoln	Town Car	1990	$22,000	t7762	8	3/8395	$23,432	$5,000	$18,432
	9	Lincoln	Town Car	1988	$17,500	h6776	10	7/16/95	$16,576	$3,500	$13,076
	10	Lincoln	Mark VII	1990	$18,000	u7767	11	4/26/94	$19,786	$5,750	$14,036
	11	Toyota	Celica	1988	$7,500	u6657	11	11/3/95	$5,545	$1,000	$4,545
	12	Ford	T-Bird	1990	$17,000	a4435	12	2/1/95	$7,698	$1,500	$6,198
	13	Ford	Mustang	1990	$15,500	e7685	13	6/13/94	$8,756	$1,750	$7,006
	14										
	15										
	16										
	17										
	18										
	19										
	20										
	21										

Zoom 88%

FIGURE 10-1

The Cars database
in List view

We'll begin by sorting the database first by make, next by model, and then by year. Here's how.

1. Click Record, and then click Sort Records.
    Works displays this Sort Records dialog box:

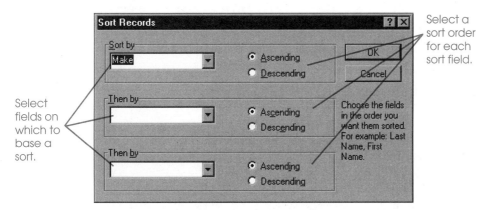

Select fields on which to base a sort.

Select a sort order for each sort field.

Choose the fields in the order you want them sorted. For example: Last Name, First Name.

When you perform a sort on multiple fields, you list the most important field first (in this case, the Make field), which Works should propose. If it doesn't, you will need to type the appropriate field name in the Sort By text box. An ascending sort, which Works proposes, is fine, so we'll go on to define the second sort field. You can use the Tab key to move to the next text box or simply click on it using the mouse.

2. Click in the Then By box, and type the next field name for the sort (or click on the drop-down list arrow and select it from the drop-down menu).

3. Click in the last Then By box, and type the next field name for the sort (or click on the drop-down list arrow and select a field name).

Because the ascending sort Works proposes would list the oldest cars first, we'll need to change the sort order for this box.

4. Click the Descending option button or use the Tab key and Down arrow key to select it.

Now Works will list, from newest to oldest, each record with the same make and model.

 TIP You can either type in the name of the field on which you want to sort, or simply select it from the drop-down menu that's present in each field sort area.

---

5. Click OK.

The result of the sort is shown in Figure 10-2.

FIGURE 10-2

A database sorted alphabetically on its first field

Records sorted alphabetically by Make

		Make	Model	Year	Price	Serial #	Stock No	Date Sold	Sold For	Dov
	1	Chevrolet	Camaro	1974	$2,350	b6567	3	4/27/95	$13,432	$5
	2	Ford	Mustang	1990	$16,500	e7995	14	6/13/91	$9,766	$1
	3	Ford	Mustang	1972	$12,250	a34de	1	7/10/95	$11,500	$3
	4	Ford	Probe	1991	$4,500	v3476	2	8/12/95	$9,876	$2
	5	Ford	T-Bird	1990	$17,000	a4435	13	2/1/95	$7,698	$1
	6	Honda	Civic	1989	$6,800	n4564	4	7/8/95	$4,656	$2
	7	Lincoln	Continental	1990	$17,500	y6756	6	5/4/95	$21,343	$15
	8	Lincoln	Continental	1966	$9,000	g4534	7	2/23/94	$19,767	$15
	9	Lincoln	Mark V	1978	$5,000	n6755	5	3/4/95	$14,543	$7
	10	Lincoln	Mark VII	1990	$18,000	u7767	11	4/26/94	$19,786	$5
	11	Lincoln	Town Car	1990	$22,000	t7762	8	3/8/95	$23,432	$5
	12	Lincoln	Town Car	1988	$17,500	h6776	10	7/16/95	$16,576	$3
	13	Toyota	Celica	1988	$7,500	u6657	12	11/3/95	$5,545	$1
	14									
	15									
	16									
	17									
	18									

Zoom 100%

If a field on which you sort contains different types of entries, such as text for some records and numbers for others, Works sorts in the following order:

- For an ascending sort, the order is text, times (such as 12:00 A.M.), numbers, and then dates (January 1, 1992).

- For a descending sort, the order is just the reverse. First sorted are dates, followed by numbers, times, and then text.

Sorting by Record

In an alphabetical sort, Works ignores differences in capitalization, so *baby* comes before *Babylon*, but *Mars* precedes *martial*. If you create a database in which capitalization is important, you have to include more information for Works.

For example, if you want *NEW YEAR* to always precede *New Year*, create a new field and use a code, such as 1 for all capitals (*NEW YEAR*), 2 for initial capitals (*New Year*), and 3 for lowercase (*new year*). You can then use the case field as the second sort field. That way, you'll be sure that duplicate entries are arranged in the order you want. Figure 10-3 shows an illustration of what we just proposed. The data listed on the left is sorted alphabetically; the data on the right is sorted by number (#).

As always, planning ahead prevents aggravation and lots of effort later on.

✔		Entry	#
☐	1	new year	5
☐	2	New Year	2
☐	3	new Year	4
☐	4	New year	3
☐	5	NEW YEAR	1
☐	6		
☐	7		
☐	8		
☐	9		
☐	10		
☐	11		
☐	12		

✔		Entry	#
☐	1	NEW YEAR	1
☐	2	New Year	2
☐	3	New year	3
☐	4	new Year	4
☐	5	new year	5
☐	6		
☐	7		
☐	8		
☐	9		
☐	10		
☐	11		
☐	12		

FIGURE 10-3

Using another value to sort by case

Finding Information

If you have 2,000 records (databases that size can develop faster than you think!), sorting will be a help, but you probably won't want to scroll through 50 screens to find what you need.

If you wish to find a particular record or group of records, or all the records that match one or more criteria, Works can do this with ease. To find specific records, all you need to do is give Works the *criteria* or information (the more the better), such as some text, a unique value, or a field entry, that it can use to locate and separate the record (or records) you're trying to find from the entire set of records.

To find records that match certain criteria, you provide Works with a "description" of the information you seek and let Works do its work.

Finding Related Records

To find one or more records that have some information in common, use the Find command on the Edit menu. You can work in either List view or Form view. Suppose, for example, we want to find all the records for Lincoln Continentals in the Cars database. We can do the following:

1. Click Edit, and then click Find.

    You will see the Find dialog.

2. Type the data you want to find. Here we typed *continental* (either uppercase or lowercase is OK).

    Make sure that the default Match setting, Next Record, is selected.

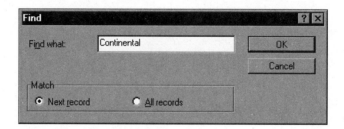

3. Click OK.

    Works highlights the first cell containing the data typed in the Find What box, which, in our example, is the Model field data for record 6 in the database.

Starting from the current location of the mouse pointer, Works scans the database and moves the selection to the next occurrence of the text typed in the Find What box. If the current selection is near the end of the database, Works skips to the top and keeps going if it doesn't find a match by the time it reaches the last record.

Notice that when you carry out a Find command and tell Works to find only the next record, the entire database remains available for viewing. In the same dialog box, you can click on All Records, and Works will display only the records in which the selected text appears. This option is a great way not only to find, but also to select, particular records from the entire database.

The Find command works the same way in Form view, but the result of selecting all records is less noticeable because you see only a single record at a time in Form view. If you were to switch to Form view, Works would display the first matching record, as shown in Figure 10-4.

Notice that the status bar indicates that we're looking at record number 6.

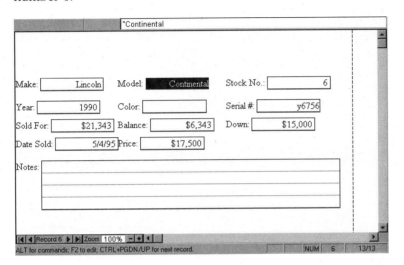

FIGURE 10-4

Finding information in Form view

In Form view you can click the Next Record button on the Navigation bar (to the left of the horizontal scroll bar), and Works displays another record that contains the text matching the text entered in the Find What box. If you were to continue scrolling to the next record until you see a blank form, this means Works has reached the end of the records containing the selected text and has no more to display.

TIP   When databases get large and you start using all the power that Works has to offer, you can become momentarily disoriented because the database might not appear in its entirety. If this happens, check the status bar. Then try choosing the Find command from the Edit menu to determine if you're actually looking at a set of *selected* records. Works continues to display the last text you searched for in the Find dialog box until you close the file or quit. If that doesn't help, use the Show All Records command on the Record menu to see all the records.

To see the entire database once again, you can click the List View button on the toolbar, click Record, click Show, and finally click All Records.

Replacing Information

Just as with the word processor and the spreadsheet, the Works database has a Replace command (on the Edit menu) that allows you to first find, and then replace, a field entry. You can use Replace only in List view.

For example, let's say we want to annotate the word *Lincoln* (in the Make field) to read *Lincoln (Pristine)*. Here's how to do it:

1. Be sure List view is active. Click Edit, and then click Replace.

2. Type the text you want to replace in the Find What box.

3. Press Tab to move to the Replace With box.

4. Type the new text to replace the occurrences of the text you entered in the Find What box.

5. Click Replace All.

The most important thing to remember about the Replace command is not to search to change individual letters, but rather to search on as much information as you can use. Always save your file before you proceed with a full-blown find-and-replace operation, to avoid unintended consequences and gnashing of teeth.

Using Wildcard Characters

Chapter 5 introduced the concept of using wildcard characters to find information in one or more spreadsheet cells. You can use the same characters, the asterisk (*) and the question mark (?), in the database to broaden a search with the Find command (on the Edit menu). The asterisk, you might recall, can stand for any number of consecutive characters, whereas a question mark can represent any one character.

For example, entering *m** in our Cars database example would cause Works to display all records having a field entry containing an M followed by any number of characters, such as Mark V, Mark VII, and Mustang. Entering *198?* in the Find What box would cause Works to display all records containing data beginning with *198* and ending in any other character, such as 1988 and 1989.

While wildcard characters can be useful in helping you find generic information, keep in mind that Works doesn't distinguish between whole words and parts of words. Use wildcard characters in the database in the same way you would use them in the spreadsheet, but always be sure to include enough specific text to narrow the selection to what you really want to find.

For example, if we were to use the Find command and type *c** to tell Works to find all Continentals in our Cars database, we'd be in for a surprise. The specification is so broad that Works would include every entry in which the letter c is followed by one or more characters, such as the records that contain Honda Civic, Lincoln Mark VII, and Chevrolet Camaro.

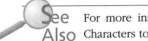

See Also For more information on *wildcard characters*, see "Using Wildcard Characters to Find Text" in Chapter 5, page 161.

Querying a Database to Find Information

You can use the database module to ask Works questions to obtain specific information. In our example we might ask, "Which cars have a price of more than $10,000?" or "Which records contain model years that are newer than 1989?" This is a tremendous time-saver in a large database. Asking such a question is called a *query* in database jargon. When you want Works to apply some "judgment" to a database search, you use criteria to query the database for specific information. And the way you query a database is through the creation of a *filter*. Just as you would filter one substance (such as rocks) from another (such as soil), you can filter out database records that contain information you want from those that contain information you don't want, and vice versa.

In the process of creating a filter, you incorporate mathematics, logic, and relational operators, such as greater than (>) and less than (<), and even logical operators, such as AND, OR, and NOT. Don't shy away from using queries even if they sound intimidating, for they can be a very powerful ally in making you a much more efficient database user.

What a Query Is and When to Use One

We could write an entire book on querying a database, the subject is so vast. Using a query is like using a set of super commands—using queries gives you the most control over what happens within your database. More than any of the other Works applications, databases (together with their ability to filter information within them) are yours to personalize. Given the way you set up your fields and the information contained in them, the type and number of questions you can ask are limited only by your own fertile ingenuity.

Fashioning a Query and Using Filters

When you use the Find command, you tell Works to search for records that contain certain information. After it finds that information, you have a group of records that are related to one another in some way.

When you use a filter to construct a query, you take the search process one step further. Here, Works not only finds the records you want, but also lets you apply several conditions to refine the search.

You can, for example, use the Find command on a personal database to give you the names of all relatives named Hubbard. With a query, you can tell Works to narrow the field by showing you any and all relatives named Hubbard who have six or more children and are over the age of 90.

> NOTE Let's state an obvious principle right now. You can only perform a query when the information the query must work with is in the database. If you don't have a field that contains the "number of children" data, you obviously cannot find relatives with a certain name that have more than a certain number of children. Although this fact is somewhat self-evident, many people try to use the query function to make gold out of straw.

We can use the Cars database to develop a feel for using filters to query a database. We might begin by querying to find all Lincolns that cost more than $9,000, as follows:

1. Click the Filters button (it's to the left of the Address Book button on the toolbar).

    You can also choose Filter from the Tools menu in either Form or List view. If this is the first filter that you've created, Works will ask you to name it. By giving a name to the query, you can use it again.

2. Type a name for the query. We entered *Lincolns>9000*.
   Works displays the Filter dialog box shown in Figure 10-5.

FIGURE 10-5
Use the Filter dialog box to construct a query.

Enter one or more AND or OR conditions.

Select a field name here.

Select a comparison operator here.

Enter criterion data here.

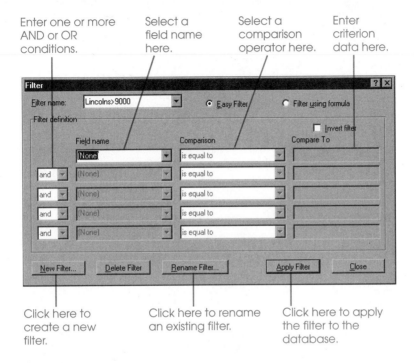

Click here to create a new filter.

Click here to rename an existing filter.

Click here to apply the filter to the database.

Now you need to provide Works with three pieces of information so that it can provide the information you seek.

❑ The first is the field you want compared (in the Field Name box).

❑ The second is how you want the field compared (in the Comparison box).

❑ The third is what you want the field to be compared to (in the Compare To box).

3. In the Field Name box, either type the field name or use the drop-down list arrow to select the field name. We selected Make.

4. In the Comparison box, select a comparison operator. We chose *is equal to* from the drop-down list.

5. In the Compare To box, type the specific data to be matched. We entered *Lincoln (Pristine)*.

TIP Your entries in the Compare To box must match exactly those in the database you are querying. Works doesn't look for partial information, so *Lincoln* will not be a valid criterion but *Lincoln (Pristine)* will be in our Cars database example.

This particular filter finds all cars that are a Lincoln (Pristine) in our example database. For this much of the filter, we could have used the Find command because this is just a simple condition of finding something equal to something else. But we want to find any Lincoln (Pristine) that costs over $9,000, not just any old Lincoln (Pristine). This means we need to specify a filter with multiple conditions. As you can see in Figure 10-6, the Filter Definition box contains the first condition we've already entered ("Make is equal to Lincoln (Pristine)") plus the AND condition we can enter by following these steps:

FIGURE 10-6
A filter with an AND
condition

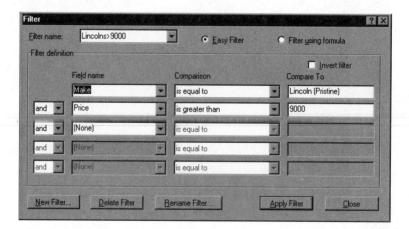

1. Select the And option.

2. Type a field name in the second Field Name box (or click the drop-down list arrow and select the field name). We selected Price.

3. Click the Comparison box's drop-down list arrow, and select a comparison operator. We selected *is greater than*.

4. Click in the Compare To box, and type criterion data. We entered *9000*.

TIP You're limited to eight filters for any one database, so feel free to delete those that you're finished with by using the Delete Query command on the Tools menu.

5. Click the Apply Filter button.

    You can see the results of our query in Figure 10-7.

		Make	Model	Year	Price	Serial #	Stock No.	Date Sold	Sol
	6	Lincoln (Pristine)	Continental	1990	$17,500	y6756	6	5/4/95	$2
	8	Lincoln (Pristine)	Town Car	1990	$22,000	t7762	8	3/8395	$2
	9	Lincoln (Pristine)	Town Car	1988	$17,500	h6776	10	7/16/95	$1
	10	Lincoln (Pristine)	Mark VII	1990	$18,000	u7767	11	4/26/94	$1
	14								
	15								
	16								
	17								
	18								
	19								
	20								
	21								
	22								
	23								
	24								
	25								
	26								
	27								
	28								

Zoom 100%

FIGURE 10-7

The results of a query using an AND condition filter

As you can see, Works did its job perfectly and instantaneously, finding only those records that met the two conditions. Records 6, 8, 9, and 10 are all records for a Lincoln (Pristine) that costs more than $9,000.

Want to see more? Suppose we query the database for all cars built from 1974 to the present that cost less than $6,000? To apply this filter, we can do the following:

1. Click the Filters button on the toolbar.

2. Click New Filter.

3. Type a name for the filter and click OK. For this one we entered *1974<6000.*

4. Select the appropriate field name, select the appropriate comparison operator, and type criterion data in the Compare To box. We selected *Year,* the operator *is greater than or equal to,* and *1974.*

5. For the AND condition, select the appropriate field name, select the appropriate comparison operator, and type criterion data in the

Compare To box. We selected *Price*, the operator *is less than*, and typed *6000* for the criterion data.

The Filter dialog box looks like this:

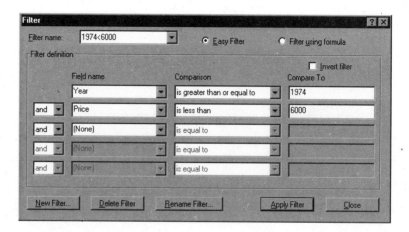

6. Click the Apply Filter button.

This filter provides the result you see in Figure 10-8. Records 2, 3, 5, and 12 meet this filter's criteria.

FIGURE 10-8

The result of the second filter with an AND condition

✓		Make	Model	Year	Price	Serial #	Stock No.	Date Sold	Sol
	2	Ford	Probe	1991	$4,500	v3476	2		
	3	Chevrolet	Camaro	1974	$2,350	b6567	3		
	5	Lincoln (Pristine)	Mark V	1978	$5,000	n6755	5		
	12	Ford	T-Bird	1990	$1,700	a4435	12		
	14								
	15								
	16								
	17								
	18								
	19								
	20								
	21								
	22								
	23								
	24								
	25								
	26								
	27								
	28								

Zoom 100%

Creating a Library of Queries

As you work, you'll find that you wish to create queries that do all kinds of filtering through various databases. If you want to reapply the last query you created (without having to create it all over again) in any particular database, you can do so by clicking Apply Filter from the Record menu.

You'll see a list of queries that have already been created for that database. Just click on the one you want to use. This way, you create a library of queries that are stored for each database.

> **TIP** Querying in Form view is exactly the same process as in List view. It's your choice as to how you want to display the results.

Editing a Filter

Queries are great because they let you impose strict conditions on filtering and selecting records. Works also gives you a way to reuse filters—an especially important feature for complex queries. Not only can you easily select any filter you have already created, but you can also select an existing filter and modify it to form a *new* query. For example, let's say we have an interested customer and want to look for Lincolns that sell for less than $18,000. We already have a query that looks for Lincolns that sell for more than $9,000, so let's edit that one by doing the following:

1. Click the Filters button.

2. Click on the Filter Name's drop-down list arrow to see the list of available filters.

3. Click the filter name for the filter you want to edit. We selected *Lincolns>9000*.

4. Select the appropriate comparison operator in the second Comparison box. We changed it to *is less than*.

5. Enter the appropriate criterion data in the second Compare To box. We entered *18000*.

6. Click Rename Filter, type a new name, and then click OK. We entered *Lincolns<18000*.

7. Click the Apply Filter button.

We just took an existing filter and modified it to perform a new query and then saved it under a unique name. It will become part of the queries "library" and be easily accessible.

Viewing Other Records

Each time you query the database, Works displays only those records you wanted to see. Where did the others go, and what if you want to see them?

Whenever you use the Find command or execute a query, Works hides all the records that don't match the criteria you specified. To see those records instead of the ones you requested, do this: click Record, click Show, and then click Hidden Records.

As you can see, this command causes Works to swap the two sets of records, hiding the current filtered set and displaying the others. You can switch back and forth as many times as you want. Each time, Works replaces the records currently on display with the alternate hidden set.

When you work with filters, Works doesn't allow you to display both the criteria- and non-criteria-matching records simultaneously. Yet if you want to compare two sets of records in a database, there's a way to do so. Apply your filter and save the file twice. Save it once under its real name and again under a temporary name.

Applying Judgment to Queries

The queries you've used so far for selecting records are the type you'll most likely need on a day-to-day basis. When you design a query with more than one field, you're entering an implied AND condition as part of your query, as if you were to say, "Show the records for all cars built after 1974 *and* priced under $6,000."

AND is only one such condition (logical operator) that Works understands. As you've seen, Works selects those records that meet *both* criteria in an AND condition filter. Works also recognizes an OR condition, in which records are selected if they meet *either* criterion specified in the filter. This means the query "Show the records for all cars built after 1975 *or* priced under $6,000" would display those records for 1974 and newer models (even those over $6,000) as well as those records for cars costing under $6,000 (even those older than 1974).

All of the operators listed in the Comparison lists can be used in either condition for filters. Table 10-1 summarizes each, and gives examples of what would be found in the Cars database.

Operator	Type of Comparison	Cars Database Example
is equal to	selects records with the exact specified Compare To data in the selected field	*Make is equal to Ford* finds all cars that are Fords
is not equal to	selects records with data other than the exact specified Compare To data in the selected field	*Make is not equal to Ford* finds all cars other than Fords
is less than	selects records with an alphanumeric value less than the specified Compare To data in the selected field	*Price is less than 10000* finds cars that sell for less than $10,000
is greater than	selects records with an alphanumeric value greater than the specified Compare To data in the selected field	*Price is greater than 10000* finds cars that sell for more than $10,000
is less than or equal to	selects records with the exact Compare To data in the selected field or Compare To data that is an alphanumeric value less than that specified	*Year is less than or equal to 1985* finds all cars that are 1985 models or older
is greater than or equal to	selects records with the exact Compare To data in the selected field or Compare To data that is an alphanumeric value greater than that specified	*Year is greater than or equal to 1987* finds all cars that are 1987 models or older
contains	selects records with any character specified for the Compare To data in the selected field	*Model contains t* finds all cars with a "t" in the model name

TABLE 10-1   *(continued)*

Filter operators and examples applied to the Cars database

TABLE 10-1 *continued*

Operator	Type of Comparison	Cars Database Example
does not contain	selects records with any character other than those specified for the Compare To data in the selected field	*Year does not contain 2* finds all cars with year models that do not contain a 2
is blank	selects records with no data in the selected field	*Serial # is blank* finds all cars with no Serial # data
is not blank	selects records containing data in the selected field	*Sold For is not blank* finds all cars that have been sold (contains data in the field)
begins with	selects records with Compare To data in the selected field that begins with the specified character	*Serial # begins with j* finds all cars that have a serial number that begins with the letter "j"
does not begin with	selects records with any character other than that specified for the Compare To data in the selected field	*Serial # does not begin with y* finds all cars other than those that have serial numbers beginning with "y"
ends with	selects records with Compare To data in the selected field that ends with the specified character	*Price ends with 9* finds all cars with a selling price that ends with the number 9
does not end with	selects records with data that ends with any character other than that specified for the Compare To data in the selected field	*Price does not end with 0* finds all cars other than those with a selling price that ends in the number 0

Using the Query Language

While you can probably formulate all your queries using the filters that we just described, there may be times when you want to use the query language and design a query formula. Here, you essentially formulate the query in Works' language rather than your own. Remember that you can always create a new query, use up to three criteria, and include all the logical operators available in the drop-down menus. To use the query language, follow these steps:

1. Click the Filters button.

2. Click the Filter Using Formula option button.

3. Type (on one line):

   ```
   ='Make'="Lincoln (Pristine)"#AND#'Year'<VALUE("1980")
   #OR#'Price'>VALUE("18000")
   ```

4. Click the Apply Filter button.

In this example, you "wrote" your query in such a way that Works could "read" it. As always, you begin the query with an equal sign to indicate that you're entering characters you want Works to evaluate. The rest of the filter's formula breaks down this way:

- Your first instruction, 'Make'="Lincoln (Pristine)", indicates the field you want to search for the first condition and encloses the data to locate in the field in double quotation marks (").

- Next comes the logical AND operator (#AND#). This tells Works to accept the next part of the formula as the filter's AND condition.

- The next instruction, 'Year'<VALUE("1980"), requests Works to locate those records with a value of 1980 or less in the Year field for those records meeting the condition in the first instruction (car makes that equal "Lincoln (Pristine)").

- Next comes the logical OR operator (#OR#). This tells Works to accept the next part of the formula as the filter's OR condition.

- The next instruction, 'Price'>VALUE("18000"), asks Works to locate those records with a price over $18,000 for those records that satisfy the same condition in the first instruction.

TIP You don't have to enter the VALUE functions, as you did in the previous example. For instance, you could have typed '*Year*'<"*1980*" for the instruction following the AND operator. However, Works converts the entry to '*Year*'<*VALUE*("*1980*"), anyway. You can see this if you click the Filters button after applying the filter and then clicking on the Filter Using Formula option button. The converted instructions appear in the formula box.

You also can use parentheses to combine instructions so that they're treated as a single conditon. Parentheses function in queries much as they do in a spreadsheet formula. If you enclosed the rest of the formula following the AND operator in parentheses, Works would interpret the query as "Search for records in which the make is Lincoln (Pristine) and the year is before 1980, or the price is greater than $18,000." This query would give you a message box telling you that no criteria-matching records could be found, which is true because the database contains only two Lincoln (Pristine)s with model years prior to 1980, and those both sell for under $18,000.

Different Types of Query Language

Databases are as varied as the people who use them. Being able to find, replace, and search using all types of logical operators allows almost anyone, in any discipline, to manage a great deal of information efficiently.

Here's a brief summary of when to use various operators when setting criteria in filters.

Greater than (>) and less than (<) These operators are used to find records in which a certain value is greater or less than a value you indicate. Although previous examples showed you how to use these operators with numeric values, you can also use them with text. Just remember to enclose the text in double quotation marks.

For example, let's say you're working with a database of dogs. You can type >24 to find all breeds taller than 24 inches, but you can also specify >"samoyed" to list all breeds that come after samoyed in the alphabet.

Combining greater than (>) and less than (<) The greater than and less than operators can be combined to find records with data in a specific range. You can use them with either numbers or text, enclosing the text in double quotation marks. Because you are entering more than one criterion, you must include the AND operator to show that you want items greater than X and less than Y. We'll use the dog database as an example again.

You can type >10#AND#<100 to find all records containing a value from 11 through 99 in the Weight field. With text, you can type >"cocker"#AND#<"doberman" to find all breeds alphabetically between Cockers and Dobermans, excluding the two you use as criteria.

The not equal to operator (<>) Typing a less than and greater than sign together creates the *not equal to* operator. You can use this operator to locate records with a value or text other than that indicated in the condition. Using the dog database, for example, you could type <>"8/17/95" to locate records with dates other than this one in the Birth Date field. For text data, you might enter <>"collie" to locate all breeds other than this one.

Logical operators The AND operator is used to find records that satisfy more than one condition. The OR operator is used to find records that match at least one condition you set up.

The following examples assume you're entering a query in a field named Grade. The form includes fields for grades, grade average, days absent, and midterm grade.

- Enter =‘Average’>"95"#AND#‘Absence’<"4" *to find all students who qualify for an A (students who have a better than 95 grade point average and were absent fewer than four days).*

- Enter =‘Midterm’>="70"#AND#((‘Average’>"50"#AND#‘Average’ <"80")#AND# ‘Absence’<"8") *to find all students who qualify for a C on the basis of a 70 or higher grade on the midterm and an average grade between 50 and 80, plus fewer than eight absences.*

Math operators You can use any of the basic math operators, as well. All of them should be familiar from the spreadsheet (and from basic math!): + (addition), − (subtraction), * (multiplication), / (division), or ^ (exponentiation). As in combined queries, use parentheses to group calculations that you want to be treated as a unit. For example:

- Enter =(‘Price’-‘Sold For’)>"1000" *in the Cars database to find all records in which the selling price was more than $1,000 below the original (selling) price.*

- In a parts inventory, enter (on hand*unit price) to find the total value of the parts you currently have in stock.

Works Functions

Use built-in functions, such as AVG, MIN, and MAX, to search for records meeting criteria that are calculated. Works includes many functions. A complete description of these functions is available in Appendix A.

Page Setup and Printing

The process of setting up pages and printing them in the database will be familiar to you because it works much the same in the other Works modules. As with the word processor and the spreadsheet, you can set page margins, switch the orientation of the paper you are printing on, and specify whether you want to print field names.

The following section deals with the Page Setup options in the Page Setup dialog box you see here, which appears when you select the Page Setup command on the File menu.

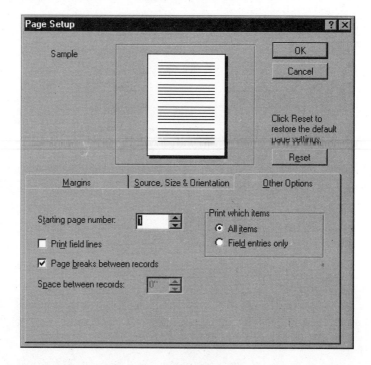

The Page Setup Options

The dialog box controlling the page setup should be familiar because you've seen it before in the word processor and spreadsheet modules.

In the Margins tab you can set the top, bottom, left, right, and header and footer margins as you do in the word processor and spreadsheet modules. The same goes for the Source, Size & Orientation tab, where you set the source of the paper; indicate its size, height, and width; and choose its orientation (landscape or portrait).

In the Other Options tab, you can set the page number of the first page, set page breaks and spaces between records (or turn them off so that more than one record goes on a page), print field lines, and choose to print fields plus data or data alone (some people prefer this approach because it is less cumbersome).

Coming Next

Throughout the last two chapters you've seen that the database is a powerful tool for managing information. In the next chapter, we'll show you how to take the records you've selected or sorted and turn them into an attractive and highly effective report.

Chapter 11

Creating
Database Reports

Databases are wonderful tools, but large ones can be a time-consuming nuisance to print, especially if you want to show only selected fields and to include calculations on selected data. With Microsoft Works for Windows 95, however, printing reports is easy. In the same way that the word processor allows you to format a document and the spreadsheet generates charts, the database produces reports. A *report* is a printed summary of database information. Using a Works report, you can select certain fields and records, print them in any order you choose, and modify their appearance so that the final output is exactly what you want.

After you've created a database, you can generate up to eight different reports for it that include the fields and records of your choice. You can name a report, duplicate it, and delete it when you no longer need it. You can also include titles, notes, labels, and calculations in your report, as well as headers, footers, and page numbers.

Although you can preview the reports you create, the Works report generator is not really meant for saving selected parts of a database for later viewing. Rather, it's an easy way to format and print the contents of a database plus the results of your queries. In fact, the report itself appears on the screen as a report definition where you see the layout of the report. To see the actual content of the database, you need to select the Print Preview command or print the report.

Creating a Standard Database Report

Works comes with a built-in design for a standard database report. You can customize the report (which we'll discuss later), but in many instances you'll find that the standard report is all you need—another major Works convenience. You can create a standard report in any Works database view, be it Form view or List view.

To demonstrate generating and printing database reports, we'll use the same Cars database example we worked with in the previous database chapters. An example of this database is shown in Figure 11-1.

✓		Make	Model	Year	Price	Serial #	Stock No	Date Sold	Sold For	
☐	1	Ford	Mustang	1972	$12,250	a34de	1	7/10/95	$11,500	
☐	2	Ford	Probe	1991	$4,500	v3476	2	8/12/95	$9,876	
☐	3	Chevrolet	Camaro	1974	$2,350	b6567	3	4/27/95	$13,432	
☐	4	Honda	Civic	1989	$6,800	n4564	4	7/8/95	$4,656	
☐	5	Lincoln	Mark V	1978	$5,000	n6755	5	3/4/95	$14,543	
☐	6	Lincoln	Continental	1990	$17,500	y6756	6	5/4/95	$21,343	
☐	7	Lincoln	Continental	1966	$9,000	g4534	7	2/23/94	$19,767	
☐	8	Lincoln	Town Car	1990	$22,000	t7762	8	3/8/95	$23,432	
☐	9	Lincoln	Town Car	1988	$17,500	h6776	10	7/16/95	$16,576	
☐	10	Lincoln	Mark VII	1990	$18,000	u7767	11	4/26/94	$19,786	
☐	11	Toyota	Celica	1988	$7,500	u6657	12	11/3/95	$5,545	
☐	12	Ford	T-Bird	1990	$17,000	a4435	13	2/1/95	$7,698	
☐	13	Ford	Mustang	1990	$15,500	e7685	14	6/13/94	$8,756	
☐	14									
☐	15									
☐	16									
☐	17									
☐	18									

Zoom 100% – + ◄

FIGURE 11-1

The Cars database information in List view

Follow these steps to create a standard report.

1. Click the Report View button on the toolbar.

When you do this, you will see this Report Name dialog box:

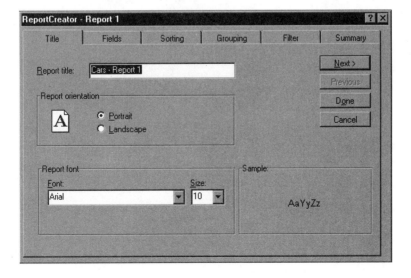

2. Click OK.

You will next see this ReportCreator - Report 1 dialog box:

Notice that the report is automatically titled Cars - Report 1. Works assigns the name of the active database file to the report.

3. Click Next.

    Notice that this activates the Fields tab.

4. Click Add All.

    The field names appear in the Field Order scroll box.

5. Click Next.

    The Sorting tab becomes active.

6. Click Next.

    The Grouping tab becomes active.

7. Click Next.

    The Filter tab becomes active.

8. Click (All Records) in the Select A Filter scroll box.

9. Click Next.

    The Summary tab becomes active.

10. Click Done.

    You'll see a box telling you that the report definition has been created and asking whether you want to preview or modify it.

11. Click the Print Preview button.

12. Click the Zoom In button.

You can see the standard report in the Print Preview window, as shown in Figure 11-2. Works uses the field widths that were set up in List view as the column widths when it creates a report. If your data displays completely in List view, it will also print without problem in a report. Be sure, however, to use Print Preview freely when creating a report, especially if you use different fonts and different sizes. When you learn to customize a report, you'll see the advantage of switching from Report view to the Print Preview window.

If you notice any problems with column width, fix them as you would with any database in List view (or as you would in a spreadsheet document window), and then use Print Preview to confirm that your solution worked.

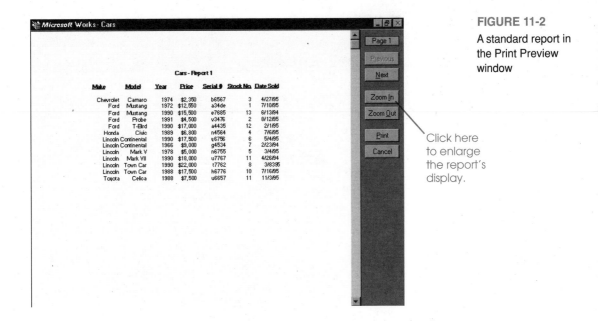

FIGURE 11-2

A standard report in the Print Preview window

When you're finished viewing the report, click the Cancel button to leave Print Preview. You should now be confident that you've created a usable report.

This report was completed with no customization, using all the fields. You could now print the report, which will include the same information that appears in the original database. This may be efficient, but not very interesting or necessarily informative. A little later in this chapter we'll turn our attention to preparing a report that you customize to meet your needs.

Naming and Saving Reports

As soon as a report is finished, you should assign a new name to it. Even though you can add a customized title in the Title tab, that's only the title of the report, not the name of the file. To name a report file, follow these steps:

1. In Report view, click Tools, and then click Rename Report.

    You'll see the Rename Report dialog box on the following page.

Type a new name
for the report here.

Then click here to
rename the report.

Recall that Works automatically assigns a name such as Report 1, which highlights in the text box near the bottom of the dialog box.

2. Type a name and click OK. We entered *Car Sales*.

The report is now named. Now the file has to be saved. When you create a report and want to save it for future reference, you save a report as you do any other Works document.

3. Click File, and then click Save.

Using a Saved Report

Let's say you open a database and then want to use a report that's already been created. Do the following:

1. Click View, and then choose Report.

You'll see the Report dialog box.

2. Highlight the report you want to open.

3. Click Preview or Modify, depending on what you want to do.

In this case, go ahead and click Preview, and then click the Cancel button in the Print Preview window.

Deleting and Duplicating Reports

The related Delete Report and Duplicate Report commands on the Tools menu work much like the Rename Report command. Delete Report, as you'd expect, eliminates a report you no longer want or need. This command is useful when you want to throw away a mistake or eliminate one or more reports when you hit the eight-report limit in the report generator.

To delete a report, choose the Delete Report command, and then select the name of the report you want to get rid of. Click the Delete button, and then click OK.

Duplicating a report follows a very similar procedure: just choose the Duplicate Report command. When you duplicate a report, Works gives it a default name, such as Report 1. Use the Rename Report command to change the name of the duplicate. Duplicating a report is the ideal way to use the work you've already done to create a new report. You'll see later on how you can modify an existing report, retitle it, and use it for another purpose than that for which the original report was intended.

Customizing a Report

As you've just seen, preparing a standard report takes little more thought and energy than a series of clicks. You get out just what you put in. On the other hand, if you wish to take advantage of the different options that the Works ReportCreator offers, your reports can take on a character of their own, making them much more effective as tools for the communication of information.

Six different areas of a report can be customized. These are represented by the tabs in the ReportCreator dialog box. You can modify options in any one of these areas, or leave them all alone and let Works create the standard report for you. The areas are:

- *Title*: You can enter the title of the report, set its page orientation (Portrait or Landscape), and select the size and type of font you want to use in the report.

- *Fields*: You can select which of the fields in the database you want to include in the report, by adding all of them in any order, adding any one field, or removing selected fields.

- *Sorting*: You can sort records on one to three fields, in ascending or descending order. The default is to sort only by the first field in ascending order.

- *Grouping*: You can group records with similar data to separate them physically on the report document, with lines, with headings, or by page.

- *Filter:* You can decide what criteria will be used to select records, as described in Chapter 10, "Using the Database to Locate Information."

- *Summary:* You can prepare a summary of data using specific functions such as average and minimum, as well as decide where the summary will appear in the report.

In the remainder of this chapter, we'll go through each one of these customization areas and also investigate other ways to modify a report.

Creating a Title

You can begin customizing a report by creating another title.

1. Make sure you're viewing the database in Report view.

2. Click Tools, and then click ReportCreator.

    When you use this command to create another report, you'll see the Report Name dialog box again, this time indicating that this is the second report you're creating. This box has room for only 15 characters. You can click OK to move on to the Title tab of the ReportCreator dialog box to customize the title and the report. After the report is created, you can simply rename it.

3. Type a name. We entered *Cars Sold by Honest Abe* in our example.

    The title can be up to 224 characters in length. Remember, if you don't customize your report, you can only use 15 characters in the Report Name dialog box.

4. Click Landscape, if you want to print the report on a wider page.

    For this report example, we'll use Landscape orientation since there are almost as many fields as there are records and Landscape will give us more room to display fields.

5. Change the Font selection, if you like. We'll leave it as Arial.

6. Change the font's size in the Size drop-down list, if you like. We changed it to 12.

    As you work with the font and size, you can see how changes will appear in the Sample area of the ReportCreator dialog box.

TIP At any point while creating a customized report, you can click Done and the ReportCreator won't go any farther or offer you any more options. The report will be finished and will include the changes you made up to that point.

7. Click Next.

Now you see the Fields tab in the ReportCreator dialog box.

Adding Fields to the Report

You can decide which of the fields in the database you want included in the customized report. As you can see in Figure 11-3, you can add one field at a time (click the field and then click the Add button), or you can click the Add All button to add all the fields at once. In our example, we'll add the Make, Model, Price, and Year fields, in that order.

Click here to add records one by one.

Click here to add all records at once.

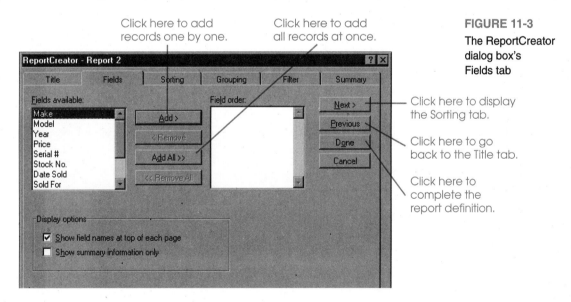

FIGURE 11-3

The ReportCreator dialog box's Fields tab

Click here to display the Sorting tab.

Click here to go back to the Title tab.

Click here to complete the report definition.

1. Click a field name, and then click Add for each field you want in the report.

Note that the order in which the fields are added is the order in which they'll appear in the report.

Here are some guidelines concerning the addition and removal of fields in the Fields tab of the ReportCreator dialog box.

❑ If you want to include all the available fields in the database report, click the Add All button.

❑ If you want to remove a field from the report, select the field you want to remove in the Field Order scroll box (only one at a time), and click the Remove button.

❑ If you want to remove all the fields from the Field Order scroll box, click the Remove All button.

❑ If you want to change the order of the fields as they appear in the Field Order scroll box, you have to click on the individual fields and click the Add button in the order you want them listed in the report.

2. If you want the names of each field to print at the top of each page in a report with more than one page, click the *Show field names at top of each page* check box, if it isn't already turned on.

If this option is not turned on, it's too difficult otherwise to track which column belongs to which field when multiple pages are necessary to print the report.

3. Click Next to see the options on the Sorting tab.

Up to now, we've assigned a title to the report and defined what fields will be included in the report and in what order. Now we'll turn our attention to sorting records.

Sorting Records in a Report

Just as you sort records both in a spreadsheet and in a database, so you can also sort records in a database report. And, just as you can sort on up to three different fields in a database, you can sort on up to three fields in a report as well. In Figure 11-4 you can see the Sorting tab and two fields that have already been defined to sort—first on Make and then on Model for records with the same Make data.

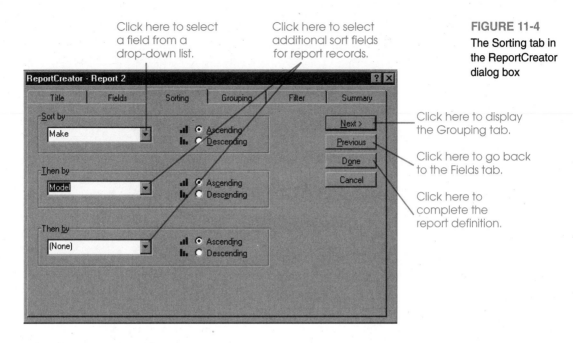

Click here to select a field from a drop-down list.

Click here to select additional sort fields for report records.

FIGURE 11-4
The Sorting tab in the ReportCreator dialog box

Click here to display the Grouping tab.

Click here to go back to the Fields tab.

Click here to complete the report definition.

Here are the steps to set up sorting in a report. When you're creating a report, you won't see the results of sorting until you're finished with the report definition.

1. Click the Sort By drop-down list arrow and click a field name.

2. Click the first Then By drop-down list arrow and click the next field name on which to sort.

3. Click Next to see the options on the Grouping tab.

 TIP To sort any field in ascending or descending order, just click the appropriate button for the corresponding sort field.

Grouping Records

Grouping is used to aggregate records under a specific heading. For example, we could group all the cars by group heading as you see in Figure 11-5, on the next page. Grouping is simply another way to assign records and fields to different categories within the report. It's another organizational tool. Notice in the figure that the Grouping tab's layout is very similar to that of the Sorting tab. In our example, Works grouped records first by Make and then by Model, based on our Sorting tab selections. Make selections on this tab, as follows:

FIGURE 11-5
The Grouping
tab in the
ReportCreator
dialog box

Click to select options that control the
appearance of record groups.

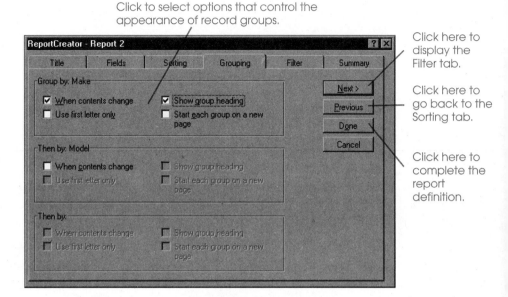

Click here to
display the
Filter tab.

Click here to
go back to the
Sorting tab.

Click here to
complete the
report
definition.

1. Click the When Contents Change check box.

    Notice that this activates the other check box options in the Group By box.

2. Click the Show Group Heading check box.

3. Click Next to see the options on the Filter tab.

Using Filters

You might recall that filters allow you to design a query, a question from you to the database to select criteria-matching records. When you design a query, you set special conditions and then the database is filtered through those conditions. You can do the same with a report: select records based on selected criteria, and then print them in a customized format.

In the Filters tab shown in Figure 11-6, you have several options open to you, all of which alter the information that will be printed in the final report.

Click here to
select a filter.

Click here to
create a new
filter.

Click here to change
conditions in an
existing filter.

FIGURE 11-6

The Filter tab in the
ReportCreator
dialog box

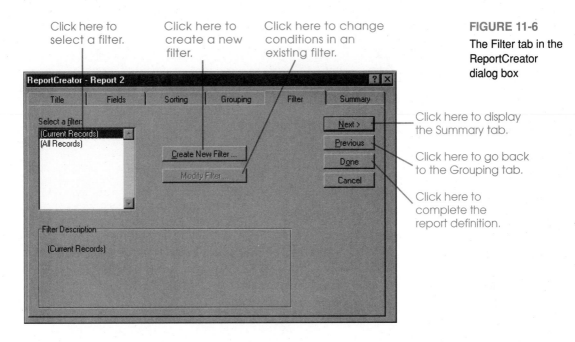

Click here to display
the Summary tab.

Click here to go back
to the Grouping tab.

Click here to
complete the
report definition.

First, you have to decide whether you want to use an existing filter or create a new one. Both options are available on the Filter tab. In our example we'll be creating a new one, which will select only specific records for the report. As you can see in Figure 11-6, you can select (Current Records) or (All Records) as a filter. These are very general filters that may serve any purpose for the person who's doing any customization.

For example, we've already titled the database (Cars Sold by Honest Abe), defined the fields we want to use (Make, Model, Price, and Year), and sorted the first three fields in ascending order. Now we'll select for the report only those cars that are of the 1985 model year or newer.

1. Click Create New Filter.

2. Type a name for the filter and click OK. We entered *Year>1985*.

3. When you see the Filter dialog box, enter the appropriate fields. We entered those that select only those cars made in 1985 or later.

4. Click OK.

    When you do this, the name of the filter (Year>1985) appears in the Select A Filter scroll box you saw in Figure 11-6, along with (Current Records) and (All Records).

5. Click Next.

See
Also

For more information on *creating a filter to query a database*, see
"Querying a Database to Find Information" in Chapter 10, page 339.

Adding Statistics

Works is nothing if not thorough and helpful. It wants to give you every
chance to include useful information in your reports, so it presents you
with the Summary tab in the ReportCreator dialog box, as you see in Figure
11-7. This portion of the report-creating process reflects the sophistication
of the Works report generator. Works' developers knew that most reports
need some statistics thrown in, so they designed this capability into the
ReportCreator.

FIGURE 11-7

The Summary
tab in the
ReportCreator
dialog box

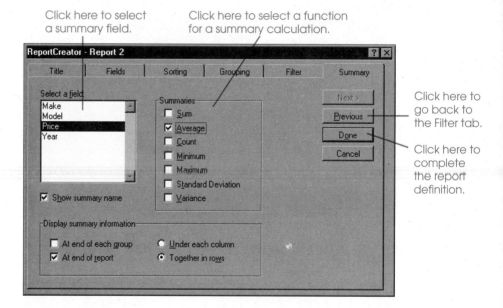

The Summary tab lists a set of standard descriptive calculations you
can choose from, such as Sum, Average, Count (number of items), Minimum, Maximum, Standard Deviation, and Variance. You can apply them
to one or more fields. The choice is yours; your selection might depend
on how you like things to look or on how accessible you want the
information to be. In our example we chose to include the average price
of a car in the report, so the Price field was selected and the Average check
box was clicked, as you see in Figure 11-7.

Once you click Done, Works wants to know if you wish to preview the report, or modify it. If you look at the screen behind this message, you'll see that the "report" you've created might not look the way you expected. This is because you're looking at the report's definition, not the actual formatted report. If you elect to modify it, you return to Report view, as you see in Figure 11-8, where you see how the report's definition appears.

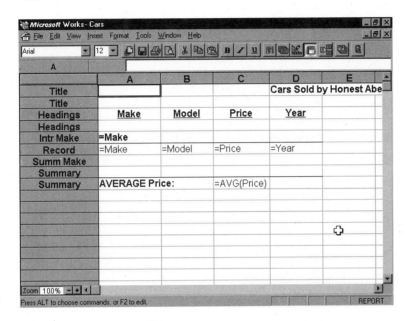

FIGURE 11-8

The customized report definition

Figure 11-9, on the next page, shows an example of the report in the Print Preview window, which reflects how it will appear when printed. In our example column C was adjusted to be wider, since it was too small (Works told us so) when we went to view it.

You can't edit a report, because it's printed directly by ReportCreator. In fact, the only way you can see what a report will look like before it's printed is by using the Print Preview command on the File menu.

When it creates a report, Works uses the field widths you set up in List view as the column widths. If your data prints completely in List view, it will also print without problem in a report. Be sure, however, to use Print Preview often when creating a report, especially if you use different fonts and sizes.

If any of the columns are too narrow to hold complete entries, Works truncates text at the right edge, and it displays and prints number signs (#####) in place of numbers in the Print Preview window. You can see any

FIGURE 11-9
The report in the
Print Preview
window

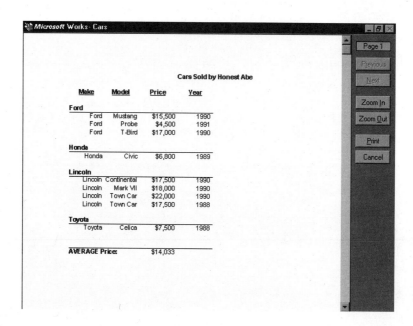

such problems in Print Preview, so catch them before printing to save yourself some frustration later. To widen columns, either drag the column boundary (in Report view), as you do in the spreadsheet document window and the database document window in List view, or use the Column Width command on the Format menu. The Best Fit button is dimmed and doesn't work in Report view.

More About Report Definitions

The report definition you see on screen is an outline of the report you created. Because Works displays the *report definition* rather than the report itself, you can modify a standard report without having to view or manipulate the actual records in it.

The parts of your report are laid out on a grid comparable to the display you see in List view (see Figure 11-8 on the preceding page). In Report view the columns are identified by letter, and the row labels (Title, Headings, and so on) tell you which elements are included in the report. Above the document window, Works displays an entry bar that you can use for entering information as well as for displaying the complete contents of any cell (for example, the formula =AVG(Price) in column D of the second Summary row). The box on the left end of the entry bar displays the letter of the column, but not the row name, where the highlight is currently located.

Here is a summary of the standard names for the row labels Works uses when creating a report (see Figure 11-8, page 369).

- *Title*: The name of your report or any other identifying text you care to include. Works boldfaces the title you type when you create a report and centers the title above the fields in the report. Titles appear only on the first page of a printed report.

- *Headings*: Field names or other identifiers you want to use for the columns in your report. Unless you change the headings, Works uses the field names you chose, displaying and printing them in bold, underlined characters centered above each column.

- *Intr Make*: A blank row or a group heading that appears before each sort break in the report.

- *Record*: The names of the fields to be included in the report, each in a separate column. Each field name is preceded by an equal sign, making it a kind of formula. When generating the report, Works uses this row to find the required data for each record you chose to include.

- *Summ Make*: Inserts a row after every specified sort break.

- *Summary*: The statistics you chose to include in the report. Each Summary row identifies and gives the formula for one statistic. By default, Works identifies the statistic by name, printing the text in boldface and the actual value of the statistic in normal type.

Working with Rows and Columns

You can add and delete rows and columns whenever you want to modify a report definition, which affects the appearance of the report. You can add new field names and entries, insert extra blank lines or columns, and make room for additional titles, text, or statistics.

Inserting and Deleting Columns

Adding and deleting columns in a report is similar to doing the same operations in List view and in the spreadsheet module. Select the column to the right of the position where you want to add a new column, and from the Insert menu choose Insert Column. To delete a column, click anywhere in the column you want deleted, click Insert, and then click Delete Column.

When you add a column, you insert a column that's the same width as the selected column.

Inserting and Deleting Rows

Adding a row to a report differs slightly from the procedure for adding rows in the spreadsheet module. You use the Insert Row or Delete Row command, as usual, but when working with a report definition you always refer to rows by *type*. Some rows in a report definition will have a Title label but no column entries. Works includes these rows, so the final printed document (the standard by which a report should be judged) has blank spaces where Works thinks it's appropriate.

Even though these rows aren't functional in the sense that they contain information, they still belong to one row type or another. Their names indicate where blank rows will appear. In our example Works inserts one blank row beneath the title, another beneath the column headings, and a third between the printed records and the summary statistics. If you were to type a report based on your own database, you might put spaces in these positions as well, to make the report easier to read.

To illustrate, suppose we want to add a subtitle row to our report. Here's how to do it.

1. Click a row to select the entire row.

   As in List view, when you select an entire row (or column), Works bypasses the dialog box that asks whether you want to insert a row or a column.

2. Click Insert, and then click Insert Row.

   Works displays this Insert Row dialog box:

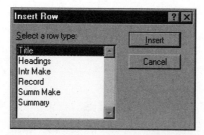

This dialog box shows the types of rows already in your report definition. The type of row we selected (Title in our example) is highlighted. Because we selected a Title row, Works will add another of the same type.

3. Click Insert to add the row.

   The new row appears above the selected one. If you add a row in the wrong place, delete it with the Delete Row command on the Insert menu. Now that we've added another Title row, we'll enter some text in it, as follows:

4. Highlight a cell in the column of the new row where you want the subtitle's text, type a subtitle, and press Enter. We entered *July, 1995*.

5. Click the Bold button (or any other style format button) to make the text boldface, if you like.

 TIP You can also adjust the vertical alignment of a text entry, by using the Top, Center, or Bottom options in the Alignment dialog box.

Our customized report example, thus far, is previewed in Figure 11-10 on the next page, with the subtitle added.

Inserting Rows and Formulas

If you prefer, you can replace the Summary rows that Works inserts with your own. These can include text or formulas—your choice. Here's how we added a Summary line that calculates the total value of all cars by adding together prices. We're also going to move the average price calculation (function) to column D.

1. In Report view, click the row label below the row where you want to insert a new one. We clicked the blank one below the last Summary line.

2. Point to the selected row, click the right mouse button, and select the Insert Row command on the pop-up menu.

3. Click a row type option in the Select a Row Type scroll box and then click Insert. We selected Summary for our example.

FIGURE 11-10

Adding a subtitle
to the report

The new
Title row
entry

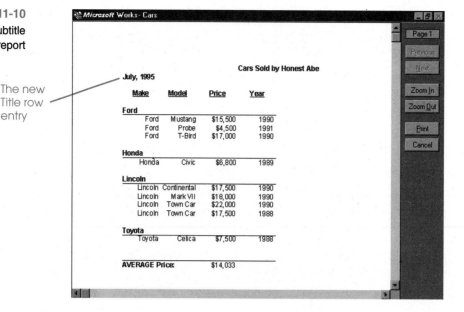

4. Click in a desired column on the newly inserted row.

5. Type a label and press Enter. We typed *TOTAL Value:*

6. Apply a font style, such as boldface, to the label if you like.

7. Click in the column that you want to place a calculated value on the row just inserted.

8. Type a function and press Enter. We entered *=SUM(Price).*
   This SUM function will sum the prices for all the cars in our example to produce a total value for this set.

9. Format the cells containing functions with a Number format option, if desired.

10. Click OK, and then click the Print Preview button.
    Our example report is shown in Figure 11-11. Notice that we moved the Average function to column D, as well.

TIP To add a header or a footer to a report, click View, and then click Headers and Footers, enter either one or both, and click OK. The text you enter will appear on each page of the report.

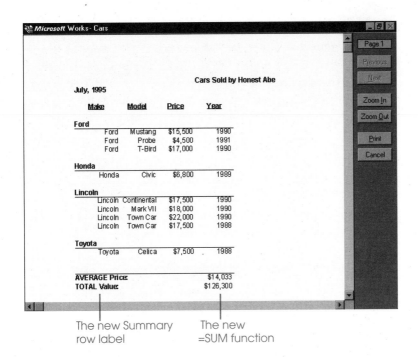

FIGURE 11-11
The report after editing and adding a function

The new Summary row label

The new =SUM function

You can insert other row types and calculations as well. Remember, the ReportCreator is there for you to define a report and to include the information you want in the way you want to see it printed. Just remember to keep viewing the report in Print Preview (click that toolbar button) to see what you have as you develop it.

Working with Field Names and Field Entries

Another way to modify a basic report definition is by adding field names, field entries, and more statistics after the report is created.

Here are the definitions that Works uses:

- *Field name*: The name of a database field. When you insert a field name, Works places the name in whatever cell you selected, whatever the row type. When you preview or print the report, the field name appears as ordinary text.

- *Field entry*: The name that refers to the entries in a field (for example, =Model). When you insert a field entry, you tell Works to replace that name with actual entries from the database records in the field you select.

- *Field summary:* A statistic (Sum, Average, Count, Minimum, Maximum, Standard Deviation, or Variance) that you insert in a report in relation to a particular field. A field summary belongs in a "Summ (field name)" row. It's an easier way of inserting formulas, like the =SUM(Price) we created in the Summ Make row in our Cars database example.

You would probably want to insert a field name to add a field you didn't include in the original report definition, or to save typing time while constructing a formula or mathematical calculation or even just while inserting text. Field entries become important only if you want to include additional data from the database. You need *both* field names *and* field entries to add extra fields to a report.

Inserting Field Names and Field Entries

Suppose, for example, we now decide to include the serial number for each of the cars in our report. Works provides the option to make such changes after the fact. Here are the steps to follow.

1. Click in a cell in the column where you want to insert a field.

2. Click Insert, and then click Field Name.

    Works displays this Insert Field Name dialog box:

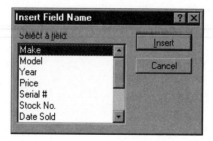

3. Click a field name, and then click Insert. We selected Serial #.

    You can add a field name (not the field itself, yet) to any part of your report. When Works inserts the name, it doesn't add any special formatting, so you must take care of the formatting on your own.

4. Apply any formatting, as necessary, to the inserted heading to make it match the others.

    Now we'll add the actual field.

5. Click the cell in the new column that's on the Record row.

6. Click Insert, and then click Insert Field Entry.

7. Click a field name in the Select A Field scroll box. We selected Serial #.

8. Click Insert.

9. Click the Print Preview button to check your report's layout.

If the Print Preview window gets crowded, you can use the scroll bars to move through the report. In our example, there's no line dividing rows, since the serial number field was added after the report was created. To use the line, the report would have to be modified by adding the serial number as part of the original design.

Inserting Field Summaries

We already created a field summary when we entered the AVG formula in the Summary Make row. Inserting summaries with the Field Summary command on the Insert menu is simple, and is similar to choosing calculations from the Statistics dialog box that appears when you create a report for the first time.

Field summaries, as mentioned earlier in this chapter, belong in Summary rows. To see how simple it is to add a summary, follow these steps:

1. Click a Summary row in an appropriate column.

2. Type a desired label for the Summary row and press Enter. We entered *How Many Cars?* in our example.

3. Apply any formatting, if you like.

4. Click in the same Summary row in the column where you want to place a calculation.

5. Type a function and press Enter. We entered *=COUNT(Make)*.

6. Click the Print Preview button to view the result in the report.

You can see the function we added at the bottom of the report in the Print Preview window shown in Figure 11-12 on the next page.

The new statistic, which counts the number of makes, appears at the bottom of the report.

FIGURE 11-12
Adding a function
to a report

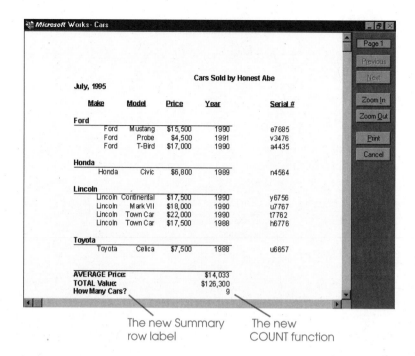

The new Summary
row label

The new
COUNT function

Formatting Reports

You can go beyond just the physical layout of records and fields by using other types of formatting tools to give your reports even more impact. Two of these are borders and shading, and both can be accessed from the Format menu when viewing the report definition in Report view. In Figure 11-13, you can see how we shaded some field titles and placed a border around the summary information at the bottom of the report.

Using these format options is identical to the way they are used to format information both in the word processor and the spreadsheet. When you work with formatting, you can also tinker with column width and alignment (also on the Format menu), depending on how you think the preview looks.

Using Borders

Here's how to use a border in our example report's report definition.

1. Select the range of cells containing the functions in the appropriate rows of the report definition.

2. Point to the selected cells, click the right mouse button, and then click Format on the pop-up menu.

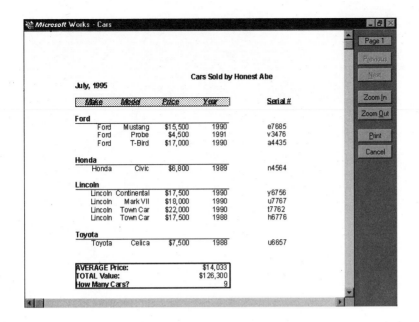

FIGURE 11-13

A preview of the
report with shading
and borders

You'll see the familiar Format dialog box with tabs for working with Number, Alignment, Font, Border, and Shading.

3. Click the Border tab.

4. Click any one of the types of line styles. We selected the thickest line style for our example.

5. Click OK.

The border will be applied to the selected area. In the report for the Cars database, we also placed an outline border around the column headings, using the thinnest line style option.

Using Shading

Here's how to use shading in our example report's report definition.

1. Select the range of cells you want to shade. We selected the first Headings row from Make to Year.

2. Point to the selected cells, click the right mouse button, and then click Format on the pop-up menu.

3. Click the Shading tab.

4. Click a desired pattern option in the Pattern box (we selected 20% shading).

5. Click OK.

The shading will be applied. If you have a color monitor, you can easily work with different foreground and background colors to make the report very impressive.

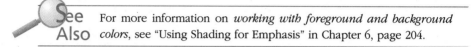

See Also For more information on *working with foreground and background colors*, see "Using Shading for Emphasis" in Chapter 6, page 204.

A final version of the report we've used for demonstration appears in Figure 11-14.

FIGURE 11-14

The final report from the Cars database

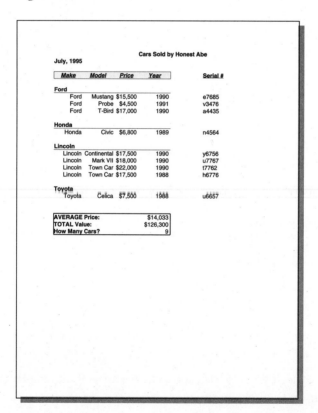

Formatting and Printing Reports

As you've seen, similar formatting options in the word processor and spreadsheet can be applied to the database—font, size and style, headings, headers and footers, and shading. Feel free to experiment with a variety of format settings. After all, formatting is a key factor in how the report presents the information to those reading the report.

Your most important ally in preparing a report for printing is the Print Preview window. Print Preview is an invaluable means of seeing what you'll get before you get it (WYSIWYG) in full-page displays. In fact, it's the only way you can see what a report will look like before committing it to paper. We've stressed that throughout this chapter, but its importance can't be overemphasized.

Working with Page Breaks

The report generator lets you insert and delete manual page breaks. You can insert page breaks either between rows or between columns.

Inserting a page break between rows is useful when you want to print groups on separate pages. For example, if you insert a page break above the headings or in the report definition, each group starts on a new page. If you do this, the titles also print on a page by themselves, so format or position them accordingly.

 TIP A smart strategy for breaking pages neatly is to create a blank Summary field name row just before the summary rows and then insert a page break before the blank row. That way, nothing is lost, things stay together as they should, and the overall report better fits your needs (with information grouped on one page).

Inserting a page break between columns is the obvious choice when you're printing a report that's too large to fit on a single sheet of paper. By inserting a vertical page break of this type, you can determine where Works will break pages between printed fields.

To insert a page break, follow these steps:

1. Place the cursor where you want the page break to occur.

2. Click Format, and then click Insert Page Break.

An Insert Page Break dialog box appears in which you can select either a row or a column page break.

3. Select a page break option, and then click OK.

A page break appears on screen as a gray, dashed line (horizontal for a row page break, vertical for a column page break).

If you want to delete a page break, select Delete Page Break from the Format menu.

TIP If you insert a page break at the end of the record in Form view, you'll have a separate page of output for each record. You can see all the pages, one by one, in the Print Preview window by using its Next button.

Page Setup and Printing

Page setup and printing methods for database reports will be familiar to you because they work much the same for documents in the other Works modules. As in the word processor and the spreadsheet, you can set page margins, the orientation of the paper you are printing on, and whether you want to print field names.

The following section deals with the Page Setup options in the Page Setup dialog box you see on the next page, which appears when you select the Page Setup command on the File menu.

The Page Setup Options

The options in the Page Setup dialog box should be familiar because you've seen them before in the word processor and spreadsheet modules.

In the Margins tab you can set the top, bottom, left, right, and header and footer margins. The same goes for the Source, Size & Orientation tab, where you set the source of the paper, as well as its size, height and width, and orientation (landscape or portrait).

In the Other Options tab, you can set the page number of the first page, set page breaks and spaces between records (or turn them off so that more than one record goes on a page), print field lines, and choose to print fields plus data or data alone. (Some people prefer this approach because it's less cumbersome.)

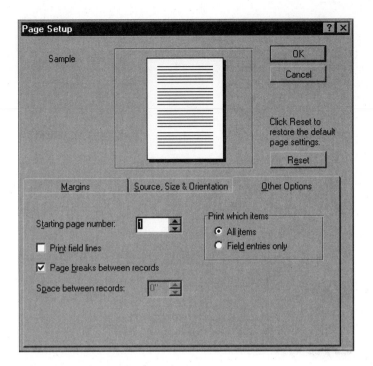

Coming Next

Another milestone reached! We're done with the three main Works modules, and you now have the tools to perform 80 percent of the tasks that personal computers are used for. But that's not all we intend to show you. Now it's time to learn about the artist in you. Welcome to Works Draw and its many graphics tools.

Part 5

Using Graphics

In This Part Here you'll discover that Works for Windows 95 is not only a word processor, a spreadsheet, and a database, but much more as well. In Chapter 12 of *Running Works for Windows 95,* you will see how Microsoft Draw gives you almost unlimited options plus a full set of tools for creating attractive graphics, which can then be placed in the documents and reports.

Draw defines these graphics as objects that can be copied, cut and pasted, edited, scaled in size, and moved all around (even to different applications) to give your documents the flair they deserve. As if Draw were not enough, Works for Windows 95 has a collection of special graphics tools that will really dress up what you've created with words and numbers. Clip-Art (an example of which you see here) . . .

. . . and WordArt, such as you see here, which lets you create different designs of text . . .

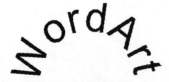

. . . and Note-It, which attaches a note to any document.

All these bring to life the documents you worked so hard at creating. Besides, they may be the most fun that Works for Windows 95 has to offer!

Chapter 12

Creating Images
with Microsoft Draw

A picture is worth a thousand words—we never tire of saying it, because it's true. Although your writing may be brilliant, how your document looks may often be as important. If you need illustrations to help make a point, or to better communicate a message, Works for Windows 95 can be your artistic ally. The key here is learning how to use Microsoft Draw, Works' drawing program.

Works offers several graphics tools, including a clip art library (a collection of ready-made illustrations) and the WordArt utility to help give your documents the visual punch they deserve. For the artistically inclined, Draw offers drawing tools to create any shape, including arcs, squares, and circles. With Draw, you can create geometric forms with ease, design your own monograms and letterheads (we'll do one here), and arrange text in circles, squares, and other patterns.

Where Is Draw, Anyway?

Unlike the other parts of Works, Draw isn't directly available on the Task Launcher; it is, however, available by selecting the Drawing command on the Insert menu in the word processor and the database modules (in Form Design view).

Typically, Draw is used in two ways:

- You create a document or a database and use the Drawing command on the Insert menu to place a drawing in the document or database. Then you use Draw's tools to modify the drawing.

- You create a drawing from scratch and then place it into the document or database.

When you insert a drawing into a document, Works inserts it at the location of the insertion point. At any time, you can go back, select the drawing, and modify it.

To start Microsoft Draw, do the following:

1. Open the word processor.

2. If you are working with an existing document, place the insertion point where you want to insert the drawing in the document.

3. Click Insert, and then click Drawing.

4. Maximize the window so that all the available Draw tools are visible.

The Microsoft Draw window appears as shown in Figure 12-1.

The blank workspace filling most of the window is the canvas on which you'll draw. On the left side is a toolbox containing buttons that represent the various drawing tools. And across the bottom are two color palettes showing available colors for drawing lines and filling shapes.

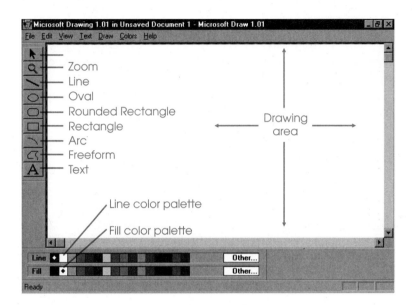

FIGURE 12-1
The Microsoft
Draw window

As usual, the title bar and control buttons are at the top of the window, and the menu bar lies just below the title bar. Notice that the name of the Draw file is Microsoft Drawing 1.01 in Unsaved Document 1—that is, the name of the word processing document appears in the title bar. That's Draw's way of telling you that any drawing you create is part of a Works word-processed document. Notice, too, that Draw includes a Help menu.

Draw: Basic Training

Basic training usually is arduous—but in basic training for Draw, you won't break a sweat. To create an image with Draw, you must first know what tools are available and how to use them. The key thing about Draw is that you can't practice enough. Be patient, let your creativity run free, and have fun; you'll find Draw to be as valuable as any other Works feature.

We'll start by reviewing the contents of the toolbox. The top two buttons, the Pointer button (with an arrow) and the Zoom button (with a magnifying glass), are "management" tools. The Pointer button (also called the Arrow) lets you select and manipulate shapes (called objects in Draw). The Zoom button lets you zoom in and out to change the display size of an object. The rest of the buttons give you access to tools that create the objects described by their labels in Figure 12-1 on the preceding page.

Drawing an Oval

First, be sure that in the Microsoft Draw window a diamond shape appears in the black square on the Line color palette (at the bottom of the window) and another appears in the white square on the Fill color palette. This will allow you to draw an outline of the selected object that is not filled. The following steps can be used to create an oval:

1. Click the Oval button (fourth from the top) and move the mouse pointer into the blank workspace.

    Notice that the mouse pointer becomes a set of cross hairs. As you create objects, you'll use the center of the cross hairs to mark your starting point.

2. Point the cross hairs pointer in the upper left corner of the drawing area.

3. Hold down the left mouse button and drag down and to the right, as you see here. Release the mouse button when the oval is egg shaped.

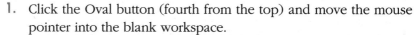
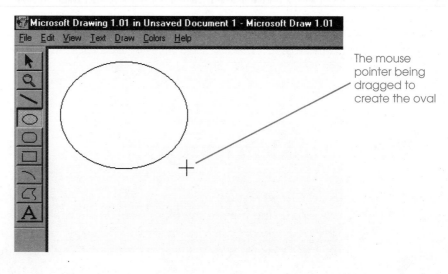

The mouse pointer being dragged to create the oval

An example of a completed oval is shown in Figure 12-2.

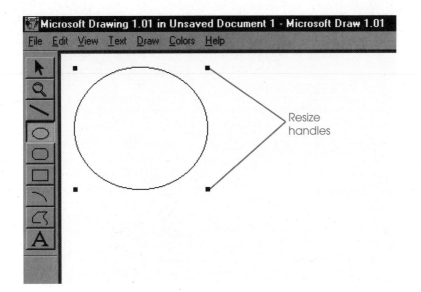

FIGURE 12-2
Drawing a
simple oval

What Is an Object?

In Draw, an *object* is a shape or an image that can be manipulated independently of other objects. For example, if you create a drawing that consists of three squares, a triangle, and some text, each of these elements is a separate and independent object in the drawing. It's also possible to group selected objects, so objects can be manipulated separately or together. Even though they're independent, they can all be used to create a drawing that's greater (in impact and meaning) than the sum of its parts or elements.

The oval is an object. Just as you can edit a document created with the word processor, you can change objects as well.

Changing the Size of an Object

When you release the mouse button after creating the oval, four small black boxes appear outside your oval. These boxes, called *resize handles*, appear at the corners of an invisible box that Draw places around each object you create. You see the resize handles only when the object is selected. To select an object, simply click anywhere inside it. To deselect it, click anywhere outside the object.

TIP Not all objects are selected by clicking inside them, because some objects (such as a line or a set of characters) have no inside on which to click. For these types of objects you have to click directly on the object itself (line or character) to select it. It may take a bit of practice to get the hang of it.

You can drag one of the resize handles to change the size (or shape) of an object. Here's how to do it.

1. Click the Arrow button in the toolbox (or click in any blank portion of the workspace).

2. Place the pointer anywhere in the oval and click to select it.

3. Point to a resize handle, such as the one in the lower right corner of the selected object, and press the left mouse button. (Notice that the mouse pointer changes to an arrowhead.) Drag the resize handle; for example, we dragged down and to the right a little, as you see here. When the object is sized the way you want it, release the mouse button.

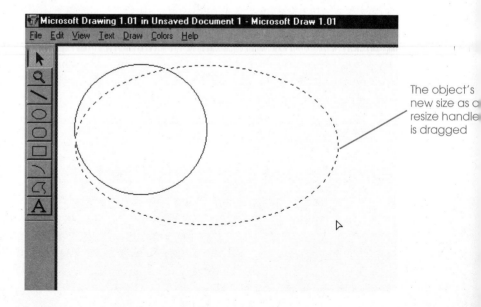

The object's new size as a resize handle is dragged

As you drag the resize handle, an outline of the oval follows to show how its changing position affects the shape of the object.

TIP To change both the vertical and horizontal dimensions of an object at the same time, drag a corner resize handle diagonally. You can drag any one of the four corner handles.

This technique applies to all objects. Simply select and drag when you want to change the size. The new shape of the oval in our example is shown in Figure 12-3.

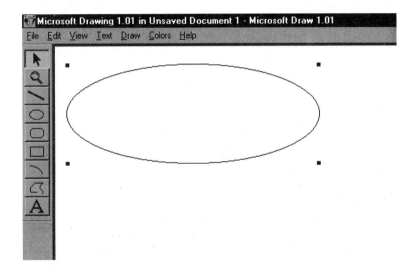

FIGURE 12-3

The resized oval object

Handling an Object

Draw refers to shapes as objects. When you manipulate a shape, Draw treats it as an independent element. Consequently, you can place objects on top of each other, group them together, and manipulate them individually or together. Let's look at some of the possibilities.

1. Click on the Rectangle button.

2. Place the cross hairs on the oval and draw a rectangle that extends beyond the border of the oval, as you see on the following page.

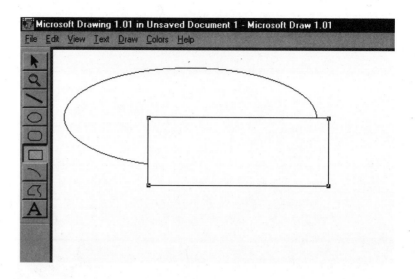

Notice that the rectangle is the selected object. If you want to select the oval, you can just click on it.

To move the rectangle, do the following:

1. Click the Arrow button, and then select the rectangle.

2. Drag the dashed outline of the rectangle until it's completely off the oval, and then release the mouse button.

    Both the oval and the rectangle are now separate but whole and unchanged, as shown in Figure 12-4.

FIGURE 12-4

Moving a
selected object

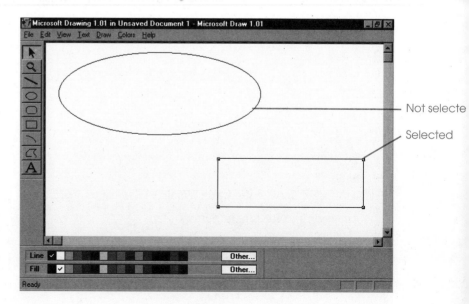

Selecting Multiple Objects

Objects stand alone and are independent of other objects. When you want to do something to an object, you must first select it. In Draw, if you want to do the same thing to more than one object at a time, you can do that as well. Here's how to select multiple objects.

1. Be sure the Arrow tool is active.

2. Place the mouse pointer in a blank area of the drawing area above and to the left of the objects you want to select.

3. Hold down the left mouse button and drag the pointer down and to the right to expand a dashed selection rectangle, as shown in Figure 12-5. When the objects are enclosed in the dashed selection rectangle, release the mouse button.

    When you release the mouse button, the dashed selection rectangle disappears. Both objects are selected. You can tell both are selected because both display resize handles.

Selection rectangle

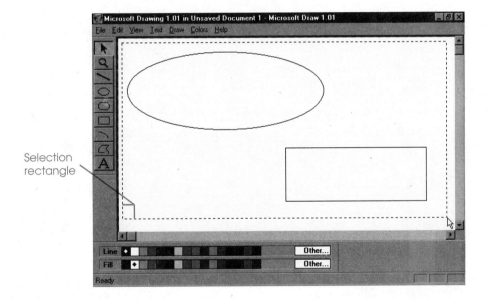

FIGURE 12-5

Selecting more than one object

Although both objects are selected, they're still separate objects. However, by selecting them together, you can work with both at the same time.

Selecting more than one object with the Arrow tool this way is a good method to use when the objects are near each other. If objects are scattered

all around a window, though, selecting them using this method is imprac-
tical. So let's look at an alternative way.

1. Select the first object.

2. Press and hold the Shift key, click another object, and then click
   any other object you want to select with the two already selected.
   Finally, release the Shift key.

   You can select as many objects as necessary. If you want to deselect
   a particular object, while leaving the others selected, simply press and
   hold the Shift key and click on that object. If you want to deselect all the
   objects, click outside of any selected object.

Managing Multiple Selections

Once you've selected a group of objects, you can move them, change their
color, copy them, or delete them. To move and change the color of selected
objects, do the following:

1. Place the Arrow tool on any selected object.

2. Press the left mouse button and drag the objects in any direction.
   Then release the mouse button.

   As you drag the objects, dashed outlines of both follow the
   mouse pointer, as you see here:

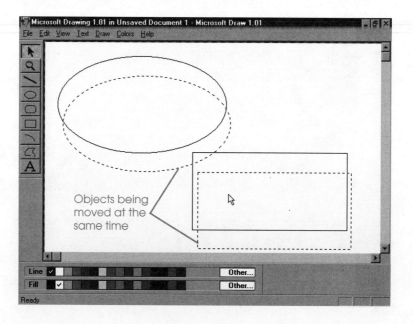

After you release the mouse button, the selected objects are in new positions, maintaining their original relationship to one another. Both remain selected.

3. Point to the color palette labeled Fill.
   The current fill color (white) is indicated by a diamond shape.

4. Click on any other color.
   After you select a color, a diamond shape appears on the color in the palette, and Draw fills the selected objects with the color you select. You can fill with other colors with just a click.

NOTE If the only thing that changed was the color of the object's border, you clicked in the Line color palette and not in Fill. Try again.

To see how managing multiple objects differs from managing individual objects, do the following:

1. Click in any blank area of the workspace to deselect the objects. Be sure you click well outside the objects.

2. Click an object to select it.

3. Click a different color in the Fill color palette.
   This time only the selected object changes color.

TIP If you've been wondering about the difference between the Line and Fill color palettes, try using them. Select an object and change white for the fill and a bright color, such as red, for the line. Fill refers to the internal color of an object and Line refers to its perimeter or border.

Combining Objects

Objects are, by definition, independent of one another. But separate objects can be combined to create one object.

1. Select the objects you want to group, using the selection rectangle. Notice the positions of the resize handles.

2. Click Draw, and then click Group (or use the keyboard shortcut Ctrl+G).

When you carry out the command, a single set of four resize handles appears around the objects. Draw is now prepared to treat the objects as one. When you click on one, the other is selected as well. If you were to point to one of the resize handles, drag it, and then release the mouse button, Draw would adjust the sizes and shapes of the objects. The shapes' original relationship to one another would still be maintained.

When objects are grouped, they're considered as one. To ungroup the objects, you can use the Ungroup command on the Draw menu (or the Ctrl+H keyboard shortcut).

Working with Patterns and Lines

Works provides additional options for changing the look of objects. You can fill a shape with a pattern as well as a color, and you can even change the style and thickness of a line.

As you see in Figure 12-6, we've created several shapes (and some shapes *within* shapes) containing different fill patterns and using lines of varying thicknesses.

FIGURE 12-6

Examples of
pattern and line
style options

Here's how to fill an object.

1. Select the object.

2. Click Draw, and then click Pattern.

3. Click on the pattern you want from the choices shown here on the Pattern menu:

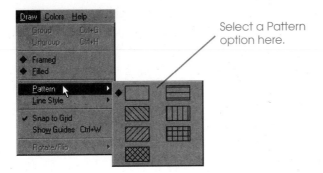

Select a Pattern option here.

The oval within an oval you see in Figure 12-6 was created by drawing a smaller oval within a larger one and then using the Pattern and Line Style options, with different fill colors.

Here's how to change the style of a line.

1. Select the object.

2. Click Draw, and then click Line Style.

3. Click the style you want to use from the menu that appears.

    You can apply a style to a straight line or to a line that outlines an object.

Using Draw to Create an Image

Drawing programs are among the most enjoyable, and often the most frustrating, computer applications to use. On the one hand, you have instant shapes available in a variety of colors. On the other hand, your efforts may not produce the image you've envisioned. Not everyone is a Michelangelo, so bear in mind that clip art is easy to use and can be modified as well.

We'll begin creating an image by turning on the display of guidelines that can be used to help line up objects. To do this, click Draw, and then click Show Guides (or use the Ctrl+W keyboard shortcut).

TIP To start with a new, clear Draw window, click File and then click the Exit and Return command. If you have any objects in the window, a message box appears, asking if you want to save the image. Select the No button to exit without saving. Then open the Draw window again, as you did previously.

Draw displays two dotted guidelines, one horizontal and one vertical, in the center of the window. These guides are comparable to the movable straight edges on drafting equipment. They indicate your position relative to the top left-hand corner of the drawing. Because the guides are movable, and because objects "snap to" them like filings to a magnet when you move the objects close enough, you can use the guides to help position text and images with a high degree of precision.

To use the guides, place the pointer on a guide and press the left mouse button. If you point to the vertical guide, a decimal number appears above a right-pointing arrow to tell you how far the guide is from the left edge of the drawing area and in which direction Draw is measuring. The same type of information appears to the left of a downward-pointing arrow when you point to the horizontal guide and press the left mouse button. Its decimal number represents the distance from the top edge of the drawing area.

To move a guide, point to it and drag it in the direction you want it to go. To start off, though, leave the guides where they are.

 See Also For more information about *working with ClipArt*, see "A Look at ClipArt" in Chapter 13, page 415.

Creating a Drawing

We'll demonstrate drawing techniques by creating the image shown in Figure 12-7.

FIGURE 12-7
The image we will
create using Draw

The drawing area available to you is much larger than the visible portion you see in the window, but to simplify matters and to ensure that the drawing will fit neatly on stationery, we can create the drawing within a single window. For your own purposes, you'll probably want to create drawings closer to the actual size you need.

The outline of an umbrella will be the centerpiece of the logo. We'll use the Arc tool to make an outline. To begin, we'll turn off the Filled option, as follows:

1. Click Draw.

2. If a diamond-shaped mark appears next to the Filled command, click it to turn the option off. If a diamond-shaped mark *doesn't* appear next to the Framed command, click it to turn it *on*.

Creating an Object Outline

If you've ever tried drawing the two halves of a heart, a butterfly, or a pair of scissors, you know that it can be very difficult to make both halves identical. With Draw, the process is much easier because you can use the tools to create regular shapes. To use an even faster method and for greater precision, however, make half of the drawing, copy the object, and then flip it to create a mirror image.

The logo will consist of five curves across the bottom edge of the umbrella, so we'll start there. Then we'll make the top curve of the umbrella fit exactly in one try. Here is how to do it.

1. Click the Arc button in the toolbox.

2. Place the center of the cross hairs about a quarter of an inch above the intersection of the two guides.

3. Press the left mouse button and drag to create a small arc extending from the starting point to the horizontal guideline, as you see in Figure 12-8. Then release the mouse button.

FIGURE 12-8

Drawing a small arc

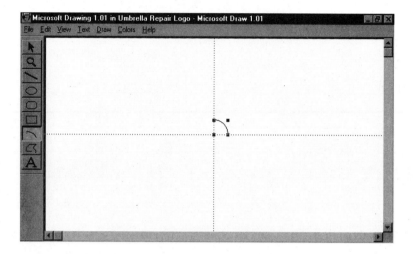

Now we can make Draw do most of the work.

4. With the arc selected, click Edit, and then click Copy to copy the arc to the Clipboard.

5. Click Edit, and then click Paste.

Another arc appears on the drawing area. The copy of the selected object stored on the Clipboard was pasted back to the drawing. This is the way to duplicate an object.

Flipping an Object

Now we'll flip this copy of the arc to create the first curve, by doing the following:

1. Click Draw, and then click Rotate/Flip.

    A menu opens, with four choices: Rotate Left, Rotate Right, Flip Horizontal, and Flip Vertical.

2. Click Flip Horizontal to make a side-to-side mirror image of the arc.

3. With the flipped copy of the arc selected, and the original arc not selected, point to the new arc by placing the Arrow tool directly on it, drag the arc into position next to the original, as you see in Figure 12-9, and then release the mouse button.

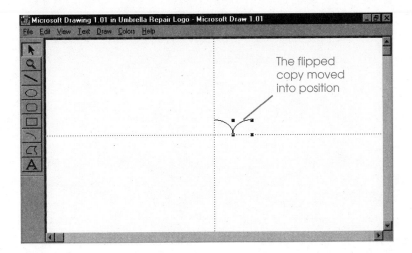

FIGURE 12-9

Dragging a flipped copy of the arc into position

The original arc copy is still on the Clipboard because it hasn't been replaced by anything yet.

4. Click Edit, and then click Paste (or press Ctrl+V) to paste another copy of the arc onto the drawing area.

5. Drag the new copy, without flipping it, and place it next to (to the right of) the arc that was flipped and pasted.

6. The Arrow tool can now be used to select both pasted halves of the curves.

7. Click Draw, and then click Group to make the two halves into a single object.

8. Click Edit, and then click Copy to copy the selected group (curve) to the Clipboard.

9. Paste the copy onto the drawing area, and drag it into position to the right of the existing arcs, as shown on the following page.

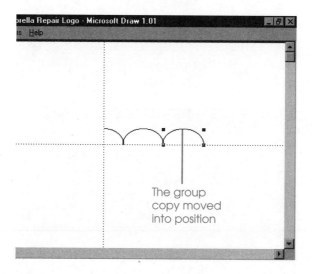

The group
copy moved
into position

Positioning Objects

This process is a bit long, but hang in there. The results will be worth it.
Here's how to draw the rest of the umbrella.

1. Click the Arc button again.

2. Position the cross hairs close to the top of the window on the
   vertical guide.

3. Drag the mouse pointer to draw a new arc extending to the outside
   edge of the smaller curves, as you see here:

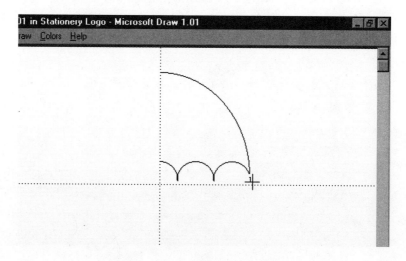

This is the right half of the top of the umbrella.

4. Click the Line button in the toolbox.

5. Make part of the umbrella's handle by drawing a vertical line straight down the center of the drawing area, following the guide, as you see in Figure 12-10.

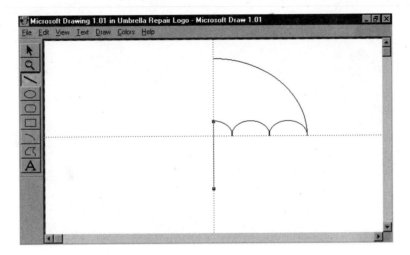

FIGURE 12-10

Drawing a line to add part of the umbrella's handle

Now we can make the other half of the umbrella by flipping the image. Because it's preferable to work with all the elements as a single object, we'll need to group them, as follows:

6. Click the Arrow button, and drag a selection rectangle around all the objects.

7. Click Draw, and then click Group.
   Now we can copy the group of objects.

8. Copy the group to the Clipboard and then paste the copy onto the drawing area.

9. Click Draw, click Rotate/Flip, and then click Flip Horizontal to flip the copy.

10. Drag the rest of the umbrella into position.

11. Add a handle to the umbrella by creating a small circle (use the Oval tool) and moving it to the end of the vertical line.
    Remember to point directly to one of the lines on your drawing to move the new group. The drawn logo is shown in Figure 12-11 on the following page.

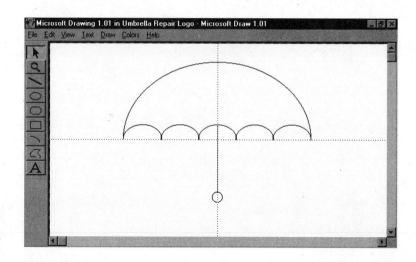

Adding Text to an Image

You can always add text to an image. To do this, you need to use the Text
tool and the Font dialog box, as follows:

1. Click the Text button.

2. Click anywhere in the drawing area.

3. Type the text you want to place on the drawing and press Enter.
   We typed *RAINGEAR* in all capital letters.

   Notice that the text is surrounded by handles (see Figure 12-12.)
   Yep, it's another object! Draw treats all the letters as a single object.

Selected
text object

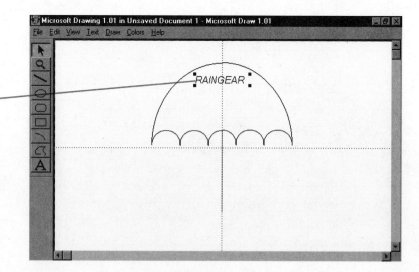

4. Apply any formatting you like to the text. We italicized it by using the Ctrl+I key combination.

5. Use the Arrow tool to drag the text object and place it where you like. We centered it in the umbrella, as you see in Figure 12-12.

We added additional text objects, changed their font sizes, and centered them under the first text object (RAINGEAR) as you see here:

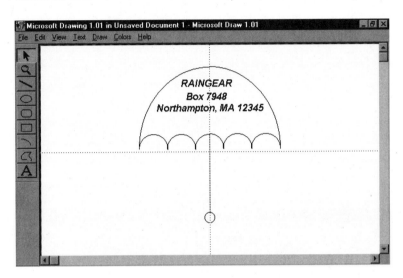

We also selected each text object (all three lines) and grouped them as one object by clicking Draw and then Group.

Grouping text objects allows you to format all of them at the same time. This is what we did to apply boldface and italic to the three text lines. To complete the logo we filled the umbrella's handle by selecting it and clicking the black square in the Fill color palette.

Saving an Image

You can save the current status of an image by selecting the Update command on the File menu. Although you can't save the image in a file like the documents you create in other Works modules, this stores the image with the document to which you've linked it by inserting the drawing. If you don't select the Update command, you'll be asked if you want to save the image when you select the Exit and Return command on the File menu to return to the original document.

Working with an Image within the Word Processor

Since a drawing can't exist independently of the word processor or the database, let's return to the word processor, by doing the following:

1. Click File, and then click Exit and Return.

    If you've made any changes to the image, you'll be asked if you want to save them, so click Yes.

 TIP You can return to Draw for more editing and refining of the image by double-clicking on the object in the word-processed document.

2. Notice that Works inserts an image at the current position of the insertion point as shown in Figure 12-13.

FIGURE 12-13

The Draw image in the word processor's document window

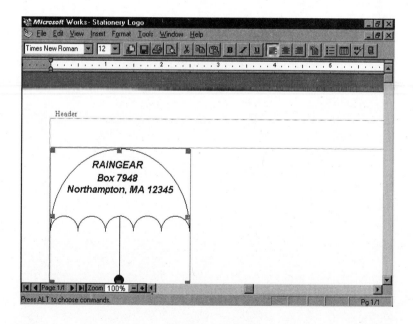

After centering the image on the page and clicking the Print Preview button, you can see in Figure 12-14 that we have created a distinctive and perfectly centered logo.

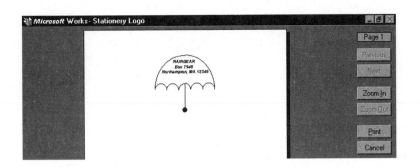

FIGURE 12-14
The inserted image
in a preview of
the document

Scaling a Drawing

If you want, you can use the resize handles in the word processor's document window to shrink a picture to an appropriate size after it's placed in a document. Simply drag on either side to increase or decrease the horizontal or vertical size (which alters the proportions as well), or drag on one of the corners to increase or decrease both simultaneously.

This is a more than adequate way to resize an image visually, but it's not precise. If you want to be more precise, you can go to the Picture command on the Format menu in the word processor. Here's how to do it.

1. Select the drawing, if necessary, by clicking on it once.

2. Click Format, and then click Picture.

   Works displays this Format Picture dialog box:

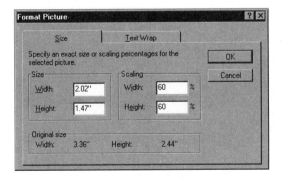

You can use the Size tab in this dialog box to make adjustments to the object's sizing and scaling.

❑ You can adjust both the height and the width of the image.

❑ You can adjust the scale of both the height and width.

409

How does scale differ from size? *Size* is the actual measured dimensions of the object, which in this case is expressed in inches. *Scale* is a percentage of the original size of the image.

If you keep an image within the bounds of a single Draw window, Works can usually import it into a document at or near its full size. Works scales down drawings larger than a single window to fit within the margins of the page. For the umbrella logo, Works didn't need to scale down the image when inserting it.

Once an image, scaled or not, is in a document, you can decide on a specific size that suits your preferences. For this example, we will scale the drawing (to 75 percent of the original), as follows:

3. Type a percentage in both the Height and Width text boxes in the Format Picture dialog box's Scaling box. We entered *75* for our example.

4. Click OK.

When Works displays the image again, check the edges to be sure you haven't lost any of the drawing. If you specify a larger size than Works can accommodate, it clips the drawing at the edges; this most often occurs with text. If this happens, increase the scale of the drawing until all of it appears.

When you scale a drawing, you can specify different percentages to alter the ratio of height to width. If you do, however, be sure to preview the result before printing. Uneven scaling can be desirable in some situations, but in others you might find squares printing out as rectangles or pies turning into eggs!

An image can be positioned by using the Left Align, Center Align, or Right Align buttons on the toolbar, or by using the Paragraph command on the Format menu and clicking on the Indents & Alignment tab.

Combining Text and Objects

In the umbrella example we've been working with, text will follow the object, since the logo, logically enough, goes at the top of the page. But suppose you want to have an object embedded in text. How do you combine the two?

One of the best ways to integrate text and objects is to wrap the text around the object, as you see in Figure 12-15.

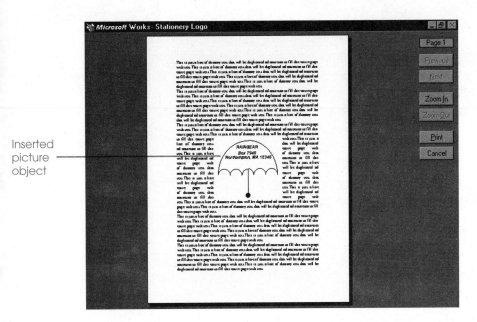

FIGURE 12-15

Wrapping text
around an image

Inserted
picture
object

Here's how you do it.

1. Click the object you want to wrap text around.

2. Drag the object to the approximate position where you want it to be located in the document.

3. Click Format, and then click Text Wrap.

   You'll see the Format Picture dialog box again, except this time with the Text Wrap tab showing.

4. Select Absolute.

   This option keeps the image object in place while the text flows around it, as you see in Figure 12-15. The In-Line option increases the spacing above and below the object as necessary.

5. In the Picture Position area, enter values where you want the picture to be located, including the page number on which you want it to appear.

   Horizontal is the measurement from the left edge of the page, and Vertical is the distance from the top of the page.

Editing an Image

Sometimes—perhaps often—you won't be satisfied with an image when you print it. You'll need to tweak it a little until it's just right. You can easily return to Draw and to the image you want to edit. All you need to do is to simply point to the image in the document and double-click it. That's all. When you double-click, Works opens the Draw window and displays the image you selected. You can move back and forth between the Draw and document windows whenever you want. To get back to the word processor (or the database) document, simply select the Exit and Return command on the File menu in the Draw window.

Coming Next

Draw is a simple yet powerful tool. However, it's only one of the graphics tools in Works. In the next chapter we'll explore ClipArt, Note-It, and WordArt—additional tools to add visual impact to all your Works projects.

Chapter 13

Special Touches with ClipArt, Note-It, and WordArt

You already know how Microsoft Works for Windows 95 can help you produce stunning documents, informative spreadsheets, and well-organized databases. And you don't have to sweat the details, either, because Works gives you access to an expansive set of symbols that let you complete your work with special flourishes.

E

ach of the utilities covered in this chapter—ClipArt, Note-It, and WordArt—can be used to add a special look to a Works document. Indeed, they set Works apart from other integrated packages. In this chapter, we'll describe what these tools are and how to use them.

A Look at ClipArt

Works comes with a library of about 100 different ClipArt images in the ClipArt Gallery, ranging from an image of a professor lecturing to a graphic picture of a computer, both shown in Figure 13-1. A *clip art* image is a little graphic picture that you can insert and manipulate in a document to enhance the final product. As you can see, the Microsoft ClipArt Gallery window offers categories of ClipArt on the left (such as Academic, Animals, and so on) plus a variety of buttons on the right that allow you to insert, locate, and organize ClipArt images. At the bottom of the ClipArt Gallery, you can see the highlighted image's filename (in this case *Professor*) as well as the path where the image is located.

Select an image here.

Select a category here.

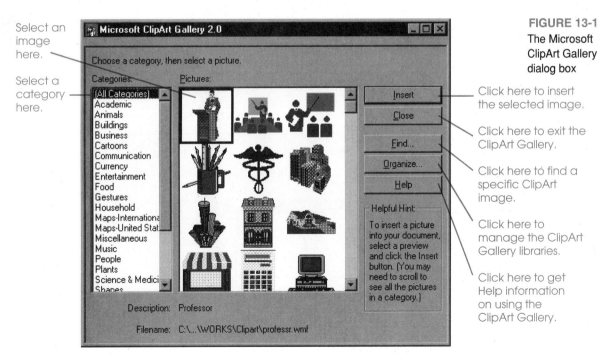

FIGURE 13-1
The Microsoft ClipArt Gallery dialog box

Click here to insert the selected image.

Click here to exit the ClipArt Gallery.

Click here to find a specific ClipArt image.

Click here to manage the ClipArt Gallery libraries.

Click here to get Help information on using the ClipArt Gallery.

The command for using ClipArt is located on the Insert menu. You simply place the insertion point in a document where you want a ClipArt image to appear, select ClipArt from the Insert menu, select an image to insert, and then continue working with your document. When you use ClipArt for the first time, Works displays the Add New Pictures dialog box, which lets you add installed packages of images to the ClipArt Gallery. After the package or packages are added, you go straight to the Microsoft ClipArt Gallery dialog box when you select the ClipArt command.

As you can see, the Gallery's images are organized by general categories, such as food, music, and people. To see any one set of images, click once on the category name and then use the scroll bars to see all the images for that category in the Gallery window. Then double-click the image you want to insert at the location of the insertion point in the document.

As with any object, once it's inserted in a document, it can be aligned, moved, and resized as you see fit.

TIP   Once an image is inserted in a document, double-clicking on the inserted image will return you to the ClipArt Gallery. There you can change the image or click Organize to further work with the ClipArt collection.

Organizing ClipArt Images

ClipArt goes far beyond just letting you see and insert images into documents. When you choose the Organize button in the ClipArt Gallery window, you see four different options in this Organize ClipArt dialog box:

Click here to add images to the ClipArt Gallery.

Click here to make recent changes current.

Click here to change an image's description and other properties.

Click here to make changes to the category list.

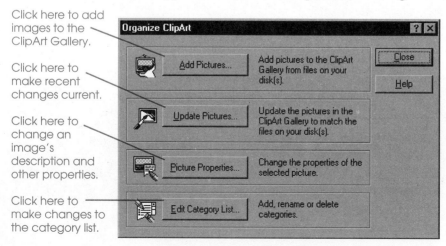

The Add Pictures option lets you add a picture to the ClipArt Gallery from another location. For example, Word for Windows (another Microsoft product) comes with a collection of clip art. If you wanted to add any one of those images to your Works ClipArt Gallery, you would use this option, provide the location of the file, and click OK. The image would then be placed in the ClipArt Gallery.

The Update Pictures button lets you keep the ClipArt Gallery current. It does this by ensuring that any changes you've made in images belonging to the Gallery (such as modifications or deletions) are reflected in the Gallery window. For example, if you deleted the file for the image of the cup holding pencils that you see in Figure 13-1 on page 415, you would click Update Pictures to remove the image from the window. The next time you open the ClipArt Gallery window, the pencil holder won't be there. When you update the ClipArt Gallery, Works provides you with a message telling you that the ClipArt database was updated. That means that the Gallery is current—that all new images that should be there are, and that those no longer being used are gone.

The Picture Properties button gives you information about any image; but most important, it allows you to add ClipArt to categories, add descriptions to images, and create new categories. Using these tools you can easily customize the ClipArt Gallery. To give you a feel for this feature, we'll demonstrate examining the properties of a file, and then we'll provide a description of the image beyond the title and assign it to a new category, as follows:

1. With a new word processor document open, click Insert, and then click ClipArt.

2. Click Cartoons, and then click an image. We selected the light bulb image you see in Figure 13-2 on the following page.

3. Click Organize, and then click Picture Properties.
   The Picture Properties dialog box appears.

4. Type a description in the Description box. Notice in Figure 13-3 on the following page that we entered *Ideas are worth a dime a dozen - do it* in our example.

5. Click Academic to place this image in the Academic category.

FIGURE 13-2

Selecting the light
bulb image

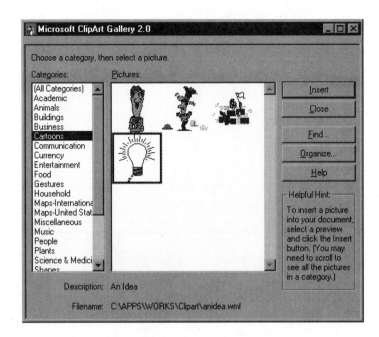

6. Click OK, and then close the Organize ClipArt dialog box.

7. Now click the Academic category and you'll see that the image you
   placed in this category is there.

FIGURE 13-3

The Picture
Properties
dialog box

Enter a
description
here.

Select a
category for
the selected
image.

Click here to
create a new
category.

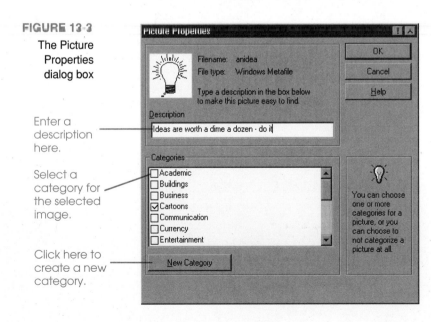

The Edit Category List button in the Organize ClipArt dialog box displays this Edit Category List dialog box:

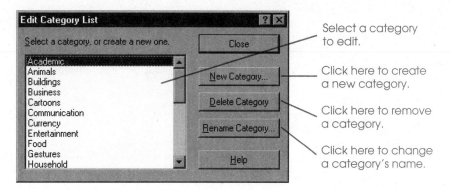

Select a category to edit.

Click here to create a new category.

Click here to remove a category.

Click here to change a category's name.

Here is where you work with categories: create a new one, delete an existing one, or rename an existing one. Why would you want to make these changes in categories? Perhaps you find that a category name is no longer relevant to the type of work you do and the name of the category needs to be changed. Or the category itself contains images that are of no use to you or your company and need to be deleted. Remember, all the images in the ClipArt Gallery are available under the (All Categories) category option, so you can always build a new category full of whatever images (including those from other applications) you want. Works gives you a warning about deleting a category, so you get a second chance to confirm that this is exactly what you want to do.

These three options in the Edit Category List dialog box are easy to use and can add a great deal of power to your use of ClipArt. Such lists help keep things organized and give you the flexibility you need to personalize your work.

Finding ClipArt

If you have a special request for a particular ClipArt image, you can use the Find button in the ClipArt Gallery dialog box to help you search for it. Works searches the descriptions for images (like the one you just entered). The more complete and accurate your description (the default ones tend to be short and general), the easier it will be for Works to find what you're looking for.

To find an image, follow these steps:

1. Open the ClipArt Gallery, if necessary.

2. Click Find in the ClipArt Gallery window.

    When you do this, you see the Find ClipArt dialog box, as shown in Figure 13-4.

FIGURE 13-4
The Find ClipArt
dialog box

Click here to select a search by description.

Click here to select a search by filename.

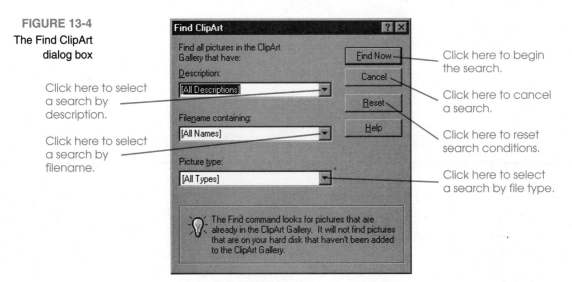

Click here to begin the search.

Click here to cancel a search.

Click here to reset search conditions.

Click here to select a search by file type.

You can search for an image by description, by the name of the file, or by the type of file. In this example, we'll search by description.

3. Type a description in the Description box, and click Find Now. We typed *man*.

    Works searches the libraries for the description and returns to the ClipArt Gallery window with a matching image, or images. For example, when you search by the word *man*, you would see the two images shown in Figure 13-5 (one called Man Talking and the other called Man With Too Many Hats). In both cases, Works found the image, since the word searched for is in the title of each image.

4. Go ahead and close the ClipArt Gallery window.

TIP A picture must be part of the Gallery for Works to find it. If you have added pictures, don't forget to select the Update Pictures button in the Organize ClipArt dialog box so that the images become part of the Gallery.

It's important to remember that as powerful as this tool is, Works will track only those images located in the Works ClipArt Gallery, rather than *all* the images on the hard drive. To do that, you must first add the images to the ClipArt Gallery. You might also notice that Works titles this search (Results of Last Find), which appears in the list of categories. This means you can always return to the image or images last found, simply by clicking this option.

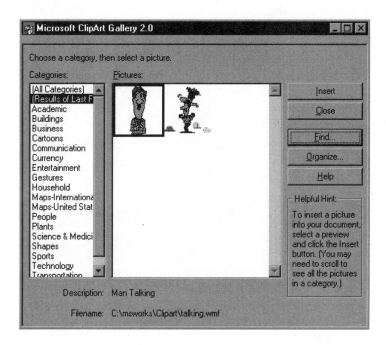

FIGURE 13-5
Found images in the ClipArt Gallery

Using Note-It

In addition to drawings, Works also lets you embed the electronic equivalent of self-sticking notes in word-processed documents.

Note-It is useful for drawing a reader's attention to comments, notes, questions, and even editorial judgments in a word-processed document or database. Note-It places a picture in the document window, such as a balloon, a check mark, or a sheet of paper with a folded corner, as you see in Figure 13-6 on the following page. When you double-click on a selected Note-It image in a document, you see the contents of the note.

FIGURE 13-6
Selected Note-It
image options

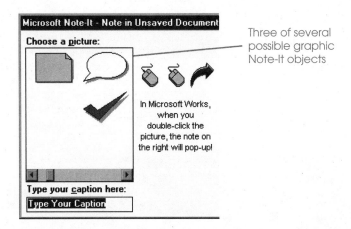

Three of several
possible graphic
Note-It objects

The example of a Note-It that we'll show you inserts a check mark to call attention to an answer on a true-false test that needs to be changed. By the way, we used the Works Tests Wizard to create the test document you see in Figure 13-7. We'll insert a Note-It in this document.

FIGURE 13-7
A test form
generated by the
Tests Wizard

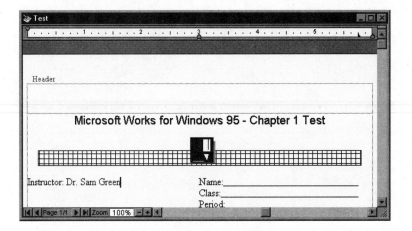

Here's how we did it.

1. We ran the Tests Wizard, which created the test document you see in Figure 13-7.

2. Now place the insertion point where you want the Note-It to appear. In this example, we'll put it just to the right of the instructor's name (Dr. Sam Green).

3. Click Insert, and then choose Note-It.

   This displays the Microsoft Note-It dialog box you see here:

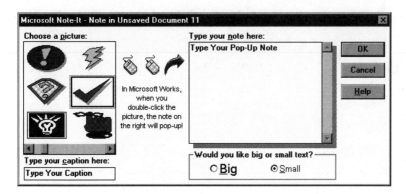

4. Click once on the picture you want to use.

   We selected the big check mark from the 58 available pictures. You have to use the horizontal scroll bar at the bottom of the Choose A Picture scroll box to see them all.

5. Type the text you want to use for the note in the Type Your Note Here box. In our example, we typed *Be sure to read directions aloud!*

6. Select the size of text you want in the note (Big or Small).

7. Enter a caption if you want one. We elected not to enter one.

8. Click OK to return to the original document.

   You'll see the inserted Note-It picture shown in Figure 13-8 on the following page. To see the contents of a note, as illustrated in Figure 13-9 on the following page, double-click on the Note-It picture.

See Also For more information about *using TaskWizards to generate documents,* see "Creating a True or False Test Form" in Chapter 2, page 70.

FIGURE 13-8

Inserting a Note-It
in a document

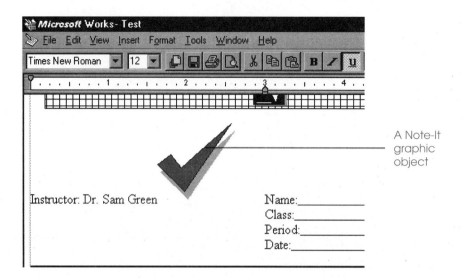

A Note-It
graphic
object

FIGURE 13-9

Displaying
Note-It text

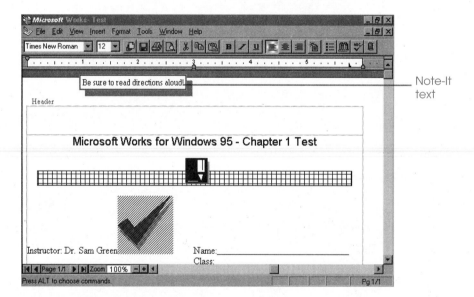

Note-It
text

Working with Note-It Objects

Note-It produces objects that, like other Works objects, can be edited, resized, moved, and deleted. To edit a note, click Edit, point to the Microsoft Note-It Object command, and then click the Edit command.

You'll be back in the Microsoft Note-It dialog box and can make whatever changes you might want. You can do the same thing by selecting the Note-It object, pointing to it and clicking the right mouse button, and then clicking the Edit command.

To change the size of a note, simply select it and drag any one of its resize handles, just as you did when you learned how to resize a drawing in the previous chapter. You can also change other formatting options for a note (since it's an object like the other images we've been dealing with here). Just select the object, point to it and click the right mouse button, and then click Format Picture. You'll see the same Format Picture dialog box you saw in Chapter 12 that allows you to change the size of the Note-It object as well as wrap text around it.

To move a note, simply drag it to a new location. The content of the note will remain the same. Bear in mind that moving it to a new location separates the note from the context within which it was created, thus potentially diminishing the note's meaning.

To delete a note, simply select it and press the Del key.

 TIP If you insert a note into a database, you should be aware that the picture representing the note will be the same size as the height of the database field. For example, a check mark or a balloon will be reduced to fit the field size. You can either increase the field size (which might look awkward) or resize the picture. The latter approach is usually the best.

Working with WordArt

If you like ClipArt and Note-It, you'll *love* WordArt. Why? Because it provides you with almost unlimited tools to modify text, with effects such as the one shown in the letterhead logo in Figure 13-10 on the next page.

With WordArt, you enter text, choose the design in which you want the text to appear, and then select the size and font. The text is inserted into a document as an object; like any other object, it can be resized, moved, and edited. WordArt is a separate program that's integrated into Works. When you start it, you'll see this toolbar above the document window:

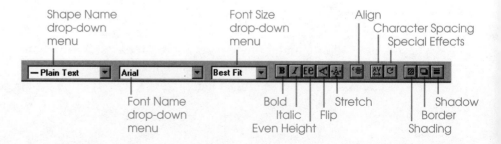

Here's a guide to the WordArt toolbar, and what each box and button does.

Toolbar Element	What It's Called	What It Does
 — Plain Text ▾	Shape Name	Click the drop-down list arrow to select a shape from the list to apply an effect to the WordArt text.
 Arial ▾	Font Name	Click the drop-down list arrow to select a font from the list.
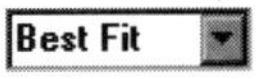 Best Fit ▾	Font Size	Click the drop-down list arrow to select a font size from the list. When you select the Best Fit option, Works selects a font size that best fills the WordArt object's box.
 **B**	Bold	Click the Bold button to apply boldface.
 *I*	Italic	Click the Italic button to apply italics.
 Ee	Even Height	Click the Even Height button to make all letters the same height, regardless of capitalization.
 Flip	Flip	Click the Flip button to turn the WordArt object on its side.
 Stretch	Stretch	Click the Stretch button to spread the text both vertically and horizontally so that it fills the WordArt object's box.
 Align	Align	Click the Align button to select an alignment option that aligns text within the WordArt object's box. If you don't select an alignment, the WordArt text is automatically centered.

TABLE 13-1   *(continued)*

Guide to the WordArt toolbar

TABLE 13-1 *continued*

Toolbar Element	What It's Called	What It Does
	Character Spacing	Click the Character Spacing button to see options for adjusting the amount of spacing between characters.
	Special Effects	Click the Special Effects button to see options for rotating the WordArt text.
	Shading	Click the Shading button to see options for choosing a pattern or color for the WordArt text.
	Shadow	Click the Shadow button to see options for choosing a shadow for the WordArt text.
	Border	Click the Border button to see options for choosing a border thickness for the WordArt text.

Many of these buttons display dialog boxes with straightforward options that can help you produce highly customized effects. For example, in Figure 13-11 the WordArt text on the left was rotated 20 degrees. The example on the right shows one of several shadow effects available.

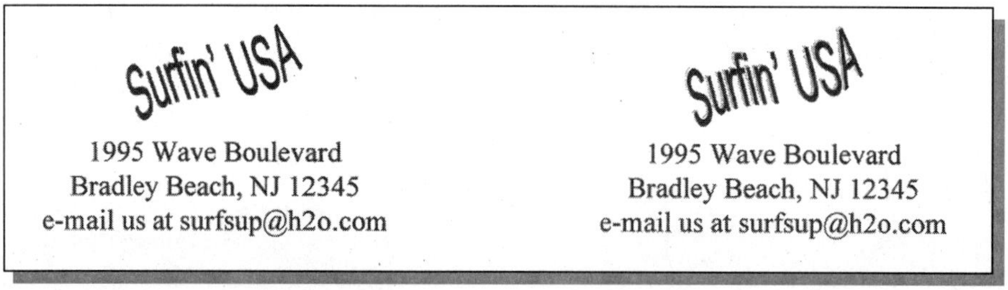

FIGURE 13-11
WordArt text showing rotation and shadow examples

Surfin' USA

1995 Wave Boulevard
Bradley Beach, NJ 12345
e-mail us at surfsup@h2o.com

Surfin' USA

1995 Wave Boulevard
Bradley Beach, NJ 12345
e-mail us at surfsup@h2o.com

Creating WordArt

To demonstrate WordArt, we'll work through an example to create a logo for a surfing shop as shown in Figure 13-10 on page 426.

Here's how to do it:

1. In a new word processing document click Insert, and then click WordArt.

   When you do this, you see the dialog box over the document window, as shown in Figure 13-12.

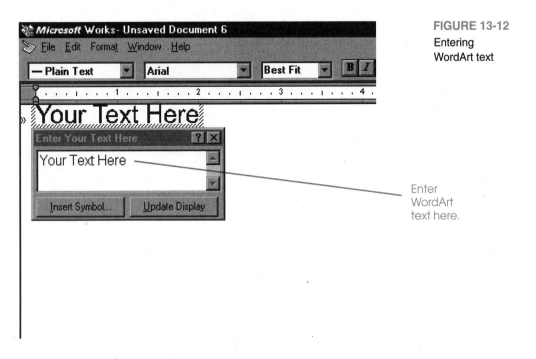

FIGURE 13-12

Entering WordArt text

Enter WordArt text here.

2. Type the text you want to format as WordArt in the Enter Your Text Here dialog box. We entered *Surfin' USA*.

3. Click the Shape Name box, on the left end of the WordArt toolbar.

   You'll see the drop-down menu of shapes shown in Figure 13-13 on the next page. We selected the Wave 1 option, the option to which the mouse pointer is pointing in Figure 13-13. Each of these shapes shows you how text will look when formatted using WordArt. The name appears in the Shape Name box after you select the option. You can select any of the patterns for creating words that are shaped.

4. Select the font you want to use. We used the default, Arial.

5. Select the font size you want to use. We selected 30 point.

   The default, Best Fit, fits the WordArt to the size of the WordArt box you first created; this may result in very small text. You can size

FIGURE 13-13
WordArt shapes
for text

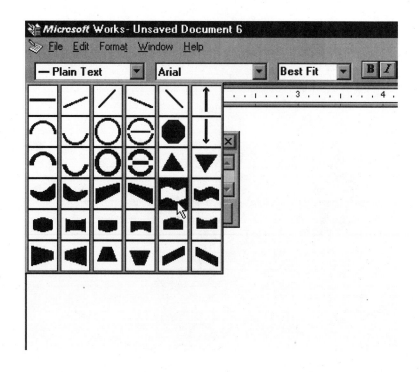

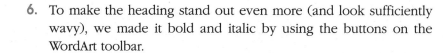

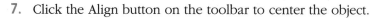

the WordArt box by dragging its resize handles. When you increase the size of the font, the size of the box adjusts automatically. If you do increase the font size, you might see a dialog box asking you if you want to resize the WordArt object. Click Yes.

6. To make the heading stand out even more (and look sufficiently wavy), we made it bold and italic by using the buttons on the WordArt toolbar.

7. Click the Align button on the toolbar to center the object.

8. Click anywhere in the document.

    The object inserts in the document at the insertion point location.

9. Select the object, and then click the Center Align button on the word processor's toolbar.

    The WordArt object centers on the page.

10. Finally, we added the rest of the address, as shown in Figure 13-10 on page 426. We used Arial 10-point for the address text, and then we centered the text.

TIP You can't save a WordArt object itself as art for an Easy Text entry, so you can't just click to insert the entire address. Rather, save the WordArt object in a document file, and then use the Easy Text command to insert the remaining address text.

To make Works work even better for us, we saved this as a custom template named *surfin*. The logo is designed; the template is available. When someone wants to write a letter, he or she has only to open the template document and go to work.

See Also For more information about *creating spreadsheet templates*, see "Using Templates" in Chapter 7, page 252.

TIP When you're done with WordArt, simply click where you want to work next. Be sure, though, that you don't accidentally click on the Enter Your Text Here dialog box, on a button on the WordArt toolbar or in a dialog box, or on the WordArt object you've created.

Inserting Symbols

So far we've discussed how to create all types of interesting text effects, but there's more we can do. Work allows you to insert a variety of different symbols into your documents, such as ®, ½, and ©. Here's how to do it:

1. Click Insert, and then click WordArt.

2. In the Enter Your Text Here dialog box, place the insertion point where you want the symbol to appear.

3. Click Insert Symbol.

You will see this Insert Symbol dialog box:

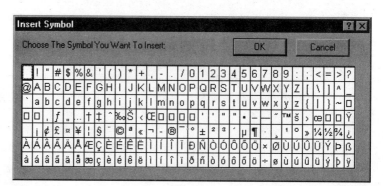

The selection of symbols depends on the font you're using. Selecting a different font will result in a set of different symbols in the dialog box, so be adventurous and try out several alternatives before you decide.

4. Select the symbol you want to use in the WordArt.

TIP With the Insert Symbol dialog box open, you can position the mouse pointer over a symbol and press and hold the left mouse button to see an enlarged view of the image. This way you can see how the symbol will appear when printed.

5. Click OK.

The symbol is inserted at the insertion point location in the Enter Your Text Here dialog box. You can alter its size if necessary for greater legibility or better impact.

Coming Next

Now you're an artist! Using these tools, plus Microsoft Draw, you can create virtually anything you can imagine. Simply take your time, save often, let your creativity run free, and practice. You'll find that Draw, ClipArt, Note-It, and WordArt are useful, fun, and helpful in your work and in your hobbies. Now we'll move on to Works Communications—the gateway to the world of telecommunications.

Part 6

Using Works Communications

In This Part You *know* what's all the rage these days: using telecommunications, posting e-mail, surfing the Internet, and cruising bulletin boards. Part of the power of Works for Windows 95 is in equipping you with the tools you need to do all your computer chores. You don't have to go outside of Works for anything—even to acquire the software you need to connect to another computer and make happen all these wonderful things you hear about.

In Chapter 14, you'll get in touch by learning what is necessary to get on line, how to set up your modem for the transfer of information, how to send and receive a file, how to capture text that appears on the screen, and how to write a script that will automatically allow you to sign on. With this information, you'll be able to take advantage of Microsofts's new online service, The Microsoft Network, CompuServe, and any one of several commercial information providers. And you'll be able to do all this by using Easy Connect, Works for Windows 95's brand-new way of speeding you through calling and connecting.

Chapter 14

Getting in Touch

You can go around the block, around the country, or around the world—maybe even someday around the universe—with your computer and Microsoft Works for Windows 95. It's true! Amazingly, you can reach all these places with a few clicks of a mouse button.

The word processor, spreadsheet, and database modules of Works allow you to choose the Dial This Number option on the Tools menu and dial any number. Dialing a phone number is only one way that Works and your computer can help you connect to and communicate with other computers. Another, much more powerful way is through telecommunications, which lets you become part of the large and growing group of people who rely on computer-to-computer hookups to gather information, transfer files, bat ideas back and forth, and in hundreds of other ways just keep in touch with one another.

If you think telecommunications is reserved for sophisticated PC users, think again. Even the most naive user can take advantage of commercial information providers such as CompuServe or America Online and find out the closing price of Marvel stock, the weather in Seattle, or how many games the New York Yankees are back—and best of all, connect to the mother of all networks, the Internet.

Communicating with Computers

Before you can use your computer for any type of communications, it must be set up to "connect" to another computer. Your version of Works uses the communications module to do this.

After you've installed a modem, computer communications boils down to several operations that you perform in sequence. Here are the general steps:

1. Set up your computer and modem to communicate.

2. Have your computer dial the phone number to connect to the other computer.

3. Log on to identify yourself, using an account number and password, if necessary.

4. Telecommunicate to your heart's content!

When you finish communicating, you log off to tell the remote computer that you're finished. Then you disconnect or hang up so that the phone lines are free to use again.

What You Need to Go On Line ·

You need four things to get started in the telecommunications business:

- A computer (almost any kind will do)
- A modem
- Communications software
- An open phone line

You already have the computer (or are about to buy one). In any telecommunications activity, the computer acts as a sender and receiver of information.

The second thing you need is a modem, a piece of hardware that handles the three C's of remote computing: calling, connecting, and communicating. Although your computer can process information perfectly well, without a modem it can't pass information to other computers through the phone lines.

The word *modem* is short for *modem*odulator/*demo*dulator, which describes exactly what a modem does. To send information, a modem modulates the electrical signal output from a computer—in a sense, embedding the data in a sound wave that can travel over a telephone line much as radio stations "embed" music in their AM and FM signals. When receiving information, the modem demodulates the incoming carrier wave, retrieving the bits of data and reconstructing them in a form the computer can use.

No matter how sophisticated any part of your telecommunications system is, if your modem doesn't do the job, you're stuck. For example, some modems have filters that screen out some of the noise that invades every line. When you're talking, this interference, which sounds like static, is simply a nuisance. But when you're transferring data, it can be a disaster because it corrupts transmissions; either what you send doesn't get to its destination, or what does gets there fails to match what you've sent and thus is unusable.

Since the modem is a critical piece of equipment in your telecommunications efforts, you want to get the best model you can afford. For all practical purposes, "best" translates into fastest, and modems are getting faster (and cheaper) every day. Modem speed is sometimes expressed as *baud rate,* which is the number of bits per second (bps) that data is transmitted. Whereas the fastest modem available used to be 300 bps, which was typical only five years ago, today 14,400 bps modems (almost

10 times faster) are the most commonly used. Even now this type is being quickly replaced with 28,800 bps modems.

So if you can afford a 14,400 bps modem (which sells for about $80 retail), go for it. And if you can afford the approximately $250 for a 28,800 bps modem (you can find some as low as $150 to $170), that would be even better. Be aware that 28,800 bps modems are not yet in wide use—although that's rapidly changing. Until they are in wide use, those with 28,800 bps modems might not be able to take full advantage of the speed because the modem needs to adjust down to fit whatever rate of transmission the receiving computer's modem can handle. So, the rule is to check the specifications of the modem connected to the computer you want to connect to and see what the highest baud rate is that it can handle. Then, buy a modem that can at least match that speed.

The third thing you need is communications software (included in Works), which performs the translation between the information as it appears to you and as it's sent.

Finally, you need a telephone connection to where you want to send (or from where you want to receive) information; in other words, you need a phone line. It may be a dedicated line just for telecommunications or a regular line that you also use for faxing documents and talking on the phone. If you have only one line for both voice and data, your voice line will be tied up when you're transmitting. Most people who are serious about telecommunicating end up with two phone lines.

TIP If you have Call Waiting, you should disable it before you log on. Do that by lifting the receiver, pressing the star button (*), and pressing *70*. If that doesn't work, check with your phone company. Typically, you can set up this dialing sequence within the communications software so that it's done automatically during the connecting and logon procedure.

Speaking the Language of Communications

When you connect your computer to another computer via a modem, you must ensure that the two computers "speak" the same language, transmit at the same speed, and follow the same rules of etiquette. If you don't, one computer might transmit in a "dialect" the other one can't understand. Or, it might transmit too quickly for the other one to comprehend.

Rules of etiquette (or "protocol") in telecommunications are needed for the same reason they're needed in everyday life—to avoid conflicts, They prevent both computers from trying to transmit at the same time and, essentially, shout each other down.

The Works communications module and comparable communications programs are your means of ensuring that communications sessions proceed smoothly. The communications module takes care of all aspects of a communications session, from establishing the initial connection to making sure that both computers talk at a rate and in a way that the other understands.

Although you won't actually connect to another computer in this chapter, you can start Works Communications to see the menus, commands, and features described in this chapter.

Starting Works Communications

To load the Works communications module, click the Communications button in the Task Launcher dialog box or click File, click New, and then select the Communications button. You'll see the Unsaved Communication 1 window as shown in Figure 14-1.

FIGURE 14-1
The opening
Communications
window

Toolbar

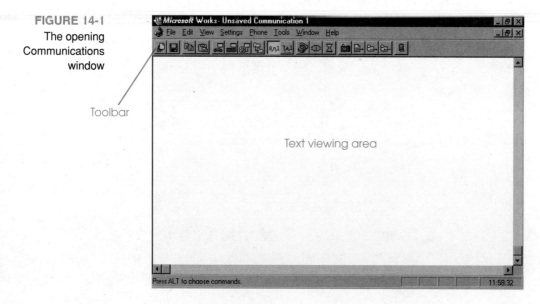

Text viewing area

Things have been made much easier for you with Windows 95, since it likely will automatically detect the presence of a modem connected to your computer as well as deduce the communications port that it uses. If it doesn't, you'll have to install it manually by using the Add/Remove Hardware utility in the Control Panel folder.

Using the Communications Toolbar

Like all the other Works modules we've discussed, the communications module contains a toolbar that offers buttons galore to make your work easier and more efficient. This toolbar, which you see here, is especially handy since so much of the telecommunications terminology and procedures can be confusing to a new user.

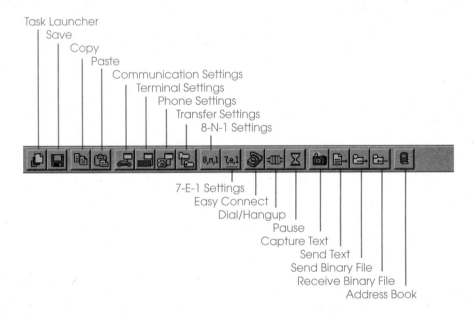

As we explained in Chapter 1, you can add buttons for commands you use often and remove buttons that you never use. In either case, you're undoubtedly familiar with many of the buttons you see here (such as Save and Copy), but there are new ones as well.

What each button does is summarized in Table 14-1 on the next page.

Button	What It's Called	What It Does
	Task Launcher	Displays the Task Launcher, which gives you access to Works modules, TaskWizards, and existing files
	Save	Saves the active file with its current name
	Copy	Copies highlighted text and stores it on the Clipboard
	Paste	Inserts Clipboard contents into the Communications window at the insertion point
	Communication Settings	Adjusts communication settings, such as the modem and the port it's connected to
	Terminal Settings	Adjusts terminal settings, such as the type of terminal and the font you want to use
	Phone Settings	Adjusts phone settings, such as redial and autoanswer
	Transfer Settings	Changes transfer options, such as the protocol you use to transfer files
	8-N-1 Settings	Changes communication settings to 8 data bits, no parity, and 1 stop bit
	7-E-1 Settings	Changes communication settings to 7 data bits, even parity, and 1 stop bit
	Easy Connect	Connects to another computer using an existing phone number

TABLE 14-1   *(continued)*
The Works Communications toolbar

TABLE 14-1 *continued*

Button	What It's Called	What It Does
	Dial/Hangup	Connects to or disconnects from the computer to which you are connected
	Pause	Temporarily suspends communications
	Capture Text	Saves incoming text as a file
	Send Text	Sends text from an ASCII file to another computer
	Send Binary File	Sends a document as a binary file to another computer
	Receive Binary File	Receives and saves a binary file sent to you by another computer
	Address Book	Opens the default Address Book file

Getting Ready to Communicate

Setting up for communications means telling Works about your modem (if not already successfully detected by Windows 95), specifying the phone number of the computer you want to call, and ensuring that both computers will use the same communications settings when sending and receiving data.

Most, if not all, of the information you need for setup should be listed in the documentation for your modem and for the remote computer. If you're connecting two independent personal computers, such as yours and someone else's, be sure to use the same settings for both.

To set up for communications, you use the aptly named Settings menu, which you see on the following page.

If you've never tried communications, some of the terms you see here and in the command dialog boxes might look a bit unfriendly, but don't let them intimidate you. The Works communications module, as well as popular telecommunication services such as CompuServe, wouldn't exist if you needed a Ph.D. in nuclear physics to get started.

We'll take it nice and slow, step by step, from the beginning.

Dialing Up

Once Windows 95 has identified your modem, you can adjust all the important settings using the Settings menu. Open the Settings menu and choose Phone, Communication, Terminal, or Transfer to display the corresponding tab in the Settings dialog box.

The following sections describe the options available on each tab.

Selecting Phone Options

The Phone tab you see here allows you to have Works automatically redial a number that's busy:

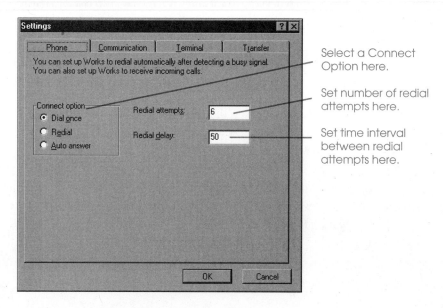

Select a Connect Option here.

Set number of redial attempts here.

Set time interval between redial attempts here.

You can have Works redial the telephone number a specific number of times before quitting. You can also specify a set amount of time for it to wait between tries.

Selecting Communication Options

The Communication tab you see here lets you define the device that Works will use when connecting:

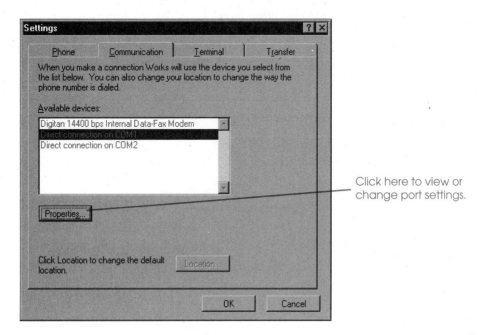

Click here to view or change port settings.

The Properties button allows you to set important parameters for communicating in the COM1 Properties dialog box shown in Figure 14-2 on the next page, including the speed at which you send information (the baud rate) and the amount sent (data bits). The settings in the COM1 Properties dialog box refer to communications port 1, which in this example is where the modem makes its connection.

This is an important group of settings, without which you can't connect to another computer. They determine how fast your modem sends and receives data, the type of error checking it uses, and the number of bits (binary 1s and 0s) it uses to represent each character.

The Port Settings tab proposes standard settings (such as 8 bits, no parity, and so on), so you might not need to tinker with these at all. If you do, however, you should be able to find the appropriate settings in the

FIGURE 14-2

The COM1
Properties
dialog box

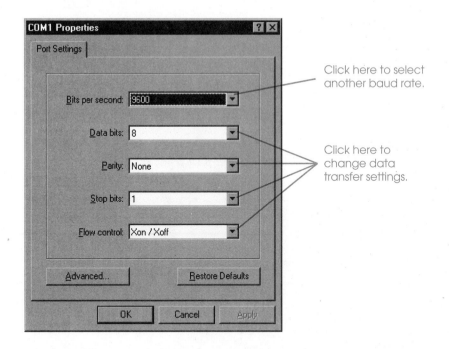

Click here to select
another baud rate.

Click here to
change data
transfer settings.

documentation for your particular computer. Here's what all these settings mean:

- Bits Per Second determines the speed of transmission. Your modem is rated for a certain speed, such as 1200, 2400, 4800, 9600, 14,400, or 28,800. Faster modems can communicate with slower ones, but slower ones need an exact match or need to connect to a slower modem to communicate successfully. Works Communications goes up to an astounding 921,600 bps!

    Although this parameter is referred to interchangeably as bps and baud rate, technically *bps* describes transmission speed more accurately than does the older term *baud rate*.

- Data Bits refers to the number of *bi*nary digi*ts* used to represent each character. During transmission, each data bit is sent as a high or low "blip" in a data stream. Most transmissions use either 7 or 8 data bits. You can use the two toolbar buttons (8-N-1 Settings and 7-E-1 Settings) to switch settings here if necessary.

- Parity indicates a form of error checking to determine whether a character has been transmitted correctly.

- Stop Bits tells the receiving computer where each character ends. Stop bits are timing intervals between characters.

■ Flow Control keeps the temporary storage location from overflowing, which can cause a possible loss of data, while you're transferring a file. Xon/Xoff, a standard flow control method, causes the communications module to send a signal to the remote computer that pauses transmission when the buffer (a reserved portion of memory) is full. You might have to choose either Hardware or None if the remote computer uses a different type of flow control or none at all.

Selecting Terminal Options

Terminal emulation refers to the way your computer behaves while connected to another computer. Back in the early days of communications (all of a decade ago), large computers dealt with specific types of terminals, which were smaller units with far less "brain power" than the mainframes that accepted their output and fed them input. The terminal options available in Works are shown here:

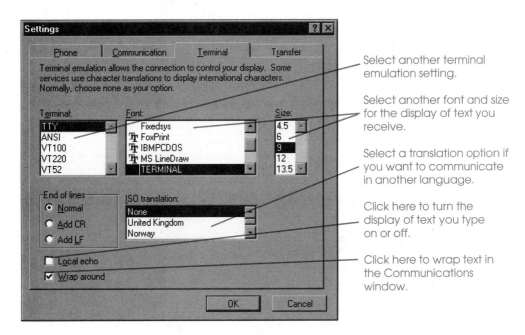

Select another terminal emulation setting.

Select another font and size for the display of text you receive.

Select a translation option if you want to communicate in another language.

Click here to turn the display of text you type on or off.

Click here to wrap text in the Communications window.

When you're using a personal computer to communicate, you often have to tell it to emulate (imitate) a particular type of terminal, by sending and receiving formatting codes and displaying characters as the terminal would do. Again, your documentation should tell you which type of terminal to emulate. Works proposes TTY as the default.

Here's an explanation of the various options available on the Terminal tab in the Settings dialog box:

- Terminal matches the type of computer you have with the type of computer you're communicating with.

- End Of Lines allows you to change some characteristics of incoming text. Select Add CR (for *carriage return*) if there are lines of text that don't begin at the left edge of your screen, or Add LF (for *line feed*) if lines of text are overwriting each other.

- Local Echo displays the characters you type. Communications is unlike other Works modules in that you don't always see what you type. Turn on the Local Echo option if your typing doesn't appear on the screen.

- Wrap Around moves words that don't fit at the window's right edge down to a new line.

- Font and Size let you change the font and the size of the text that appears on the screen when you receive messages.

- ISO Translation is used to specify a different country if you're going to send and receive information in a different language. The country you choose determines the characters Works uses. Your choice must be one that the remote computer can recognize.

Selecting Transfer Options

Finally, the Transfer tab shown here gives you a choice of four *protocols,* or agreements between computers on how data should be sent:

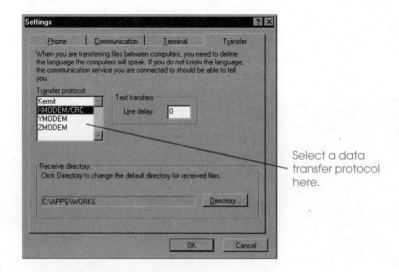

Select a data transfer protocol here.

Here are the various options:

- Kermit (not related to the famous frog) is the slowest of the four, but the most reliable. Because of this, it's often used to communicate between different types of personal computers.

- XMODEM/CRC is the most common; it's very reliable, but slow.

- YMODEM is faster than XMODEM/CRC (since it sends more information at a time), but it doesn't work well if your phone connection is not good.

- ZMODEM is even faster than YMODEM and is as reliable as XMODEM/CRC. Z is a good choice, but less common than X or Y.

Which one is best for you? Most of the time, the location to which you're trying to send or receive files will indicate which transfer protocol you should use. If in doubt, try Kermit. It's very popular, and most computers use communication software that can understand it.

TIP When you type a phone number, type all the numbers you would dial, including such digits as 9, for accessing an outside line, and 1, for calling out of your local dialing area. You can use parentheses, spaces, or hyphens to separate the parts of a phone number for readability, but they're not necessary.

Setting Modem Properties

A modem is a modem is a modem. Right? Wrong. Modems vary by make, model, and speed, as well as by the types of commands they use to start and end phone connections. That's why there's a separate Modem command on the Settings menu. When you click it, you'll see the dialog box shown in Figure 14-3 on the next page that indicates the properties of the installed modems. You can see in the figure that there is one modem installed (Digitan 14400 bps Internal Data-Fax Modem) and that through this dialog box you can add a new modem or remove an existing one.

FIGURE 14-3

The Modems
Properties
dialog box

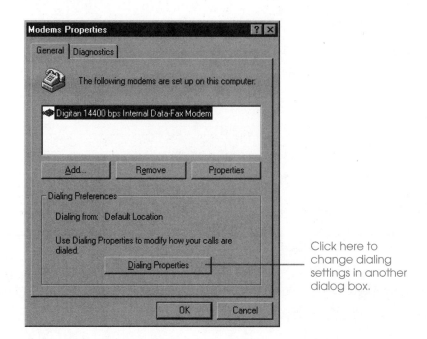

Click here to
change dialing
settings in another
dialog box.

If you click the Dialing Properties button, you'll see the settings for
the default dialing location (as shown in Figure 14-4) including where
you're dialing from, your area code, your location, and how you dial (using
1 as a prefix or some other combination of numbers). All these options are
there to ensure that when it does come time to dial, you can get through
without any difficulty.

FIGURE 14-4

The Dialing
Properties
dialog box

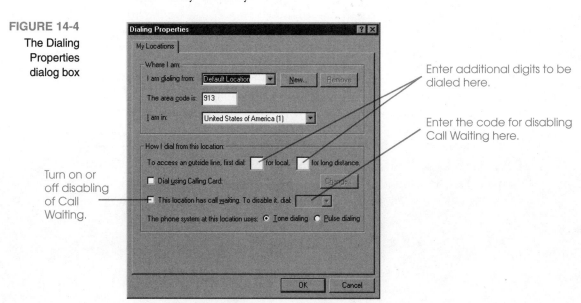

Enter additional digits to be
dialed here.

Enter the code for disabling
Call Waiting here.

Turn on or
off disabling
of Call
Waiting.

TIP An important character to remember when entering numbers is the comma. Use a comma to tell Works to pause for two seconds before dialing the next digit. For example, if you dial 9 for an outside line, you can type the phone number as *9,18005551234* to have Works pause after the 9.

Saving Your Settings

Even though it's unlikely, you might need to make a variety of adjustments before you can communicate successfully using Works. After you've finished all that work, the last thing you want to do is have to do it over again.

Luckily, you can save the settings in a file by choosing the Save command from the File menu. When you choose this command, Works displays a familiar-looking Save As dialog box, which asks you to type a name for the settings file and, if you want, to specify a drive or folder. Although the file you save isn't one that you can display and work with as you can a letter or other document, the communications module saves it with the extension .WCM.

The next time you want to connect with the same computer, simply choose the Open command from the File menu and specify the filename; Works reads all your settings, including any phone number, and is ready to go.

Connecting with Easy Connect

Windows has done it again! Using Easy Connect (on the Phone menu and the communications module's toolbar), Works handles virtually every piece of information needed to connect, except for the telephone number of the computer you want to dial up. After you choose Easy Connect, you'll see the Easy Connect dialog box as shown in Figure 14-5 on the next page. Here you just fill in the number you want to call plus the name of the destination (since Works will save this information for you for later use). Then click OK, verify what you entered, click Dial, and then your modem should dial and connect you after verifying that you entered the correct numbers. The high-pitched sound from your PC speaker or modem means that the modem is trying to connect. Then you'll hear other sounds, including some loud hissing. Finally, when you do connect, your modem may provide an audio signal of several beeps.

FIGURE 14-5
The Easy Connect
dialog box

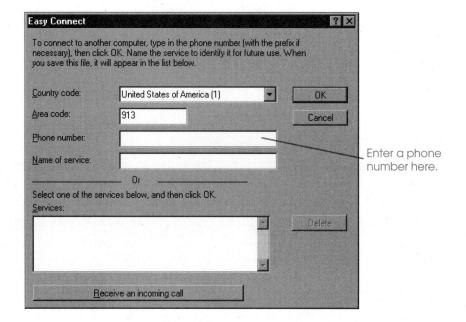

Enter a phone number here.

In Figure 14-6, you can see how we connected to the University of Kansas, which is waiting for our ID account number so that we can be connected to its remote computer. Note, also, in the bottom right corner that we've been on line for 16 seconds.

TIP Once you've used Easy Connect, that same connection will be available at the bottom of the Phone menu. You can just click Phone, and then the name of the destination to connect to the same location easily and quickly.

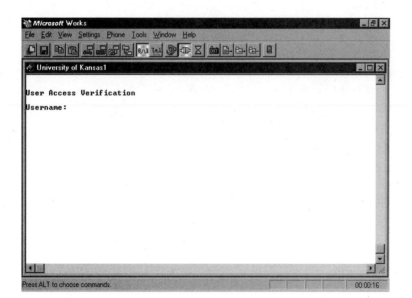

FIGURE 14-6
Connecting to a
remote computer

🪟 Windows and the Internet

One of the things that Microsoft has done with Windows 95 is include its new on-line system, named The Microsoft Network, or MSN. Using this service, you can connect to the Internet and join the thousands of people who do everything from visiting the Library of Congress to ordering fine wines. All you need to do to get on the Internet with Windows 95 is start MSN (click the icon on your desktop), join, and then use the special browsing software that MSN provides.

The Internet is simply a network of networks. It was originally funded by the U.S. Department of Defense, and there is some "Net" lore that claims it was built in a decentralized fashion (no one owned or controlled it) to make it immune to the effects of a nuclear war. Some 30 years later, it's the playground of millions of people, and millions more are joining every year. Using the Net, there's almost nothing you can't learn, see, or hear. It takes some exploring and the right equipment (most, if not all, of which you already have)—and lots of time. Try it. You'll have a blast and learn a lot as well.

Sending a File

The Works communications module provides you with a ready means of transferring your Works files from place to place simply by establishing a phone connection between your computer and the remote computer. No need to send that document through the mail, pay for a stamp, or have it get lost in the shuffle; simply send it as an electronic file and it's there in minutes.

Computer files can travel in either of two forms: as text files or as binary files. Text files are also known as ASCII files. ASCII, short for *A*merican *S*tandard *C*ode for *I*nformation *I*nterchange, is a set of codes used to translate letters, numbers, and punctuation marks into a form that all computers can handle. ASCII files can contain tabs, carriage returns, and other simple formatting, but they can't include any unusual or program specific formatting, such as superscripts, italics, or graphics.

Binary files, on the other hand, can contain all manner of codes, text formatting, and unusual characters. Program files, such as Works itself, are always binary files. Document files you create with Works are also binary files, although you can save them as Text or Text (DOS) files in the Save File As Type option of the Save As dialog box.

It doesn't matter which type of file you want to send, the procedures are the same. To send a file, first get ready by doing the following:

1. Be sure you have a file available that you want to send, and be sure you know whether it's in ASCII or binary format.

2. Connect to the computer to which you want to send the file.

3. Click Tools, and then click Send Text (or click the Send Text button on the toolbar). When you do this, you'll see the Send Text dialog box on the following page.

4. Locate the file you want to send.
   In this example, we're sending a file named *Margolis* located in the *Letters* folder.

5. Click OK.

Although you won't see the file itself being transferred, you can tell that Works is working because a little indicator on the screen tracks the progress of the transfer. That's all there is to it!

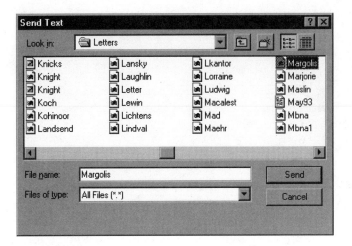

Receiving a File

You can receive text from another computer as well and then save it to your disk. This is often referred to as *downloading*; sending a file to another computer is called *uploading*.

As with sending a file, during receiving (downloading) the contents of the file aren't displayed on either computer's screen. Rather, Works displays a status box that indicates how much of the file has been received.

To receive and save a file, follow these steps:

1. Connect to the computer from which you want to receive the file.

2. Click Tools, and then click Receive File (or click the Receive Binary File button on the toolbar).

   Works shows you the Receive File dialog box.

3. Enter a name for the file you're about to receive.

   It can be the name given it by the sender, or a new name more suited to your needs or your file organization system.

4. Click OK.

As with sending a file, a status box keeps you informed about the file transfer.

TIP If you want to cancel the transfer of a file before the job is done, click the Cancel button, and then click OK. The transfer is terminated, with no harm done to the file or either computer.

Capturing Text

You just learned how you can save text you receive as a file that was sent to you. You might also want to save text transmitted in a session that appears on your screen but that isn't sent to you as a file. For example, you might be connected to the Internet where you're reading a recipe. As text rolls by on screen, you can capture it to a file.

To do this, use the Capture Text command on the Tools menu or click the Capture Text button on the toolbar to start the process. Once you do this, you'll see a Capture Text dialog box. Enter a filename, and any text that you see on the screen will become part of the file that you just named. You must choose the Capture Text command *before* you receive the text you want to save. Only the text that is received after you choose the command is saved.

To capture text and save it as a file, follow these steps:

1. Click Tools, and then click Capture Text (or click the Capture Text button on the toolbar).

2. Select the drive on which you want to save the text as a file.

3. Select the folder in which you want to save the text as a file.

4. Type a name for the file.
    Works saves all captured text as an ASCII (text) file. This is the only file type available for captured text.

5. Click OK.

While Works captures text, you'll see the word *CAPT* displayed on the status line. You should also look to the status line for other tips about what's going on during your communication session. For example, when you're not connected, you'll see the *Offline* message. When you are connected, the status line reads *Online*.

If, in the middle of a session, you want to stop the capture process, select End Capture Text from the Tools menu.

Using Scripts

A script is a saved set of commands that Works can invoke at any time. Think of a script as a tape recording of instructions. When you create it, you describe each instruction. When you're finished, you can play the instructions back to help you accomplish a particular task.

Recording a Script

You can record a sequence of steps for a particular task, such as those for logging on, in the Works communications module.

    Here, we'll show you how to create a script for a sign-on sequence so that each time we want to log on, we can simply select the name from the Tools menu and the logon procedure will be carried out.

1. Click Tools, and then choose Record Script.

   You'll see this Record Script dialog box:

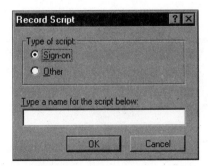

   You can select this to be a sign-on script (for connecting) or some other script for doing tasks such as entering commands to a remote computer.

TIP If you're creating a script to sign on to another computer, you don't need a name, since Works will assign a name based on the destination. If you want to create another script, enter a name in the script name box.

2. Click OK.

   Everything you do from here on in becomes part of the script.

3. When you finish recording all the steps in the logon procedure, choose End Recording from the Tools menu.

Works saves the recording in the exact sequence that you selected. The next time you choose the script from the Tools menu, Works asks if you want to connect. Click OK to use the recorded logon script to connect to the other computer.

You can also record tasks other than logging on. To do this, follow these steps:

1. Click Tools, and then choose Record Script.

2. Select the Other option in the Record Script dialog box.

3. Type a name of 15 characters or fewer in the box labeled *Type a name for the script below*.

For example, if you're going to record the steps to view stock market quotes, you might name the script *View Quotes*.

4. Click OK.

5. Perform the exact steps needed to accomplish the task.

6. Click Tools, and then choose End Recording when you've finished recording all the steps.

Works saves the recording for you to play back later.

TIP To cancel a recording in progress, choose Cancel Recording from the Tools menu or press the Esc key. Works stops the recording and doesn't save it.

Playing Back a Script

A script is only useful when you play it back. To do this, click Tools, and then select the script name at the bottom of the menu. Then click OK to connect.

For an alternative method, you can do this:

1. Click File, and then click Open.

2. Select the communications file you want to open by working your way through different levels of folders if necessary.

3. Double-click the icon representing the script.

Logging Off

You must take care of two simple but important tasks when ending a communications session: logging off and then hanging up.

If you're communicating with a remote computer that requires you to log on, remember to end your session by logging off. Logging off is never difficult—it can be as simple as typing *bye, exit,* or *quit.* Regardless of how it's done, logging off tells the remote computer that you're officially checking out. Be sure to log off if you're connected to a computer on which you pay for connect time. If you hang up without logging off, you might end up paying for time you didn't use.

Your final step in ending a communications session is to choose the Hang Up command from the Phone menu or click the Dial/Hangup button on the toolbar. Hanging up disconnects you from the remote computer, the same way you end a phone call by hanging up the phone. Until you feel confident about hangup procedures, you might be sure you've properly hung up by picking up the handset and listening for a dial tone if you have a single phone line.

Coming Next

That's the end of Part 6 and your primer on connecting to other computers using Works. Now we'll move to the most advanced material in this book—sharing information created with different modules. It might be advanced, but it's not difficult. It even turns out to be a real time-saver, and, best of all, it's fun!

Part 7

SELECT EDITION

Working Together

In This Part Now it's time for some real-life applications. In Chapter 15, you'll become acquainted with how a form letter is created, as well as how lists are made and envelopes created. Then it's to Works for Windows 95 and some of its most useful features. If you ever had to enter the same information in more than one place, you were using the wrong tools. Once you create that dynamic drawing, or that spreadsheet that shows you are only days away from profitability, inserting it into another document is only a question of using the Cut, Copy and Paste tools, with your understanding of how linking and embedding operate with different Works for Windows 95 applications.

For example, if you want to insert a chart created using the Chart tool into a word processor document, it can be done with ease. What's more impressive is that once you select a chart, anytime you change the original data on which the chart is based (using the spreadsheet), the chart in the major document (the word processor) will change as well. As shown in Chapter 16, when objects are linked, they are bound until told otherwise. Once an object is linked, there is a connection between documents that will be maintained unless it is broken by you.

Now you have the works—the ability to use the Works for Windows 95 word processor, spreadsheet, and database, plus its graphics and telecommunications tools, to do your own work more effectively and enjoy your hobbies and leisure-time activities.

Chapter 15

Sharing Information Among Modules

ou've learned the basics of using Microsoft Works for Windows 95 to create documents, spreadsheets, and databases, as well as to communicate with others via telephone lines and even to send files anywhere you want. You've also explored how to use Microsoft Draw to jazz up a document with drawings and clip art, and you've used the spreadsheet's charting feature to produce a graph. These are some of the ways of using the different parts of Works in an integrated fashion.

More often than not, real-life work requires that you be able to combine information of different types and even from different sources. Besides importing drawings and charts, you might need to include rows and columns of spreadsheet values in a financial statement created with the word processor, or you might need to move inventory balances from a database file into the spreadsheet where you track your need for new materials. Also, you certainly don't want to have to retype information in a new module once you've entered it in another!

In this chapter, we'll show you how to move data easily between Works modules.

Moving and Linking Information Between Modules

Within any of the four Works modules, you can cut and paste or copy and paste information freely. Between the word processor and the spreadsheet (not the database), you can also use a more sophisticated Paste Special procedure that lets you create a *link* between the copied information and the original information in the spreadsheet. After you create such a link, Works can update the information in the word processor whenever you change the same or related information in the contributing spreadsheet.

Knowing roughly what Works does when you use data-transfer commands will make you feel more confident about moving data from place to place. All you need is a basic understanding of the three data-transfer mechanisms Works supports: cut and paste (or copy and paste), linking, and embedding. We'll deal with cut and paste in this chapter, and linking and embedding in the next.

Cutting, Copying, and Pasting Information

Both the cut and paste and copy and paste operations use the Clipboard as a temporary storage place for information you want to duplicate or move. Cut and paste moves the information from one location to another, whereas copy and paste duplicates it. Other than this distinction, these operations work in exactly the same way. In general, here are the steps you follow in any cut and paste or copy and paste operation.

1. Select the information you want to place in a different document.

2. Cut or copy the information to the Clipboard.

3. Select the location in the receiving document where you want to paste the information.

4. Paste the contents of the Clipboard into the receiving document.

Because Works is both integrated software and a Windows-based program, you can use the Clipboard as a way station whether you're moving information within a document, between documents in the same module (such as the word processor), between documents in different modules, or even between documents in different applications. For example, if you want to move the information from the Works spreadsheet to Microsoft Access (a separate database program), the cut and paste procedure is exactly the same as if you were moving the data within the same module or the Works application.

Cut and paste and copy and paste are simple ways to move data from one module to another. Because modules differ in the way they treat data, however, you'll see some differences in the way Works handles the information.

Working with Shared Information

Here are brief descriptions of the results when you cut and paste data between Works modules. The examples describe the process of transferring data between the modules.

- *Spreadsheet to word processor:* If you paste the contents of multiple cells into a word-processed document, Works arranges the incoming data into a table-like format.

- *Database to word processor:* If you paste one or more database records into a word-processed document, Works arranges the data in rows and columns separated by tab spaces.

- *Word-processed table to spreadsheet:* If you paste a table with entries separated by tab spaces into a spreadsheet, Works places each entry in a separate cell.

- *Word-processed table to database:* If you paste a word-processed table with entries separated by tab spaces into a database, Works reads across the table and turns each row of entries into a separate database record. If you're working in List view, Works places each entry in a separate cell. If necessary, Works also creates fields with default names (Field 1, Field 2, Field 3, and so on) for the entries. If you're working in Form view, you can paste the table into a blank form with the Paste Record command, and Works creates default field names and fills in as many blank forms as there are rows in the table.

- *Word-processed text to spreadsheet or database:* If you paste a string of text such as words, a sentence, or a paragraph into either the spreadsheet or the database, Works inserts the entire string into the highlighted cell or field.

- *Database to spreadsheet:* If you paste database records into a spreadsheet, Works inserts field entries in columns and records in rows.

The following sections show you how to transfer information between modules.

Pasting Data from the Spreadsheet

We'll begin by looking at how to transfer information from the spreadsheet to the word processor.

> **TIP** When you share data among modules by cutting, copying, and pasting, remember to use the toolbar buttons to save yourself some time and effort.

1. Select the cells containing the data you want to transfer.

2. Click the Copy button on the toolbar to copy the selection to the Clipboard.

3. Switch to the word processor document (using the Window menu or clicking on any part of the window).

4. Place the insertion point where you want to insert the data.

5. Click Edit, and then click Paste Special.

   When you do this, you'll see this Paste Special dialog box:

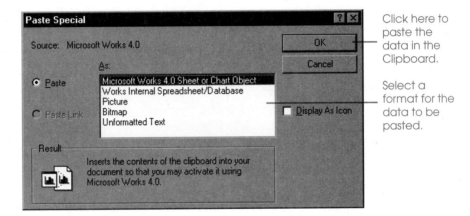

Click here to paste the data in the Clipboard.

Select a format for the data to be pasted.

The Paste Special dialog box lets you specify a format for the spreadsheet data you paste into the word processor. As you can see, you can paste the data as an object (which can't be edited) or in one of several other formats, including Unformatted Text. The Paste command on the Edit menu pastes information as an object that can't be edited.

6. Select a format.

7. Click OK.

An example of spreadsheet data transferred to a word-processed document is shown in Figure 15-1 on the following page.

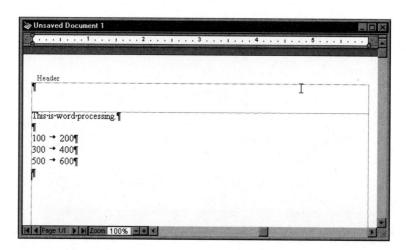

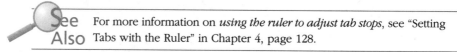

FIGURE 15-1

Pasting spreadsheet data into the word processor

Works pastes in the values copied to the Clipboard, adding tab characters to align the cell contents in the word-processed document. By default, Works sets the tab stops .5 inches apart. You can alter these settings by dragging the tab markers to the left or right on the ruler.

> **See Also** For more information on *using the ruler to adjust tab stops*, see "Setting Tabs with the Ruler" in Chapter 4, page 128.

Pasting Data from the Database

The process of pasting information from the database to the word processor is similar to pasting data from the spreadsheet. Here's an example for you to follow.

1. Switch to the database document using the Window menu.

2. Click the List View button on the toolbar, if necessary, to see your records in List view.

3. Select the records you want to copy.

4. Click the Copy button on the toolbar.

5. Return to the word processor document.

6. Place the insertion point where you want to paste the data.

7. Click the Paste button on the toolbar.

Now the word-processed document in our example contains the data from both the spreadsheet and the database, similar to that shown in Figure 15-2.

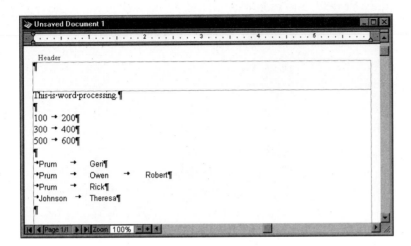

FIGURE 15-2

Pasting database records into the word processor

When you paste records from the database, Works again separates fields with tab spaces.

Formatting Pasted Data

After you've pasted spreadsheet data or database records into a word-processed document, you can select the information and format it in any way you like, as long as you didn't transfer it as an object. For example, you can select the copied spreadsheet values or database records and use the toolbar buttons or menu commands to format the numbers as you like.

Pasting Text from the Word Processor

Although you're more likely to paste from the spreadsheet or the database to the word processor than the other way around, you can move text from a word-processed document into either a spreadsheet or a database. To see how this works, do the following:

1. Select text in a word-processed document.

2. Click the Copy button on the toolbar.

3. Switch to the database window.

4. If you're in List view, select the cell in the first field of the next empty row, and then click the Paste button on the toolbar. If you're in Form view, move to a new record, highlight the dotted line for the first field, and then click the Paste button on the toolbar.

    When you paste a block of word-processed text in a database with List view active, Works inserts the text in the field you selected.

To see what happens when you paste from the word processor into the spreadsheet, follow these steps:

1. Switch to the spreadsheet, and click the cell where you want to insert data.

2. Click the Paste button.

    You don't have to copy the data again from the word processor, because the text you copied earlier is still on the Clipboard.

As in the database List view, Works pastes the incoming text into the cell you selected.

Pasting Tables to the Spreadsheet

Now let's see what happens when you move a table from the word processor to the spreadsheet.

1. Click the Task Launcher button and click Word Processor, or open an existing word-processed document that contains a table. An example is shown in Figure 15-3.

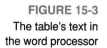

FIGURE 15-3

The table's text in the word processor

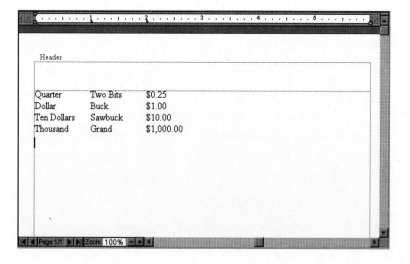

2. Select all the text in the table you want to copy.

3. Click the Copy button.

4. Switch to an open spreadsheet document in the spreadsheet module.

5. Click a cell.

6. Click the Paste button.

The example spreadsheet document is shown in Figure 15-4, with the table that was created in the word processor now nicely formatted in the spreadsheet. As you can see, each table entry becomes a cell entry in the spreadsheet.

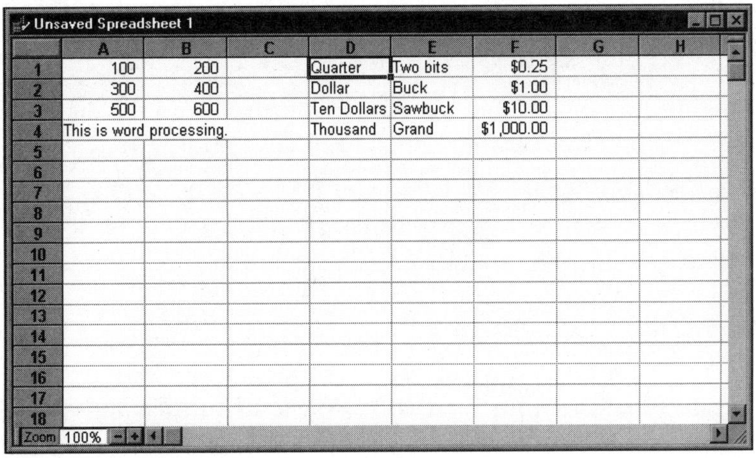

FIGURE 15-4
Copying a table into the spreadsheet

Pasting Tables to the Database

Now let's look at how to move the table created in the word processor into a database.

1. Open a new or existing database document.

2. Click the Paste button.

The copied information appears in the database as shown in Figure 15-5 on the following page.

FIGURE 15-5

Copying a table to
the database

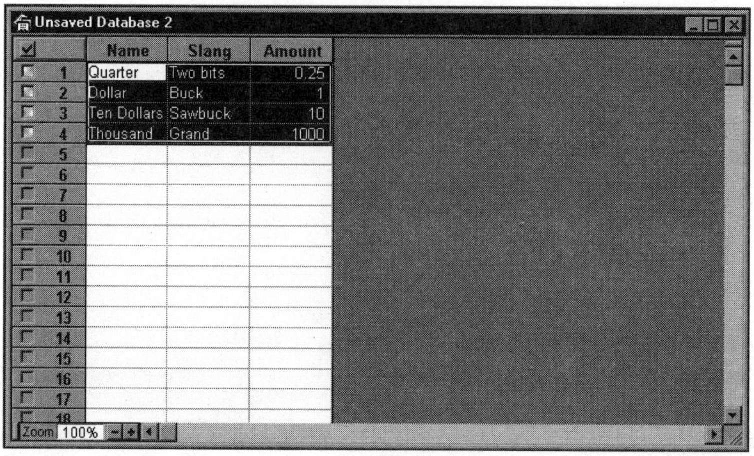

☑		Name	Slang	Amount	
☐	1	Quarter	Two bits	0.25	
☐	2	Dollar	Buck	1	
☐	3	Ten Dollars	Sawbuck	10	
☐	4	Thousand	Grand	1000	
☐	5				
☐	6				
☐	7				
☐	8				
☐	9				
☐	10				
☐	11				
☐	12				
☐	13				
☐	14				
☐	15				
☐	16				
☐	17				

Creating a Form Letter

A common task involving the word processor and the database is writing
personalized form letters (if that's not a contradiction in terms).

To produce a form letter, you need two types of Works documents.
First, you need a basic word-processed letter and, second, you need a
database of names and other information that you'll draw from to personalize the letter.

After you've created these two documents, you can put the form letter
together on your own or with the help of a TaskWizard. The Wizard
ensures that the form letter is constructed correctly. But doing it on your
own isn't so difficult and allows you much more flexibility. It also teaches
you how to do things for yourself rather than being too dependent on a
TaskWizard tool.

To create a form letter, start with a word-processed document containing the text for the body of the letter. To turn the document into a form
letter, you insert *placeholders* that show Works where you want the personalized information to appear. Each placeholder is the name of an
existing database field, such as First Name, that you've already created. On
screen, a placeholder is distinguished from surrounding text by chevrons
that look like << and >>.

Using the Form Letter TaskWizard is easy as long as your database
fields match the fields used by the Address Book TaskWizard, and as long
as you don't want to include more than the address, or the address and a
salutation.

If you want to use different field names in your database, or if you want to insert personalized information in the body of your letter, you must create your own form letter and insert different fields using the Field command on the Insert menu. This command lets you select existing fields in a database and insert placeholders wherever you want them in a document.

The basic steps for creating a form letter are as follows:

1. Create the database with all the fields you want included.

2. Tell Works which database you want to use.

3. Create the letter you want to use, with the placeholder names (corresponding to the database field names) inserted in the letter.

4. Print the word-processed document, and the form letters will print with the personalized information from the database integrated into the text.

To demonstrate, we'll create a personalized form letter that notifies job applicants about the time and place of their interview. The steps are as follows:

1. Create a database of names, addresses, and appointment dates and times. In ours, we created the following eight fields:

```
Last Name
First Name
Street
City
State
Zip
Date of Appt
Time of Appt
```

We created first and last name fields so that we can sort on the Last Name field separately if we want to.

2. Create records. We created two records by entering the data shown in Figure 15-6 on the next page.

3. Click the Task Launcher button, and open the word processor.

FIGURE 15-6
The database for
form letters with
two records

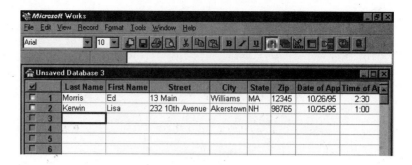

4. Type the current date and press Enter twice. In our example we entered *October 20, 1995*.

5. Click Insert, and then click Database Field.

    You see the Insert Field dialog box.

6. Click the Use A Different Database button, click Names, and then click OK.

    You'll see this Insert Field dialog box, which lists all the fields in the database:

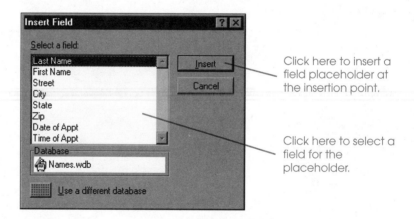

7. Click First Name and click Insert; click Last Name and click Insert again.

8. Click Street and click Insert; click City and click Insert; click State and click Insert; click Zip and click Insert; and finally click Close.

   The six inserted field placeholders occupy one line, as shown here:

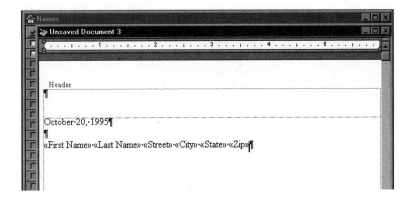

9. Place the insertion point to the left of the opening chevrons (<<) for the Street field, and press Enter.

10. Place the insertion point to the left of the opening chevrons (<<) for the City field, and press Enter.

11. Place the insertion point to the right of the closing chevrons (>>) for the City field, and type , (to insert a comma).

12. Move the insertion point to the end of the current line (following the Zip field), and press Enter twice.

13. Type a salutation and press the Spacebar. We typed *Dear*.

14. Click Insert, click Database Field, click the First Name field, click Insert, and then click Close.

15. Type a comma, and then press Enter twice.

16. As we've done thus far, we continue typing text and inserting field name placeholders so that the document looks like the one shown in Figure 15-7 on the next page.

FIGURE 15-7
The completed
letter including
database field
placeholders

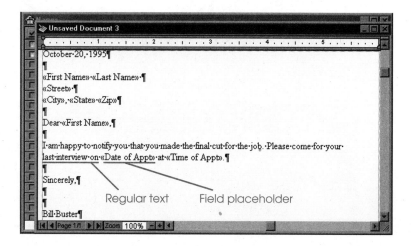

As you click Insert, you're entering the fields into the word processor document.

TIP If you want to get fancy and format text inserted from the database, simply format the placeholders in the letter and Works will print it that way. For example, if you apply bold to *<<Date of Appt>>*, the date of the appointment will print bold in all the form letters that are generated.

Now we're ready to preview or print the form letters, as follows:

1. Click Tools, and then click Form Letters.
    You'll see the Form Letters dialog box.

2. Click the Printing tab, and the dialog box will look like the one on the following page.

3. Click Print if you want to print the letters, or click Preview if you want to preview them first.
    In this example, we clicked Preview. This will display the same Print Preview window that you've seen throughout *Running Works for Windows 95.*

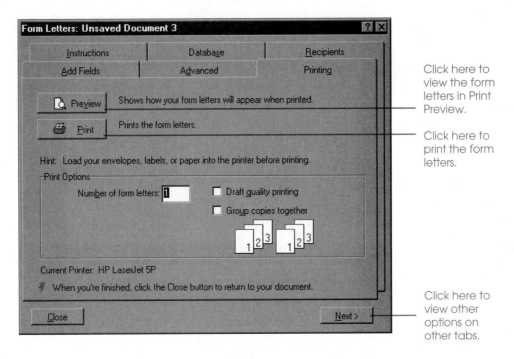

Click here to view the form letters in Print Preview.

Click here to print the form letters.

Click here to view other options on other tabs.

4. When Works asks you if you want to preview all the records, click OK.

In Figure 15-8, you can see a form letter for the first record in the Print Preview window. Notice how the data from the Names

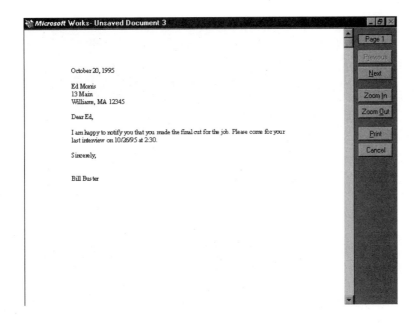

FIGURE 15-8
The preview of a form letter

database has been integrated into the form letter. Very easy, very useful, and very cool.

Print Preview shows you what your integrated and fully personalized letter looks like. If you click the Next button in the Print Preview window, you'll see the next completed form letter.

See Also   For information about *selecting specific records to merge by using a query*, see "Querying a Database to Find Information" in Chapter 10, page 339.

Bear in mind that you can reuse information in a letter or database as the need arises. A letter file can also be called a template (or boilerplate), and you can use it with several databases. For example, you might have other applicants to interview. Simply save the letter for later use, and select a different database next time. You can also use the same database to print envelopes for the form letters.

Creating Envelopes and Mailing Labels

Printing envelopes and mailing labels needn't be a nightmare. It can be as easy as printing form letters. You use both the word processor and a database of names and addresses. You use the word processor to create the envelope document or mailing label template containing the database fields you want to print, and you use the database to supply the information for the addressees.

Printing Envelopes

The ability to print envelopes is also printer dependent since some computer printers come with envelope feeders, while some can print envelopes from a separate bin. But in general, here are the instructions for printing envelopes.

1. Insert the envelopes into your printer tray or bin or envelope feeder. If you have an envelope feeder, then click Tools, click Options, click the General tab, and then click Use Printer's Envelope Feeder.

2. Click Tools, and then click Envelopes.

3. Click the Printing tab.

4. Select the options you want to use and click Print.

Printing Mailing Labels

Using mailing labels is easier than you might think because Works does most of the work for you. Although a mailing-label document doesn't look much like a document in the traditional sense, it's your starting point for printing labels. The document itself is simply a set of database fields arranged in columns and rows so that the information prints on sheets of labels. Take the following steps:

1. Open a new word processor document.

2. Click Tools, and then click Labels.

3. Click Labels (one copy of several labels) or Multiple Copies Of One Label (more than one copy of the same label) in the Labels dialog box, depending on what you want to do.

    We clicked Labels. When you do this, you'll see the Labels dialog box shown here:

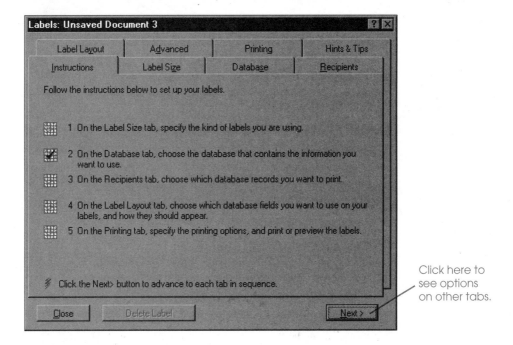

Click here to see options on other tabs.

4. Follow the instructions you see in the dialog box, including defin-
    ing label size, what database you want to use, which of the records
    in the database you want to print, which fields you want to print
    and how they should appear, and what printing options you want
    to use. You can click Next to move from tab to tab in this
    dialog box.

In Figure 15-9 you can see what the labels for the two records in our
database look like in the Print Preview window. Just as they should!
Notice that not all the available fields were used, but only those relevant
to a label. For example, date of appointment and time of appointment
didn't need to be included.

FIGURE 15-9

Two labels
prepared using the
Labels command
on the Tools menu

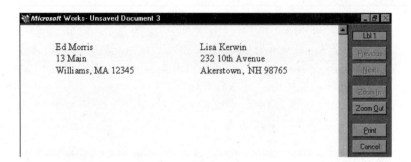

Coming Next

Works has some additional amazing tools in its arsenal. It can connect
documents so that when you change one, the other responds in kind.
That's what we'll turn our attention to next.

Chapter 16

Linking and Embedding Objects in Documents

Linking and embedding data are two ways that Works can help you update and incorporate information quickly and easily. *Linking* data means establishing a connection between an object, such as a chart, and a Works document or database file. When you create such a link, changes you make in the original (source) document are automatically reflected in the receiving (target) document, spreadsheet, or database. Sometimes linking is referred to as *dynamic linking*, since the relationship between the object and the document that contains the object is a dynamic or changing one. Basically, linking means that when you update the original, you also change a copy of the original, no matter where the copy is located.

Embedding means creating an object in a document that is proprietary to another application. Without leaving the current application, embedding an object allows you to create and edit an object with the application tools that are germane to the object. An example of embedding an object is creating a graphic image for a document in the word processor module, using the graphics tools from a drawing application that are available to you in the word processor module.

The primary difference between linking and embedding is the location of the original information. With linking, the original information resides in its own separate document. With embedding, by contrast, the original information resides in the document.

For example, a chart created with the spreadsheet can be linked to a word-processed document. Even though the chart image is visible in the word-processed document, the original chart resides in the spreadsheet file, not the word-processed document's file. However, if you embed a spreadsheet table into a word-processed document (using the Insert menu), the table stands alone as an object in the word-processed document and isn't connected to any other application.

In this chapter, we'll describe how you can link and embed objects in your documents.

Linking Objects

You link information from a source document (where the object is created) to a destination, or target, document, where the object is pasted. You can also link the object from the source to several different destinations.

For example, if you link a chart created with the spreadsheet to a word-processed document, Works in effect writes an internal "note" to itself, linking the information even after you've closed the document or quit Works.

Because the link is permanent, it ensures that any changes you make to the chart or to the data in the spreadsheet are automatically reflected in the word-processed document. You can link the same chart to a database as well.

To show you how easy linking is, let's look at a simple but very useful example: between a chart created with the spreadsheet and a document created with the word processor.

Before we begin, remember the following rule: when you create information in one Works application to be linked to another application, you must save and name the source document (the file that contains the information to be linked).

Linking Spreadsheet Data to a Document

You link spreadsheet data pretty much like you copy and paste. You select and copy a chart to the Clipboard as usual, but then you paste it into a word-processed document using the Paste Special command instead of the Paste command. The Paste Special command (available in the word processor, spreadsheet, and database modules) establishes a link between the original document (and module) and the pasted copy. With this link, the copied information has a direct line to the source document, and Works can update the copy whenever you change the original.

For example, let's say that we have a completed report containing text and also a chart showing how a widget-manufacturing company has done over the past two years.

The simple line chart that shows the sales trend is shown in Figure 16-1 on the following page.

See Also For more information on *creating charts for spreadsheet data*, see Chapter 8, "Creating Charts," page 255.

FIGURE 16-1

A simple line chart

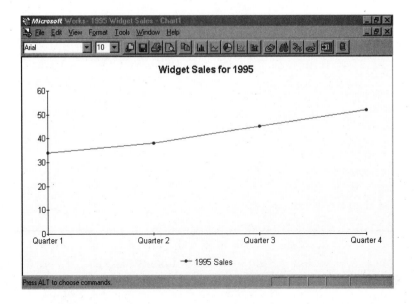

We now have a source document (the chart) and the destination document (the word-processed report). Now let's look at how to link them.

You can insert a chart into a word-processed document by following these steps:

1. Open the spreadsheet that contains the chart to link.

2. Switch to the word-processed document.

3. Move the insertion point to the location where the chart is to appear.

4. Click Insert, and then choose Chart.

When you do this, you see this Insert Chart dialog box:

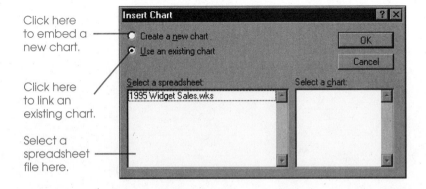

484

5. Click the Use An Existing Chart button.

6. In the Select A Spreadsheet scroll box, click the name of the spreadsheet that you used to create the chart.

 When you do this, Works lists the charts that are attached to that spreadsheet.

7. In the Select A Chart scroll box, highlight the name of the chart you want to insert.

8. Click OK.

As you can see in Figure 16-2 (which shows the document in the Print Preview window, letting us fit the entire page on one screen), the chart is inserted into the word-processed document.

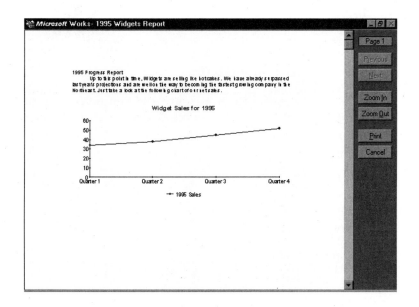

FIGURE 16-2

Inserting a chart in a word-processed document

By inserting the chart into the word-processed document, you linked the data in the spreadsheet (which you used to create the chart) to the chart that appears in the report.

Want proof? You can switch to the spreadsheet and change the value in any cell. (Use an extreme change to make sure you can see the change.) Now go back to your report. Notice anything different? As you can see in Figure 16-3 on the next page, any change made to the original data in the spreadsheet is reflected in the chart in the report. Once again, we're showing you the document example in the Print Preview window.

FIGURE 16-3

The effect on linked
data when a
change is made to
the source
document

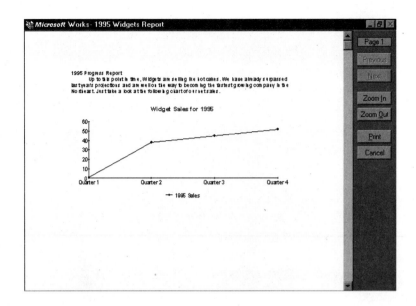

Verifying a Dynamic Link

Let's say that you get some new sales figures and you want to update the
spreadsheet on which the chart (now in the final report) is based. Remember
ber that even if the report isn't open, the link still exists. This means that
any change made to the spreadsheet is reflected in the chart, which, in
turn, is reflected in the report.

You can always make changes to a spreadsheet and save it without
ever opening or doing anything to the report to which the chart is linked.
This can be done as follows:

1. Open a spreadsheet file.

2. Change a value.

3. Save the spreadsheet.

4. Now open the word-processed document that contains the linked
    chart.

    Works displays the dialog box you see in Figure 16-4. This gives
    you the opportunity to update the document before you open it. To
    do so, click Yes.

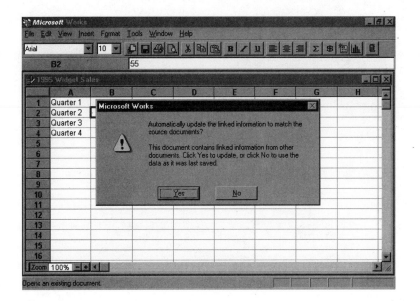

FIGURE 16-4
Confirmation that
data is linked
between two
documents

A few moments later the report will appear, complete with updates based on the linked spreadsheet data.

Editing a Linked Object

The easiest way to edit a linked object is to open its source application or module. You can open the source module that you used to create an object by double-clicking on the object. For example, if you are working in a word-processed document containing a chart that needs to be changed, simply double-click on the chart to open the spreadsheet module. Any changes you make are reflected in the chart as it appears in the word-processed document.

TIP The Paste Special command on the Insert menu lets you paste linked information into a word-processed document as an object, database, spreadsheet, picture, or bitmap, or as unformatted text. Depending on what you want to do with the information, you can select the appropriate alternative.

Editing a Link

In addition to editing linked data, you might sometimes want to edit the link itself. For example, say you want to save a spreadsheet under a new name or in a different folder. You do this type of editing with the Links command on the Edit menu. Let's explore that now.

1. If necessary, highlight the linked data in an open word-processed document.

2. Click Edit, and then choose the Links command.
    Works displays this Links dialog box:

Click here to update changes.

Click here to select another source file.

Click here to turn off the automatic update feature.

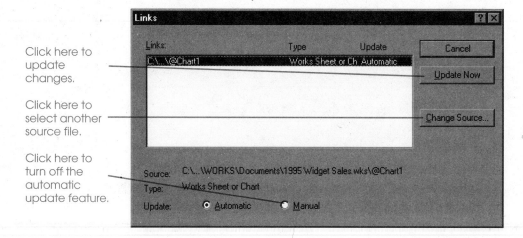

In the box labeled Links, Works identifies the source document, the type of document it is, and whether the update is automatic or manual. The other options are as follows:

■ You can select an Automatic update, which Works does without waiting for your OK, or a Manual update, which Works does only if you tell it to. The Manual update is a good idea when you want to see what the destination document looks like before you make the changes.

■ You can click Update Now to refresh the highlighted information.

■ You can click Change Source to alter the identification of the source document. For example, you can change the drive letter or folder if you've moved the file.

Embedding Objects

Embedding allows you to create and modify (without a particular association) objects associated with another application. Unlike the process used to link data, you don't leave the application module that contains the embedded object to do any of your work.

The best way to show you how to embed objects is to work through some examples. If you read Chapter 13, you already know how to insert a drawing in a document, and you also know how to use ClipArt, WordArt, and Note-It. These objects are all embedded in the document where you insert them. In this section, we'll show you how to embed and work with a chart in a word-processed document. We'll also show you how to create objects within a word-processed document.

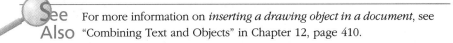

See Also For more information on *inserting a drawing object in a document*, see "Combining Text and Objects" in Chapter 12, page 410.

Creating and Embedding a Spreadsheet

You can create and embed a spreadsheet within a word-processed document without ever leaving the word processor. For instance, suppose you're in the middle of a report and want to insert information to be arranged in a spreadsheet format. The finished report looks something like what you see in Figure 16-5.

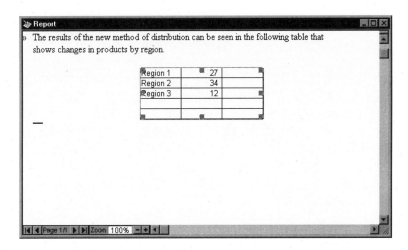

FIGURE 16-5

Spreadsheet data inserted in a word-processed document

Here's how we prepared this report.

1. Place the insertion point where you want to embed the spread-sheet.

2. Click Insert, and then click Spreadsheet.

   When you do this, you see this Insert Spreadsheet dialog box:

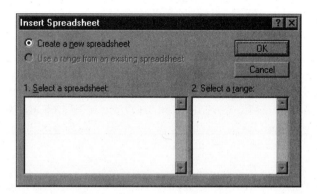

3. Make sure the Create A New Spreadsheet option button is selected.

   If you already created a spreadsheet you want to use, you would select a spreadsheet filename and click the Use A Range From An Existing Spreadsheet option button; that range would form the basis for the inserted spreadsheet/table.

4. Click OK.

   When you do this, Works places a mini-spreadsheet right into the word processor document as you see in Figure 16-6. It contains only three columns and five rows, but you can use the standard drag techniques to increase its size.

5. Enter the information you want in the spreadsheet.

6. Click anywhere outside the spreadsheet (or press the Esc key) to embed it in the word processor.

You'll notice that, like any object, the spreadsheet can be dragged, moved, and resized. And, like any object, when you double-click it, the original application used to create the object is revealed (along with the appropriate toolbar!). When you're done making any changes, simply click once again in the word processor window—and your document returns to normal.

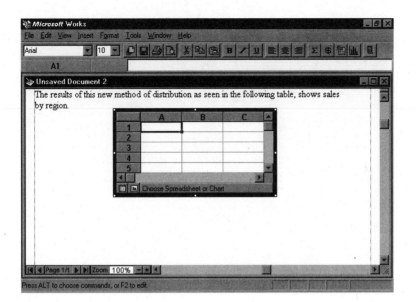

FIGURE 16-6
Embedding a
spreadsheet within
a word-processed
document

Creating and Embedding a Chart

If you can embed a new spreadsheet/table combo, isn't charting just one step away? It certainly is. The spreadsheet toolbar contains all the buttons and other features that you became familiar with in Chapter 8.

You can create a chart from an existing spreadsheet by clicking the New Chart button on the spreadsheet toolbar and then selecting the chart options you want in the New Chart dialog box. It's that simple to embed a chart into a word-processed document. As you can see in Figure 16-7 on the following page, the buttons for switching from a spreadsheet to a chart and back again are in the lower left corner of the chart object area. Simply click whichever one you want. Clicking outside the chart object embeds the chart in the word-processed document. Notice also that the chart toolbar becomes active in the module's window as well as the chart menu bar, which is evidenced by the missing Insert menu.

If you want to create a chart without first creating a spreadsheet, you go through the same procedures for embedding a spreadsheet, including embedding the table and then generating the chart. Works will remind you that before you can create a chart, you first must have data on which to base it.

See
Also For more information on *using the chart toolbar*, see "The Chart Toolbar" in Chapter 8, page 260.

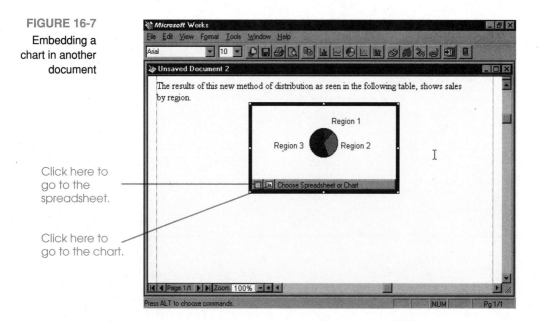

FIGURE 16-7

Embedding a
chart in another
document

Click here to
go to the
spreadsheet.

Click here to
go to the chart.

Creating and Embedding Other Objects

Now all that's left before you become a linking and embedding expert is
knowing how to embed other types of objects into a word-processed
document. What might these other objects be? Anything from a sound to
a picture created with Paintbrush.

To insert other types of objects, follow these steps:

1. Place the insertion point where you want to insert the object.

2. Click Insert, and then click Object.

   When you do this, you'll see the Insert Object dialog box shown
   on the next page, which lists all the possible types of objects that you
   can insert into your document.

   This list differs from computer to computer since it, in part,
   depends on what types of applications the computer supports.

   You can select the type of object you want to insert. You can
   also specify whether you want the object to be a new creation or you
   want to create the object from an existing file.

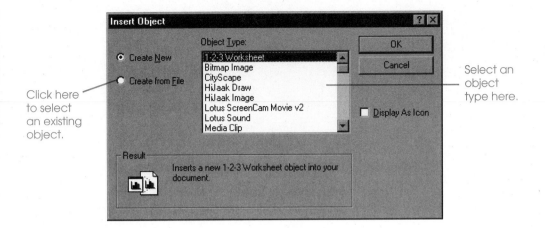

Click here to select an existing object.

Select an object type here.

For example, if you click the Create New button and click Microsoft Note-It from the Object Type box, Works gives you the Note-It dialog box. (Choosing such object types as ClipArt, Drawing, Note-It, and WordArt from the Insert Objects dialog box is just like selecting the respective menu command from the Insert menu.)

3. Click the appropriate option to indicate whether this will be a new object or whether you want to import one from an existing file.

   If you want to use an existing file, Works asks you to identify the complete path to the file.

4. Click the type of object you want to insert.

5. Click OK.

Works takes over from there and inserts the identified object.

That's All!

Ta-da! You're done with *Running Works for Windows 95,* but we certainly hope that you're not done running Works. We trust that this book has helped you master some of the important basic techniques for using Works.

Part 8

Appendixes

In This Part *Running Works for Windows 95* is over, but your learning has just begun. These three appendixes provide you with additional information, including a summary of spreadsheet and database functions, keystroke shortcuts, and details on how to install Works 4.0 for Windows 95. While these might not be the first things you want to read when you start using this book, you will certainly want to familiarize yourself with the content of these appendixes so that you know where to go when you need the information they contain.

Appendix A

Built-In Spreadsheet and Database Functions

One of the best things about Works, and what helps make it such a workhorse, are the built-in functions you can use instead of defining your own formulas to do the same work.

Every function has a name and must be typed in the following format:

```
=FunctionName(Argument0,Argument1, . . . ArgumentN)
```

- FunctionName is the name of the function. Function names are shown in capitals in this appendix.

- Argument0,Argument1, . . . ArgumentN represent arguments or values used in the calculation. Arguments can be numbers, cell references, range references or names, field names, or other functions.

Regardless of form, however, all arguments must represent numbers.

For example, if cell B3 is included as an argument, B3 must contain a numeric value.

All functions, like all formulas, begin with an equal sign (=) to indicate that they are to be calculated rather than interpreted as text or values. Arguments, if used, are always enclosed in parentheses. If a function takes multiple arguments, the arguments must be separated by commas.

People tend to shy away from using functions because they feel intimidated by them and think that functions are too complicated. Our advice is to try them! What can you lose? You'll be amazed at how much time you can save with them and how much more powerful a tool Works becomes.

Works organizes these functions into eight categories, as follows:

- Financial functions

- Date and time functions

- Math and trig functions

- Statistical functions

- Lookup and ref functions

- Text functions

- Logical functions

- Informational functions

The following descriptions provide a reference to the Works functions, organized by category.

Financial Functions

CTERM(Rate,FutureVal,PresentVal)

CTERM calculates the number of compounding periods required for an investment to grow from the entered present value (PresentVal) to the entered future value (FutureVal), given a fixed interest rate (Rate) per compounding period.

DDB(Cost,Salvage,Life,Period)

DDB uses the double-declining balance method of calculating depreciation of an asset. Cost is the original cost of the asset. Salvage is the expected value at the end of the asset's life. Life is the number of years or other time periods the asset is expected to be usable. Period is the time period for which you want to calculate the depreciation. The function calculates depreciation for a given period according to the formula

$$\frac{value*2}{life}$$

FV(Payment,Rate,Term)

FV calculates the future value of an annuity in which equal payments earn a fixed rate per term, compounded over the entered number of terms.

The function assumes that the first payment is made at the end of the first period and calculates future value according to the formula

$$\frac{Payment*((1+Rate)^{Term}-1)}{Rate}$$

IRR(Guess,RangRef)

IRR gives the internal rate of return (profit) on the series of cash flows represented by RangeRef. Guess is an estimate of the yield. RangeRef is the reference to the cell range containing the values to be calculated.

NPV(Rate,RangeRef)

NPV returns the net present value of a series of payments at a fixed interest rate per period. Rate is the interest rate per period. RangeRef is the range of cells containing the values to calculate. If the interest rate is annual, but the payment periods are more frequent, divide the rate by the number of periods (such as 12).

The function uses the formula

$$NPV = \sum_{i=1}^{n} \frac{Payment[i]}{(1+Rate)i}$$

PMT(Principal,Rate,Term)

PMT calculates the payment per period on a loan or investment with a fixed interest rate over the entered term.

Principal is the amount of the loan or investment. Rate is the interest rate. Term is the length of the loan or investment. The rate and the term must correspond to the same periods. If the rate is annual, but the payment is monthly, divide the rate by 12. The function uses the formula

$$PMT = \frac{present\ value * rate}{1-(1+rate)^{-term}}$$

PV(Payment,Rate,Term)

PV calculates the present value of a series of equal payments earning a fixed rate of interest over a specific term.

Payment is the amount per period. Rate is the interest rate. Term is the number of periods. The function assumes that the first payment is made at the end of the first period. The function uses the formula

$$PV = \frac{payment * (1-(1+rate)^{-term})}{rate}$$

RATE(FutureVal,PresentVal,Term)

RATE returns the fixed interest rate per period needed for an investment to grow from its present value to an expected future value in the number of terms entered.

FutureVal is the value expected at the end of the term. PresentVal is the current value of the investment. Term is the number of periods to be considered. The function uses the formula

$$RATE = \left(\frac{future\ value}{present\ value}\right)^{\frac{1}{term}} -1$$

SLN(Cost,Salvage,Life)

SLN calculates the straight-line depreciation for an asset. Straight-line depreciation assumes a linear reduction in value, so the depreciation amount is the same for any period.

Cost is the initial cost of the asset. Salvage is its estimated salvage value. Life is the number of periods the asset is expected to remain useful. The function uses the formula

$$SLN = \frac{cost-salvage}{life}$$

SYD(Cost,Salvage,Life,Period)

SYD calculates depreciation of an asset according to the sum-of-the-years-digits method, in which the greatest allowances for depreciation are made in the earliest years in the life of the asset.

Cost is the initial cost of the asset. Salvage is the estimated salvage value of the asset. Life is the estimated useful life of the asset. Period is the period for which depreciation is to be calculated. The function uses the formula

$$SYD = \frac{(cost-salvage)*(life-period+1)}{\left(\frac{life*(life*+1)}{2}\right)}$$

TERM(Payment,Rate,FutureVal)

TERM calculates the number of periods required for an annuity to grow to the entered future value at a fixed interest rate and a fixed payment per period.

Payment is the amount per period. Rate is the interest rate. FutureVal is the desired future value. If the interest rate is annual, divide the rate by 12 for a monthly payment period.

Date and Time Functions

DATE(Year,Month,Day)

DATE converts a date to a constant number between 1 and 65534, representing the days from January 1, 1900, through June 3, 2079. The values for Year, Month, and Day must be numbers.

For example, =DATE(1992,1,20) returns 33623 for January 20, 1992. Year can also be a number from 0 (for 1900) through 179 (2079), Month can be 1 through 12, and Day can be 1 through 31. If the day or month are outside the normal ranges, the function corrects for the error. It does not return ERR.

DAY(DateSerialNumber)

DAY returns the number of the day of the month for the date entered as DateSerialNumber. Using the preceding DATE example of 33623 for January 20, 1992, =DAY(33623) returns 20. DateSerialNumber can be entered either as a number between 1 and 65534 or as a date surrounded by single quotation marks, for example, =DAY('1/20/92').

MONTH(DateSerialNumber)

MONTH returns the number of the month for the date entered as DateSerialNumber. DateSerialNumber can be entered either as a number between 1 and 65534 or as a date surrounded by single quotation marks, for example, =MONTH('1/20/92').

YEAR(DateSerialNumber)

YEAR returns the number of the year for the date entered as DateSerialNumber. DateSerialNumber can be entered either as a number between 1 and 65534 or as a date surrounded by single quotation marks.

TIME(Hour,Minute,Second)

TIME converts a time to a number between 0 and 0.99999, representing the hours, minutes, and seconds between 12:00:00 a.m. and 11:59:59 p.m.

MINUTE(TimeSerialNumber)

MINUTE returns the number of the minute, from 0 through 59, for the time entered as TimeSerialNumber. Enter TimeSerialNumber as a number between 0 and 0.99999, representing the times between 12:00:00 a.m. and 11:59:59 p.m., or enclose the time in single quotation marks.

SECOND(TimeSerialNumber)

A function that converts a number for the second of the time represented by TimeSerialNumber. SECOND returns a value in the range of 0 to 59.

HOUR(TimeSerialNumber)

HOUR returns the number of the hour of the day (0 through 23) for the time entered as TimeSerialNumber. Specify time as a number between 0 and 0.99999, representing the times between 12:00:00 a.m. and 11:59:59 p.m., or enclose the time in single quotation marks.

NOW( )

NOW returns a serial number representing the current date and time. The number returned consists of an integer plus a decimal. The integer is the serial number representing the date; the decimal is the serial number representing the time.

Math and Trig Functions

ABS(x)

ABS gives the absolute value of x. For example, ABS(–3)=3. X cannot be 0.

ACOS(x)

ACOS gives the arccosine (inverse cosine) of the angle whose cosine is x. X must be a value between –1 and +1. The function returns a value between 0 and p radians (0 through 180 degrees).

ASIN(x)

ASIN gives the arcsine (inverse sine) of the angle whose sine is x. X must be a value between –1 and +1. The function returns a value between –p/2 and p/2 (90 degrees through 90 degrees).

ATAN(x)

ATAN gives the arctangent (inverse tangent) of the angle whose tangent is x. The function returns a value between –p/2 and p/2 (90 degrees through 90 degrees).

ATAN2(x-coordinate,y-coordinate)

ATAN2 gives the arctangent of an angle defined by X and Y coordinates. X is the X coordinate and y is the Y coordinate. Otherwise, the function returns a value between –p/2 and p/2 as shown in the following table:

If x is	If y is	Function returns
++	++	0 through p/2
–	++	p/2 through p
–	–	–p through –p/2
++	–	–p/2–0

COS(x)

COS gives the cosine of x, an angle expressed in radians.

EXP(x)

EXP returns the value of the constant 2.71828 . . . , the base of the natural logarithm raised to the power of x.

INT(x)

INT gives the integer part of the value x. The INT function truncates the decimal portion of a number without rounding up or down.

For example, =INT(3.14) and =INT(3.99) both produce the same value, 3.

LN(x)

LN gives the natural logarithm (base e, the constant 2.71828) of x.

LOG(x)

LOG gives the base 10 logarithm of x.

MOD(Numerator,Denominator)

MOD gives the remainder after the numerator is divided by the denominator.

For example, =MOD(10,3) produces 1 because 10 divided by 3 has a remainder of 1.

PI( )

PI returns the value of pi rounded to nine decimal places (3.141592654).

RAND( )

RAND returns a random number. The number is a decimal from 0 up to, but not including, 1.

ROUND(x,NumberOfPlaces)

ROUND rounds the value x to the number of places entered.

SIN(x)

SIN returns the sine of x, an angle expressed in radians.

SQRT(x)

SQRT returns the square root of x. X must be a positive value.

TAN(x)

TAN returns the tangent of x, an angle expressed in radians.

Statistical Functions

AVG(RangeRef0,RangeRef1, . . .)

AVG returns the average of the values in the ranges listed as arguments. RangeRef0,RangeRef1, and so on are sets of values. They can be entered as numbers, cell or range references, or formulas. Text is always treated as 0. Blank cells are also treated as 0 if they occur in cell references; in range references, they are ignored.

COUNT(RangeRef0,RangeRef1, . . .)

COUNT returns the number of cells in the ranges referenced. RangeRef0,RangeRef1, and so on can be numbers, cell or range references, or formulas. The function counts cells containing not only numbers, but also text and the values ERR and N/A, which are returned by other functions. Blank cells are counted only if they occur in cell (not range) references.

MAX(RangeRef0,RangeRef1, . . .)

MAX returns the largest (maximum) value in the ranges referenced. RangeRef0,RangeRef1, and so on can be numbers, cell or range references, or formulas. The function ignores blank cells in range references, but treats them as 0 in cell references.

MIN(RangeRef0,RangeRef1, . . .)

MIN returns the smallest (minimum) value in the ranges referenced.

STD(RangeRef0,RangeRef1, . . .)

STD calculates the population standard deviation of the values in the ranges referenced. Referenced ranges can be numbers, cell or range references, or formulas. Blank cells are ignored in range references but treated as 0 in cell references. To calculate the standard deviation of a sample, use STD(ranges)*SQRT(COUNT(ranges)/(COUNT(ranges)1)), where ranges include RangeRef0,RangeRef1, . . . for the functions involved.

SUM(RangeRef0,RangeRef1, . . .)

SUM totals the values in the ranges referenced. RangeRef0,RangeRef1, and so on can be numbers, cell references or ranges, or formulas. Blank cells are ignored in range references and treated as 0 in cell references.

VAR(RangeRef0,RangeRef1, . . .)

VAR calculates variance, the degree to which the values in the referenced ranges deviate from the mean for all values. RangeRef0,RangeRef1, and so on can be numbers, cell or range references, or formulas. Blank cells are ignored in range references and treated as 0 in cell references. To calculate sample variance, use the formula VAR(ranges)*(COUNT(ranges)/(COUNT(ranges)1)), where ranges includes RangeRef0,RangeRef1, . . ., as described above.

Lookup and Ref Functions

CHOOSE(Choice,Option0,Option1, . . .)

CHOOSE selects the value of Choice to return the value of the option whose position in the list of arguments corresponds to Choice.

For example, in the function =CHOOSE(2,20,30,40,50) the function returns 40, because its position corresponds to 2 (20=0,30=1,40=2,50=3).

COLS(RangeRef)

COLS returns the number of columns in a range.

For example, =COLS(A1:C1) returns 3 because the range covers three columns—A, B, and C.

HLOOKUP(LookupValue,RangeRef,RowNum)

HLOOKUP uses the value (LookupValue) to retrieve an entry from a predefined table. LookupValue is a value in the top row of the table. RangeRef is the range comprising the table. RowNum is the number of rows that the function is to go below the LookupValue to retrieve the desired entry.

For example, if a table in cells A1 through C4 contains the following:

	A	B	C
1	1	2	3
2	10	20	30
3	40	50	60
4	70	80	90

the formula =HLOOKUP(2,A1:C4,2) returns 50. The function first reads across the top row of the range defined by A1:C4 to find the LookupValue (2) and then goes down the number of rows defined by RowNum (2) to retrieve the table entry (50).

INDEX(RangeRef,Column,Row)

INDEX returns the value of the cell at the intersection of the entered column and row. Column and row numbers begin with 0, so the intersection of column 0 and row 0 is the first value in the entered range.

ROWS(RangeRef)

ROWS returns the number of rows in a range.

VLOOKUP(LookupValue,RangeRef,ColNum)

VLOOKUP uses the value (LookupValue) to retrieve an entry in a specific column within a predefined table. For example, if a table in cells A1 through C4 contains the following:

	A	B	C
1	1	20	60
2	3	30	70
3	4	40	80
4	5	50	90

the formula =VLOOKUP(2,A1:C4,2) returns 30. The function first reads down the leftmost column of the range defined by A1:C4. When it finds a number equal to the LookupValue, it goes across the entered number of columns (2) and retrieves the value in the cell at that location. The function returns 0 if the target cell contains text.

Text Functions

EXACT(TextValue0,TextValue1)

EXACT compares two strings of characters and gives 1 (True) if they match or 0 (False) if they do not.

For example, if cells A9 and G9 contain Buy and cell D9 contains Sell, then:
=EXACT(A9,G9) equals 1 (true)
=EXACT(A9,D9) equals 0 (false)
=EXACT("Fred",D9) equals 0 (false)

FIND(FindText,SearchText,Offset)

FIND finds one string of text within another string of text and returns the number of the character at which FindText occurs, starting from 0 (zero) at the left end of the string.

For example, if cell A10 contains the text Gertrude Stein, then:
=FIND("Stein",A10,0) equals 9
=FIND("eat","The Beatles",4) equals 5
=FIND("Hello","Goodbye",0) equals ERR

LEFT(TextValue,Length)

LEFT gives the first (or leftmost) character or characters in a text string. Length specifies how many characters you want LEFT to extract.

For example, if cell A1 contains Madonna, then =LEFT(A1,1) equals M. If cell F19 contains #NEW8778, then =LEFT(F19,4) equals #NEW.

LENGTH(TextValue)

LENGTH determines the number of characters in a string of text. When the LENGTH function counts the number of characters, it also counts blank spaces and punctuation marks.

For example, if cell B5 contains the text London, England, =LENGTH(B5) equals 15.

LOWER(TextValue)

LOWER converts all uppercase letters of text in TextValue to lowercase. TextValue references the cell that contains text.

For example, if cell B12 contains the text K.D. Lang, then =LOWER(B12) equals k.d. lang.

MID(TextValue,Offset,Length)

MID gives a specific number of characters from a text string, starting at the position entered. TextValue references a cell that contains text. Offset is the position of the first character you want to extract from TextValue. Length is the total number of characters you want MID to extract.

For example, if cell B12 contains the text Paul Newman, =MID(B12,0,4) equals Paul.

N(RangeRef)

N gives the entry in the first cell in a range as a value. If the first cell contains text, N gives the value 0 (zero). RangeRef is a cell or range reference, or a range name.

For example, if cell B25 contains the text PAID and cells B26 and B27 contain $45.00 and $36.00, respectively, =N(B25:B27) equals 0 (zero).

PROPER(TextValue)

PROPER capitalizes the first letter of each word and any text that follows any character other than a letter in a text string. TextValue references the cell that contains the text.

For example, =PROPER("This is a title") returns This Is A Title.

REPEAT(TextValue,Count)

REPEAT repeats text as many times as you specify. TextValue can be a reference to a cell that contains text.

For example, if cell A3 contains Sales, =REPEAT(A3,2) returns SalesSales.

REPLACE(OldText,Offset,Length,NewText)

REPLACE exchanges one string of text for another. OldText references a cell that contains text. Offset is the number of the character within OldText at which to begin replacing OldText characters with NewText. NewText is the text that you want to replace OldText with. NewText can be a reference to a cell that contains text.

For example, this formula replaces the five characters after the fifth character in OldText with NewText: =REPLACE("abcdefghijk",5,5,"*") returns abcde*k.

RIGHT(TextValue,Length)

RIGHT returns the last (or rightmost) character or characters in a text string. TextValue references a cell that contains text.

For example, if cell D5 contains the text string Sale Price, =RIGHT(D5,5) returns Price.

S(RangeRef)

S gives the text in the first cell in a range. RangeRef is a cell or range reference, or a range name.

For example, if cell C10 contains the text string CA and cells C11 and C12 contain 95678 and 90266, respectively, =S(C10:C12) returns CA.

STRING(x,DecimalPlaces)

STRING gives the value converted to text with the entered number of decimal places. X references a cell that contains a value. DecimalPlaces is the number of decimal places you want Works to display for the value that is converted to text.

For example, if cell B3 contains the value 345, =STRING(B3,2) returns 345.00 (as text).

TRIM(TextValue)

TRIM removes all spaces from TextValue except for single spaces between words.

For example, if cell E2 contains the text Monthly   Status   Report, then =TRIM(E2) returns Monthly Status Report.

UPPER(TextValue)

UPPER converts text to uppercase.

For example, if cell A4 contains the text sell, =UPPER(A4) returns SELL.

VALUE(TextValue)

VALUE gives a number entered as text as its corresponding numeric value.

For example, if cell K5 contains $554.00 entered as text (that is, when you highlight the cell, $554.00 is displayed on the entry bar with a double quotation mark preceding it), =VALUE(K5) returns 554 as a value, not text.

Logical Functions

AND(Logical0,Logical1, . . .)

AND returns 1 (True) if all of the arguments are TRUE (nonzero), and it returns 0 (False) if one or more arguments are FALSE (zero).

For example, if the range B1:B3 contains the values TRUE, FALSE, and TRUE, =AND(B1:B3) equals 0 (False).

FALSE( )

FALSE returns the value 0, meaning False. This function is the complement of TRUE( ).

For example, =IF(A1>0,TRUE(),FALSE()) returns 1 (True) if the value in cell A1 is greater than 0; otherwise, the IF function returns 0 (False).

IF(Cond,ValueIfTrue,ValueIfFalse)

IF returns one of two results, depending on the outcome of a specific condition. Cond is the condition to evaluate and is often an expression that includes an operator such as greater than (>), less than (<), or equal (=); ValueIfTrue is the value that is returned if the outcome of the condition is true. ValueIfFalse is the value returned if the outcome of the condition is false.

NOT(Logical)

NOT reverses the value of its argument. If Logical is FALSE, NOT returns 1 (True). If Logical is TRUE, NOT returns 0 (False).

For example, =NOT(1+1=3) equals 1 (True).

OR(Logical0,Logical1, . . .)

OR gives 1 (True) if one or more of the arguments are TRUE. It gives 0 (False) if all of the arguments are FALSE.

For example, =OR(1+1=1,2+2=5) equals 0 (False).

TRUE( )

TRUE returns the value 1, meaning True. *See also* FALSE.

Informational Functions

ERR( )

ERR returns the value ERR. This function is usually used to display ERR in a selected cell under a specific condition. ERR takes no argument.

For example, =IF(A1<0,ERR( ),A1) displays ERR if the value in cell A1 is less than 0; otherwise, the IF function that contains the ERR function displays the value in cell A1.

ISERR(x)

ISERR determines whether the argument is the error value ERR. If the argument produces ERR, the function returns 1. Otherwise, the function returns 0. The ISERR function can be used to control the propagation of the ERR error message through related formulas in a spreadsheet.

For example, =IF(ISERR(C15),0,C15) returns 0 if cell C15 contains an error, but otherwise returns the value in cell C15.

ISNA(x)

ISNA determines whether the argument is the value N/A (not available). If it is, the function returns 1. This function is similar to the ISERR function in helping prevent the propagation of one value (N/A) throughout related formulas in a spreadsheet.

NA( )

NA returns the value N/A (not available). Works treats N/A as a numeric, not text, value. It is used mainly to test formulas. *See also* ISNA.

SELECT EDITION

Appendix B

QuickStrokes

Although Works provides a graphical environment that makes a mouse or trackball so convenient for working within its modules, keystroke shortcuts can also help make your work go faster. Very often, however, it can be equally convenient to use keystroke alternatives to select commands, navigate through documents, or format content, especially when your hands are already on the keyboard for entering data. Here you will find many keyboard shortcuts—for the sake of convenience, we'll call them QuickStrokes—to help you perform a variety of Works tasks.

Getting Help

Display the Help Index	F1

Choosing Commands

Activate the menu bar	Alt or F10
Open a menu on the menu bar	Underlined letter in the menu name
Choose a command on a menu	Underlined letter in the command name
Activate a shortcut menu	Shift+F10
Close a menu without choosing a command	Esc

Closing Windows

Close the active window	Ctrl+F4
Quit Works	Alt+F4

Switching Between Windows

Go to the next window	Ctrl+F6
Go to the previous window	Ctrl+Shift+F6
Open the Start menu	Ctrl+Esc
Switch between open programs	Alt+Tab

Choosing Options in a Dialog Box

Move to the next option	Tab
Move to the previous option	Shift+Tab
Open a list box	↓

Choose an option	Alt+underlined letter in the option name
Confirm all options	Enter
Cancel and close a dialog box	Esc

Moving and Highlighting

Right, left, down, or up	→, ←, ↓, or ↑
One screen down	PgDn
One screen up	PgUp
Beginning of a line or row	Home
End of a line or row	End
Beginning of a document	Ctrl+Home
End of a document	Ctrl+End
Specify a bookmark, range, or field	Ctrl+G
Begin highlighting text or range	Shift+any arrow key

Undoing

Undo the last change	Ctrl+Z
Remove the highlight	Any arrow key
Remove the font style	Ctrl+Spacebar

Formatting

Bold	Ctrl+B
Italic	Ctrl+I
Underline	Ctrl+U
Center	Ctrl+E
Left align	Ctrl+L
Right align	Ctrl+Shift+R
Open the Font list box	Ctrl+Shift+F
Open the Font Size list box	Ctrl+Shift+P

In the Word Processor

Justify a paragraph	Ctrl+J
Apply a hanging indent	Ctrl+Shift+H
Undo a hanging indent	Ctrl+Shift+T
Apply a nested indent	Ctrl+M
Undo a nested indent	Ctrl+Shift+M

Add a line before paragraph   Ctrl+0 (zero)
Remove line before paragraph Ctrl+0 (zero)

In the Spreadsheet

Apply Comma format   Ctrl+, (comma)
Apply Currency format   Ctrl+4
Apply Percent format   Ctrl+5

Making Changes

Cut   Ctrl+X
Copy   Ctrl+C
Paste   Ctrl+V
Delete next character or selection Del

In the Entry Bar

Activate the entry bar   F2
Confirm entry bar change   Enter
Cancel entry bar change   Esc

In the Spreadsheet

AutoSum   Ctrl+M

Repeating Commands

Repeat the last format   Ctrl+Y
Repeat the last search   Shift+F4
Repeat the last paste   Ctrl+V

Printing

Print preview   Alt, F, V
Print   Ctrl+P

Saving Work

Save a document   Ctrl+S

Appendix C

Installing Microsoft Works for Windows 95

What You Need to Run Works

Works for Windows 95 runs on most personal computers, but Works does take lots of room on your hard drive. Here's exactly what you will need to make Works go for you.

- A personal computer with at least a 486 microprocessor and at least 4 megabytes of RAM; the more RAM you have above 4 megabytes, the faster Works will run

- A VGA monitor or better

- At least 15 megabytes of hard disk space for a complete installation; four megabytes for a minimum installation

- Microsoft Windows 95 installed on your system; Works will not run with any other version of Windows

- A mouse

Installing Works

It's an absolute cinch to install Works. Just follow these instructions step by step, and you will soon be up and running.

1. Be sure that your computer is turned on.

2. Close any open applications.

3. Insert the Microsoft Works Setup disk 1 or the Works CD in your computer's disk drive. Be sure to close the disk drive door.

4. Click the Start button.

5. Click Run.

6. Type *a:\setup*. Substitute the CD drive letter for *a* if the setup disk is not in drive A.

7. Click OK.

Works will set itself up and create a listing on the Programs menu.

Changing the Installation

1. Be sure that your computer is turned on.

2. Close any open applications.

3. Insert the Microsoft Works Setup disk 1 or the Works CD in your computer's disk drive. Be sure to close the disk drive door.

4. Click the Start button.

5. Click Run.

6. Type *a:\setup*. Substitute the CD drive letter for *a* if the setup disk is not in drive A.

7. When you see the setup screen, click Add/Remove.

8. Click on those components you want to add (there should be a check in the box for those) and those you want to remove (there should be no check in the box).

9. Click Continue and answer any questions that Works asks.

10. Click OK.

Removing Works

If you want to remove Works from your hard disk, you can do it with the Add/Remove Programs utility available with Windows 95. Here's how to do it.

1. Be sure that your computer is turned on.

2. Close any open applications.

3. Click the Start button.

4. Click Settings.

5. Click Control Panel.

6. Double-click the Add/Remove Programs icon.

7. Click the Microsoft Works 4.0 name to highlight it in the list in the Add/Remove Programs dialog box.

8. Click the Add/Remove button.

9. Click the Remove All button in the Microsoft Works 4.0 Setup dialog box.

Index

cut and paste, *continued*
  See also drag-and-drop editing;
    Paste command

D

data,
  buffer, 447
  charts require, 491
  combining applications, 40–42
  cut and paste, 465
  database, 302–5, 325–29
  duplicating cell, 182–83
  embedding, 489–93
  entering and editing, 325–29
  formatting pasted, 469
  linking between modules, 482–88
  pasting between modules, 465–71
  protection, 188–90, 314–16
  spreadsheet, 181–85
  transfer between documents, 40–42
  See also sharing information
database, 32–37
  adding fields, 311–13
  adding records, 310–11, 326
  Address Book, 10
  ClipArt (*see* ClipArt)
  components, 297–98
  creating a, 301–9
  data, 302–5
  data to spreadsheet, 466
  data to word processor, 466, 468–69
  definition of, 297
  deleting fields, 313–14
  deleting records, 311
  editing, 309–16
  entering data, 302–5
  fields (*see* fields)
  files, 33, 298
  fill series, 314
  filter operators, 346–48
  finding information, 335–39
  fonts (*see* fonts)
  form letters using a, 473–78
  forms (*see* database forms)
  formulas, 326–29

database, *continued*
  formulas for report summary,
    373–75, 377–78
  Form view (*see* Form view)
  functions, 326–29, 499–512
  hidden records, 346
  hiding information, 315–16
  highlighting key combinations, 310
  labels and descriptions, 324–25
  linking objects in, 482–88
  lists, 334–35
  List view (*see* List view)
  Navigation buttons, 305
  Note-It notes in, 425
  Personal Address Book
    TaskWizard, 67–69
  planning, 301–2
  printing, 381–83
  protection, 314–16
  queries (*see* queries)
  reorganizing fields, 317–19
  replacing information, 338
  report definition display, 369–71
  reports (*see* reports)
  Report view, 34, 306, 357–58
  sample session, 33–37
  search criteria, 335–39
  split screen view, 308–9
  standard reports, 356–61
  TaskWizards list, 45–50
  titles, 359, 361, 362–63
  toolbar, 306–7
  views, 298–301
  wildcards in searches, 338–39
  word-processed table to, 466
  word-processed text to, 466
Database button, 33
database forms,
  designing, 316–25
  protecting, 314–15
  reorganizing, 321
  TaskWizard, 52–54, 67–69,
    75–77, 297
database Form view. *See* Form view
database List view. *See* List view
database management system. *See*
    database
database reports. *See* database; reports

E

functions, *continued*
    text, 508–511
    values in parentheses, 226, 350,
        351, 499
    what-if-analysis, 245–48
    working with, 216–23
    See also formulas; *and Appendix A*
FV function, 500

G

gallery. *See* ClipArt Gallery
General number format, 198, 200, 303
General tab, 10
Go To,
    command, 181, 211, 260
    dialog box, 95, 149, 278
go to chart from spreadsheet, 492
Go to First Page button, 95
Go to First Record button, 305
Go to Last Page button, 95
Go to Last Record button, 305
Go to Next Record button, 305
Go to Previous Record button, 305
go to spreadsheet from chart, 492
Grade Book TaskWizard, 47, 72–74
graphics libraries. *See* ClipArt; Note-It
greater-than operator (>), 220, 347,
        350–51
greater-than-or-equal-to operator
        (>=), 220, 347
gridlines display, 185–86
    in charts, 262, 268, 282–83
Group command (Ctrl+G), 398
grouping,
    records, 361, 365–66
    text objects, 407
    and ungrouping objects, 395–98
guided tour of Works, 5–6
guidelines display, Draw, 399–400
gutter between columns, 137–38

H

handles,
    field sizing, 320
    object or shape, 391–95, 406
hanging indent (Ctrl+Shift+H),
        131, 516
Hang Up command, 459
hard disk, managing the, 80–81,
        520–21
hardware for Works, 520
headers, 162, 291, 374
    codes, 164–65
    document, 20
    margins, 135, 163–64
    running, 164–65
Headers and Footers command,
        291, 374
headings,
    report definition, 369, 371
    spreadsheet, 186–88, 197, 209, 213,
        273–74
headline font, 119
Help (F1) key, 515. *See also* Help
        menu
Help on Help command, 16–17
Help Me Find A Document Button,
        78–79
Help menu,
    Help Topics, 12–14
    Hide Help, 17
    Navigation buttons, 15–16
    Step-by-Step, 13–14, 16
Help screen, 17
    buttons, 15–16
    context-sensitive, 17–18
    Index, 13, 14–15, 515
    jump words, 16
    underlined jump words, 16
Help Topics dialog box, 13
Hewlett-Packard LaserJet page mar-
        gins, 164
Hidden Records, 346
Hide Help command, 17, 20
Hide Record command, 315–16
hiding cells, 190–92
hiding fields and records, 315–16
Highlight (F8) function key, 96

key combinations, *continued*
  inserting information, 164–65
  keyboard commands, 94
  making changes, 517
  moving around dialog boxes, 515–16
  moving around spreadsheet, 178–79, 181–82
  moving around the word processor, 23, 94, 96
  moving and highlighting, 516
  printing, 517
  QuickStrokes, 515–17
  repeating commands, 517
  saving work, 517
  spreadsheet highlighting, 178–79, 516
  switching between windows, 515
  undoing, 516
  word processor, 516–17
  word processor highlighting, 23, 96, 516
  See also QuickStrokes
keystroke selection actions, 96–97
keywords, using Help, 14–15

L

labels,
  charts, 258–59, 276
  database, 324–25
  database report row, 370–71
  mailing, 47, 479–80
  report field, 375–80
  from spreadsheet text, 258–59
Labels TaskWizard, 47
  Return Address, 48
landscape orientation, 136, 213, 291–92
language,
  ISO Translation, 448
  query, 349–52
laser printers, 144
last column, 182
last find, ClipArt, 421
Last Record button, 305, 326
Launcher, Works for Windows 95, 2

Launch Works Forum command, 19
leader characters, 129–30
leading zeros, 201
ledger, electronic. *See* spreadsheet
Left Align button, 114, 119–20
Left Align (Ctrl+L), 516
left-aligned tab stop, 128–29, 130–31
left and right panes, 309
Left arrow key (←), 516
LEFT function, 508
left indent control, 125–26
left one cell (←), 181
left one character (←) key, 94
left one word (Ctrl+←), 94
left one screen (Ctrl+PgUp) key combination, 182
left tab, 128–29, 130–31
left to beginning of block (Ctrl+←), 182
legends, chart, 274–76. *See also* titles
Legend/Series Labels dialog box, 275–76
length,
  of document names, 20, 110
  page, 140
  of text lines on screen, 90
LENGTH function, 509
less-than operator (<), 220, 347, 350–51
less-than-or-equal-to operator (<=), 220, 347
letterhead stationery, 47, 56
  WordArt logo, 425–26
Letterhead TaskWizard, 47
letters, form. *See* form letters
Letter TaskWizard, 47, 61–64
levels, Help screen, 14
library,
  ClipArt, 415–21
  queries, 344–45
limits. *See* number
line before paragraph (Ctrl+0 [zero]), 517
Line Between Columns, 137–38
line breaks, 90, 165
line charts, 256, 261, 264–65
  stacked, 267–68, 282
Line color palette, 389, 397
line feed (Add LF), 447–48

M

O

Q

T

Works for Windows 95 Templates

Get more than 200 letter and spreadsheet templates to use with Works for Windows 95 for only $19.95. The 3.5-inch disk contains ready-to-use business letters, general-use letters, and spreadsheets, including:

9 different categories of spreadsheet templates:

· Financial	· Personnel	· General management
· Purchasing	· Legal	· Retail
· Marketing	· Sales	· Operations

17 different categories of letter templates:

· Announcements	· Proposals	· Apologies
· Letters of reference	· Appointments	· Reminders
· Appreciation	· Reservations	· Business letters
· Social invitations	· Introductions	· Sympathy
· Invitations	· Thank-yous	· Letter formats
· Transmittals	· Orders	

Please send me the Running Works for Windows 95 disk including more than 200 letter and spreadsheet templates. I am enclosing a check or money order for $19.95.

_____
NAME

_____
STREET ADDRESS

_____
CITY   STATE   ZIP

Make check payable to Works for Windows 95 Disk and mail this coupon to:
Running Works for Windows 95 Disk   P.O. Box 1465   Lawrence, KS 66044

Overnight delivery? Please add $15.
Thanks, and have fun with Works!

You can use a TaskWizard to create a time card. See "Starting a TaskWizard," page 45.

You can include a header, such as your company name. See "Creating Headers and Footers," page 162.

DROID Temporary Personnel

Employee Time Card

Last Name		First		MI	

SSN		Today's Date			

Pay Period From: To:

Day of Week	Reg. Hours	Overtime	Holiday	Sick Leave	Day Total
Monday	8.00	.25			8.25
Tuesday	8.00	.25			8.25
Wednesday	8.00	.25			8.25
Thursday	8.00	1.25			9.25
Friday	7.5				7.5
Saturday					
Sunday					
Monday					
Tuesday					
Wednesday					
Thursday					
Friday					
Saturday					
Sunday					

	Reg. Hours	Overtime	Holiday	Sick Leave	Total Hours
Bi-Weekly Totals	39.5	2.0			41.50

XXXXXXXXXXXXXXXXXXXX
XXXXXXXXXXXXXXXXXXXXXXXXXX
XXXXXXXXXXXXXXXXXXXXXXXXXXX
XXXXXXXXXXXXXXXXXXXXXXXXX
XXXXXXXXXXXXXXXXXXXX

Please sign your time card here

You can copy parts of the spreadsheet to cut back on the time you spend typing identical cell entries. See "Moving and Copying Data," page 184.

You can use formulas to automatically calculate cells in rows and columns. See "Building a Formula," page 216.

More ideas inside back cover.